McNae's Essential Law for Journalists

McNae's

Essential Law for Journalists

Twenty-third edition

Mark Hanna   Mike Dodd

OXFORD
UNIVERSITY PRESS

OXFORD
UNIVERSITY PRESS

Great Clarendon Street, Oxford, OX2 6DP,
United Kingdom

Oxford University Press is a department of the University of Oxford.
It furthers the University's objective of excellence in research, scholarship,
and education by publishing worldwide. Oxford is a registered trade mark of
Oxford University Press in the UK and in certain other countries

© National Council for the Training of Journalists 2016

The moral rights of the authors have been asserted

Twentieth edition 2009
Twenty-first edition 2012
Twenty-second edition 2014

Impression: 2

Public sector information reproduced under Open Government Licence v3.0
(http://www.nationalarchives.gov.uk/doc/open-government-licence/open-government-licence.htm)

Published in the United States of America by Oxford University Press
198 Madison Avenue, New York, NY 10016, United States of America

British Library Cataloguing in Publication Data

Data available

Library of Congress Control Number: 2016930495

ISBN 978–0–19–874835–9

Printed in Great Britain by
Bell and Bain Ltd, Glasgow

To my wife Linda, my son Rory, my father Michael and my mother Mary

Mark Hanna

For my good friend Sarah Perry—and all the other young people taking their first steps on the road to careers in journalism—with hopes that this book helps

Mike Dodd

Preface

It has become rare for there to be a quiet or static time in the evolution of laws and regulatory frameworks which govern or affect the UK's journalism. There are usually, for example, significant developments in privacy or defamation law each year, and this updated edition of *McNae's Essential Law for Journalists*—the 23rd edition—explains these. But other recent events have been particularly momentous and far-reaching, and this edition covers these too.

These include the jailing in 2014 of Andy Coulson, former editor of the *News of the World*, for phone-hacking offences—referred to in ch. 35—and the launch later that year of the Independent Press Standards Organisation (Ipso) to replace the Press Complaints Commission (PCC), which was discredited by its failure to comprehend or sufficiently investigate the extent of phone-hacking by some journalists.

When this preface was written some privacy lawsuits brought in the civil courts by victims or alleged victims of phone-hacking remained unresolved. The actions were against News Group Newspapers, which owns *The Sun* and owned the *News of the World*, and Mirror Group Newspapers. For updates on these cases, check this book's Late News section and www.mcnaes.com. But the Crown Prosecution Service (CPS) announced in December 2015 that—after securing nine convictions of journalists, including Coulson, in the previous three years for hacking offences—its involvement in the Metropolitan Police's criminal investigations into the hacking had come 'to a close'. This means that the long shadow of the hacking scandal will start to recede unless further offences come to light. Hacking was perpetrated by a tiny fraction of the UK's journalists, but a large proportion of this workforce is affected by the creation of the Ipso system, explained in ch. 2.

After the Metropolitan Police in 2011 re-opened its inquiries into the hacking, it also began investigating—in Operation Elveden—what the CPS described as 'the unlawful provision of information by public officials to journalists'. By late 2015 this had led to more than 30 public officials being convicted—mainly for the common law offence of 'misconduct in public office'—because, without the knowledge or permission of the public agencies which employed them, they corruptly sold or otherwise leaked 'inside' information to journalists. Those jailed included police and prison officers. By late 2015 Elveden had also led, according to *Press Gazette* research, to some 34 journalists who worked for tabloid national newspapers being arrested and/or charged. Only two of these were convicted of conspiring to commit misconduct—and one of those convictions was being appealed. The high acquittal rate in the cases brought against journalists, and the protracted ordeals of those acquitted and of those against whom charges were ultimately not laid or pursued, has led to the CPS being criticised as having been over-zealous in Elveden and of having had a chilling effect on the freedom of the press to explore newsworthy information. But as ch. 35 explains, Elveden brought home to the UK media the need for very careful consideration, before any use of a public official as a confidential source of information, of whether there is a demonstrable, 'public interest' justification for investigating or publishing the information. That justification might protect the journalist, and possibly the source, from prosecution. The shadow cast on UK journalism by Elveden is darker and may be more enduring than that of the hacking scandal, as it has had some form of impact on all the UK's news media—including broadcast organisations. This is because public officials—including police officers—now fear prosecution for 'misconduct' and so are less likely to leak information to journalists, even if no payment is made or offered, and even if the leak would be in the public interest because it would tell the public of wrongdoing, inefficiency or negligence within a public agency.

A revised form of the Editors' Code of Practice, which Ipso uses to adjudicate on complaints against media organisations in its membership, took effect on 1 January 2016—see ch. 2. The revised Code includes new definitions of 'public interest' journalism and can be seen in full in Appendix 2 of this book. As various chapters point out, the Code is not law—but demonstrable adherence to the Code not only offers some protection against Ipso reaching an adverse adjudication, but might also help guard against losing privacy lawsuits and being convicted of data protection or bribery offences. The revision of the Code also changed the wording of other clauses and some of their numbering. For example, its main protection of privacy was in clause 3 but is now in clause 2. For convenience, when referring to Ipso or PCC adjudications issued before 2016 we use the new numbering of clauses when referring to Code content cited in those adjudications. But readers who look up pre-2016 adjudications elsewhere should bear in mind that the numbering of the Code's clauses has changed on several occasions since it was first published in 1991.

Journalists working in broadcast media are not affected by the creation of Ipso. But changes in the regulatory regime governing the BBC seem likely in that—as ch. 3 notes—the BBC Trust may be abolished. Again, check www.mcnaes.com for updates.

The need for better law to protect journalists' relations with confidential sources—and for journalists themselves to take much greater care to protect their sources—was dramatically illustrated by the discovery in 2014 that the Metropolitan and other police forces had, when investigating alleged leaks of information to the media, secretly been getting journalists' 'communications data' from phone companies, without any requirement for a judge to authorise this. The data can show who journalists have communicated with by phone and email. The fact that the police could so easily gain this data came as a shock to many in the UK media. Protests quickly led to new law in 2015 requiring such access to be approved by a judge, as ch. 34 explains.

Our Late News section refers to the important judgment in December 2015 by the Investigatory Powers Tribunal that the former law on access to communication data by police or other official agencies was incompatible with safeguards under Article 10 of the European Convention on Human Rights, which should protect journalists' rights to freedom of expression, and to receive and impart information. That judgment might prove valuable by influencing the drafting of future law governing such access. But it is alarming that—before 2014—there was no official focus on the ease with which police could then obtain journalists' communications data (although previous editions of *McNae's* had warned about this power). Media organisations remained concerned that the draft Investigatory Powers Bill—unveiled by the government in late 2015 to govern future access to such data by official agencies and other surveillance methods they use—lacked adequate safeguards for journalists' Article 10 rights.

In our work on this edition of *McNae's* we were struck, as we have been before, by the casual approach of successive UK governments to the protection of media freedoms and to the formulation of law directly affecting the media. The pre-2015 lack of adequate protection for journalists' communication data is one example of this.

Another is the way in which new, wide-ranging reporting restrictions were introduced in July 2015 to govern what is published about cases of 'human trafficking for exploitation'. As ch. 10 explains, an amendment made by the Modern Slavery Act 2015 to the Sexual Offences (Amendment) Act 1992 means it is now illegal in reports of crime or court cases to identify anyone who is or says they are a victim or intended victim of such a trafficking offence. Because these include non-sexual offences, and because the definitions of 'trafficking' and 'exploitation' are broad—for example, involving travel within the UK, not just from abroad—this law extends automatic provision of anonymity to new categories of victims/alleged victims of crime. It is a criminal offence for anyone—including the media—to publish anything which breaches the anonymity. Yet the government's Explanatory Notes to the 2015 Act do not explain this extension of anonymity, and no announcement of the change was made to the media. We only discovered this amendment to the 1992 Act because we can check for updates to statute via a paid-for commercial database of legislation. The government's own legislation website—legislation.gov.uk, which is free to use—is hopelessly out of date in many respects and by early 2016 was still not showing the amendment. But at least the provision in 2015 in another statute of lifelong anonymity for victims/alleged victims of female genital mutilation *was* announced. Ch. 10 explains this measure too.

Other changes in law covered in this edition include the planned major departure from the principle of open justice to be implemented in the 'trial by single justice on the papers' procedure, explained in ch. 6, which is due to affect how magistrates' courts deal with many summary cases, and reform of the provision of anonymity for juveniles concerned in court proceedings, explained in ch. 9.

In ch. 30, on the Freedom of Information Act 2000, we note that in 2015 the government launched a review of that statute's provisions, and that journalists and others were campaigning against proposals to weaken the legislation. The fact that such proposals are being seriously considered in the review—which is being carried out by an 'Independent Commission on Freedom of Information'—is a depressing example of how some in the government apparently want a tamer media rather than one with strong rights to investigate the effects of government policies and the workings of its departments, the health service, councils and other public authorities. When the main text of this book was completed the Commission had begun to consider evidence. Check our Late News section and www.mcnaes.com for updates about the review.

On the bright side, UK journalists have continued to break major stories from information gained through the 2000 Act and from confidential sources, and have continued to challenge reporting restrictions imposed needlessly or invalidly by the courts, when media organisations can spare resources to do this. Our aim continues to be that *McNae's* be a guide to what journalists can and should do, ethically and legally, as well as describing what the law and ethical codes prevent them from doing. This is why in this edition we have used the heading 'Remember your rights' to stress some points.

This book covers the law in England, Wales and Northern Ireland which it is essential for journalists to know. A chapter on www.mcnaes.com provides an introduction to Scottish law most relevant to journalists.

This edition follows the practice in previous editions of using the term 'media organisations' to encompass the publishers of newspapers, magazines and websites, and broadcasters. As we have acknowledged, the term is not wholly satisfactory, especially where the point being made also applies to freelance journalists, or to any individual 'blogger' or 'tweeter', but we feel it remains the most practical option to reflect the technological convergence in how journalism is published.

Acknowledgements

As authors we are grateful to the NCTJ's chief executive Joanne Butcher and NCTJ staff for support as we wrote this edition. We owe a great debt to Felicity Boughton, publishing editor for higher education (law), at Oxford University Press for all her guidance.

We also owe particular thanks for help and suggestions to: Amanda Ball, the NCTJ's principal examiner, who is a senior lecturer at Nottingham Trent University; Karen Nicholson, who also lectures at Nottingham Trent and who is chief examiner of the NCTJ media law examinations board; and to the rest of our fellow members on that board, including Brian Pillans, a lecturer at Glasgow Caledonian University for his advice on Scottish law. We owe similar debts of gratitude to Colm Murphy, head of the school of media, film and journalism at Ulster University, for helping us update the chapter on Northern Ireland law.

Our thanks also go to the large number of lawyers, barristers and solicitors who have so freely given us their help and guidance, but particularly to: Heather Rogers QC of One Brick Court; Caoilfhionn Gallagher of Doughty Street Chambers; Hugh Tomlinson QC, Gavin Millar QC and Guy Vassall-Adams of Matrix Chambers; Gervase de Wilde, a former national newspaper journalist turned barrister, of chambers 5RB; and Simon Westrop, head of legal at Newsquest Media Group.

We also thank: the Judicial College for permitting use of diagram material; the Regulatory Funding Company for permitting reproduction of the Editors' Code of

Practice; Ofcom for allowing us to cite extracts from its Broadcasting Code; and crime reduction charity Nacro for kindly giving us permission to reproduce on www.mcnaes.com its chart on rehabilitation periods.

We owe thanks too to our employers—in Mark's case, the Department of Journalism Studies, Sheffield University, and in Mike's, the Press Association—for their support and encouragement.

The main body of the text of this edition was completed in early December 2015 but it was possible to add to the Late News section until mid-March 2016. As we have indicated, the book's website carries updates.

Readers should feel free to email us with their comments about this edition and its website.

Mark Hanna, chair of the NCTJ Media Law Examinations Board
Email: M.Hanna@sheffield.ac.uk

Mike Dodd, legal editor, Press Association, and member of the NCTJ Media Law Examinations Board
Email: m_dodd@msn.com

This book bears the name of its first author, the late Leonard McNae, who was editor of the Press Association's Special Reporting Service.

Summary Contents

Detailed Contents

Late News

Major press groups object to Impress bid for recognition as a regulator

The News Media Association (NMA) objected in March 2016 to the application by the Independent Monitor for the Press (Impress) to be 'recognised' as a regulator of the press.

The NMA represents most of the national, regional and local press—the majority of which are already signed up to the Independent Press Standards Organisation (Ipso) regulation system and do not want to be part of a 'recognised' system.

Impress applied in January 2016 to the Press Recognition Panel, after 10 relatively small publishers signed up as Impress members, including hyperlocal organisations.

The NMA said that 'recognition' of Impress would be perverse and irrational, as it had failed to attract applications from mainstream press groups, had no editorial code of standards of its own but had 'adopted' the Editors' Code of Practice (used by Ipso) over which Impress had no control and it relied for its funding on one single wealthy donor—Max Mosley. Impress said it would begin handling complaints relating to its members in April 2016 and has pledged to be a regulator 'wholly independent' of the press (*Media Lawyer*, 21 January and 15 March 2016; Impress website).

Ch. 2, Press regulation, refers to the Impress application and explains the possible legal consequences of there being a 'recognised' regulator. The case which led Mr Mosley to campaign about press ethics is featured in chs. 25 and 26.

Ipso censures *The Sun*

The Sun newspaper's article headlined '1 in 5 Brit Muslims' sympathy for jihadis' was misleading, Ipso announced in March 2016.

The article published four months earlier reported the results of a survey of British Muslims and generated more than 3,000 complaints.

Ipso ruled it breached clause 1 of the Editors' Code, covering accuracy.

The article said 'nearly one in five British Muslims has some sympathy with those who had fled the UK to fight for IS [so-called Islamic State] in Syria' but noted that the survey showed that 'a clear majority of the 2.7 million Brits who follow Islam are moderate'.

The question about sympathy asked respondents about those 'who leave the UK to join fighters in Syria'.

Complainants argued that, as the question did not mention IS, those who responded to the question might not have intended for their answers to be understood as relating to those joining IS; a number of British Muslims had left the UK to fight *against* IS, or alongside anti-Assad forces or various Sunni groups.

Ipso said: 'The newspaper had failed to take appropriate care in its presentation of the poll results, and as a result the coverage was significantly misleading, in breach of Clause 1.' (*Muslim Engagement and Development v The Sun*, Ipso adjudication issued 17 February 2016; *Media Lawyer*, 29 March 2016).

The Sun found to have identified teenage victim

The Sun breached the Sexual Offences (Amendment) Act 1992 by inadvertently identifying the victim of a sexual offence. Former editor David Dinsmore denied the charge, but was found guilty by the chief magistrate, District Judge Howard Riddle, at Westminster magistrates' court in March 2016. The case was brought by Durham police and arose from a *Sun* article published after footballer Adam Johnson's arrest in 2015 for illegal sexual activity with a 15-year-old girl. Johnson was jailed for this in March 2016. The article showed part of a photo of him with the girl in which her face was obscured. The article did not name her and warned that anyone who identified her online would face prosecution. But, Mr Riddle heard, some social media users identified her because they recognised similarities between the original photo, from when it had been visible on a private Facebook account, and the altered version used by *The Sun*. Mr Riddle said he was satisfied that Dinsmore and *The Sun* staff thought they were complying with the law because they took extensive steps to change the photo to obscure the girl's image, including changing the colour and length of her hair, and the background in the photo. Dinsmore, who in 2015 became chief operating officer of News UK which owns *The Sun*, told the court that the test staff applied was 'Can this person be identified by a man or woman on the street?' He was ordered to pay £1,000 in compensation to the girl and £1,300 in costs. He apologised to the girl (Durham Constabulary press release; *Press Gazette*, 7 March 2016).

See www.pressgazette.co.uk/sun-story-led-identification-sexual-adam-johnson-sexual-offence-victim

Ch. 10 explains the ban on identifying the victims of sexual offences and the risks of jigsaw identification.

TV cameras to be used in Crown court pilot study

Television cameras are being allowed into Crown courts for the first time. Sentencing remarks made by senior judges were to be filmed in a pilot scheme due to start in late spring 2016. This footage was not to be broadcast but the historic move could pave the way for the first live coverage of sentencing in Crown court cases. Until now filming has only been allowed at the Court of Appeal and Supreme Court. The three-month pilot was taking place at the Old Bailey, and courts at Southwark in south London, Manchester (Crown Square), Birmingham, Bristol,

Liverpool, Leeds and Cardiff. The cameras would film only the judge—filming of all other court users, including defendants and court staff, remained banned (Ministry of Justice press release, 20 March 2016; *Media Lawyer*, 21 March 2016).

Ch. 11 explains the normal ban on photography and filming in courts.

Public has right to take notes at open court hearings

Members of the public attending hearings in open court have the right to take notes—and judges should interfere with that right only when it is believed that it would interfere with the course of justice—for example, by allowing someone to brief a witness about the evidence being given by others. Lord Justice Burnett, sitting in the Divisional Court (part of the High Court) with Mr Justice Sweeney, said: 'The common law has long upheld the principle that open justice is central to the rule of law.' While the open justice principle might be curtailed in limited circumstances, generally dictated by statute or rules of court, none applied in this case, he said: 'There is no primary or secondary legislation that governs note-taking in the Crown Court. Neither is the topic governed by any practice direction.' The decision (*Ewing v Crown Court Sitting at Cardiff & Newport & Ors* [2016] EWHC 183 (Admin)) should help any journalist who is forced to sit in the public seats at a court and then told by ushers, clerks or security staff that note-taking is not allowed, and reporters should cite it to anyone who tries to stop them taking notes (*Media Lawyer*, 10 February 2016).

Ch. 14 explains the principle of open justice.

Incedal trial restrictions

Media organisations lost a challenge over continuing restrictions on reporting a terrorism trial which was held in conditions of unprecedented secrecy. The case centred on what should now be allowed to be reported following the Old Bailey trial of law student Erol Incedal, who in 2015 was acquitted of plotting to target individuals such as former Prime Minister Tony Blair or carry out a 'Mumbai-style' outrage using a Kalashnikov but jailed for possessing a bomb-making manual. His friend Mounir Rarmoul-Bouhadjar, also aged 28 and from south London, was jailed as well after admitting possessing the same manual. Much of Incedal's trial was in private, with only a small group of journalists being allowed to attend but barred from reporting on anything they saw or heard. In addition, parts of the trial were held in secret, with the press as well as the public excluded. Rejecting the media's challenge to the trial judge's refusal to lift reporting restrictions which had covered those parts of the trial which were held in private, the Lord Chief Justice, Lord Thomas, in the Court of Appeal, emphasised the importance of open justice, but said that the trial judge had made the correct decision 'in the interests of national security' (*The Guardian*, 1 April 2015 and 9 February 2016; *Media Lawyer*, 9 February 2016).

Ch. 15, Challenging the courts, refers to an earlier challenge over whether Incedal and Rarmoul-Bouhadjar could be named in coverage—see p. 182.

Celebrity wins privacy injunction

A well-known person in the entertainment world won an injunction to stop *The Sun on Sunday* reporting a couple's tale of a sexual threesome with him. The Court of Appeal held that the man, who is married to and has children with another high-profile showbusiness figure, was entitled to regard his extra-marital sexual liaisons as private. His relationship with his partner was—despite his occasional sexual encounters outside it—a committed and loving one, so there was no 'false image' to correct about their marriage, the Court said. In addition, disclosure of his 'open marriage' would be devastating for him, and 'a factor to place in the balance' was the effect it would have on his children if they were to learn of these matters from schoolfriends or the internet (because of material the newspaper wanted to publish). Also, such disclosure would not advance 'public debate', the Court added. The decision suggests that newspapers are now rarely likely to win against such privacy claims, especially if a claimant argues his/her children would suffer if the material were published. The newspaper criticised the judgment as a blow against the freedom of the press to tell the truth and said that the celebrity had regularly used his children as 'photogenic baubles' to enhance his image, but was now using them as 'human shields' to cover up behaviour of which he appeared to be ashamed (*PJS v News Group Newspapers Ltd* [2016] EWCA Civ 100; *Media Lawyer*, 22 March 2016; *The Sun on Sunday*, 27 March 2016).

Ch. 26 explains privacy law.

MGN loses bid to appeal on hacking damages

The Supreme Court rejected an application by Mirror Group Newspapers to appeal over record phone-hacking damages totalling £1.2 million awarded in a case brought by eight celebrities. The Court said that the newspaper group did not raise an arguable point of law. The decision means that the damages originally awarded by Mr Justice Mann, who assessed them on the basis that the hacking involved was 'so serious and so prolonged', were expected to provide a framework for resolving similar actions which were still going through the civil courts (*Media Lawyer*, 23 March 2016).

Ch. 26 on privacy refers to this case, and ch. 35 explains the risks of being charged with hacking or intercepting.

Journalist wins FoI battle to name council tax debt councillor

Dale Haslam, a reporter with the Newsquest paper *The Bolton News*, won a three-and-a-half year battle using the Freedom of Information Act 2000 to discover from Bolton council the name of a councillor who had been summoned to court for non-payment of council tax. The council, refusing to name the councillor, had cited the section 40 (personal data) exemption in the Act. But in March 2016 Judge Kate Markus QC, in the Upper Tribunal, ordered it to give Mr Haslam the councillor's name, saying it was 'not reasonable' for a councillor to expect not to be identified in these circumstances. There were 'powerful factors' as to why a councillor's default in paying council tax was a serious matter of public concern, both over the individual's ability to perform his key functions and in terms of public accountability, she said (*Haslam v Information Commissioner and another* [2016] UKUT 0139 (AAC); *Bolton News*, 17 March 2016; *Panopticonblog. com*, 18 March 2014).

See www.theboltonnews.co.uk/news/14373965.REVEALED__Labour_councillor_finally_admits_not_paying_council_tax_after_three_year_battle_to_name_ him/

Ch. 30 explains the Freedom of Information Act 2000.

No change to FoI law, says government

Ministers have made clear there will be no major changes to the Freedom of Information Act 2000 after an outcry over potential curbs. The government said that introducing routine fees for making requests for information would be 'inappropriate' after a review by an Independent Commission found that the legislation was 'generally working well'. The Commission's report praised the legislation for 'enhancing openness and transparency', but suggested that some changes were needed to improve 'clarity and certainty'. But there was no need for the Act to be 'radically altered' or for the right of access to information to be restricted. The Commission's conclusions represent a victory for national newspapers and a wide range of other organisations which campaigned against any restrictive change to the Act (*Media Lawyer*, 1 March 2016).

Ch. 30 explains the Freedom of Information Act 2000.

Use of confidential sources under further threat

The UK government has said it intends to protect journalists' rights to have confidential sources who supply the media with information. But the Investigatory Powers Bill 2015–16 seems to undermine what protection there was. The Bill is designed to regulate surveillance activity by official agencies—for example, surveillance of suspected terrorists. But media lawyers warn that its measures will, if made law in the form proposed, give police and other official agencies greater powers to access journalists' private communications data as well as other information, which will put the confidentiality of journalists' sources at greater risk.

In addition, lawyers have warned that, because the Bribery Act 2010 can be used by the authorities, journalists now paying confidential sources for leaks of information to expose wrongdoing or inefficiency will be unable to use the public interest defence accepted by the juries which acquitted journalists charged in Operation Elveden. This was the Metropolitan police's investigation into payments by journalists to public officials. The Elveden charges included conspiracy to commit or aiding and abetting misconduct in public office, a common law offence used because Elveden investigated events which occurred before the 2010 Act came into force. Operation Elveden has now closed—the announcement was made by the Metropolitan police on 26 February 2016.

Also, lawyers have warned that a journalist using an unofficial police 'contact' to gain information now risks being charged with conspiracy to commit, or aiding and abetting, an offence created in section 26 of the Criminal Justice and Courts Act 2015, covering 'improper' conduct by police officers. No money needs to change hands for the offence to take place, because the Act can be breached if a police officer exercises power or privileges, when he/she knows or ought to know that it is improper to do so, in order to gain a benefit or detriment for someone else. The government said this offence was created to 'supplement' the common law misconduct offence (Explanatory Notes to the 2015 Act; *Media Lawyer*, various dates, including 26 February and 14, 16 and 22 March 2016).

Ch. 34 explains the law on protection of journalists' sources. Ch. 35 outlines Elveden and explains the risks of being charged with bribery or 'misconduct'.

The Sun's battle in RIPA powers case

The legal regime in the Regulation of Investigatory Powers Act 2000 (RIPA) under which police obtained three *Sun* journalists' communications data breached their rights to freedom of expression under Article 10 of the European Convention on Human Rights, the Investigatory Powers Tribunal has ruled.

The case arose because the Metropolitan police used the 'authorisation' powers in section 22 of RIPA to get data from phone companies to seek to discover which of its officers had apparently leaked information to the newspaper about the 'Plebgate' episode. This concerned allegations that Andrew Mitchell, then government Chief Whip, used abusive language to police officers in Downing Street. The data included which phone accounts were used to call or text the journalists, what numbers they had rung or texted, and times and durations of calls.

The Sun and the journalists complained to the Tribunal that their Article 10 rights to have confidential sources were breached by this use of the Act. The Tribunal said:

> We have held that the use of the section 22 power in this investigation was indeed both necessary and proportionate in respect of three out of the four authorisations challenged, but are compelled to hold that the legal regime in place at the relevant time did not adequately safeguard the important public interest in the right of a journalist to protect the identity of his source.

But the Tribunal refused to order any compensation for the newspaper or its journalists, saying that its judgment itself was 'just satisfaction'. The legal code under which police obtained the data—which included records of calls made to *The Sun's* newsdesk—has since been reformed to require police to make an application to a Crown court judge if they want access to journalists' communications data and to notify the media organisation or journalist concerned so that the application can be challenged at a court hearing (*News Group Newspapers Ltd and others v Commissioner of the Police of the Metropolis* [2015] UKIPTrib 14_176-H; *Media Lawyer*, 4 February 2016).

Ch. 34 refers to this case and relevant law.

McNae's at a glance

McNae's Essential Law for Journalists contains a range of features to help you find the information you need quickly—in class and on the job. This short guide outlines these features and how they can help you.

glossary Glossary terms are highlighted in the text and defined in the glossary at the back of the book and on www.mcnaes.com.

Chapter summaries introduce each chapter and outline the content—and why it matters to a journalist.

Cross-references point out related information in other chapters, helping you navigate key areas and understand the full picture.

Case studies appear throughout the text to provide context and examples of how the law and ethical codes have been applied to real-life situations.

These features offer advice from the authors on applying media law and ethical codes on the job, and reminders about relevant content elsewhere in the book.

These features offer advice from the authors on asserting your rights.

The website that accompanies this book, www.mcnaes.com, contains regular updates from the authors, as well as self-test resources, writing tips and additional chapters and information on a range of key topics.

Each chapter features a summary of the essential points—ideal for revision and as an at-a-glance reminder.

A list of useful websites is included at the end of each chapter to help students and journalists find information quickly

www.mcnaes.com

McNae's Essential Law for Journalists is accompanied by a free-to-use website—www.mcnaes.com—that features extra resources for both students and journalists.

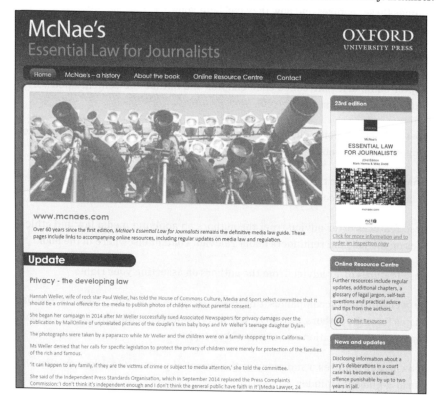

Updates

Whether you are studying or a working journalist, keep your knowledge up-to-date at www.mcnaes.com with regular updates from the authors on key changes affecting media law and ethics.

Online-only chapters

Access additional online chapters on

> The incitement of hate
>
> Scottish media law
>
> Terrorism and the effect of counter-terrorism law

as well as extended chapters on family law and the Official Secrets Acts.

Additional material

Find additional detail and resources on a range of topics, including media coverage before trial, reporting on juveniles, challenging the courts and privacy.

Self-test questions

Test your media law know-how and get instant feedback with chapter-related questions—ideal preparation for exams or to refresh your knowledge.

Glossary

Need to check a key term at court or on the way to class? Download the *McNae's* glossary for on-the-go access to essential legal terms. The glossary is also available to download as flashcards for ready-made exam preparation.

Extra resources

Writing tips—including how to avoid clichés and advice on commonly confused words—from the experts at Oxford University Press.

www.mcnaes.com also features regular discussion pieces and information on the history of *McNae's*, as well as key news from OUP and the authors.

Part 1

The landscape of law, ethics and regulation

1

Introduction

Chapter summary

The UK media enjoy freedoms which are the envy of journalists in oppressed societies. Nevertheless, the UK has more laws affecting journalism than is the case in some other democracies, and so a sound, thorough knowledge of legal matters is especially important for UK journalists, particularly in their role as 'watchdogs' acting on the public's behalf. This chapter explains how the UK's laws are made and how the European Convention on Human Rights helps safeguard freedom of expression. It also outlines the distinction between criminal and civil law, and between solicitors and barristers.

▶ Free but with restrictions

Although the UK has a 'free press' in comparison to the authoritarian censorship which stifles liberty in some other nations, the description must be qualified because of the many and growing restrictions on what can be published. This book covers the increasing number of laws affecting journalism.

The importance of freedom of expression, and of the journalist's position as a watchdog ensuring a properly informed public in a democratic society, have been stressed by both the UK courts and the European Court of Human Rights in Strasbourg.

The senior law lord, Lord Bingham, said in 2000 in a case in the House of Lords, predecessor of the Supreme Court:

ch. 21, p. 289, The nature of press conferences, explains this case

❝ In a modern, developed society it is only a small minority of citizens who can participate directly in the discussions and decisions which shape the public life of that society. The majority can participate only indirectly, by exercising their rights as citizens to vote, express their opinions, make representations to the authorities, form pressure groups and so on. But the majority cannot participate in the public life of their society in these ways if they are not alerted to and informed about matters which call or may call for consideration and action. It is very largely through the media, including of course the press, that they will be so alerted and informed. The proper functioning of a modern participatory democracy requires that the media be free, active, professional and enquiring. (*McCartan Turkington Breen v Times Newspapers Ltd* [2001] 2 AC 277) **🙰🙰**

It is the journalist's job to help safeguard freedom of expression and a free media, by reporting accurately and ensuring that people are properly informed about what is being done in their name by those who claim to govern them. It is also the job of journalists to safeguard the principle of an independent judiciary by reporting what is going on in the courts which apply the laws intended to safeguard the interests of all.

To do all this, journalists must know the law: where it comes from, what it says and what it allows them to do—or stops them doing.

The UK has a vibrant and wide-ranging media—newspapers, magazines, radio and television stations, and of course the ever-growing internet, with the myriad text and audio-visual sites it offers—and the law applies to all of them. Many are also subject to regulatory systems. This book explains how reporting restrictions, libel and privacy laws limit what may be published—and the financial consequences of mistakes or recklessness in journalism. But it also emphasises the freedoms which exist to publish and investigate. Only by knowing what is and is not possible, and what may or may not be done, can journalists, broadcasters, website operators and those who work with them keep the freedoms and variety of platforms they have now, campaign for greater freedom—and ensure that their work is not discredited or curtailed by some foolish but expensive error.

chs. 2 and 3 focus on codes of ethics

Journalists' ethics are under increasing scrutiny. The observance of ethical codes should be an integral part of how journalists operate, to help produce respected, fair journalism and preserve freedoms. Failure to respect these codes risks the creation of new and punitive laws aimed at curbing malpractices and limiting everyone's freedoms.

◗ Sources of law

→ glossary

The main sources of the law have traditionally been custom, precedent and statute.

Custom

→ glossary

When the English legal system began to take shape in the Middle Ages, royal judges were appointed to administer the 'law and custom of the realm'. This developed into the **common law**.

Precedent

As judges applied the common law to the cases before them, their decisions were recorded by lawyers. This process continues. Records of leading cases give the facts considered by a court and the reasons for its decision. The UK has a hierarchy of courts, so a decision made by a lower court can be challenged by appeal to a higher court. The decisions made by the higher courts—precedents—are binding on all lower courts, thus shaping their future rulings. Precedents evolve and develop the common law.

Figure 1 is a diagram of the hierarchy of the courts in England and Wales. The nature and role of these courts is explained further in later chapters.

A **Supreme Court** judgment binds all other UK courts, apart from—in most respects—Scottish criminal courts. But the Supreme Court can refuse to follow its own precedents, which otherwise can only be overturned or reversed by legislation.

Below the Supreme Court, the Court of Appeal's decisions bind the High Court and the lower courts, and High Court decisions bind all lower courts.

 → glossary

 chs. 8, 12 and 13 explain the roles of the Court of Appeal and High Court

 Ch. 37 explains Northern Ireland's courts, and the www.mcnaes.com chapter on Scotland outlines that nation's courts system.

Figure 1 Hierarchy of the courts

Fam = Family (civil); Ch = Chancery (civil); QBD = Queen's Bench Division (civil and criminal)—see chs. 8, 12 and 13 for these High Court roles

Statutes and statutory instruments

→ glossary

Common law can be modified or replaced by statutes—Acts of Parliament, which are primary legislation. But British governments have made increasing use of secondary legislation known as **statutory instruments**. Parliament frequently uses Acts to enshrine broad principles in legislation, but delegates the detailed framing of the new law to the departmental Minister concerned, who sets its detail out in statutory instruments in the form of regulations or rules. Statutory instruments must be approved by Parliament.

European regulations and directives

The UK is part of the European Union, so EU treaties and other EU law are part of UK law. The EU's Council and its Parliament agree regulations and directives which are binding on member states as part of the EU's *raison d'être* of encouraging trade between member states by harmonising their laws. EU regulations apply in the form in which they are drawn up, but member states decide how directives should be implemented through their own legislation.

The European Court of Justice, based in Luxembourg, clarifies—for the national courts of EU member states—interpretation of EU legislation. It can, for example, rule on allegations that a member state has infringed EU law to gain advantage in trade and penalise a state for such infringement. This court is not to be confused with the European Court of Human Rights.

▌ The European Convention on Human Rights

After the Second World War the horrors of the repression and genocide inflicted by the Nazi Party prompted western European nations to create the Council of Europe to promote individual freedom, political liberty and the rule of law. The Council's work led to the European Convention for the Protection of Human Rights and Fundamental Freedoms—usually called the European Convention on Human Rights—which sets out rights which must be protected by signatory states, and to the foundation of the European Court of Human Rights (ECtHR), which sits in Strasbourg. The rights the Convention guarantees include the right to respect for privacy and family life, in Article 8, and the right to freedom of expression, in Article 10. Forty-seven states have adopted the Convention, and any of their citizens can take a case to the Strasbourg court to argue that the state has failed to protect them from, or to sufficiently compensate them for, a breach of a Convention right. The Convention has very wide application, as a state will be held to have breached a right if its legal system fails to stop or to offer an adequate remedy for a violation of an individual's rights by a private body or individual as well as by a state authority or body.

The Human Rights Act 1998

The Human Rights Act 1998 came into force on 2 October 2000, putting the Convention into UK law and greatly increasing its influence on UK courts. Individuals can require any UK court to consider their rights under the Convention in the context of any case.

The Act requires any UK court determining a question in connection with a Convention right to take account of the ECtHR's decisions, requires new UK legislation to be compatible with Convention rights, and says old and new legislation must be construed so far as possible to conform with them.

It is unlawful for UK public authorities to act in a manner incompatible with the Convention.

Convention rights

Adopting the Convention directly into UK law has required judges systematically to consider Convention rights, which conflict in many cases.

For journalists, the most important part of the Convention is Article 10, which says in part: 'Everyone has the right to freedom of expression. This right shall include freedom to hold opinions and to receive and impart information and ideas without interference by public authority.'

Article 10 makes clear that restrictions on this right have to be justified, necessary in a democratic society, proportionate and 'prescribed by law'.

Journalists wanting to exercise their Article 10 rights might find themselves facing a claim under Article 8—the right to respect for privacy and family life—such as someone seeking an injunction to stop publication of a story about his/her personal life, or seeking damages if the material has been published.

Weighing competing rights

The methodology a court should use to decide in any particular case whether one Convention right should prevail over another was detailed in *Re S (A Child) (Identification: Restrictions on Publication)* [2004] UKHL 47. In that House of Lords judgment, Lord Steyn said:

> First, neither article has as such precedence over the other. Secondly, where the values under the two articles are in conflict, an intense focus on the comparative importance of the specific rights being claimed in the individual case is necessary. Thirdly, the justifications for interfering with or restricting each right must be taken into account. Finally, the proportionality test must be applied to each. For convenience I will call this the ultimate balancing test.

Lord Steyn was emphasising that the particular circumstances of each case must be intensely considered to decide which Convention right—and therefore which party to the argument—prevails in each matter to be decided.

see ch. 15, p. 182

see www. mcnaes.com, ch. 13, for more detail on the *Re S* judgment

Articles 2,
3, 6, 8 and
10 are
set out in
Appendix 1,
pp. 461–462

In some judgments relevant to the media, Article 2 (the right to life) and Article 3 (the prohibition of torture and inhuman or degrading treatment or punishment) are cited and, by their very nature, can have great weight—for example, if it is argued with justification that someone's name or address should not be published to protect him/her from violent criminals or vigilantes.

Divisions of the law

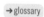

see chs. 4–9
for more
detail about
the criminal
justice
system, a
huge source
of news for
journalists

→ glossary

There are two main divisions of law—criminal and civil.

Criminal law deals with offences which harm the whole community and thus are considered to be offences against the sovereign. A Crown court case in which John Smith is accused of an offence is listed as *R v Smith*. 'R' stands for Regina (the Queen) or Rex (the King), depending on the monarch at the time, and 'v' for 'versus'.

A lawyer talking about this case would generally refer to it as 'The Queen (or the King) *and* Smith' (italics added).

Civil law concerns disputes between individuals and organisations, and includes the redress of **torts**—that is, wrongs suffered. Medical negligence, defamation and breach of copyright are all torts. A case in which Mary Brown sues John Smith will be known in writing as *Brown v Smith*. Lawyers will speak of the case as 'Brown *and* Smith'.

In practice, the two divisions overlap: many acts or omissions are criminal offences for which an individual may be prosecuted and punished as well as civil 'wrongs' for which the injured party may recover compensation—for example, a motorist in a road accident may be prosecuted for dangerous driving and sued by someone who was injured in the crash.

Civil and criminal law cases have different terminologies. In criminal courts a defendant is prosecuted, pleads guilty or not guilty, is acquitted or convicted and, if convicted, is sentenced—for example, fined or jailed. In civil courts a claimant sues a defendant or respondent, who admits or denies liability, is found either to be liable or not liable and, if liable, is ordered to pay damages.

Civil courts also resolve disputes between couples such as divorce actions.

> Chs. 12 and 13 explain the civil courts, which have newsworthy cases. Other chapters cover civil laws, such as privacy and copyright, which journalists can be accused of infringing.

The legal profession

Lawyers are either solicitors or barristers.

By tradition and practice, solicitors deal directly with the client—a defendant in a criminal case or someone seeking advice or representation in a civil case. Solicitors advise, prepare the client's case and take advice, when necessary, from a barrister specialising in a particular area of the law. Solicitors may represent their clients in court, and solicitor-advocates may appear in the higher courts.

Barristers are known, singly or collectively, as 'counsel'. A barrister wears a wig and gown in the higher courts, the Crown courts and county courts, but not in magistrates' courts. Barristers who have been practising for at least 10 years may apply to the Lord Chancellor for appointment as a Queen's Counsel and, if successful, use the letters QC after their names.

▶ High offices in law

The constitutional position in the UK and other democracies is that the nation's 'executive' (the government) is separate from the judiciary (the judges), to help ensure that the judiciary is independent of political influence and that the government is subject to the rule of law, just as other organisations and citizens are.

The head of the judiciary is the Lord Chief Justice.

The UK government is advised on law by the Attorney General, which is a political role with holders attending Cabinet meetings. The Attorney General also has a prosecution role—he/she approves the instigation of, and may personally conduct, prosecutions in certain important cases. These include, as ch. 18 explains, proceedings against media organisations for contempt of court.

➡ Recap of major points

- The media are the eyes and ears of the general public, and free media are an essential element in maintaining parliamentary democracy.
- The European Convention on Human Rights has codified fundamental freedoms, including that of freedom of expression.
- Sources of UK law include custom, precedent, statutes and statutory instruments, and European Union regulations.
- The two main divisions of the law are criminal law and civil law, and journalists need to use correctly the legal terms appropriate for the type of court case they are reporting.

((•)) Useful Websites

www.parliament.uk/about/how/laws/
    UK Parliament—'Making laws'

www.echr.coe.int
    European Court of Human Rights—the 'Official Texts' link leads to the Convention

www.judiciary.gov.uk/
Judiciary of England and Wales—information on judges and the courts system

www.lawsociety.org.uk/law-careers/becoming-a-solicitor/
Law Society information on solicitors

www.barcouncil.org.uk/about-the-bar/about-barristers/
Bar Council site—'About barristers'

www.attorneygeneral.gov.uk
Attorney General's Office

Press regulation

Chapter summary

People aggrieved by what newspapers or magazines and their websites publish about them, or by how journalists have treated them, may want a watchdog body to intervene in or adjudicate on their complaint. A new watchdog—the Independent Press Standards Organisation (Ipso)—began operating in 2014, replacing the Press Complaints Commission (PCC). Ipso uses the Editors' Code of Practice to adjudicate on complaints. This chapter introduces and outlines the Code.

▶ Introduction

There are no state controls in the UK on who can own or run newspapers, magazines, their online versions or any kind of news website—publications defined by the term 'the press'. Anyone with the resources can launch a new publication. These liberties help keep the UK's media relatively free from state influence. Newspapers, magazines and websites are free to be partisan about social and political issues. Editors may use leader columns, news stories and features to campaign on any issue, from environmental law to local hospital closures. They and their journalists may also publish, subject to the restraints of libel and other laws, their own fierce criticisms of those in the news, or anyone else. The lack of any requirement for these media sectors to be impartial contrasts with the position of the broadcasting industry, as the next chapter explains.

But newspaper and magazine owners recognise that irresponsible journalism could lead Parliament to introduce a statutory system of regulation, specifying standards of accuracy, fairness and so on, or even to establish an official tribunal to hear complaints against publications, impose financial penalties, or force editors to publish corrections or replies.

The UK broadcasting sector has such a statutory system, as explained in the next chapter. But broadcast journalism in its routine form may be tamer than the ch. 35 outlines the phone-hacking scandal

daily output of the press, which can be raucous and more likely to probe, and tends to set the nation's news agenda.

The press industry created the Press Complaints Commission in 1991 to keep the threat of statutory regulation at bay. The PCC was—it can be argued—better than the Press Council, its predecessor, because it developed a faster service—which remained free of charge—for handling complaints. Also, PCC adjudications and guidance established the Editors' Code as the standard, succinct set of rules for editors and journalists in the press. But revelations by *The Guardian* in 2011 about the huge scale of the phone-hacking by the *News of the World* sounded the death knell for the PCC, which had failed to understand or probe the extent of that criminality. The revelations led Prime Minister David Cameron to appoint senior judge Lord Justice Leveson to hold a public inquiry into 'the culture, practices, and ethics of the press'.

Controversy after Leveson reported

see Useful Websites at the end of this chapter for the Leveson Report

The Leveson Report, published in 2012, called for a new regulator which should be more independent of the industry than the PCC was, with better investigatory powers and the ability to fine the newspapers, magazines and websites it regulates if they seriously or systemically breach its code of ethics.

A deep concern among the press was that Leveson's proposed regulatory system included an overseeing 'recognition body', to be created by statute (and therefore in a form decided by politicians) which would conduct periodic reviews of the effectiveness—in terms of promoting standards in journalism—of any regulator funded by the press. Critics said the concept offered potential for future governments to interfere with press freedom, by exercising influence through the role of, or powers granted to, the 'recognition body'—for example, by giving it powers to insist that a regulator impose tighter rules on the press, with harsh penalties for breaching them. Nevertheless, in late 2013 the government, with cross-party support in the House of Commons, put in place a Royal Charter creating a legal framework for a model of regulation close to that proposed by Leveson.

The Royal Charter model has been rejected by all major newspaper and magazine publishers, which see it as a step closer to state-run statutory regulation. Most major newspaper and magazine groups, including the vast majority of the regional and local press, agreed to establish and fund—and be bound by the decisions of—the Independent Press Standards Organisation (Ipso). It operates a self-regulatory system created by these press groups to adjudicate on complaints against their journalism or journalistic activity. Ipso has no connection to the Charter model, but has some of the features Leveson wanted a regulator to have.

Press regulation is now fragmented as five national newspapers—the *Financial Times*, *The Guardian*, *The Observer*, the *Independent* and the *Independent on Sunday*—and the *London Standard* are owned by groups which have so far decided against joining the Ipso system. Each of these groups has its own system to consider complaints.

A Panel waiting for a role

The shunning by major press groups of the Royal Charter model meant that the Press Recognition Panel—which, because of the Charter, came into existence in November 2014 and had a board appointed to run it—twiddled its thumbs for months. By early 2016, when the main text of this book was completed, no regulator existed other than Ipso, and the press groups which fund the Ipso system did not want it to apply for 'recognition' (meaning that Ipso will not be subject to periodic reviews by the Panel).

The Independent Monitor for the Press (Impress) project—see Useful Websites at the end of this chapter—which has supporters who include some journalists and philanthropists, is pledged to regulate press organisations 'in compliance with Leveson's criteria'. In January 2016 it announced it had 10 publishers signed up as members—including hyperlocal and investigative organisations—and applied to the Panel for 'recognition'. But Impress, should it become a Panel-recognised regulator, will only be able to consider complaints against publishers in its membership. This means that, as far as can currently be foreseen, it will have no power to adjudicate on complaints against any of the UK's major press organisations as they have either joined Ipso or decided to run their own complaints systems. By early 2016 it remained very unlikely that any major press group would sign up to 'recognised' regulation.

Law created to drive the press into 'recognised' regulation

Sections 34–39 and 41–42 of the Crime and Courts Act 2013 created the position that any press organisation not signed up to a Panel-recognised regulation system was, from November 2015, exposed—to some extent—to a greater likelihood of having to pay 'exemplary' (punitive) damages in privacy and defamation cases it might lose in the courts.

 Ch. 19 explains defamation and ch. 26 explains privacy law.

Also, sections 40–42 of the Act could lead to a press party which wins such a case—for example, successfully defending its exposure of a major criminal—being deprived of the right to recover its costs from the losing party, unless that press organisation is in such a 'recognised' system.

The government's (Leveson-inspired) rationale behind these provisions was that they would help drive the press into 'recognised' arbitration schemes offering financial compensation for people with valid complaints against the press. Leveson favoured such arbitration as it would be cheaper for claimants than seeking redress in the courts. But the press fears that cheap arbitration will encourage spurious complaints which are time-consuming to deal with, or complainants with valid complaints to seek financial redress rather than be satisfied by adjudications and/or corrections and/or apologies, which is all Ipso currently offers.

The 'costs' provisions will only come into force if the Secretary of State for Culture, Media and Sport activates them. Also, the courts will only be able to apply these provisions if the Recognition Panel has by then 'recognised' a regulator—for example, Impress. They cannot be applied in the absence of such an approved regulator.

A press group hit financially by this provision under the 2013 Act—through refusal to join a 'recognised' regulator—may decide to argue in the UK courts, and possibly in the European Court of Human Rights, that such financial discrimination breaches the right to freedom of expression guaranteed by Article 10 of the European Convention on Human Rights.

 Check www.mcnaes.com for updates on press regulation.

❚ The Independent Press Standards Organisation

Under the Ipso system a person or organisation aggrieved by what has been published or how journalists have behaved should complain first to the relevant editor. A complainant who remains dissatisfied should then contact Ipso and will be asked to state what part or parts of the Editors' Code have allegedly been breached. Ipso offers what the PCC did—a free process involving guidance, mediation and, if the complaint remains unresolved, a ruling. Ipso's complaints committee decides to what extent it needs to make such an adjudication.

The Code is discussed in detail below and in other chapters. Its clauses are reviewed by the Editors' Code of Practice Committee—the Code Committee—which consists mainly of editors but which, as part of the response to the Leveson report, now includes people independent of the press.

The Code was originally created as part of the PCC system. The continuity in its use means that the PCC's jurisprudence—its adjudication decisions, based on the Code—will continue to be valuable guidance for journalists, and so this book draws on it. But Ipso is not bound by that jurisprudence.

Ipso does not offer financial redress to those whose complaints are upheld (and nor did the PCC). In 2015 Ipso consulted on whether it should pilot an independent arbitration scheme which could offer financial redress. But there is little enthusiasm for arbitration among much of the press, as explained earlier.

✳ Remember

Ipso has the contractual power to fine any member publication—newspaper, magazine or website—up to £1 million for a serious or systemic breach of the Code. The PCC did not have this power.

Compliance procedures

The Ipso system puts much greater emphasis than the PCC did on member publications having formal compliance procedures, so that they can demonstrate—for example, in annual reports—what ethical training they give their journalists and how complaints are handled, as they should, ideally, be resolved without need for Ipso involvement. This means that publications have, to a greater extent, adopted the formal internal procedures, including 'audit trails', which major broadcast organisations already had for making and recording decisions on ethical issues.

 See the Additional Material for ch. 2 on www.mcnaes.com for more detail of the Ipso system.

▶ The Ipso complaints process

Ipso may rule that a complaint was not justified or that, even if it was, an editor's response, such as a private or published apology or an offer to publish a correction, was enough to resolve the issue. It might negotiate a resolution to a problem. It might also intervene before anything is published, as the PCC did—for example, in cases in which people want the press to leave them alone. But if Ipso decides to proceed to a formal adjudication, it will require an editor to publish any adverse adjudication, which it can also publish on its website. This public acknowledgement that the Code was breached is the redress for those whose complaints are upheld. This was the redress under the PCC system. In any case in which Ipso imposes a financial penalty on the media organisation for the breach, the complainant will have the additional satisfaction of knowing that this has occurred.

Ipso, because of its contractual powers to impose financial penalties, can also specify where a signed-up organisation publishes an adverse adjudication, to ensure suitable prominence.

Ipso also publishes adjudications which do not uphold a complaint, because adjudications illustrate how it interprets the Code. Generally, it will not consider a complaint about a published article from anyone not featured in or affected by it. But it can start an investigation without such a complaint if it considers that the article's content or activity by journalists needs such scrutiny, or that significant inaccuracy may have been published on a general point of fact.

▶ The scope of the Editors' Code

see
Appendix 2,
pp. 463–468

The Editors' Code—reproduced in full in Appendix 2 and also used by some UK press organisations not in the Ipso system—has 16 clauses. These set out ethical standards to, for example, uphold accuracy, to protect people's privacy and children's welfare, to prevent harassment, intrusion into grief or shock, and excessive detail in coverage of suicides, and to govern how journalists make inquiries at hospitals and use undercover tactics involving secret filming, subterfuge or misrepresentation.

In this book most of the Code's clauses are featured with case studies in relevant chapters—for example, ch. 27 has a focus on news-gathering, and so features clause 2 on privacy, clause 3 on harassment, clause 4 on intrusion into grief or shock, and clause 6 on children's welfare. This book's index entry for the Editors' Code lists pages featuring each clause. This chapter deals with the other clauses of wide application and clauses governing comparatively rare practices or specialist work in journalism.

see Useful Websites at the end of this chapter for the Codebook, Ipso and PCC sites

The Editors' Codebook, produced by the Code Committee, is online and offers guidance on the Code and adjudications. It is also useful to browse Ipso's website for adjudications and the PCC's archive of cases.

The Code does not deal with issues of taste and decency—the industry's position has been that, as these are subjective matters, rulings on them could compromise freedom of expression.

✳ Remember

→ glossary

see ch. 26, p. 340, Relevance of ethical codes, on judges and the Code, and ch. 28, p. 362, The Information Commissioner's Office guidance

Breaching the Editors' Code is not a criminal offence or a civil **tort**. But observing its requirements is ethical conduct and can help journalists avoid legal problems. Judges ruling on claims of media intrusion into privacy or of breach of data protection law must take relevant codes into account.

- Note that, for convenience, all references to the Code in this book adopt the clause numbering used in the latest version, which took effect from 1 January 2016, although earlier versions had different numbering.

Public interest exceptions in the Editors' Code

Some clauses or sub-clauses in the Code are marked with an asterisk, which indicates that breaches of these parts can be justified if an editor can demonstrate that what was done was 'in the public interest'.

The Code says 'the public interest' includes, but is not confined to:

- detecting or exposing crime, or the threat of crime, or serious impropriety;
- protecting public health or safety;
- protecting the public from being misled by an action or statement of an individual or organisation;
- disclosing a person or organisation's failure or likely failure to comply with any obligation to which he/she/it is subject;
- disclosing a miscarriage of justice;
- raising or contributing to a matter of public debate, including serious cases of impropriety, unethical conduct or incompetence concerning the public;
- disclosing concealment, or likely concealment, of any of the above.

The Code says editors seeking to rely on public interest exceptions 'will need to demonstrate that they reasonably believed publication—or journalistic activity taken with a view to publication—would both serve, and be proportionate to, the public interest and explain how they reached that decision at the time'. This wording means there is a requirement for there to be an 'audit trail'—for example, a record that there was **prima facie** evidence of a serious matter which gave → glossary rise to the editor's 'reasonable belief' that it was 'in the public interest' for his or her journalists to probe deeper—and records that careful decisions were made to ensure the investigation itself complied with the Code, which includes a requirement for such activity to be 'proportionate' to the investigation's aim. This 'reasonable belief' and careful approach are necessary under the Code to justify investigative methods—for example, as explained later, deception—or publication of material which would otherwise be deemed a breach of the Code.

It may be that the investigative journalism finds that there is nothing which needs exposure and so nothing is published. But if there is a complaint about the methods used, the 'audit trail' helps prove to Ipso why the 'reasonable belief' existed that such activity was necessary 'in the public interest' to discover what was true. Being able to prove there was such 'reasonable belief' could also be important in data protection law, explained in ch. 28, and—as ch. 22 explains—would help the media organisation use the 'public interest' defence successfully against a defamation lawsuit, if material was published.

Use of the term 'in the public interest' in the Code denotes that the journalism has a particularly high potential to be beneficial to society. But the Code also says: 'There is a public interest in freedom of expression itself.'

It stresses the need to protect young people, adding: 'An exceptional public interest would need to be demonstrated to over-ride the normally paramount interests of children under 16.'

> The Code's clause 6, covering the welfare of children, is explained in ch. 27, pp. 350–351, Protecting children's privacy and welfare, and clause 7, covering children in sexual offence cases, is explained in ch. 10, p. 118, Ethical considerations.

Accuracy and opportunity to reply

Clause 1 of the Code says: 'The Press must take care not to publish inaccurate, misleading or distorted information or images, including headlines not supported by the text.' It adds that 'a significant inaccuracy, misleading statement or distortion' must be corrected promptly and with due prominence, and, where appropriate, with a published apology, and that in cases involving Ipso due prominence should be as it stipulates.

see Late News section, Ipso censures *The Sun* for inaccuracy

It adds that the press 'while free to editorialise and campaign, must distinguish clearly between comment, conjecture and fact', and that a 'fair opportunity to reply to significant inaccuracies should be given, when reasonably called for'.

Many complaints to Ipso allege breaches of clause 1. It is not subject to the public interest exception—there is no public interest in inaccuracy.

👁 Case study

Ipso ruled that the *Ayrshire Post* breached clause 1 (accuracy) in an April 2015 article about a secure psychiatric unit. The article covered a report by Healthcare Improvement Scotland about its inspection visit to Ayr Clinic. Ipso said that while the article included some accurate details, its description of the inspection report as a 'shocker' and the article's claim that the clinic had been 'rapped on the knuckles' went beyond legitimate interpretation. The inspection report was positive, finding the clinic to be 'very good' in all areas, and the only recommendations it made were minor issues. The newspaper had failed to take care not to publish distorted information, Ipso said (*Partnerships in Care v Ayrshire Post*, issued 27 July 2015).

Coverage of suicides

see also ch. 16, p. 212, Ethical considerations when covering deaths

Research has found that news of suicides may prompt others to take their own lives in the same way. To minimise this risk, clause 5 of the Code says reports of suicides should avoid giving excessive detail about the method used.

Deception (subterfuge and misrepresentation)

Clause 10 of the Code says:

ch. 28 explains data protection law and ch. 35 explains hacking (interception) offences

" i) The press must not seek to obtain or publish material acquired by using hidden cameras or clandestine listening devices; or by intercepting private or mobile telephone calls, messages or emails; or by the unauthorised removal of documents or photographs; or by accessing digitally-held information without consent.

ii) Engaging in misrepresentation or subterfuge, including by agents or intermediaries, can generally be justified only in the public interest and then only when the material cannot be obtained by other means. "

It makes clear that journalists should normally be open and transparent when seeking information or comment by declaring from the outset to anyone unfamiliar with them that they are journalists.

see also p. 19, Recording phone calls

It also means that normally photography or filming must be done openly, and that eavesdropping by using 'bugs', or audio-recording by hidden microphones, will breach the Code because the activity is 'clandestine'. Irrespective of the Code, using hidden cameras or microphones could breach privacy law, as chs. 26 and 27 explain.

But this clause is subject to the public interest exceptions, so that if the story or journalistic activity is justified by a sufficient public interest, a journalist may pose as someone else, or use other kinds of subterfuge or hidden cameras or microphones, without breaching the Code. Such methods are common in investigative journalism. But the Code's wording means that misrepresentation and subterfuge should only be used when a public interest exception applies and—a further requirement—when it is reasonable to believe that an open approach would not work.

👁 Case study

Ipso ruled in 2015 that a freelance reporter was justified in using a hidden camera and deception to record views about Islam held by Magnus Nielsen, a UKIP candidate in the General Election. The reporter attended a rally where Mr Nielsen was a speaker. After the speech the reporter, without disclosing he was a journalist, approached Mr Nielsen and discussed the issues with him, secretly filming him. The *Daily Mirror* published the reporter's investigation. Mr Nielsen complained that it was a smear and his speech had been quoted selectively to distort his message. But Ipso said there was no breach of clause 1 (accuracy) or clause 10 (clandestine devices and subterfuge). The newspaper had provided historical screenshots of Mr Nielsen's Facebook page, which showed that posts about Islam had subsequently been deleted. Ipso said it was reasonable for the journalist and newspaper to believe they would be unable to ascertain Mr Nielsen's true views of Islam without employing subterfuge, which was justified in the public interest to prevent the public being potentially misled by Mr Nielsen's actions (*Nielsen v Daily Mirror*, 24 July 2015).

'Fishing expeditions'

The Code does not permit subterfuge or misrepresentation—including using hidden cameras or recording devices—or infringement of privacy in 'fishing expeditions'. A 'fishing expedition' is an investigation launched without sufficient prima facie grounds to justify such methods. An editor who authorises their use needs to be able to demonstrate from records that there was prima facie evidence to give rise to a reasonable belief that, for example, the investigation's target was or could be committing a crime or guilty of serious impropriety, or was or could be misleading the public or putting people's health or safety at risk. An editor will also need to be able to demonstrate that the methods used were proportionate and necessary.

→glossary

Recording phone calls

Journalists, particularly those involved in investigations, may decide to record their own telephone calls—for example, when they are interviewing the target of their inquiries. The recording may be needed as proof if the subject sues for defamation over what is published. In the UK it is legal for one party in a phone conversation to record it, even if the other is unaware this is being done.

Ipso has ruled that recording an interview given with consent does not constitute a breach of clause 10 (*Yates v Mail Online*, issued 15 June 2015), so this does not require a 'public interest' justification. Similarly, the PCC said that journalists who record calls they make or legitimately receive were not regarded as using a clandestine recording device under clause 10, even if they did not tell the other person the call was being recorded (*Messrs Lewis Silkin on behalf of Mrs Isobel Stone*, Report 49, 2000).

ch. 35 explains the law on hacking and interception

A journalist who fails to declare in such a call that he/she is a journalist may breach the Code's ban on subterfuge and misrepresentation, unless the 'public interest' exception applies and it was reasonable to conclude there was no other way to obtain the information.

Intercepting a phone call—using external technology to hack directly, or 'tap', into a phone system to listen to or record other people's conversations or messages—is illegal in most circumstances.

Discriminatory material

Clause 12 of the Code says the press must avoid prejudicial or pejorative reference to an individual's race, colour, religion, sex, gender identity or sexual orientation, or to any physical or mental illness or disability, and that details of an individual's race, colour, religion, gender identity, sexual orientation, physical or mental illness or disability must be avoided unless genuinely relevant to the story.

  See Useful Websites at the end of this chapter for guidance on reporting mental illness.

Financial journalism

Clause 13 of the Code seeks to prevent journalists making personal profit by anticipating movements in share prices on the basis of information leaked to them by business contacts. It says journalists 'must not use for their own profit financial information they receive in advance of its general publication, nor should they pass such information to others'. It also bans journalists from dealing in shares or securities about which they have recently written, or intend to write, as what they publish might affect market prices and it would be unethical for them to take financial advantage of this power. It says journalists must not write about shares or securities in which they or close relatives have a significant financial interest without disclosing it to their editor or financial editor.

Payments to witnesses

Media organisations covering high-profile stories may pay people, including the victims of notorious crimes, for the exclusive right to publish their accounts of events. In the case of crime victims, those accounts would be more than the evidence they can give in court, which would not have exclusive value. An account could, for example, include descriptions not limited by court rules on evidence. Clause 15 of the Code aims to prevent these 'chequebook journalism' deals interfering with the process of justice. The risk of contempt of court which can arise from these deals, or from a reporter interviewing anyone due to testify in a trial, is explained in ch. 18.

The first part of clause 15 says: 'No payment or offer of payment to a witness—or any person who may reasonably be expected to be called as a witness—should be made in any case once proceedings are active as defined by the Contempt of Court Act 1981.' The ban applies until a case ceases to be active or the suspect pleads guilty or there is a verdict.

The second part says that:

> [W]here proceedings are not yet active but are likely and foreseeable, editors must not make or offer payment to any person who may reasonably be expected to be called as a witness, unless the information concerned ought demonstrably to be published in the public interest and there is an over-riding need to make or promise payment for this to be done; and all reasonable steps have been taken to ensure that no financial dealings influence the evidence those witnesses give. In no circumstances should such payment be conditional on the outcome of a trial.

It says a payment or an offer of payment made to a person later cited to testify in proceedings must be disclosed to the prosecution and defence.

Payments to criminals

Clause 16 of the Code says: 'Payment or offers of payment for stories, pictures or information, which seek to exploit a particular crime or to glorify or glamorise crime in general, must not be made directly or via agents to convicted or confessed criminals or to their associates—who may include family, friends and colleagues.' This recognises that people, particularly crime victims, are likely to condemn a deal under which criminals or those close to them profit from tales of wrongdoing. But the clause also recognises that press payment to a criminal may be justified by the Code's public interest exceptions.

➡ Recap of major points

- The Editors' Code sets standards for journalists working for newspapers, magazines and websites.
- It has clauses to uphold accuracy and to protect people's privacy.
- It permits undercover reporting, but only if justified by special 'public interest' factors.

- The Independent Press Standards Organisation, which adjudicates on complaints against editors and journalists in member organisations in newspaper, magazine and online sectors, requires editors to publish adverse adjudications.

((•)) Useful Websites

www.ipso.co.uk/
 Ipso

http://pressrecognitionpanel.org.uk/
 Press Recognition Panel

www.editorscode.org.uk/
 Editors' Codebook

www.pcc.org.uk
 PCC website

www.pcc.org.uk/advice/editorials-detail.html?article=NDIwMA==
 PCC guidance on the reporting of mental health issues

www.levesoninquiry.org.uk/about/the-report/
 Leveson Report

http://impressproject.org/
 Impress Project

3

Broadcast regulation

Chapter summary

Television and radio journalism in the UK is regulated by statute. The Office of Communications (Ofcom), the independent regulator, adjudicates on complaints against broadcast journalists. Ofcom's Broadcasting Code says commercial broadcast organisations must be impartial when covering politics and social issues, and must be accurate, treat people fairly, respect privacy, and avoid causing harm and offence. Ofcom can impose substantial fines for breaches of the Code. The BBC is also required to be impartial and ethical. It is subject to the Code in some respects, but also has a system of self-regulation.

▌ Introduction

In the UK commercial broadcasters—those funded by advertising revenue—are regulated as regards ownership and journalistic output. As the previous chapter explained, newspaper, magazine and online-only publishers are free to be politically partisan. But broadcasters and their journalists must, when reporting news, be impartial about politics and social issues, although they are free to cover them in depth. The regulatory system also requires broadcasters to observe 'due accuracy' in news and other ethical norms. The regulator, the Office of Communications (Ofcom) can levy substantial fines on any broadcaster which seriously breaches journalistic standards.

Why regulate broadcasters?

Historically, broadcast media have been seen as having particular potential to influence, offend or harm their audiences. The emotional impact of moving images and sound, particularly on children in the audience, can be greater than that of printed text and still pictures—for example, if a programme has sexual content, or shows death or violence. Also, the ability of television and radio to air material instantaneously means they have great potential to provoke immediate public disorder or violence.

Television is also seen as having great potential—because moving images and sound can often portray intimate or harrowing experiences more vividly than photographs or text—to intrude into the privacy of those being filmed.

Politicians also decided that broadcasting must be regulated because, for decades, transmission was only possible on analogue wavelengths. These are relatively scarce, so the consensus was that a regulator was needed to vet broadcasters and specify requirements for quality in programmes and diversity in output.

These justifications for regulating broadcast media have lost some force as technological advances mean that newspapers, magazines and other publishers can 'webcast' audio-visual material on websites, so the power of moving images and sound is no longer exclusive to TV and radio. Digital transmission also allows many more channels, giving the public greater freedom of choice.

There is also an argument that regulating broadcast journalism is a societally beneficial counterbalance to the unregulated, partisan journalism of newspaper, magazine and website-only publishers, although it could also be said that regulation means broadcast journalism tends to have less impact than newspapers.

▌ Ofcom—its role and sanctions

Commercial broadcasters cannot transmit without a licence from Ofcom, which began operating in 2003, replacing previous regulators. It is structurally independent of the government, although the Secretary of State for Culture, Media and Sport appoints its chair and non-executive members of its main board. Ofcom, which for 2015/16 had a budget of £114.3 million, is funded mainly by licence fees paid by broadcasters and other charges it imposes, but has some government funding. It has a range of duties, including regulating phone services. The Communications Act 2003 makes Ofcom responsible for ensuring the existence of a wide range of TV and radio services of high quality and wide appeal, and for maintaining plurality in broadcasting. When deciding on applications for national, regional or local broadcast licences, it considers what programming is being proposed and whether the applicant is 'fit and proper'. Ofcom monitors whether broadcasters comply with the conditions of their licences—for instance, by meeting a 'public service' obligation to provide news. Licences are granted for set durations—for example, 12 years—and can be renewed.

The 2003 Act and the Broadcasting Act 1996 require Ofcom to draw up standards for programme content. These are detailed in the Ofcom Broadcasting Code. Anyone aggrieved by a programme's content or by how they were treated when it was made can—as long as the programme has been broadcast—complain to Ofcom, which assesses complaints against the standards set in the Code. Ofcom does not regulate all aspects of the BBC's output. Web content, even on sites run by broadcasters, is not subject to Ofcom regulation, as it is not defined in UK law as 'broadcast' material.

If Ofcom upholds a complaint, it can direct that a programme should not be repeated, or that the broadcaster must air a correction or a statement of Ofcom's findings. It can impose a fine if it considers a breach of the Code to be serious or reckless. If broadcasters consistently breach the Code, Ofcom can shorten or suspend their licences, or, in the worst cases, revoke them. Ofcom used this power in 2012 to close Press TV, the controversial news channel broadcasting in English from the UK, funded by the Iranian government. Press TV failed to respond to concerns that it had breached its licence because it did not control its own editorial content, which, it had indicated, was controlled from Tehran. Press TV also failed to pay a £100,000 fine imposed by Ofcom after it breached fairness and privacy sections of the Broadcasting Code by screening an 'interview' with a *Newsweek* journalist without his consent—he was under duress and being held in an Iranian prison.

Ofcom cannot shorten, suspend or revoke the licences of the BBC, S4C or Channel 4—they are public service broadcasters. But it can fine the BBC or S4C up to £250,000 for a Code breach. For other broadcasters, the maximum fine is £250,000 or 5 per cent of the broadcaster's 'qualifying revenue'.

👁 Case study

The highest regulatory fine imposed for unethical broadcast journalism is £2 million, paid by Central Independent Television, part of the ITV network, after a 1998 Independent Television Commission ruling that scenes in *The Connection*—a documentary which claimed to show a new heroin-smuggling route from Columbia to the UK—were fabricated. The ITC said this was 'a wholesale breach' of the trust viewers placed in programme-makers. *The Connection* had won awards before its authenticity was questioned in an investigation published by *The Guardian* newspaper, which led to the ITC's findings (ITC press release and *The Guardian*, 18 December 1998).

▌ The scope of the Broadcasting Code

The Broadcasting Code has rules on: protecting under-18s (section 1); avoiding harm and offence (section 2); covering crime (section 3); covering religion (section 4); due impartiality and due accuracy, and undue prominence of views and opinions (section 5); covering elections and referendums (section 6); fairness (section 7); protecting privacy (section 8); commercial references in television programming (section 9); and commercial communications in radio programming (section 10).

The Code covers all broadcast output, not just journalism.

((•))
see Useful Websites at the end of this chapter for the Code's full text

see also
pp. 27–28,
Imitation
of harmful
behaviour

▌ Protecting under-18s

Section 1 of the Code says: 'Material that might seriously impair the physical, mental or moral development of people under 18 must not be broadcast' (rule 1.1). Broadcasters must take all reasonable steps to protect those under 18 (rule 1.2), it says, adding: 'Children must also be protected by appropriate scheduling from material that is unsuitable for them' (rule 1.3). 'Children' here is those under 15.

The TV watershed

Rule 1.4 says television broadcasters must observe the 9pm 'watershed' marking the transition for free-to-air TV channels between the times of day—from 5.30am to 9pm—when children are most likely to be watching and later slots for which the audience is assumed to be more adult. Material unsuitable for children must not, in general, be broadcast pre-watershed, and the transition to post-watershed material must not be unduly abrupt (rule 1.6).

For pre-watershed broadcasts clear information should, if appropriate, be given about content which might distress children (rule 1.7)—for example, news anchors can warn if footage about to be shown portrays violence. Violence or its after-effects must be 'appropriately limited' in pre-watershed broadcasts and be justified by context (rule 1.11).

Rules also limit the pre-watershed televising of offensive language (rules 1.14–1.16) and portrayal or discussion of sexual behaviour (rule 1.20).

Times when children are likely to be listening to radio

The term 'watershed' is not used for radio. But the Code says radio broadcasters must have particular regard to what is aired when 'children are particularly likely to be listening' (rules 1.5–1.6). Rules on content involving violence, offensive language, sexual material and so on apply to radio at such times—for example, breakfast time.

see Useful
Websites at
the end of
this chapter
for Ofcom
guidance on
these rules

Protecting children

The Broadcasting Code's rule 1.28 says broadcasters must take 'due care' over 'the physical and emotional welfare and the dignity' of children under 18 who take part or are involved in programmes, irrespective of any consent they, their parents or guardians give. Ofcom guidance says that 'due' means 'appropriate to the particular circumstances'. Rule 1.29 says that such children must not be caused unnecessary distress or anxiety by involvement in programmes or by broadcast of them.

Other elements of the Code's protection of children are dealt with elsewhere in this book.

See too: p. 32, Informed consent, about children; ch. 10, p. 119, Ethical considerations, on children in sexual offence cases; ch. 27, pp. 315–352, Protecting children's privacy and welfare. See also Additional Material for ch. 4 on www.mcnaes.com about teenagers involved in 'pre-trial investigations' into crime.

Harm and offence

Section 2 of the Broadcasting Code says in rule 2.1 that 'generally accepted standards' must be applied to the content of television and radio broadcasts to avoid including harmful or offensive material. Material which may cause offence includes: pictures or sounds of distress, humiliation or violation of human dignity; offensive language; violence; sex; and discriminatory treatment or language. Material likely to cause offence must be justified by context, and appropriate information should be broadcast where it would help avoid or minimise offence (rule 2.3)—for example, a warning that news footage shows people distressed and badly injured after a terrorism attack

Section 2 says context includes the programme's editorial content, the time of the broadcast, and the likely size and composition of the potential audience.

👁 Case study

In 2014 Ofcom ruled that Sky News breached section 2.3 of the Code by showing during a live broadcast a reporter at the scene of an air disaster picking through items from a dead passenger's suitcase. All 298 people on the Malaysian Airlines jet had died after it was shot down over the Ukraine by a Russian-made missile, believed to have been fired for or by secessionist rebels. Reporter Colin Brazier told viewers: 'Here are, I think it's a small girl's bag by the look of things … a set of keys … toothbrush.' He quickly put them back and said: 'We shouldn't really be doing this, I suppose really.' More than 200 viewers complained that showing this was offensive. Sky and Mr Brazier quickly apologised. Ofcom's report said Brazier's actions were 'capable of causing considerable offence' but that, taking into account the apologies and that news crews at the crash site were in an emotionally charged situation, it considered the matter resolved (*Ofcom Broadcast Bulletin*, No. 263, 6 October 2014).

((•))
see Useful Websites at the end of this chapter for Colin Brazier's account of what happened

The Code says demonstrations of exorcism, the occult, the paranormal, divination or related practices which purport to be real (as opposed to entertainment) must be treated with due objectivity, and if they are for entertainment, this must be made clear (rules 2.6 and 2.7).

There is also a general rule (2.2) that factual programmes or items, or portrayals of factual matters, must not materially mislead the audience, because this could cause harm or offence (though accuracy in news output is regulated under the Code's section 5: see pp. 29–31, Due impartiality and due accuracy).

Imitation of harmful behaviour

Programmes should not include material which, taking into account the context, condones or glamorises violent, dangerous or seriously anti-social behaviour and is likely to encourage others—particularly children—to copy it (rule 2.4, and see also rules 1.12 and 1.13).

Methods of suicide and self-harm must not be included in programmes except when justified editorially and by context, to avoid people imitating them (rule 2.5).

 For the rationale of rule 2.5, see ch. 2, p. 18, Coverage of suicides, about similar provision in the Editors' Code.

Photosensitive epilepsy

Broadcasters must take precautions to maintain a low level of risk to viewers who have photosensitive epilepsy (rule 2.12), who can be affected by broadcasts of flashing lights, including news footage of photographers using flash equipment.

▶ Crime

Section 3 of the Code says material likely to encourage or incite the commission of crime or to lead to disorder must not be included in television or radio services (rule 3.1). Descriptions of criminal techniques with detail which could enable the commission of crime must not be broadcast unless editorially justified (rule 3.2).

Broadcasters must use their best endeavours not to broadcast material which could endanger lives or prejudice the success of attempts to deal with a hijack or kidnapping (rule 3.6).

✳ Remember

Police dealing with kidnaps may ask news media to observe a news 'blackout' to help preserve the victim's life. Also, coverage of an anti-terrorist or hostage recovery operation should not include broadcasts of live material which might alert the terrorists to armed police or special forces launching a rescue operation.

Payments to criminals

see pp. 32–33, Public interest exceptions

Section 3 forbids making any payment or promise of payment, directly or indirectly, to 'convicted or confessed criminals' for a programme contribution by the criminal relating to his/her crime, unless doing so is in the public interest (rule 3.3). As with similar provision in the Editor's Code—see ch. 2, p. 21, Payments to criminals—this is to avoid distressing victims of crime and outraging the public.

Payments to witnesses

Section 3 also prohibits broadcasters making or offering payments to witnesses in 'active' criminal cases, or to anyone who might reasonably be expected to be called as a witness, though they can be paid expenses (rule 3.4). If a criminal case is not 'active', but is likely and foreseeable, payment should not be made to anyone who might reasonably be expected to be a witness unless there is a clear public interest. Any payment should be disclosed to the defence and prosecution if the person becomes a witness (rule 3.5).

These rules are to ensure broadcasters do not jeopardise the administration of justice or commit contempt of court.

ch. 18 explains contempt law and 'active'

Religion

Section 4 of the Broadcasting Code says the views and beliefs of those belonging to a particular religion or religious denomination must not be subject to abusive treatment. Rule 4.7 says religious programmes containing claims that a living person (or group) has special powers or abilities must treat such claims with due objectivity. They must not be broadcast when significant numbers of children may be expected to be watching or listening.

Due impartiality and due accuracy

see p. 36, The BBC

Section 5 of the Code sets out impartiality and accuracy requirements for broadcasters other than the BBC, which has its own regulatory requirements on these matters.

Rule 5.1 says: 'News, in whatever form, must be reported with due accuracy and presented with due impartiality.'

The Code says impartiality means not favouring one side over another, and the qualification 'due' means adequate or appropriate to the programme's subject and nature. It adds: 'So "due impartiality" does not mean an equal division of time has to be given to every view, or that every argument and every facet of every argument has to be represented. The approach to due impartiality may vary according to the nature of the subject, the type of programme and channel, the likely expectation of the audience as to content, and the extent to which the content and approach is signalled to the audience.'

Politicians may not be used as newsreaders, interviewers or reporters in any news programme unless, exceptionally, this is editorially justified and the individual's political allegiance is made clear (rule 5.3).

Owners of broadcast organisations may not use them to project their own views on 'matters of political or industrial controversy and matters relating to current public policy'. The Code offers a general definition of such matters in this section.

Rules 5.5–5.12 require the providers of television programme services, teletext services, national radio and national digital sound programme services to preserve due impartiality on such matters in their output. This may be achieved over a series of programmes 'taken as a whole' rather than in a single programme.

The Code seeks to ensure the presentation of a diversity of opinion in respect of major political and industrial controversy and major matters of current public policy, saying 'an appropriately wide range of significant views must be included and given due weight in each programme or in clearly linked and timely programmes. Views and facts must not be misrepresented' (rule 5.12).

👁 Case study

In 2014 Ofcom ruled that Bangla TV, a channel for UK communities of Bangladeshi heritage, broke the Code's impartiality requirement in a news item, broadcast on 26 and 27 October 2013, about Lutfur Rahman, who was then executive mayor of Tower Hamlets, London. A news reporter, introduced by a newsreader as 'our chief reporter', said in the item: '"I will serve the people" was his promise to the people. The people have recognised that he has kept his promise.... He has reached to the pinnacle of his success through his unparalleled contribution and determination.' Ofcom, adjudicating on a complaint that the item—which included an interview with Rahman—was an 'advertorial' for him, said that it breached rule 5.1, noting that the item did not include any viewpoint alternative to the positive content about him (*Ofcom Broadcast Bulletin*, No. 249, 3 March 2014). In 2015 an Electoral Commissioner, ruling in the High Court that Rahman was guilty of illegal electoral practices, removed him from the office of mayor (*Erlam and others v Rahman and another* [2015] EWHC 1215 (QB)).

Any personal interest of a reporter or presenter which would call the due impartiality of the programme into question must be made clear (rule 5.8).

'Personal view' and 'authored' programmes

Rule 5.9 says: 'Presenters and reporters (with the exception of news presenters and reporters in news programmes), presenters of "personal view" or "authored" programmes or items, and chairs of discussion programmes may express their own views on matters of political or industrial controversy or matters relating to current public policy. But alternative viewpoints must be adequately represented either in the programme, or in a series of programmes taken as a whole. Additionally, presenters must not use the advantage of regular appearances to promote their views in a way which compromises the requirement for due impartiality. Presenter phone-ins must encourage and must not exclude alternative views.'

'Personal view' programmes are defined as those presenting a particular view or perspective. These could involve a person who is a member of a lobby group and is campaigning on a subject expressing highly partial views, or 'the considered "authored" opinion of a journalist, commentator or academic, with expertise or a specialism in an area which enables her or him to express opinions which are not necessarily mainstream'. The Code says a personal view or authored programme or item must be clearly signalled as such at the outset.

Accuracy considerations

Ofcom guidance says that the clarification of the term 'due' in respect of impartiality (see earlier in the chapter) also applies to the accuracy requirement.

Significant mistakes in news should normally be acknowledged and corrected on air quickly, with corrections appropriately scheduled (rule 5.2). Views and facts must not be misrepresented (rule 5.7).

see Useful Websites at the end of this chapter for this guidance

✳ Remember

A journalist who, to produce a dramatic effect, edits footage or an audio recording in a way which, when it is broadcast, misrepresents a sequence of events will breach the Code. It will also be breached if a broadcaster stages and airs a reconstruction of a news event while failing to make clear to the audience that it is not the real event.

Undue prominence of views and opinions

Rule 5.13, which applies to local radio services and local digital sound programme services, including those at community level, says their broadcasters 'should not give undue prominence to the views and opinions of particular persons or bodies on matters of political or industrial controversy and matters relating to current public policy' in programming when 'taken as a whole', by which it means programming 'dealing with the same or related issues within an appropriate period'.

It defines 'undue prominence of views and opinions' as a significant imbalance of views.

 Section 6 of the Code sets out specific requirements for broadcasters to maintain impartiality during election and referendum periods—see ch. 32.

▌ Fairness

Section 7 of the Code sets out general principles on how programme-makers should treat people or organisations participating or featured in programmes.

Rule 7.1 says: 'Broadcasters must avoid unjust or unfair treatment of individuals or organisations in programmes.'

The section details 'Practices to be followed'. A failure to follow these which leads to unjust or unfair treatment will be a breach of the Code.

Practice 7.2 says broadcasters and programme-makers should be fair in dealings with potential contributors to programmes unless doing otherwise is justified.

Informed consent

Practice 7.3 says people or organisations who agree to take part in programmes should do so on the basis of 'informed consent', which requires that a person invited to contribute to a programme should normally be told:

- its nature and purpose, and what it is about, and be given a clear explanation of why he/she has been asked to contribute and when and where it is likely to be broadcast;
- the kind of contribution he/she is expected to make—live, pre-recorded, interview, discussion, edited, unedited, etc;
- the areas of questioning and, wherever possible, the nature of other likely contributions.

It lists other information the person should be told and says the public interest or other provisions might justify withholding all or some of this information.

If a contributor is under 16, the parent or guardian's consent should normally be obtained. Those under 16 should not be asked for views on matters likely to be beyond their capacity to answer properly without such consent (practice 7.4).

 See the Additional Material for ch. 3 on www.mcnaes.com for a case study on 'informed consent'.

The Code says guarantees given to contributors—for example, about the content of a programme, confidentiality or anonymity—should normally be honoured (practice 7.7).

 See ch. 34 for cases in which journalists ethically kept secret the identities of their sources.

Getting and airing the other side of the story

Practice 7.11 says that if a programme alleges wrongdoing or incompetence or makes other significant allegations, those concerned should normally be given an appropriate and timely opportunity to respond. Where a person approached to contribute to a programme chooses to make no comment or refuses to appear, the broadcast should make this clear—and give that person's explanation if it would be unfair not to do so (practice 7.12).

▌ Public interest exceptions

→ glossary

Ofcom accepts that programme-makers may be justified in breaching some of the Code's provisions 'in the public interest'. It uses the term **warranted** to indicate when there must be a public interest or some other exceptional justification to merit breaching the usual rules.

- Section 8 says that examples of public interest include:
  - revealing or detecting crime;
  - protecting public health or safety;
  - exposing misleading claims made by individuals or organisations; or
  - disclosing incompetence that affects the public.

 There are similar public interest exceptions in the Editors' Code—see ch. 2, pp. 16–17, Public interest exceptions in the Editors' Code.

Deception and misrepresentation

The Broadcasting Code says in practice 7.14 that:

> [B]roadcasters or programme makers should not normally obtain or seek information, audio, pictures or an agreement to contribute through misrepresentation or deception. ...

But it adds that it may be warranted to use material gained by such tactics if it is in the public interest *and* the material cannot reasonably be obtained by other means.

Thus, a journalist who lies about the nature of a programme in order to trick a criminal into taking part will not breach the Code if the programme's purpose is to expose sufficiently serious offences. Similarly, giving a false reason to a public institution when seeking consent to film its activities will not be a breach if the public interest is sufficient, such as exposing incompetence affecting the public. The public interest can justify journalists misrepresenting themselves—for example, by posing as members of another profession or an uninformed citizen. But in all such instances, if a complaint is made, Ofcom will consider whether what was done was proportionate (not excessive) and whether there was any other way the material could reasonably have been obtained.

Secret filming and recording—deception and privacy

The Code says in practice 7.14 that 'surreptitious'—secret or undercover—filming or recording is a type of deception. Under the Code material gained in this way should not normally be broadcast unless the person filmed or recorded consents.

Surreptitious filming or recording includes using long lenses or recording devices, or leaving an unattended camera or recording device on private property without the full and informed consent of the occupiers, or deliberately continuing a recording when the other party thinks it has ended (section 8).

- But practice 7.14 says that it may be warranted to use, without consent, film or audio gained surreptitiously if it is in the public interest and the material could not have reasonably been obtained in another way.

Practice 7.14 adds that if an individual or organisation filmed or recorded surreptitiously is not identifiable in the programme as broadcast, their consent to be included in it is not required (though their right to privacy would need to be taken into account).

Surreptitious filming or recording can violate privacy—for example, by recording private conversations without consent—even if the person is not identified, or the conversations included, in what is broadcast.

Section 8 of the Code, on protecting privacy, says that any infringement of privacy in programmes, or in connection with obtaining material included in programmes, must be with the consent of the person and/or organisation or be otherwise warranted (rule 8.1 and practice 8.5). Ofcom will deem a failure by programme-makers to observe the 'practices to be followed' in section 8 as breaching the Code if it leads to an unwarranted infringement of privacy.

Practices 8.13 and 8.14 say surreptitious filming or recording should only be done when warranted and that normally it will only be warranted if:

→ glossary

- there is **prima facie** evidence of a story in the public interest; and
- reasonable grounds to suspect that further material evidence could be obtained; and
- it is necessary to the programme's credibility and authenticity.

for
explanation
of this term,
see ch. 2,
p. 19,
'Fishing
expeditions'

The requirement for prima facie evidence is to prevent arbitrary 'fishing expeditions'.

👁 Case study

Ms Rachel Gray, a worker at Gillman Funeral Services, South London, owned by Funeral Partners Ltd (FPL), complained to Ofcom that she was treated unfairly and that her privacy was infringed by an edition of ITV's *Exposure* programme entitled 'The British Way of Death'. It showed that a lack of refrigeration facilities at Gillman's led to some bodies decomposing. Footage shot by an undercover reporter showed Ms Gray placing, as a joke, a shopping bag over one body's head, singing 'Big Spender'—a song associated with striptease—as she undressed another body, to amuse a colleague, and referring to another body as 'Chelsea scum'. FPL's chief executive described some of Ms Gray's behaviour in the footage as totally unacceptable. ITV said it filmed covertly after gathering prima facie evidence of callous treatment of the deceased at Gillman's, adding that the programme's commentary recognised that some 'gallows humour' there was understandable. Ofcom ruled that Ms Gray was not treated unfairly, and that ITV's right to freedom of expression and the public interest in the programme's subject matter outweighed her expectation of privacy (*Ofcom Broadcast Bulletin*, No. 236, 27 August 2013).

Ofcom guidance says broadcasters should take care not to infringe the privacy of bystanders who might inadvertently be caught in a recording—for example, it might be necessary to obscure the identities of those recorded incidentally.

Recording phone calls

Practice 8.12 of the Code says broadcasters can record telephone calls if they have, from the outset of the call, identified themselves, and explained to the other person the call's purpose and that it is being recorded for possible broadcast (if that is the case) unless it is warranted not to identify themselves or give such explanation. This means that failing to tell the person that the call is being recorded for broadcast, failing to explain its purpose or broadcasting a recording of it without the person's consent can be justified if the journalism is 'in the public interest'.

Ofcom might class recording a phone call without the other person's knowledge as a surreptitious recording, and therefore—if the intention is to broadcast it—practices 7.14 and 8.13 apply. But Ofcom guidance says it is acceptable for journalists to record their own calls for note-taking purposes.

 See Useful Websites at the end of this chapter for Ofcom guidance, and see ch. 35, p. 440, Regulation of Investigatory Powers Act (RIPA) 2000, as regards the illegality of the interception of phone calls.

▌ Privacy in general

Section 8 of the Code includes general provisions for protecting people's privacy in relation to journalists openly filming or audio-recording. These are explained in ch. 27, which also explains the Code's use of the term 'legitimate expectation of privacy' and its restrictions on 'doorstepping'.

Practice 8.2 says the location of a person's home or family should not be disclosed without permission, unless it is warranted.

▌ Financial journalism

Appendix 4 of the Code sets out 'binding guidance' on how journalists working for commercial broadcasters must operate to comply with legislation on investment recommendations.

▌ Other parts of the Broadcasting Code

Section 9 regulates commercial references in television programming and section 10 regulates commercial communications in radio programming. These rules seek to ensure there is a distinction between editorial and advertising content, and set out specific principles of editorial independence as regards television—for example, news and current affairs programmes on television must not be sponsored (rule 9.15). With the exception of relevant 'product placement' rules for television, these sections do not apply to BBC services funded by the TV licence fee as they do not carry advertising.

◗ The BBC

The BBC, the biggest broadcasting organisation in the world, has nine national TV channels plus regional programming, 10 national radio stations and more than 40 regional and local radio stations, plus its website.

The legal basis for the BBC's independent existence is its Royal Charter, which is renewed every 10 years, and the accompanying Agreement. The Agreement says the BBC must do all it can to ensure that controversial subjects are treated with due accuracy and due impartiality in all relevant output. These aspects of its output, including its journalism, are regulated by the BBC Trust, the Corporation's governing body. So complaints about inaccuracy or lack of impartiality in BBC output cannot be considered by Ofcom, only by the BBC itself. Also, Ofcom does not regulate the BBC's online output or its World Service.

The BBC has an Editorial Complaints Unit. Complainants unhappy with its decisions can appeal to the Trust, which publishes its appeal findings online. In other respects—for example, if it is alleged that material broadcast was unfair or offensive—Ofcom regulates the BBC, using relevant parts of the Broadcasting Code. So, while the BBC can consider complaints about all such matters, complainants can contact Ofcom if they are dissatisfied with the BBC's response. In late 2015, when the main text of this chapter was completed, there was debate about whether the Trust should be abolished so that Ofcom could become the sole, ultimate regulator for the BBC's output.

The BBC's Editorial Guidelines set out standards for its journalism.

see Useful Websites at the end of this chapter for these Guidelines

    Check www.mcnaes.com for updates on the future of the BBC Trust.

➡ Recap of major points

- Broadcast journalism is regulated by the Office of Communications (Ofcom).
- Broadcast organisations must comply with the Broadcasting Code, which requires them to avoid harm and offence, to be fair and to protect people's privacy.
- Ofcom can fine broadcasters for the worst transgressions of the Code and can close a commercial broadcaster which persistently or recklessly flouts it.

- There must be 'due accuracy' and 'due impartiality' in all broadcast news.
- The BBC is regulated by the BBC Trust, not by Ofcom, as regards accuracy and impartiality.

((•)) Useful Websites

www.ofcom.org.uk/about/what-is-ofcom/
  What is Ofcom?

http://stakeholders.ofcom.org.uk/broadcasting/broadcast-codes/broadcast-code/
  Ofcom Broadcasting Code

http://stakeholders.ofcom.org.uk/broadcasting/guidance/programme-guidance/bguidance/
  Ofcom's guidance on the Code

www.theguardian.com/media/2014/jul/22/mh17-sky-news-reporter- colin-brazier-crash-victims-luggage
  Colin Brazier's article on air crash site

www.bbc.co.uk/aboutthebbc/
  About the BBC

www.bbc.co.uk/editorialguidelines/
  BBC Editorial Guidelines and Guidance

www.bbc.co.uk/editorialguidelines/guidance/secret-recording
  BBC guidance on secret recording

www.bbc.co.uk/complaints/
  BBC complaints system

www.bbc.co.uk/bbctrust/
  BBC Trust

www.bbc.co.uk/academy/journalism
  BBC Academy—provides training content for broadcast journalists, including on impartiality and ethics

Part 2

Crime, courts and tribunals

4

Crime—media coverage prior to any court case

Chapter summary

This chapter explains how police investigations are driven by the standard of proof needed to convict someone of a crime. Reporters should understand police powers to arrest and to detain. There is a strong public interest in media reporting of crime and police investigations, but the media must be wary of contempt of court law, made 'active' when a suspect is arrested and in other circumstances. There may be libel risks in identifying suspects before they are charged.

▌ Standard of proof in criminal law

Those accused of crime enjoy 'the presumption of innocence'. This legal principle means that those charged with crimes are not required to prove themselves innocent—the prosecution has to prove guilt 'beyond reasonable doubt', the standard of proof necessary in law for a conviction. Police and other agencies which investigate crime need clear evidence to meet this standard.

▌ Arrests

Under the Police and Criminal Evidence Act 1984 a police officer can arrest a person who has committed, is committing or is about to commit an offence (however minor), or anyone of whom there are reasonable grounds for suspicion. But the officer must have reasonable grounds for believing the arrest is necessary to achieve one of the purposes specified in the Act—for example, to allow 'prompt and effective investigation' of a crime, or to stop a person from obstructing the highway. Police may use 'reasonable force' to make an arrest. An arrest automatically makes the case 'active' under the Contempt of Court Act 1981, limiting what can be published about it.

✳ Remember

The 1981 Act, explained in ch. 18, safeguards the fairness of trials. That chapter explains what types of material, if published about an active case, can breach the Act. A breach is a contempt offence, for which a media organisation can be heavily fined.

▌ Police questioning of suspects

An arrested person is usually taken to a police station. A suspect who goes to a police station voluntarily may be arrested there. Police sometimes tell the media that someone is 'helping with inquiries'.

- Journalists should check whether the suspect is helping police voluntarily or is under arrest, as newsrooms need to know if the case is 'active'. If it is 'active', contempt law affects what can be published.

Limits to detention by police, prior to any charge

→ glossary

To protect civil liberties, no one should normally be held under arrest for more than 24 hours, and if they have not been charged within that period, they must be released. This period runs from the time of arrest or from when the suspect was taken into the police station, depending on circumstances. A police superintendent can authorise the detention of someone suspected of an **indictable offence** for a further 12 hours. Police can then ask a magistrates' court to authorise the person's detention for another 36 hours. If a further application is made, the court cannot extend this detention beyond a maximum of 96 hours since it began. But people suspected of terrorism can be detained for 14 days without charge.

False imprisonment

An arrested person who later sues the police for damages, alleging unlawful arrest or 'false imprisonment', must prove that the police grounds for detaining him/her were unreasonable.

 The Additional Material for ch. 4 on www.mcnaes.com explains the *habeas corpus* procedure in which police and official agencies can be required to justify to the High Court why a person is being detained.

 Ch. 36 explains that photo-journalists covering tense incidents may be threatened with arrest.

The Crown Prosecution Service

Most prosecutions are the responsibility of the Crown Prosecution Service (CPS), a government department, with bases serving each of the 43 police areas in England and Wales. The head of the CPS is the Director of Public Prosecutions.

> ((•)) See Useful Websites at the end of this chapter for the CPS site.

The CPS is independent of police, but has the duty to advise and direct them in investigations, except those into the most minor crimes. It decides, in all major cases involving police investigation, whether a suspect should be prosecuted, and if so, on what charge(s).

- A charge is a formal accusation, giving the alleged offender basic details of the crime allegedly committed, including, for example, details of the property allegedly stolen, its value and the owner's name, and, for a violence offence, the name of the alleged victim. It means the case will be prosecuted and go to court.

Usually a suspect is charged at a police station. He/she should be given the charge in written form, but may already have been charged orally, before the document was ready. A charge makes a case 'active' under the Contempt of Court Act 1981 if it is not active already because of an arrest.

The case ceases to be 'active' if an arrested person is released without charge, unless he/she is released on **police bail** because officers want more time to complete investigations. A suspect on bail must return to a police station on a specified date, when he/she may be charged, released without charge, or re-bailed.

→ glossary

>   The www.mcnaes.com chapter on Scotland provides an outline of its prosecution system.

Decisions on whether to prosecute

When considering if a suspect should be prosecuted, CPS lawyers assess whether there is 'a realistic prospect of conviction'. If the case passes that test, they consider if it is in the public interest to prosecute. In almost all serious cases, consideration of the public interest leads to a decision to prosecute.

Limits to detention by police, after any charge

Once someone is charged police must stop questioning him/her, except in limited circumstances. The person, if under arrest, must by law be taken before a magistrates' court on the day he/she is charged or on the following day, except Sundays,

Christmas Day or Good Friday. Alternatively, after being charged the person may be released on police bail to attend court.

In all major cases lawyers employed by the CPS conduct the prosecution in the courts, although police have power to prosecute in some cases.

▌ Other prosecution agencies in the public sector

Various other governmental agencies investigate and prosecute offences—for example, local authorities may investigate and prosecute property landlords for breach of tenants' rights, and the Serious Fraud Office, a government department, investigates and prosecutes serious and complex fraud.

▌ Laying or presenting of information; summonses; service of written charge

The decision whether to prosecute may be taken quickly—for example, soon after an arrest. But it might not be taken for months if time is needed to gather evidence. A prosecution can begin with a charge. It can also begin by 'laying' or 'presenting'—either term is used—'information' before a magistrate. In this procedure an allegation that a crime has been committed is made orally or in writing to a magistrate who will, without at that stage full consideration of evidence, issue a summons to be served on the alleged perpetrator.

- A summons is a formal document, issued by a magistrates' court, setting out one or more crime allegations in similar detail to a charge. It requires attendance at court on a specified date to respond to the allegation(s).

The summons makes the case active under the Contempt of Court Act 1981, as ch. 18 explains.

For public prosecutors—including the CPS—the laying or presenting of 'information' has been replaced with a streamlined procedure called 'written charge and requisition' in which the prosecuting agency serves (usually by post) such documents on the accused person. The requisition is formal notification of the date he/she must appear at the magistrates' court. Summonses and requisitions are used routinely for minor offences if these cannot be resolved by a 'fixed penalty'. In 2015 the 'trial by single justice on the papers' procedure, which involves service of 'written charge and notice', was launched in a pilot project in part of London. Any service of a written charge makes a case 'active' under the 1981 Act.

 Ch. 6, p. 64, Many cases dealt with by post, explains fixed penalty offences and trial by a single justice 'on the papers'.

▌ Arrest warrants

Magistrates can issue an arrest warrant if sworn, written information is laid before them that a person has committed an indictable offence, or any summary offence punishable by imprisonment, or in relation to any offence if the suspect's address is not sufficiently established for a requisition or summons to be served.

 → glossary

offence categories are explained in ch. 5

- An arrest warrant is a formal document in which a magistrate empowers any police officer to arrest a suspect, wherever he/she is in England or Wales, to be taken to the magistrates' court.

It can be used for a suspect 'on the run'. The terms of an arrest warrant may allow for a person to be released on bail, after being arrested and completing formalities at a police station, to appear at the magistrates' court at a future date.

The issue of an arrest warrant makes the case 'active' under the 1981 Act if it has not already become active because of the issue of a summons or service of a written charge. A UK arrest warrant is needed for police to get a European Arrest Warrant for the extradition to the UK of a suspect who has fled to another EU state.

▌ 'Private prosecutions'

Any citizen can, by laying information before a magistrate, start a prosecution, seeking to prove that an accused individual is guilty of a specified crime. The police and the CPS may have been aware of the allegation but concluded there was no or insufficient evidence. The capacity for any citizen to start a 'private prosecution' is seen as a fundamental right to counter-balance any inertia or partiality by police or other official agencies. But a magistrate can refuse to issue a summons if the allegation is deemed frivolous. A private prosecution may quickly become unsustainable because, for example, an individual citizen lacks the investigatory powers of the police. The CPS can take over a 'private prosecution', and therefore also withdraw the case, and the Attorney General can also stop private prosecutions.

ch. 1, p. 9, High offices in law, explains the Attorney General's role

The Royal Society for the Prevention of Cruelty to Animals regularly conducts private prosecutions for cruelty to or neglect of animals.

▌ The risk of libel in media identification of crime suspects

The media may discover that someone is being investigated by the police or another agency—for example, that the person is under arrest. A media report which includes the suspect's name, or other detail identifying him/her in this context, may allow that individual successfully to sue the publisher for libel if the

chs. 19 and
20 explain
defamation
dangers

investigation does not lead to a prosecution. Publishing a statement that someone is under investigation, even when this is factually correct, may be defamatory because it creates an inference that he/she is guilty.

👁 Case study

In 2011 Bristol landlord Chris Jefferies won 'very substantial' settlements in libel actions against eight national newspapers for articles published after one of his tenants, landscape architect Joanna Yeates, was found dead. Police arrested Mr Jefferies at one stage, but later released him. The newspapers published defamatory material about him. But then another man was charged with murdering Joanna and subsequently convicted. Louis Charalambous, Mr Jefferies' solicitor, said of the libellous coverage: 'Christopher Jefferies is the latest victim of the regular witch hunts and character assassination conducted by the worst elements of the British tabloid media' (*Media Lawyer*, 29 July 2011).

As ch. 18 explains, what was published about Mr Jefferies also led to two newspapers being convicted of contempt of court.

If the media are officially given the name of a person under investigation or arrest by a spokesperson for a governmental agency—for example, the police, CPS or a local council—it can safely be published because the report will be protected by the libel defence of qualified privilege if its requirements are met. Ch. 21 explains this.

In reality, media organisations reporting high-profile investigations, especially if a celebrity or public figure is a suspect, may choose—because of the fierce competition to break news—to publish the suspect's name before it is known if he/she will be charged and without any qualified privilege. They might decide that the person is unlikely to sue for libel because, for example, a celebrity or politician may not wish to alienate the media or stir up more publicity. Or the media might take the risk of naming the person because police leaks indicate that a charge is sure to follow. If the person is charged, a libel action over pre-charge publicity becomes less likely as any damage this caused to the person's reputation will usually be outweighed by, or indistinguishable from, damage caused by reports of the consequent court case, which the media can safely publish.

▌ Police guidelines on naming of suspects and victims

Guidance issued to police forces in 2013 by the College of Policing states that generally police should not give to the media the name of a person under investigation prior to any charge unless naming him/her is justified by 'a policing purpose' such as avoiding a threat to life, or preventing or detecting crime, or as a matter of public interest and confidence. Forces may provide non-identifiable information such as the age, gender, offence and a general location of arrest.

The College guidance says that when an adult is charged, unless legal restrictions apply, his/her name, address, occupation and details of the charge(s) should be released.

> ((•)) See Useful Websites at the end of this chapter for the College guidance.

The guidelines say that, unless there is an overriding public interest factor, personal information about crime victims and witnesses should only be released with their agreement and if no legal restrictions apply.

> See the Additional Material for ch. 4 on www.mcnaes.com for law banning the disclosure of identities of police informants, including 'investigation anonymity orders', ethical considerations when journalists accompany police 'raids' to arrest or search, and ethical considerations in media coverage of crime and of juveniles involved in 'pre-trial investigations'.

▌Teachers given anonymity

The Education Act 2011 gives automatic lifelong anonymity to teachers in respect of any allegation that they have or may have committed an offence against a pupil at their school.   → glossary

The ban makes it illegal to publish any detail likely to lead members of the public to identify the teacher as being the subject of such an allegation. But the anonymity ends if he/she is charged with an offence or a court agrees to an application that it should be lifted in the interests of justice.

The anonymity also ends if the Education Secretary publishes information about the individual in connection with an investigation or decision relating to the allegation, or if the General Teaching Council for Wales publishes information about the individual in connection with an investigation, hearing or decision on the allegation.

This law was created because teachers complained that they were vulnerable to false allegations. But it is controversial in that it made them the first—and so far the only—group of people in UK legal history to be given automatic anonymity by law in respect of an allegation against them.

A teacher may waive his/her anonymity, by giving written consent—for example, to a media organisation—to being identified. But the consent is not valid if it is proved that it was obtained by unreasonable interference with his/her peace or comfort. The anonymity also ends if the teacher himself/herself publishes information about the allegation—for example, on a social media page.

ch. 17 explains employment tribunals

The anonymity provisions are in section 13 of the Act, which amended part of the Education Act 2002. The section makes it unlawful, for example, to identify a teacher who has been accused of assaulting or sexually abusing a child at his or her school if that teacher has not been charged with a criminal offence—even if the accusation is referred to in public, for example at an employment tribunal hearing at which the teacher claims unfair dismissal.

Publication of anything which breaches the anonymity is punishable by a fine, for which no maximum is specified, and those liable to be prosecuted are the same as for breach of the anonymity provision for victims of sexual offence victims— see ch. 10, p. 115, Liability for breach of the anonymity provision. It is a defence for anyone accused of publishing such information to show that at the time he or she was not aware, and did not suspect or have reason to suspect, that the publication included the information in question, or that he or she was not aware and did not suspect or have reason to suspect, that the allegation had been made.

➡ Recap of major points

- Covering crime stories presents contempt of court dangers for the media, because an arrest, an oral charge, service of a written charge, or the issue of a summons or an arrest warrant makes a case 'active' under the Contempt of Court Act 1981.

- There could well be libel risks if a suggestion is published, prior to any charge, that a suspect is guilty of a crime if what is published identifies the suspect.

- But if the police or another governmental agency, in an official statement, identifies a person as a suspect, it is safe to report the statement.

- Some police informants are protected by anonymity orders.

- Teachers accused of an offence against a pupil have anonymity unless they are charged.

((•)) Useful Websites

www.cps.gov.uk/
Crown Prosecution Service

www.cps.gov.uk/about/principles.html
Code for Crown Prosecutors

www.npcc.police.uk/documents/reports/2013/201305-cop-media-rels.pdf
College of Policing, *Guidance on Relationships with the Media*

Crimes—categories and definitions

Chapter summary

All criminal cases begin in magistrates' courts. The most serious—for example, charges of murder, rape or robbery—progress to a Crown court. Journalists must know the different categories of crimes, to understand when reporting restrictions affect what can be published in court stories. They also need to know the legal definitions of some crimes to avoid libel problems when referring to offences.

▶ Categories of criminal offences

Criminal charges—and therefore the offences they allege—are grouped into three categories: indictable-only, either-way and summary.

(1) **Indictable-only offences** are the most serious crimes, punishable by the longest prison terms—for example, murder, rape, robbery. Such cases are processed initially by a magistrates' court, but cannot be dealt with there because the maximum jail sentence which magistrates can impose (six months) would be too lenient for a defendant convicted of a serious offence. So indictable-only cases progress quickly to a Crown court, as explained in ch. 7. If the defendant admits the charge there, or a jury finds him/her guilty, the judge will sentence. The term 'indictable-only' derives from 'the indictment', the document used at a Crown court to record the charge(s).

→ glossary

→ glossary

(2) **Either-way offences** include theft, sexual assault and assault causing grievous bodily harm. These charges can be dealt with either at a Crown court or by magistrates, hence the term 'either-way'. For this category, magistrates may—after hearing an outline of the case—decide it is so serious that only a Crown court can deal with it. As ch. 7 explains, if magistrates decide they can deal with the case, the defendant may nevertheless exercise the legal right of those charged with either-way offences to choose trial by jury at Crown

→ glossary

ch. 8 explains Crown courts

court. Either-way offences are regarded as being less serious than indictable-only offences, but nevertheless include distressing, harmful crimes.

✳ Remember

Confusingly, indictable-only and either-way charges are sometimes referred to collectively as 'indictable' charges, because both categories share the possibility of jury trial at Crown court. But, as stated earlier, magistrates can decide to deal with an either-way case in their summary proceedings—that is, as if it were a summary offence.

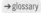

(3) **Summary offences** are comparatively minor offences, and include common assault, drunkenness and speeding offences. Summary charges are dealt with in magistrates' courts, except in some cases in which a defendant faces both summary and either-way or indictable charges arising from the same event, in which instance a Crown court may deal with all of them. People charged with a summary offence have no right to a jury trial. 'Summary proceedings' means 'proceedings in a magistrates' court', with the term 'summary' indicating the relative speed of the process.

▌ Defining criminality

There are two elements in most crimes:

- an act which is potentially criminal—which lawyers refer to as the *actus reus*; and
- a guilty mind—the *mens rea*, which means that the act was carried out, or planned or attempted, with guilty intention—that the perpetrator knew he/she was acting, or intending to act, unlawfully.

Generally, the prosecution must prove both elements. In the crime of murder, the *actus reus* is that of unlawfully killing someone, and the *mens rea* is that the act was done with intent to kill or cause grievous bodily harm. If there is no such intent, a killing may be a lesser crime—for example, manslaughter.

Strict liability

Some offences are of **strict liability**. Strict liability, when it applies in law, removes or strictly limits the defences to the charge. Strict liability means that a motorist who exceeds the speed limit commits an offence even if he/she did not realise how fast he/she was driving. A motorist who drives with too much alcohol in his/her blood commits an offence even if he/she did not intend to breach the alcohol limit. Strict liability can be seen as a practical, societal solution to deter dangerous or anti-social conduct for which, in many cases, it would be impossible to prove that *mens rea*—a guilty mind—existed.

Journalists must understand this concept, not least because some criminal offences arising from publishing material are strict liability offences, meaning it is not a defence to say 'Sorry, I didn't intend to ...'—for example, publishing material which breaches the Contempt of Court Act 1981.

see ch. 18, p. 233, Contempt of Court Act 1981—strict liability

▌ Definitions of crimes

A victim of theft may tell friends he/she has been 'robbed'. A journalist who makes this colloquial error when reporting a court case will seem foolish and—worse—the error could lead to a defamation action.

chs. 19 and 20 explain defamation

If a defendant is guilty of a minor theft, but is wrongly reported as guilty of robbery, the mistake suggests to the public that he/she committed a much worse crime, in that robbery—because it involves violence or threatened violence—is generally regarded as worse than theft.

The crime definitions in the following list are simplified. For fuller definitions, see the Crown Prosecution Service's Legal Guidance section, listed at the end of this chapter under Useful Websites, or *Blackstone's Criminal Practice.*

Crimes against people

Murder The unlawful killing of a human being with the intention of killing or causing grievous bodily harm. An adult convicted of murder must be sentenced to life imprisonment. Indictable-only.

Manslaughter Killing by an unlawful act likely to cause bodily harm but without the intention to kill or cause grievous bodily harm. Manslaughter can be a charge in its own right. A jury in a murder trial might in some circumstances find the defendant not guilty of murder but convict him/her of manslaughter as an alternative. Indictable-only.

Corporate manslaughter An offence for which the senior managers of an organisation, including a company, a government department or a police force, can be convicted if its activities cause a person's death in the circumstance of a gross breach of a duty of care owed to that person and the way in which the organisation's activities were managed or arranged by its senior management was a substantial element in that breach. Indictable-only.

Infanticide The killing of an infant under 12 months old by its mother, when her mind is disturbed as a result of the birth. Indictable-only.

Assault; common assault; battery; assault by beating The way these offences evolved in case law led their definitions to overlap. These charges are likely to be used in cases in which no, or only transient or trifling, bodily injury is allegedly caused. 'Assault' and 'common assault' can mean an unlawful infliction of force/violence, or a hostile act—for example, a threatening gesture—which puts another person in fear of immediate violence. Journalists should not assume that

→ glossary

an assault charge necessarily alleges that a physical attack occurred. Either type of act must be proved as intentional or reckless. A push can be a common assault. Battery can also be expressed as a charge of 'assault by beating'. They are summary offences, unless the assault allegedly involved racial or religious motives, in which event they are either-way.

Assault occasioning actual bodily harm (ABH) An assault—that is, a threat and/or attack, see earlier—which caused more than transient and trifling harm. The harm could be psychiatric illness. Either-way.

Wounding or inflicting grievous body harm (GBH) These charges are in section 20 of the Offences against the Person Act 1861. It must be proved that the defendant intended or foresaw causing some harm and—depending on which charge the prosecution sees as accurately describing the injury—that the harm caused was a wound or grievous (that is, serious) harm which was not, or not only, a wound. Either charge, in full form, includes the term 'malicious'—for example, 'malicious wounding'. A 'wound' is the slicing through or breaking of skin and can be a mere cut. But a wounding charge tends to be used only if the wound is serious. A GBH charge tends to be used, for example, if the harm includes broken bone, or led to substantial loss of blood and/or extended medical treatment and/or permanent disfigurement and/or permanent disability. These charges are either-way.

Wounding 'with intent'/inflicting grievous body harm 'with intent' Under section 18 of the 1861 Act, the wounding or GBH is deemed to have been 'with intent' if there is intent to cause GBH or to resist 'lawful apprehension'. Such a charge is indictable-only. It carries a maximum penalty of life imprisonment.

Rape Indictable-only. See definitions of sexual offences in ch. 10, which also explains that victims of these offences must have anonymity in media reports.

Crimes against property or involving gain

Theft Dishonest appropriation of property belonging to another with the intention of permanently depriving the other of it (Theft Act 1968). Either-way. The act of theft is stealing. Do not refer to this offence as robbery.

Robbery Theft by force (that is, violence), or by threat of force. Indictable-only.

Handling Dishonestly receiving goods, knowing or believing them to be stolen, or dishonestly helping in the retention, removal, disposal or sale of such goods. Either-way.

Burglary Entering a building as a trespasser and then

- stealing or attempting to steal from it; or
- inflicting or attempting to inflict grievous bodily harm to anyone in it; or
- making trespassing entry to a building with:
  - intent to steal; or

- intent to inflict GBH; or
- intent to do unlawful damage.

Generally, burglary is an either-way charge, but in some circumstances it is indictable-only.

Aggravated burglary Burglary while armed with a firearm, imitation firearm, or any other weapon or explosive. Indictable-only.

Fraud Under the Fraud Act 2006, there are now general offences of fraud, defined as conduct 'with a view to gain or with intent to cause loss or expose to a risk of loss' involving either:

- a dishonest making of a false representation (for example, using a credit card dishonestly or using a false identity to open a bank account); or
- a dishonest failure to disclose information when under a legal duty to disclose (for example, failure when applying for health insurance to disclose a heart condition);
- dishonest abuse of a position (for example, an employee swindling money from his/her employer).

The Act also includes a fraud offence of obtaining services dishonestly. These statutory fraud offences are either-way, but if deemed to be of sufficient 'seriousness or complexity', they are treated procedurally as indictable-only (as explained in ch. 7). Conspiracy to defraud is indictable-only.

Blackmail Making an unwarranted demand with menaces with a view to gain. This offence could be a threat to disclose embarrassing secrets or photos involving the victim unless money is paid. But it could also be another type of extortion such as a threat to contaminate goods on a supermarket company's shelves unless money is paid. Indictable-only.

Taking a vehicle without authority Sometimes referred to as 'taking without owner's consent' (TWOC). It can cover conduct known as 'twocking' or 'joyriding' in which perpetrators abandon a car after using it. This offence does not involve an intention to deprive the owner permanently of the vehicle and so should not be described as theft. Summary.

Aggravated vehicle taking When a vehicle has been taken (as above) and someone is injured, or the vehicle or other property is damaged because of how it was driven. Either-way.

Motoring crimes

Driving under the influence of drink or drugs Driving a motor vehicle when the ability to do so is thus impaired. Summary.

Driving with excess alcohol When alcohol in the driver's body exceeds the prescribed limits—80 milligrammes of alcohol in 100 millilitres of blood; 35 microgrammes of alcohol in 100 millilitres of breath; or 107 milligrammes of alcohol in 100 millilitres of urine. Summary.

Causing death by careless driving when under the influence of drink or drugs The driver is unfit to drive as a result of drink or drugs, or has consumed excess alcohol or failed to provide a specimen. Indictable-only.

✳ Remember

It may not be fair or accurate (and therefore could be a libel problem) to describe a driver with more than the prescribed limit of alcohol as 'drunk'. He/she may only be marginally over the limit. It is safe to use the term 'drunk' if and as it is expressed in evidence or if—in the case of a convicted defendant—the evidence clearly supports this.

Other noteworthy crimes

→ glossary

Perjury Knowingly giving false evidence after taking an oath as a witness to tell the truth in court, or in an affidavit, or to a tribunal. Indictable-only.

Perverting the course of justice Concealing evidence or giving false information to police. Indictable-only.

Wasting police time A lesser offence, committed by a person knowingly making a false report that a crime has been committed or falsely claiming to have information material to an investigation. Summary.

➡ Recap of major points

- There are three main categories of criminal offences:
  - indictable-only, which can only be dealt with by a Crown court;
  - either-way, dealt with by a Crown court or a magistrates' court—see ch. 7;
  - summary—almost all such cases are dealt with by magistrates.
- If an offence is of 'strict liability', the defendant can be convicted even if he/she had no clear 'intention' to do wrong.
- A media organisation which fails to report an offence or charge accurately might be successfully sued for libel by the defendant.

((•)) Useful Websites

www.cps.gov.uk/legal/
    Crown Prosecution Service, 'Legal guidance'

Magistrates' courts— summary cases

Chapter summary

Magistrates' courts deal with about 95 per cent of all criminal cases and send the rest—the most serious—to Crown courts. Hearings in which magistrates try or sentence defendants are called 'summary proceedings'. Offences with which they deal include burglaries, sexual assault and dangerous driving. Magistrates can jail convicted defendants for up to six months for a single offence. This chapter also explains bail and details the automatic reporting restrictions on what the media can publish from pre-trial hearings at magistrates' courts.

▸ Who are magistrates?

The role of magistrates originated in the twelfth century. They still use the ancient title of 'justice of the peace'. Most are volunteers and part-time—that is, lay magistrates. There are about 21,500 lay magistrates, who are trained and paid expenses. In 2015 there were 204 magistrates' courts in England and Wales, but there are plans to close about a quarter of them.

If lay magistrates try a criminal case, there must be at least two of them. A trial in a magistrates' court is known as a **summary trial**, reflecting the fact that mag- →glossary istrates dispense quick and relatively informal justice whereas the higher courts, having more serious and complex cases, have slower processes.

 See Additional Material for ch. 6 on www.mcnaes.com, 'More about magistrates'.

One magistrate is sufficient for some court duties. When a court hearing has more than one magistrate, one acts as chair and announces decisions. Magistrates are advised on law by a justices' clerk or one of his/her staff of legal advisers, who sits in front of the magistrate(s) in court.

District judges

There are also about 140 professional (that is, salaried) magistrates called district judges, appointed after at least five years' experience as a lawyer or legal executive. Most are in city districts with high caseloads. A district judge tries cases on his/her own. For convenience, this book refers to 'magistrates' (that is, plural) sitting in court, because two or three lay magistrates sit in many hearings.

ch. 4 explains categories of charges and see pp. 61–64, Sentencing by magistrates

→ glossary

→ glossary

▶ The taking of pleas

Defendants facing summary charges are asked, usually during their first appearance in the magistrates' court, how they plead. If they plead guilty to a charge, this means they are convicted of it. Sentencing usually takes place at a later date, to enable preparation of a 'pre-sentence report'.

A contested case will in most instances be adjourned for summary trial. When it is first adjourned, the magistrates must decide, unless the charge is a minor one, whether to grant bail.

Defendants who deny either-way charges can ask magistrates to try them. The allocation (mode of trial) procedure is outlined in the next chapter, which explains that a denied either-way charge is tried at a Crown court if the defendant wishes or if magistrates decide it is too serious for them to try.

▶ Bail

Bail is the system by which a court grants a defendant his/her liberty until the case's next hearing.

The court may impose conditions—for example, that the defendant should live at his/her home address and/or surrender his/her passport and/or report to a police station once a week and/or not contact someone who is a witness.

The Bail Act 1976 has a general rule that a defendant must be granted bail unless:

- the court is satisfied there are substantial grounds for believing that if bail is granted,
  - the defendant will abscond, or
  - he/she will commit another offence, or
  - he/she will obstruct the course of justice (for example, by interfering with witnesses), or
  - he/she will, or will be likely to, cause mental or physical injury to an associated person or cause him/her to fear such injury;
- the court decides the defendant should be kept in prison for his/her own protection (for instance, if the alleged crime has so angered the local community that a mob may attack him/her);

- the defendant is alleged to have committed an **indictable** offence when he/ →glossary
  she was on bail granted in an earlier case;
- the defendant is already serving a jail sentence;
- there is insufficient information to decide on bail.

A court must give reasons for refusing bail.

A defendant charged with murder can only be given bail by a Crown court judge.

Evidence and previous convictions aired

When deciding on bail, the court is told of the defendant's relevant previous conviction(s) and some details of prosecution evidence about the charge(s) faced. A defence lawyer arguing for bail may outline defence evidence.

Surety

In some cases, a court will insist that the defendant has a surety before bail is granted.

A surety is someone—for example, a relative or friend of the defendant—who guarantees that the defendant will 'surrender' to bail—that is, appear at court as required. The surety agrees to forfeit a sum of money, fixed by the court, if the defendant absconds.

If the defendant absconds, a surety who fails to pay the sum can be jailed.

Failure to surrender

It is a criminal offence for a defendant to fail to surrender to bail, which will probably result in the court issuing an arrest warrant.

Appeals

If magistrates refuse bail, a defendant can apply for bail to a Crown court judge. The prosecution, if the alleged offence is serious, can appeal to a Crown court judge to challenge a decision by magistrates to grant bail.

▶ Reporting restrictions for pre-trial hearings

When a denied charge is heading for a summary trial, magistrates may hold at least one pre-trial hearing to consider any dispute between prosecution and defence on admissibility of evidence or about other questions of law, to make rulings about such matters and to decide on bail.

Section 8C of the Magistrates' Courts Act 1980 imposes automatic restrictions →glossary limiting contemporaneous reporting of these pre-trial hearings.

see ch. 7,
pp. 74–76,
Allocation
procedure
in either-
way cases

The restrictions are intended to prevent the risk of prejudice should a case originally due to be tried by magistrates end up being tried by a Crown court jury. Parliament anticipated that, because of changes to integrate the courts system, a case—even if a magistrates' court starts preparing to try it—may end up being tried at a Crown court with a 'related' either-way or indictable-only case. Also, a magistrates' court may initially agree in the allocation procedure to try an either-way case but later in a pre-trial hearing decide that a Crown court should try it after all because the alleged offence is more serious than it first appeared.

The type of material aired in a pre-trial hearing which could, if published contemporaneously by the media, subsequently prejudice a jury's verdict at Crown court is outlined in the next chapter. It includes evidence ruled to be inadmissible.

- The section 8C reporting restrictions ban media reports from referring to evidential matters aired in pre-trial hearings at magistrates' courts, so that if the case is later sent to Crown court for trial, people who later become jurors will not have read or heard about evidence which may not be presented during the trial.

The scope of the section 8C reporting restrictions

The section 8C restrictions automatically apply to reports of pre-trial hearings at magistrates' courts in cases due for summary trial.

They ban publication of:

- any ruling by magistrates on admissibility of evidence and other questions of law, and of any order to discharge or vary such a ruling;
- applications for such rulings and for such orders, including legal argument and discussion about whether such a ruling or order should be made.

The Act defines a pre-trial hearing as one relating to a charge due to be tried by magistrates to which the defendant has pleaded not guilty and which takes place before magistrates start hearing prosecution evidence at the trial. So section 8C could cover a defendant's first appearance at court, as well as any other pre-trial hearing, but does not prevent contemporaneous reporting of the plea.

While the restrictions are in force, the media can only report seven categories of information from pre-trial hearings about admissibility of evidence or other questions of law. These are (in simplified form):

- the names of the court and the magistrates;
- the names, ages, home addresses and occupations of the defendant(s) and witnesses;
- the charge(s) in full or summarised;
- the names of solicitors and barristers in the proceedings;
- if the case is adjourned, the date and place to which it is adjourned;

- any arrangements as to bail;
- whether **legal aid** was authorised to pay for the defendant(s) to be represented by a lawyer.

It is also safe to publish that reporting restrictions are in force—this is not prejudicial.

 →glossary

The effect of the restrictions is to ban publication of any reference to evidence, except as it is encapsulated in the wording of the charge(s), or to other prejudicial matter aired in the hearing.

As regards 'arrangements as to bail', it will be safe to report, unless the court orders otherwise, whether bail was granted, and, if it was granted, any bail conditions and surety arrangement.

 see also
ch. 7, p. 68,
Types of
prejudicial
matter

→glossary

But the media should *not* report in most instances if or why the prosecution opposed bail, or the reasons the magistrates gave for refusing it, as doing so could be prejudicial.

It would be safe to report that someone was remanded in custody for his/her own protection because it was feared, for example, that his/her life would be at risk if he/she were to be released.

The home addresses which may be published are those current when the report is published and former addresses which were current during events that gave rise to the charge(s).

✳ Remember

A report which refers to a defendant's former address or includes a picture or footage of it should make clear that he/she no longer lives there. Failing to do so could cause the current occupants to sue for libel because people think they are linked to the court case.

The explicit ban in section 8C on publishing pre-trial argument and rulings about admissibility of evidence and other questions of law is a 'belt and braces' approach, since its limitation of reports to the seven categories cited earlier has the same effect.

A media report of a pre-trial hearing can safely include neutral descriptions of the court scene and neutral background information.

See ch. 7, pp. 69–70, The scope of the section 52A restrictions, about such neutral material.

When do the section 8C restrictions cease to apply?

The magistrates can lift the section 8C reporting restrictions, wholly or in part, to allow the media to publish contemporaneously fuller reports of these pre-trial applications and of any ruling or order made in them. If any defendant objects, the court can lift the restrictions only if satisfied that doing so is in the interests of justice. If there are objections, these applications and any representations made to the court about them (that is, argument in court about whether the restrictions should be lifted) cannot be reported until the case is 'disposed of', even if restrictions are lifted earlier in other respects.

The section 8C restrictions automatically lapse when the case is 'disposed of', which happens when all defendants in the case are acquitted or convicted of all charges in the case, or if the court dismisses the case or the prosecution decides not to proceed with it.

So, at the end of the trial, a media organisation could publish a report of evidence ruled inadmissible some weeks or months previously in a pre-trial hearing, or of any ruling made in it.

Liability for breach of the section 8C restrictions

A proprietor, editor or publisher can be prosecuted and fined for breaching these restrictions. There is no longer a maximum of £5,000 for the fine which can be imposed—see p. 63, Fines and the removal of the £5,000 limit.

▸ Procedure in summary trials

Though reporting restrictions cover pre-trial hearings, what is said in a trial at a magistrates' court can usually be reported fully as it occurs.

No restrictions under the 1980 Act apply, but they could apply under other law, explained in chs. 9–11.

The usual summary trial procedure is as follows.

see also ch. 4, p. 41, Standard of proof in criminal law

- The prosecutor makes an opening speech, describing the alleged crime.
- Witnesses testify, after swearing an oath or affirming that their evidence is true.
- Prosecution witnesses are called first. Each is asked questions by the prosecutor to elicit their evidence-in-chief (that is, evidence given during questioning by the side which called them). The defence can cross-examine them. The prosecution may then re-examine them.
- When prosecution evidence ends, the defence may submit, for any or all charges faced, that there is no case to answer—that is, that the prosecution cannot meet the standard of proof required.
- If the magistrates agree with this submission, they dismiss the charge. Otherwise, or if there is no such submission, the trial continues.
- Defence witnesses are called. These may include the defendant, though he/she cannot be compelled to testify.
- Defence witnesses are questioned to elicit their evidence-in-chief. They can be cross-examined by the prosecutor and then re-examined by the defence.
- When the court has heard all witnesses, the defence may address the court in a closing speech, arguing how facts and law should be interpreted. Either

side can address the court twice in total, in opening or closing speeches. The defence has the right to make the last speech.

- If the magistrates feel a charge is not proved, they acquit the defendant.
- If they find him/her guilty on any charge, he/she is convicted of it, and the magistrates sentence the defendant, or adjourn to sentence at a later date.

! Remember your rights

There are court rules on what case material journalists can see to help them report a trial and a national protocol on what prosecution material can be released to them to help coverage of cases—see ch. 14, pp. 168–175, Journalists' access to case material in court proceedings.

Hostile witnesses and leading questions

Normally, to ensure witnesses tell of events in their own words, leading questions are not allowed to be put to them when they give evidence-in-chief.

- But a witness who refuses to testify or retracts a statement made to investigators can be ruled by the court to be 'a hostile witness'—that is, someone who can be asked leading questions by the side which calls him/her.
- A leading question is one which suggests what answer is expected. 'Did anything happen after that?' is not a leading question; 'Did you then see a man with a knife?' is.

'Bad character'

As a general rule, prosecutors in trials cannot refer to a defendant's previous 'bad character' because—to comply with the principle of the presumption of innocence—the focus is on evidence for the charge(s) being tried, not any past crime.

But evidence of previous offences and other reprehensible behaviour can be introduced to correct a false impression given by the defendant, or as evidence that he/she follows a distinctive method when committing offences of the kind with which he/she is charged, or if the defendant's evidence has attacked another person's character.

ch. 4, p. 41, Standard of proof in criminal law, explains this principle

▶ Sentencing by magistrates

In sentencing hearings for an admitted offence, the prosecution gives magistrates details of the crime. If there is dispute about the facts of an admitted offence, the magistrates must accept the defence version unless the prosecution proves its version in a **Newton hearing**.

→ glossary

Otherwise, defendants who admit an offence and those convicted at trial are sentenced in the same way, as follows.

The court will consider any written statement the victim of the crime provides. Before sentence is passed, the defendant's lawyer can make a speech in mitigation, citing any extenuating circumstances while asking for leniency.

A defendant may ask for other offences to be 'taken into consideration'.

- Offences to be 'taken into consideration', which should not be confused with previous convictions, are crimes which the defendant admits although he/she has not been charged with them.

The defendant brings these to the court's attention to be sentenced for them as well as for the charged offence(s). By admitting uncharged crimes—for example, burglaries—the defendant removes the possibility of being prosecuted for them in future, giving the opportunity of a fresh start.

Magistrates may also consider a 'pre-sentence report' about the defendant's background, prepared by a probation officer.

> 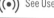 See Useful Websites at the end of this chapter for details about the Probation Service.

Jail sentences

Magistrates can jail a defendant for up to six months for a single offence and for up to 12 months for more than one offence if they decide that jail terms should run consecutively, depending on penalties specified for an offence.

- Consecutive sentences are two or more jail terms ordered by the court to run one after the other, imposed when the defendant is convicted of more than one crime. If a sentence of six months is made consecutive to one of three months, the defendant is sentenced overall to nine months.
- Concurrent sentences are those where the defendant is sentenced overall only for the length of the longest sentence imposed. In the example just given, this would be six months.

Courts can give a suspended sentence to a defendant deserving leniency.

- A defendant given a suspended sentence does not have go to jail unless he/she commits a further offence or breaches a requirement of the suspended sentence—for example, doing unpaid community work—during the period for which the sentence is suspended.

So, a jail term of six months can be suspended for two years. If the defendant commits no other offence in that time and does not breach any requirement, the suspended sentence lapses.

see ch. 21 for defamation considerations in court reporting

✳ Remember

A report which inaccurately portrays a suspended sentence as an immediate jail term could create a libel problem, as an offender might sue for the inference that the crime was worse than it was.

Committal for sentence

Magistrates dealing with a defendant who has pleaded guilty to an either-way charge or one convicted of an either-way charge in a summary trial can, in most instances, **commit him/her for sentence** to the Crown court if they believe, because of what they are told of the case and/or about any previous conviction(s), their punishment powers are insufficient. A Crown court judge can impose longer jail terms.

→glossary

Fines and the removal of the £5,000 limit

Some offences can be punished by a fine but not by a jail sentence, though failure to pay the fine could lead to such a sentence.

For years it was the case that, broadly speaking, the maximum fine which magistrates could impose was £5,000, where law specifies this. Most fines are much lower. But for decades there have been exceptions in certain statutes—for example, an employer can be fined up to £20,000 for a health and safety breach. Now there are more exceptions, because in 2015 a section of the Legal Aid, Sentencing and Punishment Act 2012 was put into effect to abolish the general £5,000 limit on magistrates' fining power. This means that for a wide range of offences there is now no specified limit on the fine.

Other types of sentence

((•))

for more detail on community orders, see Useful Websites at the end of this chapter

- *A community order, which is sometimes referred to as a 'community sentence' or 'community punishment'*—The court orders a defendant to obey one or more requirements, at least one of which (for an adult defendant) should normally be deemed by the court to be punitive, which could include:
  - unpaid work in the community under a probation officer's direction, now branded 'community payback';
  - a curfew, with a requirement that the offender wears an electronic 'tag' to monitor whether he/she obeys it;
  - a fine;

  and one or more non-punitive elements, eg a requirement to attend treatment for drug or alcohol dependency.

  Failure to comply with any requirement in the order could be punished by a jail sentence of up to six months.
- *A conditional discharge*—This means that the court has not immediately imposed or specified punishment, but states that if the offender commits any other offence within a period specified by the court, such as a year, he/she is liable to be punished for the first offence as well as for the subsequent conviction.
- *An absolute discharge*—This means that the court feels that no punishment, other than the fact of the conviction, is necessary.

As well as imposing a sentence a court can order an offender to pay compensation to a crime victim.

Binding over and restraining orders

Since the fourteenth century, courts have had power to 'bind over' a person 'to keep the peace'. This can be used to resolve, without trial, minor allegations of assault, threatening behaviour, or public disorder, in that the prosecution may drop a charge if the defendant agrees to be 'bound over'. A binding over can also follow a conviction. A witness can also be bound over, if, for example, he/she seems to have been involved in a fracas. When binding over, the court specifies an amount which the person must pay if he/she breaches the peace—for example, by violent or threatening conduct—within a specified period. The order is a preventative, civil law measure, not a punishment, and is *not* a conviction and should not be reported as such.

A court may impose a restraining order on a defendant, even one acquitted at trial, to protect another person—for example, an ex-partner—from harassment. The order may ban the defendant from any contact with that person.

Section 70 committal

Magistrates can make an order under section 70 of the Proceeds of Crime Act 2002 committing the case of a convicted offender to a Crown court hearing to assess what money or property he/she has gained from crime and, if necessary, to make a confiscation order. No automatic reporting restrictions apply to the committal hearing or the Crown court hearing.

▌ Many cases dealt with by post

Magistrates' courts can also deal, in open court, with minor 'fixed penalty' offences—for example, speeding. A defendant need not appear at court if he/she, having received written notice of the charge, returns a form admitting guilt and pays the fine.

▌ Trial by a single justice 'on the papers'

Law allowing a single lay magistrate or a district judge to deal with some types of case in private came into force for magistrates' courts on 13 April 2015, and soon afterwards a pilot of the new procedure began in London.

This law is in sections 16A–16F and other amended sections of the Magistrates' Courts Act 1980, created by Part 3 of the Criminal Justice and Courts Act 2015. It means that a case can be heard in private, in the absence of the defendant, and be dealt with solely by consideration of documents (that is, without any oral evidence or oral submissions) if all the following conditions are met:

- the alleged offence is summary and not punishable by imprisonment;
- the defendant was 18 or older at the time of the alleged offence;
- the defendant pleads guilty or has not responded to a 'written charge and notice' asking for an indication of plea and served on him/her by the relevant prosecuting agency;
- the defendant or his/her representative has not objected before the hearing to this procedure being used.

If no plea is indicated or there has been no response to the 'written charge and notice', the magistrate decides whether guilt is proved. A legal adviser (a court official) must be present, but a prosecutor does not have to be. This procedure—because it involves a district judge or only one lay magistrate and only documents—is officially referred to as 'trial by single justice on the papers'. It means the defendant—having agreed to it or having not responded—might not know the date or venue of the private hearing, because the case can be quickly switched from one courthouse to another if the first is too busy. After a conviction, the court can decide to sit in open court to sentence if it considers it is no longer 'appropriate' to deal with the case in private, and if so, the defendant must be summoned to appear.

! Remember your rights

Journalists may feel this new procedure, introduced to save costs, breaches the fundamental principle of open justice. Ch. 14, p. 167, says more about the procedure and explains the rights journalists have to get information from courts about all cases.

▶ Appeal routes from magistrates' courts

The defence or prosecution may contest a ruling by a magistrates' court by appealing to the High Court by means of the 'case stated' procedure. In other types of challenge, the defence can ask the High Court for a judicial review. → glossary

A defendant appealing against a conviction by a magistrates' court or the severity of the sentence imposed appeals to a Crown court.

These High Court and Crown court roles are explained in ch. 8.

➡ Recap of major points

- Trials and sentencing at magistrates' courts are known as summary proceedings.
- Automatic reporting restrictions under section 8C of the Magistrates' Courts Act 1980 limit what the media can report from pre-trial hearings.

- Magistrates can jail a convicted offender for up to six months for one offence and for up to 12 months for two or more offences.

- Many trials at a magistrates' court can be reported fully and contemporaneously, though some trials are, in the 'single justice on the papers' procedure, now being conducted in private if the case cannot lead to a prison sentence.

((•)) Useful Websites

www.magistrates-association.org.uk/
Magistrates Association

www.justice.gov.uk/about/probation
National Probation Service

www.sentencingcouncil.org.uk/search/?s=community
Sentencing Council explanation of community orders

Magistrates' courts—the most serious criminal cases

Chapter summary

Those charged with the most serious crimes—such as murder and robbery—make their first court appearance in a magistrates' court, usually having been held since arrest in police cells. Journalists may be on the court's press bench. But automatic reporting restrictions are in force in these preliminary hearings, to safeguard the defendant's right to fair trial by jury, because the case is bound for the Crown court. It is illegal for the media to breach the restrictions, but some newsworthy facts can be reported immediately from the magistrates' court. The restrictions also apply in preliminary hearings for either-way charges, such as sexual assault. Magistrates try some either-way cases.

▌ Processing of indictable-only and either-way charges

Defendants charged with the most serious crimes cannot be tried by magistrates. These cases are, as ch. 4 explains, **indictable-only**. They have an initial phase in the magistrates' court, where decisions on bail and case management may be made, but are quickly 'sent for trial' to a Crown court where, if the defendant denies the offence, a jury trial will take place. For most indictable-only cases magistrates can decide on bail. But only a Crown court judge can decide on bail if the charge is murder (when it is exceptional for bail to be given).

→ glossary

see ch. 6, pp. 56–57, Bail

A hearing at which a defendant on an indictable-only charge appears in a magistrates' court is only a preliminary hearing, known as a 'sending' hearing. But it will be newsworthy if the alleged crime is already notorious. Usually a 'sending' hearing is the defendant's first—and only—appearance before magistrates.

→ glossary

Some **either-way cases** are also sent to the Crown court for trial if in the 'allocation' procedure—explained later in this chapter—magistrates do not offer the defendant the option of summary trial or if the defendant wants trial by jury.

▌ Section 52A automatic reporting restrictions

→ glossary

Automatic reporting restrictions tightly limit what the media can publish contemporaneously from a **preliminary hearing** at a magistrates' court if it concerns any indictable-only case, or an either-way case which retains potential for jury trial. These restrictions, in section 52A of the Crime and Disorder Act 1998, replaced similar restrictions in section 8 of the Magistrates' Courts Act 1980. Their scope is set out in the next section. The restrictions prevent media reports of 'allocation' and 'sending' hearings disclosing information which could create a risk of prejudice to jury trials—and cover *any* hearing of such cases at the magistrates' courts which occurs before 'allocation' or 'sending'.

the jury system is explained in ch. 8

The concern is that people who read or hear information given at preliminary hearings may include some who months later will be called to be jurors in these cases. Justice demands that jurors try the case only on the evidence presented at the trial and should not be influenced by what they remember from pre-trial coverage.

Types of prejudicial matter

The section 52A restrictions are designed to prevent publication from preliminary hearings of:

- any reference to evidence in the case, apart from what is encapsulated in the wording of the charge(s);
- a defendant's previous conviction(s);
- any other material with potential to create prejudice.

Evidence Some evidence might be referred to in detail in an allocation or sending hearing—for example, magistrates may need to hear it to assess the risk of a defendant re-offending if given bail or, in an either-way case, to assess whether the defendant should be offered the option of summary trial. But some evidence mentioned by the prosecution or defence might not figure in the trial. When the case reaches the Crown court a judge may rule, before the trial, that some evidence is inadmissible. For example, evidence that a defendant confessed to the crime will be ruled inadmissible if the judge accepts that the confession was made under duress. If journalists covering a preliminary hearing at a magistrates' court could immediately report such evidence, a juror might remember reading about that 'confession' or some other detail of evidence aired then and not understand why it did not figure in the Crown court trial. That recollection could contaminate the jury's consideration of the case, and a defendant could be wrongly convicted.

ch. 4, p. 41, Standard of proof in criminal law, explains this principle

Previous convictions Generally, in accordance with the principle of the 'presumption of innocence', a Crown court jury is not told if a defendant has previous conviction(s). But a defendant's criminal record may be disclosed in a 'sending' hearing—for example, to help magistrates decide on bail. Magistrates will also be told about a defendant's criminal record in the allocation procedure, which will precede any 'sending' in an either-way case. Were a juror to remember a media report of these proceedings disclosing that criminal record, he/she could be prejudiced against the defendant.

Other material with potential to create prejudice could include suggestion by the prosecution in a 'sending' hearing that a defendant is guilty of more offences than the crime with which he/she is charged. For example, in a rape case police might check other unsolved rapes if they suspect that the defendant is a serial rapist, and magistrates might be told of these inquiries by a prosecutor opposing bail. The inquiries might come to nothing, but allowing the media immediately to report these unfounded suspicions could lead to a juror remembering them and passing them on to fellow jurors at the trial.

The scope of the section 52A restrictions

The section 52A restrictions list categories of information from preliminary hearings at a magistrates' court which can be published. The list is expressed here in simplified format (with explanation in italics):

- the name of the court (*for example, Doncaster magistrates' court*) and the magistrates' names;
- the name, age, home address and occupation of the accused;
- in the case of an accused charged with a 'serious or complex' fraud, any 'relevant business information'—see later;
- the charge(s) in full or summarised;
- the names of counsel and solicitors engaged in the proceedings;
- if proceedings are adjourned, the date and place to which they are adjourned;
- 'arrangements as to *bail*'—that is whether bail was granted, and if it was, any bail conditions and surety arrangement;

    → glossary

    - if bail is refused, the usual approach is that media organisations do not report why the prosecution opposed bail or the magistrates' reasons for refusing it, as such information might be prejudicial—but it would be safe to report that someone was remanded in custody for his/her own protection;
- whether legal aid was authorised to pay for the defendant(s) to be represented by a lawyer.

    → glossary

The fact that reporting restrictions are in force can be reported. The 1998 Act does not specify this, but it cannot be prejudicial to publish this fact.

Section 52A says that if the case in the preliminary hearing is classed as 'serious or complex' fraud, a report of the hearing can include 'relevant business information'.

This business information is the same as that which can be reported from Crown court hearings dealing with applications for such fraud charges to be dismissed.

 For 'serious or complex' fraud, see also p. 76, Two types of either-way case are simply 'sent', and ch. 8, pp. 80–81, 'Relevant business information'.

The scope given in section 52A to report the place to which the case has been adjourned permits, on any logical interpretation, reporting that a case has been 'sent for trial' to the Crown court specified.

If, in a hearing in which there is more than one defendant, one unsuccessfully asks for the section 52A reporting restrictions to be lifted (see later), section 52A permits the reporting of the fact that the court declined to lift them.

Reporting denials of guilt and choice of jury trial

When reporting preliminary hearings covered by section 52A the media routinely publish:

- *basic protestations of innocence* made by the defendant from the dock or through a solicitor—in an indictable-only case no formal plea is taken at the magistrates' court, but it may be made clear there that the charge is denied; in either-way cases defendants are asked to indicate how they will plead;
- *that a defendant, in an either-way case, has chosen trial by jury.*

Although publication of protestations of innocence and choice of jury trial is beyond what strict application of section 52A would permit, the media are safe in reporting these facts, because:

- it seems only fair to the defendant to quote his/her denial of guilt—if made in relation to the only charge faced or to all charges—and choice of jury trial, which too indicates denial of the charge(s);
- publishing such matter cannot be prejudicial—a jury, obviously, will know if a charge is denied.

But the media should be wary, when the restrictions apply, of reporting anything suggesting that a defendant will later enter a mixture of pleas—for example, quotes suggesting he/she is likely to admit one charge while denying another. This could be prejudicial if at trial jurors are not told of the admission but remember it from pre-trial coverage.

Describing the courtroom scene

The media routinely report, even when section 52A restrictions apply, scene-setting information: that the hearing lasted 10 minutes; what the defendant wore;

that he/she 'spoke only to confirm his/her name and address'; that guards stood on either side of him/her. Such bland material will not cause prejudice.

Background material

Media organisations publishing reports of preliminary hearings usually add some background material about the defendant and/or the alleged crime. Background material, from sources other than the court hearing, is not itself a report of those proceedings and so does not contravene section 52A. But the Contempt of Court Act 1981 would cover such material, so nothing should be published which creates a substantial risk of serious prejudice or impediment—see ch. 18. Mingling background material into a court report without sufficient care could create such a risk—for example, potential jurors who see/hear the report could draw wrong inferences about the evidence.

An option for the media, when they want to report on an alleged crime committed, say, in the previous 24 hours, but for which the alleged perpetrator has already appeared in court in a preliminary hearing, is to publish items segregated by page design or separate narrative. Each item could have its own headline/introduction—a story on the alleged incident, conforming to contempt law, not citing material from the court hearing, and, somewhere else, a separate report solely of the preliminary hearing, conforming to the section 52A restrictions.

Liability for breach of the section 52A restrictions

Section 52B of the 1998 Act says that 'any proprietor, editor or publisher' of a newspaper or periodical can be prosecuted if it breaches the section 52A restrictions. If the breach is published in any other type of written report—for example, on a website not linked to a newspaper—'the person who publishes it' can be prosecuted.

In the case of a TV or radio programme, 'the body corporate which provides the service' and any person 'having functions in relation to the programme corresponding to those of an editor of a newspaper' can be prosecuted. The penalty is an unlimited fine—see ch. 6, p. 63, Fines and the removal of the £5,000 limit.

👁 Case study

In 2013 *The Sun* newspaper was fined £3,350 after it admitted breaching the section 52A restrictions in its report of the hearing in which Oldham magistrates' court sent the case of Andrew Partington, charged with manslaughter and criminal damage, to Manchester Crown court for trial. The report—including its headline 'Gas pipe's cut, boom ... you bitch'—quoted evidence from texts, described as the crux of the prosecution case, in which Partington threatened his girlfriend. Fining *The Sun*, District Judge Jonathan

Taaffe said at Manchester magistrates' court that this was 'shoddy' journalism. He endorsed the view that it went way beyond what was permitted, and that its content and tone created a substantial risk of prejudice.
At Crown court Partington, 28, of Buckley Street, Oldham, was jailed for 10
years after admitting causing the gas blast which destroyed houses and
killed a neighbour's child (Judiciary of England and Wales press release, *The
Independent* and BBC online news, 5 April 2013). See Useful Websites at the
end of this chapter.

✳ Remember

see ch. 18,
p. 245,
Media
could face
huge costs
if 'serious
misconduct'
affects a
case

If a breach of the section 52A restrictions occurs after a trial has begun and is
serious enough—because of what is published—to cause the trial to be aborted, a
media organisation may also become liable for huge costs under section 93 of the
Courts Act 2003 which can punish 'serious misconduct'.

When do the section 52A restrictions cease to apply?

The restrictions cease to apply in three sets of circumstances.

A magistrates' court can lift the restrictions

These courts have a discretionary power to lift the restrictions, including at the
request of a defendant. If any defendant objects, the restrictions may only be
lifted if the magistrates decide that doing so is in the interests of justice. A defendant may want restrictions lifted so his/her solicitor can publicise, by means
of a full media report of the hearing, an appeal for witnesses—for example, the
defence solicitor may be seeking witnesses to help corroborate the defendant's
alibi: 'My client was at the funfair, not the crime scene. Did anyone see him at
the fair?'

→ glossary

- Even if the restrictions are lifted at a defendant's request, the media should
  not, until any trial in the case is concluded, publish reference made in the
  preliminary hearing to any defendant's previous convictions.

ch. 18,
p. 246, Court
reporting—
the section 4
defence

Pre-trial publication of previous convictions is so foreseeably prejudicial that, arguably, the section 4 defence in the Contempt of Court Act 1981, which normally
protects fair and accurate reports of court hearings, might not apply.

Section 52A says that if a defendant, whether a sole defendant or a co-accused,
objects to the restrictions being lifted, his/her representations to magistrates on
this issue, even if a lifting order is then made, should not be reported until the end
of the case, including any trial. But the fact that such a lifting order was made or
not made can be reported contemporaneously.

Once these reporting restrictions have been lifted they cannot be re-imposed (*R v Blackpool Justices, ex p Beaverbrook Newspapers Ltd* [1972] 1 All ER 388, [1972] 1 WLR 95). If magistrates decide, after a request from one defendant, to lift the restrictions, this means they are lifted in respect of all defendants in the hearing—even if any objected (*Leeds Justices, ex p Sykes* [1983] 1 WLR 132).

> For an example of a report of a hearing in which the restrictions were lifted, see *Express and Star* report in Useful Websites at the end of this chapter.

The restrictions lapse if it becomes clear there will be no 'sending'

The restrictions cease to apply to a report of an allocation hearing if the sole defendant, or all the defendants in the case, plead guilty to each either-way charge faced (and there are no indictable-only charges in the case). This means there will be no trial and no 'sending' of the case to Crown court.

The restrictions lapse after the last trial ends or if the case does not proceed

The restrictions on a report of the sending and/or allocation proceedings cease to apply at the conclusion of the trial of the defendant(s) or—if there is more than one trial—the last trial in the case.

This means that if an either-way case is tried summarily, these restrictions automatically cease to apply at the end of that trial (and do not apply to reporting of the trial itself). It also means that, for any case 'sent' to Crown court, if there the sole defendant pleads guilty or all the defendants plead guilty to all charges, or all the charges are dismissed or not proceeded with for some other reason, it can safely be construed that the restrictions no longer apply at that point, but that otherwise they cease to apply after the last verdict in the only or last trial in the case is delivered. Again, the section 52A restrictions do not affect the reporting of a trial, but only what can be reported from the earlier allocation and sending proceedings.

When the restrictions cease to apply, evidence aired or submissions made at any preliminary hearing at a magistrates' court weeks or months earlier can be fully reported. For example, the media may wish to highlight evidence which, for legal reasons, the jury did not hear, which might give a fuller picture of the defendant or throw light on how the crime was investigated.

> See Additional Material for ch. 7 on www.mcnaes.com for an example of a newspaper reporting evidence aired at a preliminary hearing months after it occurred.

Libel considerations

A report of preliminary proceedings published as soon as practicable after the section 52A restrictions are lifted or expire will be regarded as a contemporaneous report and so can enjoy the protection of absolute privilege in libel law, explained in ch. 21.

▌ Procedure in allocations hearings and whether section 52A applies

An either-way case will have at least one preliminary hearing in a magistrates' court, and if the defendant denies the charge, the allocation procedure will occur. Either-way cases include theft, burglary and sexual assault charges. A defendant in an either-way case has a right to jury trial, but may choose not to exercise it. An allocation hearing determines, for the defendant who intends to deny the charge, whether he/she will be tried summarily or by a jury. For as long as an either-way case retains potential for trial, the section 52A restrictions apply to reports of the allocation hearing. See Figure 2, which shows how an either-way case is processed.

Allocation procedure in either-way cases

In an either-way case, the defendant is asked, usually in its first hearing in the magistrates' court, to indicate how he/she intends to plead.

→ glossary

- *If the defendant indicates an intention to plead guilty*, this is automatically treated as a formal plea of guilty, convicting him/her of that offence. If this is the only charge in the case, the section 52A restrictions automatically lapse, as there will be no trial. The magistrates will sentence the defendant at that hearing or a later one. But they may decide, after hearing more detail of the offence and of the defendant's previous conviction(s), that their powers of punishment are insufficient and that the case should be committed for sentence to the Crown court for the defendant to be sentenced there. Magistrates' sentencing powers are explained in ch. 6.

- *If the defendant indicates he/she will plead not guilty*, magistrates then decide if he or she should be offered the option of summary trial. This 'allocation' decision is based primarily on whether the magistrates consider that they have sufficient power to punish the defendant, should they convict him/her. The maximum sentence which a magistrates' court can impose is six months for one offence and 12 months for more than one offence. In the allocation procedure, the magistrates are told some detail of the evidence which gave rise to the charge, so that they can assess the seriousness of the allegation—for example, what effect the crime had on the alleged victim—and are also told if a defendant has any previous conviction(s), as a defendant who already has a criminal record may well deserve a punishment more severe than a first-time offender would receive. Should the magistrates decide that either or both of these factors make the case too serious for them to try, they will send it to Crown court for trial. If this is their decision, the section 52A restrictions continue to apply.

If magistrates agree that they can try the case—that is, they 'accept jurisdiction'—the defendant is then asked if he/she wants that or jury trial.

Figure 2 Processing of either-way cases in magistrates' courts

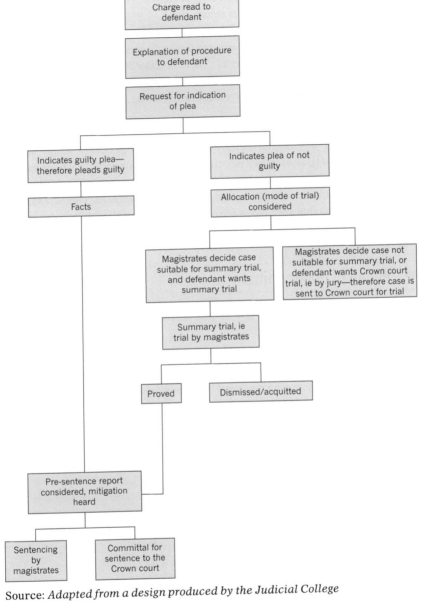

Source: *Adapted from a design produced by the Judicial College*

Magistrates may indicate to the defendant whether he/she could be jailed if convicted at their court. If the defendant chooses jury trial, magistrates will send the case to Crown court, and the section 52A reporting restrictions will continue to apply to reports of the 'allocation' hearing and the 'sending'.

If the defendant chooses to be tried by the magistrates—that is, summary trial—he/she is asked to enter a formal plea. If he/she pleads not guilty, the trial will take place in that court, most likely after an adjournment to permit preparations. The section 52A reporting restrictions continue to apply to reports of the 'allocation' hearing until that trial is concluded.

Also, other reporting restrictions, under section 8C of the Magistrates' Courts Act 1980, automatically come into force to cover subsequent pre-trial proceedings which occur before the summary trial. These section 8C restrictions, similar in format to those of the 1998 Act's section 52A, are explained in ch. 6. The section 52A and section 8C restrictions do not affect reporting of the summary trial itself.

Two types of either-way case are simply 'sent'

Two types of either-way case do not have allocation hearings but are simply 'sent' to the Crown court for trial, as if they were indictable-only offences. These are 'serious or complex' fraud cases, or cases in which the alleged offending is sexual or violent *and* a child (possibly the alleged victim) is due to be a witness. This streamlined procedure indicates that such cases are too serious to be dealt with by magistrates.

➡ Recap of major points

- An indictable-only case will be 'sent for trial' to the Crown court.
- A denied either-way offence can in most instances be tried by magistrates or by a jury. The defendant can choose trial by jury.
- Reporting restrictions in section 52A of the Crime and Disorder Act 1998 automatically apply to media reports of 'allocation' and 'sending' hearings in the magistrates' court.

((•)) Useful Websites

www.expressandstar.com/news/crime/2013/02/08/halesowen-murder-suspect-acted-in-self-defence-claim/
 Express and Star newspaper report of a preliminary hearing in which reporting restrictions were lifted

www.judiciary.gov.uk/judgments/r-v-news-grp-newspapers-ltd/
 District Judge Jonathan Taaffe's remarks when fining *The Sun* for breach of the section 52A restrictions in the Andrew Partington case

www.independent.co.uk/news/media/press/sun-fined-3000-for-oldham-gas-explosion-reporting-breach-8562354.html
 The Independent's report of *The Sun* being fined

www.bbc.co.uk/news/uk-england-21499501
 BBC report of Partington being sentenced

Crown courts and appeal courts

Chapter summary

Crown courts deal with the most serious criminal cases, including murder. Their trials lead to the tense moment when the jury announces the verdict, with the press bench full for major cases. This chapter details the work of Crown courts, the jury's role and how reporting restrictions ban the media from publishing full reports of pre-trial hearings. It also outlines the work of the High Court, Court of Appeal and Supreme Court.

▌ Roles at Crown courts

There are Crown courts at more than 70 locations in England and Wales, in administrative regions referred to as 'circuits'. The most famous is the Central Criminal Court in London—known as the Old Bailey.

In Crown court trials:

- juries decide if each charge is proved;
- judges rule on law and sentence convicted offenders.

In very rare circumstances—for example, if there is a real risk that criminals could intimidate jurors to acquit a defendant—a Crown court trial can proceed with no jury, leaving the judge to decide the verdict(s).

Who are jurors?

A Crown court jury consists of 12 people, aged between 18 and 70 (though in 2014 the government said it planned to raise the upper age limit to 75). They are selected randomly from electoral rolls for the local districts and are sent a summons to appear for jury service. Some categories of people, such as anyone jailed in the previous 10 years, are barred from being jurors.

Types of Crown court judge

Three types of judge sit in Crown courts, as follows.

- High Court judges—that is, those who can sit in the High Court and Crown courts—are referred to as, for instance, 'Mr Justice Smith' or 'Mrs Justice Smith'. They wear red robes for criminal cases. Only they can try the most serious offences, such as murder, as they are the most experienced judges.
- Circuit judges, referred to as 'Judge John Smith' or 'Judge Mary Smith', are barristers of at least 10 years' standing or solicitors who have been Recorders.
- Recorders—part-time judges—are barristers or solicitors who have held 'right of audience' (that is, the right to represent clients) at Crown court. Recorders are usually referred to as 'the Recorder', 'Mr John Smith' or 'Mrs Mary Smith'.

✳ Remember

Some cities have bestowed the title of 'Honorary Recorder of—' on the senior circuit judge, who carries out ceremonial duties.

see also ch. 1, p. 8, The legal profession, on solicitors and barristers

Lawyers at Crown court

Prosecutions at Crown court are conducted by barristers. Barristers also usually appear for the defence. Barristers are referred to as 'counsel'. Solicitors have 'right of audience' in some circumstances. A court clerk sits in each Crown court in front of the judge, to assist in procedures.

▌ Routes to Crown court

A case yet to be tried reaches a Crown court because it has been sent for trial by a magistrates' court or youth court—see ch. 7, pp. 74–76, Allocation hearings and whether section 52A applies; ch. 9, p. 92, 'Sending for trial' for homicide, 'grave' and other cases—or by a High Court judge by means of a voluntary bill of indictment, a legal process explained in the Additional Material for ch. 7 on www.mcnaes.com.

A case can also be heard by the Crown court if the case has been committed for sentence or subject to 'section 70' committal—see ch. 6, p. 63, Committal for sentence, and p. 64, Section 70 committal—or is an appeal—see p. 88, The Crown court as an appeal court.

▌ Arraignment

A defendant whose case is sent to a Crown court for trial is there asked to plead guilty or not guilty to each charge on the indictment, so formal pleas can be recorded. This process is known as 'arraignment'. At Crown court charges are referred to as 'counts'. See also pp. 83–84, Reporting the arraignment, later in this chapter.

▶ Hearings prior to jury involvement—automatic reporting restrictions

In cases in which a defendant denies guilt, there will be at least one hearing at Crown court before the jury is involved. Statutes impose automatic reporting restrictions on media coverage of certain types of these hearings. The hearings are for the judge to make rulings, some of which may determine what the jury, if the case proceeds to trial, will be told and may include bail decisions.

 →glossary

bail decisions are explained in ch. 6, pp. 56–57, Bail

The reporting restrictions are to prevent publication of information which could prejudice a trial. The principle is that potential jurors should not learn about information discussed in hearings held before the trial as it could relate to a case they might try. Material which could prejudice a jury, and which could be discussed in these hearings, includes a defendant's previous conviction(s), or evidence ruled inadmissible. For examples of what can cause prejudice if published, see ch. 7, pp. 68–69, Types of prejudicial matter, which also explains similar restrictions in section 52A of the Crime and Disorder Act 1998 which apply—for the same reason—to media coverage of preliminary hearings in magistrates' courts.

The scope of the automatic reporting restrictions

The automatic restrictions limiting media reports of some types of pre-trial hearing at Crown courts are in various statutes, but of the same format. They restrict these reports to seven categories of information:

- the name of the Crown court and the judge's name;
- the names, ages, home addresses and occupations of the defendant(s) and witness(es);
- the charge(s), or a summary of it/them;
- the names of solicitors or barristers in the case;
- if proceedings are adjourned, the date and place to which they are adjourned;
- arrangements as to bail—that is, whether bail was granted or refused, and if it was granted, any bail conditions and surety arrangement;

→glossary

- whether legal aid was authorised to pay for the defendant(s) to be represented by a lawyer.

→glossary

chs. 9–11 explain anonymity law

Witnesses are unlikely to take part in a hearing before trial. But if they do, or are mentioned in court, under these restrictions they can be named in reports, unless other law gives them anonymity.

In cases in which bail is refused, the usual interpretation of the restrictions is that the media should not report why the prosecution opposed bail or the reasons the judge gave for refusing it, as such information could be prejudicial.

Home addresses can include past addresses in events which gave rise to the charges—see ch. 6, pp. 68–69, The scope of the section 8C reporting restrictions, on care needed in references to former addresses.

Which types of hearing?

The types of hearing for which the above format of restrictions apply follow.

Unsuccessful applications for a case to be dismissed, prior to arraignment A defendant whose case is sent for trial to Crown court may apply to a judge, before arraignment, for it to be dismissed because of insufficient evidence. The reporting restrictions on such hearings are detailed in Schedule 3 to the Crime and Disorder Act 1998.

see p. 84, Selection of the jury and the giving of evidence, for meaning of 'sworn'

'Preparatory hearings' A Crown court may hold a 'preparatory hearing' in a case involving a serious offence or which will involve a complex or lengthy trial. A preparatory hearing must be held in a terrorism case. The hearings are so the judge can rule on case matters. Such a hearing, if held, marks the start of the trial and takes place shortly before the jury is sworn. If the arraignment has not yet been held, it must take place at the start of the preparatory hearing. The reporting restrictions—again, in the format set out earlier—are in section 11 of the Criminal Justice Act 1987 for preparatory hearings in 'serious or complex fraud' cases, and in section 37 of the Criminal Procedure and Investigations Act 1996 in respect of preparatory hearings in other types of case.

The same restrictions apply, generally under section 37 of the 1996 Act and—for such fraud cases—under section 11 of the 1987 Act to media reports of any application to a Crown court judge for leave to appeal against rulings made at a 'preparatory hearing' and to any such appeal in a higher court.

'Relevant business information'

Section 11 of the Criminal Justice Act 1987 allows journalists covering an unsuccessful application for a 'serious or complex' fraud case to be dismissed or, for a preparatory hearing in such a case, to include 'relevant business information' in reports of the hearing even when the automatic restrictions are in place. This means the media can report:

- any address used by the defendant for carrying on business on his/her own account;
- the name of the business at 'any relevant time'—that is, when events which gave rise to the charge(s) occurred;

- the name and address of any firm in which he/she was a partner, or by which he/she was engaged, at any such time;
- the name of any company of which he/she was a director, or by which he/she was otherwise engaged, at any such time, and the address of its registered or principal office;
- any working address of the defendant in his/her capacity as a person engaged by any such company.

'Engaged' means under a contract of service or a contract for services.

What else can be reported?

In addition to the information which the format of restrictions lists as safe to publish, it is safe to include in reports of pre-trial Crown court hearings neutral descriptions of the court scene and non-prejudicial background facts of the type outlined in ch. 7 in relation to preliminary hearings before magistrates—see pp. 69–70, The scope of the section 52A restrictions.

'Pre-trial' hearings—automatic reporting restrictions

The Criminal Procedure and Investigations Act 1996 defines a 'pre-trial hearing' as any hearing at a Crown court before a guilty plea is accepted (that is, before it becomes clear there will be no trial), or—in cases which remain contested—all hearings which occur before a jury is sworn or before the beginning of a 'preparatory' hearing. Reporting restrictions in section 41 of the Act automatically ban publication, before the conclusion of all proceedings in the case, of what is said at a 'pre-trial hearing' in:

- applications for rulings on the admissibility of evidence or any other question of law, including any rulings made by the judge;
- applications for such a ruling to be varied or discharged, including any order made.

The safest course to obey the restrictions

As can be gleaned from the earlier passages, the law enshrining these various sets of restrictions developed piecemeal. Their definitions of hearings held at Crown court before a trial overlap, and the extent to which the restrictions apply to all types of these hearings is unclear.

- A journalist's safest course, to avoid breaching the law in a contemporaneous report of a Crown court hearing held before a jury becomes involved—that is, a contested case—is to check, by asking the court clerk, what type of hearing the judge considers it to be and—unless advised it is a pre-trial hearing under the 1996 Act—to include only the categories of information listed under the heading 'The scope of the automatic reporting restrictions' plus in fraud cases 'relevant business information', and non-prejudicial background information. If told simply that it is a 'preliminary hearing', the journalist should ask for a more specific definition.

See also pp. 83–84, Reporting the arraignment, later in this chapter.

When do the automatic reporting restrictions cease to apply?

A Crown court judge can lift the restrictions, or lift them in part, to allow the media to publish contemporaneously fuller reports of such hearings.

If any defendant objects to this, the judge may lift them only if satisfied that doing so is in the interests of justice. Argument in court about whether the restrictions should be lifted cannot be reported until the 'conclusion' of all relevant trials, even if restrictions are lifted in other respects.

If the judge leaves the restrictions in place, they automatically cease to apply at the 'conclusion' of relevant proceedings. The statutes state that this is, or it can safely be construed to be, the acquittal or conviction of a sole defendant or, for multiple defendants, of all defendants in respect of all charges in all trials in the case, or when it becomes clear that, for some other reason, no relevant trial remains pending, which might be when the prosecutor decides not to proceed with the case or when all charges are dismissed for lack of evidence. But reporting restrictions under other law may still apply—see chs. 9–11.

◉ Case study

In 2014 a judge at Southwark Crown court agreed to lift reporting restrictions covering a pre-trial hearing. The case concerned an alleged multi-million-pound fraud. Because evidence was complex it was classed as a Very High Cost Case (VHCC). But, the court heard, government cuts to legal aid had reduced by 30 per cent the fees which defence barristers could claim in such cases, so no barristers were willing to represent five defendants in the forthcoming trial. A barrister representing them *pro bono* at the hearing asked Judge Anthony Leonard QC to 'stay' (end) the fraud proceedings, arguing that without barristers the defendants could not have a fair trial. Journalists from three newspapers, the *BBC* and the *Law Society Gazette* argued in a note to the judge that reporting restrictions covering the pre-trial hearing should be lifted because the legal argument relating to the legal aid cuts was a matter of considerable public interest (and so should be published contemporaneously) and because airing it would not prejudice the trial case as the issue was whether the defendants could have a fair trial. The judge agreed, ruling that the media was 'free to report anything' from the hearing, subject to the normal rules on contempt of court. Subsequently he did 'stay' the fraud case. But the Court of Appeal reversed this 'stay' decision, saying it was too early to ascertain whether the defendants could get barristers (*Media Lawyer*, 1 and 13 May 2014; *R v Crawley and others* [2014] EWCA Crim 1028).

Liability for breach of the automatic reporting restrictions

Liability and penalty for breach of the reporting restrictions under the Acts cited earlier are the same as for breach of restrictions in section 52A of the Crime and Disorder Act—see ch. 7, p. 71, Liability for breach of the section 52A restrictions. If a breach occurs after a trial has begun, and is serious enough—because of what is published—to cause it to be aborted, a media organisation may also become liable for huge costs under section 93 of the Courts Act 2003—see ch. 18, p. 245, Media could face huge costs if 'serious misconduct' affects a case.

▶ Appeals against rulings by judge—reporting restrictions

The Criminal Justice Act 2003 gives the prosecution the right to appeal against a ruling made by a Crown court judge which would terminate all or part of the case—for example, that there is no case to answer—no matter what stage the case has reached when the ruling is made. Section 71 of the Act, intended to prevent prejudice to the trial or to any linked trial, automatically bans reporting of any Crown court discussion (which, if the trial has begun, would be in the jury's absence) about such an appeal. It also restricts reports of the Court of Appeal hearing, and of any further appeal made to the Supreme Court, to the same seven categories of information listed earlier under the heading 'The scope of the automatic reporting restrictions'. These restrictions apply, unless lifted earlier, until the conclusion of all trials in the case.

In the appeal hearing referred to earlier in the case study about the 'Very High Cost Case', the Court of Appeal decided to lift the section 71 restrictions so the media could fully and contemporaneously report the arguments over the legal aid issue, and because airing it would not cause prejudice.

▶ Reporting the arraignment

If defendants in a case plead guilty at the arraignment to each charge, they are convicted of each charge, in which case the restrictions detailed earlier in this chapter cease to apply as there will be no trial.

If a sole defendant or all defendants deny the charge or charges at the arraignment, the media can safely report those pleas contemporaneously if there will be just one trial in the case.

But if a defendant or co-defendants enter a mixture of guilty and not guilty pleas, or if denied charges are to be dealt with in more than one trial, a judge may—to avoid what he/she considers a substantial risk of prejudice—make an order under section 4(2) of the Contempt of Court Act 1981 postponing publication of some of that information. A judge could do this, for example, to ban media reports of an arraignment from mentioning, until the trial ends, any charge which has been admitted (if the jury is not to be told about it) or—if the case will involve more than one trial—any charge not due to be dealt with in the first trial. Or the judge could use section 4(2) to ban any reporting of the arraignment, and of the first trial, until any further trial in the case is concluded.

For detail on section 4(2) orders and for considerations to be borne in mind even if a judge does not make such an order, see ch. 18, pp. 246–249, Section 4(2) orders.

▌ Procedure in Crown court trials

chs. 9–11 explain these restrictions and anonymity laws

The media can publish contemporaneous, full reports of what the jury is told at a Crown court trial once it has started, but must comply with any discretionary reporting restriction or any automatic anonymity for a complainant of a sexual offence

✴ Remember

Until the jury has returned all verdicts, no report of a trial should include—unless the judge says otherwise—any ruling, discussion or argument which takes place in the jury's absence. This is explained in ch. 18. To avoid libel dangers, reporting must be fair and accurate, as explained in ch. 21.

Selection of the jury and the giving of evidence

A Crown court trial can be regarded as under way when the jury is 'empanelled'—that is, when a group of potential jurors is taken into the courtroom and the court clerk selects 12 at random. These will be 'sworn'—required to swear an oath that they will try the case according to the evidence.

ch. 6, pp. 60–61, Procedure in summary trials, explains trial procedure in magistrates' courts

Soon after this the prosecution counsel 'opens the case' by outlining it. Prosecution witnesses then testify. A Crown court trial usually follows the same sequence used in magistrates' trials as regards the giving of evidence, including cross-examination, and speeches by lawyers.

At Crown court defence counsel may choose to make a speech 'opening' the defence case prior to calling defence witnesses. After all these have been heard, prosecuting counsel in most cases makes a closing speech to the jury, which is followed by the defence's closing speech.

The judge then sums up the case, to remind jurors of evidence and direct them on law. The judge will, if he/she decides that evidence is not sufficient to support a charge, direct the jury to bring in a verdict of not guilty on that charge.

Otherwise, and to consider any other charge, the jury 'retires' to a jury room to decide the verdict(s). A jury bailiff escorts jurors to and from the room, and is the only official allowed contact with them in it. The jury will have been directed to elect a foreperson to speak on its behalf.

Majority verdicts

A judge initially asks a jury to reach a unanimous verdict on each charge—that is, a unanimous decision to acquit or convict.

ch. 11 explains the legal ban on interviewing jurors about verdicts

- But if a jury has deliberated the case for at least 2 hours and 10 minutes and has failed to reach a verdict, the judge can recall it to the courtroom to tell it that a majority verdict is acceptable (for each charge).
- For a full jury of 12, majority verdicts of the ratios 11–1 or 10–2 are acceptable.
- If a jury is reduced in number for any reason—for example, because one or two jurors have fallen ill during the trial—a majority of 10–1 or 9–1 is allowed.
- If a defendant is convicted by a majority, rather than unanimously, the media should report the fact that it was by a majority decision, as this indicates that one or two people in the jury disagreed with the guilty verdict.

If the verdict is an acquittal, the court asks no questions of the jury about the ratio of the vote—so no indication is usually given of how many jurors concurred in the verdict. But if the foreperson volunteers in court the fact that acquittal was by a majority, it is by convention regarded as unfair to publish this fact, because stating that one or two jurors voted against acquittal could leave a stain on the defendant's character even though he/she is cleared of the charge.

A jury which cannot reach a verdict by a sufficient majority is known as a 'hung jury'. The prosecution then has to decide if it wants to seek a re-trial.

! Remember your rights

There are court rules on what case material journalists can see to help them report a trial and a national protocol on what prosecution material can be released to them to help coverage of cases—see ch. 14, pp. 168–175, Journalists' access to case material in court proceedings.

▶ Sentencing at Crown court

If a defendant pleads guilty at a Crown court to all charges, the judge will pass sentence, often after an adjournment. First, the judge will hear the prosecution's summary of the facts, and be told if the defendant has previous convictions and of any offences to be taken into consideration. The judge will also consider any statement from the victim(s) about the impact of a crime or—in a homicide case— a statement by bereaved relatives on the crime's effect on them. The judge will also hear mitigation.

→ glossary

→ glossary

Sentencing after a Crown court trial follows a similar pattern, though the judge, having presided at it, will not normally need to hear again detail of the offence(s).

The same sentencing procedure is used for a defendant who, after conviction in a magistrates' court, has been committed for sentence to the Crown court.

→ glossary

Crown courts frequently impose jail terms, but have the same range of other sentencing options as magistrates—see ch. 6.

If no other factors apply—for example, the defendant is not sentenced to life or to an 'extended' sentence—he/she can expect, if he/she behaves well in prison, to be released 'on licence' halfway through the term imposed by the court, which means that after release he/she will monitored by a probation officer and may be returned to prison to serve the remainder of the jail term if a licence condition is broken.

Life sentences and extended sentences

Life sentences may be imposed for murder and other serious offences. The judge will state, when sentencing, a minimum term of the life sentence which the defendant should serve—the tariff—and may pass 'a whole life order', meaning the sentence will actually be for life.

A defendant convicted of a sexual or violent offence can be categorised as a 'dangerous offender'. This law is complex, but in summary an offender can be categorised as 'dangerous' if a Crown court judge considers there is significant risk of him/her committing further offences which might cause members of the public serious harm. The offender could incur a life sentence. Other categories of 'dangerous offender' receive 'extended' sentences, meaning they will not be considered for release from prison until they have served two-thirds of their sentence.

 For the Parole Board's work and information from the Sentencing Council about different types of sentence, see Useful Websites at the end of this chapter.

▌ The Court of Appeal

Figure 1 in ch. 1, p. 5, shows the hierarchy of the court system

A defendant who wishes to appeal against a conviction or the severity of the sentence imposed by a Crown court can seek permission to appeal to the Court of Appeal Criminal Division, based in London. Permission to appeal can be granted by the Crown court trial judge or the Court of Appeal itself, or a case may later be referred to the Court by the Criminal Cases Review Commission.

The Court of Appeal may, if it allows the appeal, quash a conviction. It may decide there must be a re-trial of the case, by another Crown court jury.

Appeals are usually heard by three judges. A reporter covering a Court of Appeal hearing in which its judgment is delivered may, in cases decided by a majority rather than a unanimous decision, have to wait until each of the three judges has announced his/her own decision for that majority, and therefore the appeal result, to be revealed.

The Court has a similar procedure in appeals in civil cases. Appeals beyond the Court of Appeal go to the Supreme Court.

Journalists can visit prisoners

The right of a convicted prisoner to be visited in jail by a journalist investigating whether there had been a miscarriage of justice was upheld in *R v Secretary of State for the Home Department, ex p Simms* [2000] 2 AC 115.

> See also 'Visiting prisoners' in Additional Material for ch. 8 on www.mcnaes.com.

The Supreme Court

((•))
see Useful
Websites at
the end of
this chapter

In 2009 the Supreme Court replaced the appellate committee of the House of Lords (also known as the Law Lords) as the highest court in criminal and civil law. Its judges are referred to as 'Justices of the Supreme Court'. It only hears appeals of high significance, usually no more than 40–50 each year. Appeals are heard by several Justices, with a majority decision being binding. The court sits in the former Middlesex Guildhall.

Re-trials after 'tainted acquittal' or after compelling new evidence emerges—reporting restrictions

Under what is known as the 'double jeopardy rule', the law usually—as a protection of civil liberties—prevents someone who has been acquitted of an offence being tried for it again. But there are two major exceptions.

- If a Crown court trial convicts a person of interference with or intimidation of a juror, witness or potential witness in an earlier trial in which the same or another defendant has been acquitted, the prosecution can apply to the High Court for an order quashing that acquittal, to allow a re-trial.
- Under the Criminal Justice Act 2003, if 'new and compelling evidence' emerges after a defendant has been acquitted at Crown court of a serious charge as defined by the Act, the prosecution can apply to the Court of Appeal for the acquittal to be quashed and a new trial to be held.

see Useful
Websites at
the end of
this chapter
for CPS
guidance on
section 82

As regards applications under the 2003 Act, the Court of Appeal can make an order under the Act's section 82 imposing reporting restrictions which make it an offence to publish anything which would create a substantial risk of prejudice to a re-trial. This can ban the media from reporting the application to quash the acquittal, or anything relating to it—for example, from reporting that there are ongoing police investigations about the new evidence. The restrictions can be in force until the end of any re-trial or until the matter is otherwise dropped.

The Crown court as an appeal court

Defendants can appeal to a Crown court judge against refusal by magistrates to grant bail.

Defendants can appeal to the Crown court against conviction by magistrates, including in youth courts. In the appeal there is no jury—a judge will sit normally with two lay magistrates. The Crown court also hears appeals against the severity of sentences imposed by magistrates and may confirm a sentence, substitute a lesser penalty or increase it, but not to more than the highest sentence magistrates could have imposed.

The High Court

for the High Court's role in civil law, see ch. 12

The High Court Queen's Bench Division, which deals with criminal and other matters, has about 70 judges and has courthouses in major cities.

A defendant convicted by magistrates, or who has appealed unsuccessfully to the Crown court, may appeal to the Queen's Bench Division on the grounds that a decision was wrong in law. This procedure is known as appeal by way of 'case stated', because no evidence is given verbally to the High Court, which considers a written record of the case. The prosecution can also use this procedure to challenge an acquittal by magistrates. The High Court has wide powers to reverse, affirm or amend magistrates' decisions, including those of youth courts. It can order the case to be re-tried summarily.

Judicial reviews

ch. 15 covers media challenges to court decisions

Part of the High Court's work involves judicial reviews, hearings which can consider other types of challenge to decisions made by magistrates. The media can use the judicial review procedure to challenge discretionary reporting restrictions imposed by magistrates.

Courts martial

People in the armed forces are subject to UK law in the courts martial system, even if the alleged offence was committed in another country. These military courts are usually open to the public and media—for example, when in 2013 a Royal Marine was convicted of murdering an insurgent in Afghanistan.

 For more information on courts martial, see Useful Websites at the end of this chapter and the Additional Material for ch. 8 on www.mcnaes.com.

➡ Recap of major points

- Crown courts deal with the most serious criminal cases.
- Crown court judges rule on law and decide on punishment, and in trials juries decide whether each charge is proved.
- Automatic reporting restrictions limit what the media can report from most Crown court hearings held prior to trial.
- A defendant convicted in a Crown court may seek to appeal to the Court of Appeal and thereafter to the Supreme Court.
- Crown courts hear appeals from magistrates' courts against conviction or sentence.
- The High Court is also an appeal court for certain matters.

((•)) Useful Websites

www.gov.uk/jury-service
  Government guidance on jury service

www.gov.uk/guide-to-probation
  Government guidance on probation

www.gov.uk/government/organisations/national-probation-service
  National Probation Service

www.gov.uk/government/organisations/parole-board
  Parole Board

www.sentencingcouncil.org.uk/
  Sentencing Council

www.supremecourt.gov.uk/
  Supreme Court

www.cps.gov.uk/legal/p_to_r/retrial_of_serious_offences/
  Crown Prosecution Service guidance on section 82

www.judiciary.gov.uk/about-the-judiciary/the-justice-system/jurisdictions/military-jurisdiction/
  Courts martial

9

Juveniles in court proceedings

Chapter summary

Most juveniles charged with crimes are dealt with in youth courts by magistrates. The public cannot attend these courts, but journalists can. Reporting restrictions automatically ban identification of the juveniles involved, to protect their welfare. The term 'juvenile' covers those aged under 18. Juveniles are involved in other courts too. A court may ban media reports from identifying a juvenile involved in a case. The media may argue against this—for example, if the juvenile is a persistent offender.

▌ Juveniles and the age of criminal responsibility

ch. 13 outlines how some family law cases involve interventions by social workers

Children under the age of 10 have not reached 'the age of criminal responsibility', and so cannot be prosecuted for a crime as they are considered too young to distinguish between right and wrong. But they may be placed under the supervision of social workers.

The distinction between a 'child' (a person aged under 14) and a 'young person' (a person aged 14–17) is not important for journalists reporting courts, although some statute law uses both terms. Lawyers, courts and this chapter use the term 'juvenile' broadly to describe anyone under the age of 18.

▌ Juveniles in youth courts

Most juveniles who are prosecuted are dealt with by youth courts, presided over by magistrates or a district judge. Youth courts are usually in the same building as magistrates' courts (where adult defendants appear) but have smaller courtrooms to make juveniles feel less nervous than they might be in an adult court.

Magistrates who sit in youth courts receive special training. Procedures there, including trials, are similar to those in adult magistrates' courts, described in chs. 6 and 7.

A juvenile denied **bail** may be sent to non-secure accommodation run by the local authority, or—if the alleged offending is persistent or serious—to custody, as explained later in this chapter.

→ glossary

Youth courts' powers

Most offences dealt with by youth courts are minor. Because youth courts' sentencing powers are limited they cannot try extremely serious cases, such as homicide, and must send such cases to a Crown court, in a procedure discussed later. But a youth court has discretion, if it considers its punishment powers sufficient in a particular case, to try other offences—such as rape or robbery—which, had the defendant been adult, could only be tried by a Crown court.

Sentencing

A youth court can impose **community sentences, absolute and conditional discharges**—sentences explained in ch. 6, pp. 63–64, Other types of sentence—and can fine. A parent must pay this fine if the offender is aged under 16. A youth court can also make a 'youth rehabilitation order', a type of community sentence which can involve several requirements, such as a curfew, unpaid work or a requirement for mental health treatment.

→ glossary

Many young offenders who admit a first offence are merely made subject to an order, which means they must cooperate with a referral to a youth offender panel of trained youth workers who aim to get the offender to address his/her offending behaviour and repair harm it caused. An offender who fails to cooperate can be given a more severe punishment.

In serious cases, youth courts can make 'detention and training orders' of between four months and two years. Normally this means that the juvenile spends half the period in custody with training and the other half being supervised in the community.

The court may make 'a parenting order' requiring, for example, a parent to attend counselling and guidance sessions.

Juveniles in custody

A juvenile refused bail by a youth court, or sentenced to detention and training, can be held on **remand** or, for that sentence, in a secure children's home, a secure training centre or a young offenders' institution.

→ glossary

'Sending for trial' for homicide, 'grave' and other cases

A juvenile charged with a homicide offence, such as murder, or one of a range of firearms offences cannot be tried or sentenced by a youth court because of the seriousness of the charge. In these cases defendants make initial appearances there for decisions on bail and procedure but are then sent for trial to a Crown court.

Grave offences

The law on juvenile defendants classifies some crimes as 'grave'. These are those for which an adult offender could be jailed for 14 years or more (apart from the homicide and firearms offences referred to earlier) and certain sexual offences. In a 'grave' case the youth court considers whether its maximum power of punishment—a two-year detention and training order—would be sufficient if the defendant were to be convicted. This is similar to the allocation procedure for either-way charges in an adult magistrates' court—it determines which court is the venue for the trial. If the youth court considers its sentencing power would be insufficient, the case is sent to a Crown court for trial if the offence is denied, or committed there for sentence if the defendant indicates a plea of guilty.

→ glossary

Extended sentences and co-accused with an adult

The youth court will also send a case for Crown court trial if it considers that the defendant would, if convicted, be classed as a 'dangerous offender' for sentencing—see ch. 8, p. 86, Life sentences and extended sentences—or because the juvenile is to be tried there co-accused with an adult defendant.

Section 52A reporting restrictions

→ glossary

A youth court case which must or may be sent for trial to the Crown court has the potential of being tried by jury, so the automatic reporting restrictions of section 52A of the Crime and Disorder Act 1998 apply to all preliminary hearings of such a case in the youth court. For a case sent for trial, these restrictions normally continue in force, as regards reports of preliminary hearings, until the Crown court finishes dealing with it.

See ch. 7, pp. 68–76, Section 52A automatic reporting restrictions, for details of the section 52A restrictions and how on rare occasions they may be lifted. They are explained in relation to cases in the (adult) magistrates' courts—but apply identically in respect of such preliminary hearings at the youth court.

ch 6,
pp. 57–60,
Reporting
restrictions
for pre-trial
hearings,
explains
section 8C

Section 8C restrictions

Pre-trial hearings of a case to be tried by a youth court are covered by the automatic reporting restrictions in section 8C of the Magistrates' Courts Act 1980.

✳ Remember

Other reporting restrictions normally apply automatically to cases at youth courts, as explained later in this chapter, preventing the media from identifying juveniles involved. So, for some hearings, section 52A of the 1998 Act or section 8C of the 1980 Act *and* anonymity will apply.

Committal for sentence—'dangerous offenders'

A youth court which convicts a juvenile of a serious crime can at this stage too consider whether he/she should be classed as a 'dangerous offender'. If the answer is 'yes', there will be a **committal for sentence**—that is, the youth court will commit him/her to Crown court for a judge there to decide the sentence.   → glossary

✳ Remember

The reporting restrictions in section 52A of the 1998 Act or section 8C of the 1980 Act do not apply in respect of a trial at a youth court or a hearing which decides whether to commit for sentence. These restrictions only apply to preliminary/ pre-trial hearings.

� Admission to youth courts

Parliament has decided that the public should not be allowed inside any youth court, to avoid juveniles suffering adverse contemporaneous publicity from their involvement in the proceedings, whether they are defendants facing allegations or convicted of immature law-breaking, or witnesses or victims/alleged victims of the crime.

- But journalists are allowed into youth courts to cover cases—section 47 of the Children and Young Persons Act 1933 gives 'bona fide representatives of newspapers or news agencies' the right to attend.

Exceptions to the ban on the public having access to the youth court can be made—for example, an adult or child who is the victim of the crime may be allowed to see an offender being sentenced.

▸ Section 49 automatic restrictions on identifying juveniles

Parliament decided to shield all juveniles 'concerned in the proceedings' in youth court cases—defendants, victims/alleged victims and witnesses—from contemporaneous adverse publicity by banning the media from identifying them in any publication referring to their cases.

This automatic anonymity is bestowed by section 49 of the Children and Young Persons Act 1933.

Section 49 says (here summarised) that:

- no matter relating to any juvenile concerned in proceedings shall, while he/she is under the age of 18, be included in any publication if it is likely to lead members of the public to identify him/her as someone concerned in the proceedings.

It also says that the following matters in particular should not be included if likely to identify the juvenile:

- his/her name;
- his/her address;
- the identity of any school or other educational establishment he/she attends;
- the identity of any place of work; and
- any still or moving picture of him/her.

The definition 'concerned in the proceedings' includes a juvenile 'in respect of whom the proceedings are taken', which means that:

- section 49 anonymity applies to a juvenile who is the victim/alleged victim in the case even if he/she is not a witness—for example, because he/she is too young to give evidence.

for context, see ch. 15, p. 179, Judicial College guidance for criminal courts

But a juvenile victim/alleged victim who is dead *can* be identified by the media, because a dead juvenile is not 'concerned in the proceedings'. This point is made in the Judicial College guidance on reporting restrictions—see Useful Websites at the end of this chapter.

Section 49 says 'publication' includes 'any speech, writing, relevant programme or other communication in whatever form, which is addressed to the public at large or any section of the public'.

No identifying detail should be published

The section 49 restrictions mean that normally media reports of youth court cases should not include any detail which could identify a juvenile concerned in the proceedings. Describing a defendant as 'a 14-year-old Bristol boy' would not identify him because Bristol is large. But naming a small village as a defendant's home could well identify him/her to people who know he/she lives there. Including a juvenile's nickname or an unusual physical characteristic in a report might identify him/her to some people, while reporting that he/she is the 12-year-old twin son of a policeman will identify him/her to anyone who knows of such twins. The test is always whether, as a result of the report, any member of the public could realise who the juvenile is. Adults who figure in youth court cases as witnesses or are mentioned in evidence can be named in reports, as long as doing so does not identify a juvenile (or breach any discretionary restriction imposed by the court in respect of the adult). But a journalist may need to leave a name and detail identifying an adult out of a report to avoid identifying a juvenile—for example, a father who gives evidence about his son, the defendant, cannot be named: see pp. 102–104, Jigsaw identification, and see the Additional Material for ch. 9 on www.mcnaes.com.

The 2015 changes to section 49

In 2015 the wording of section 49 was amended to that summarised earlier in the chapter, partly to ensure that 'publication' covered the internet and partly to adopt a standardised format already used for anonymity provision in other reporting restrictions (eg those for victims of sexual offences—see ch. 10).

The change means that section 49 no longer applies merely to reports of youth court cases, but bans any publication (eg a feature on crime) from identifying a juvenile as being concerned in a youth court case.

The amendments also mean that section 49 is no longer a blanket ban on identifying the juvenile's school, in that it may be possible for a report to identify the school if it is large, without being likely to identify the juvenile. But journalists should err on the side of caution, and the safest course is to ask the court for specific permission to identify the school if this is 'in the public interest'—see p. 97, When section 49 anonymity ceases to apply, and the case studies later in this chapter. The court may give such permission—for example, to let the media highlight a problem of drug-dealing at a particular school.

When does the section 49 anonymity begin?

Section 49 refers to court proceedings. Therefore, strictly speaking, its anonymity does not take effect before the first hearing begins in the youth court. Journalists may decide, for ethical or defamation risk reasons—see ch. 4, pp. 45–46, The risk of libel in media identification of crime suspects—not to identify a juvenile being investigated by police even though section 49 applies only if or when the case reaches a youth court hearing.

 See the Additional Material for ch. 4 on www.mcnaes.com about the Ofcom rule against identifying juveniles who are under investigation and cases in which newspapers have done this.

Anonymity retained for appeal and youth rehabilitation order hearings

ch. 8 explains these Crown court and High Court appeal routes

- Section 49 anonymity also applies to reports of Crown court hearings of appeals from the youth court against conviction or severity of sentence, and to reports of High Court hearings of appeals from the youth court (or from the Crown court appeal hearings) on a point of law, so the anonymity travels up with the appeal.

- The anonymity also applies to proceedings in a magistrates' court for breach, revocation or amendment of youth rehabilitation orders if the court announces that section 49 applies.
- The section 49 restrictions do *not* apply to reports of the Crown court proceedings involving a juvenile sent there for trial or committed there for sentence. But the Crown court may make a discretionary order giving him/her anonymity under section 45 of the Youth Justice and Criminal Evidence Act 1999, as explained later.

Breaches of section 49 and who is liable

It is illegal to publish material which breaches section 49—that is, material which identifies a juvenile who should have anonymity. The punishment is a fine. There is no longer a maximum amount specified—see ch. 6, p. 63, Fines and the removal of the £5,000 limit.

Section 49 says that the proprietor, editor or publisher of a newspaper or periodical can be prosecuted for a breach, but it shall be a defence to prove that at the time of the alleged breach he/she/it (the proprietary company) was not aware, and neither suspected nor had reason to suspect, that the publication included the matter in question.

For a TV or radio programme the case will be against 'the body corporate' which provides the programme service and 'any person having functions in relation to the programme corresponding to those of an editor of a newspaper', and in the case of any other publication, any person publishing it. The Attorney General must consent to such prosecutions.

👁 Case study

In 2003 a district judge fined the *Plymouth Evening Herald* £1,500 for publishing a photograph of a 15-year-old boy convicted at a youth court of stabbing a fellow pupil. The district judge said evidence by friends and relatives that they had recognised the boy, even though his face was pixelated, meant that the paper had breached section 49 (*Media Lawyer*, 4 March 2004).

---

see ch. 21, p. 297, General protection in regulation 19

Readers' comments which breach anonymity

It is possible that a reader might post directly onto a media organisation's website a comment identifying a juvenile who should have anonymity. Law which can protect the organisation from any liability includes regulation 19 of the Electronic Commerce (EC Directive) Regulations 2002, provided the comment was deleted expeditiously after the organisation became aware of its unlawful content.

When section 49 anonymity ceases to apply

The section 49 anonymity automatically expires when the juvenile reaches the age of 18. The 2015 legislative amendments to the section make this clear, reflecting case law.

Section 49 allows a youth court to lift a juvenile's anonymity—that is, before he/she turns 18—to allow the media to identify him/her 'to any specified extent' in three types of circumstance.

(1) *To avoid injustice*—This power is rarely exercised. A youth court could use it to allow a media report of a preliminary hearing to identify a juvenile defendant whose lawyer says he/she wants publicity to help trace witnesses to prove an **alibi**—'My client John Doe was at the funfair that night, not the crime scene. Did anyone see him at the funfair?' The court might also do so to quash rumours suggesting that the victim was in fact the defendant. → glossary

(2) *Unlawfully at large*—A youth court, if asked to do so by or on behalf of the Director of Public Prosecutions, can lift section 49 anonymity to help to trace a juvenile who is 'unlawfully at large' after being charged with or convicted of a violent or sexual offence, or any offence for which a person aged 21 or more could be jailed for 14 years or more. This would let the media name and publish a photograph of a juvenile who has failed to answer bail or who has escaped from secure accommodation, and who is a potential threat to public safety.

(3) *In the public interest*—A youth court can lift the anonymity of a juvenile it convicts of any offence if satisfied that doing so is 'in the public interest'.

   • Before taking this decision it must give the prosecution and defence the opportunity to argue for or against lifting the anonymity.

   This power to lift the anonymity can be used when a youth court feels that the media should be able to identify—for the benefit of the community—a juvenile who has persistently offended or committed a notorious crime.

 See also ch. 15, pp. 197–198, Challenges to youth court anonymity, for the 'public interest' grounds the media can cite to argue in court for a convicted juvenile's anonymity to be removed.

✳ Remember

A court can only lift section 49 anonymity 'in the public interest' if the juvenile is a convicted defendant. Remember too that though section 49 anonymity expires when a juvenile turns 18, law created in 2015 means a youth court can give lifetime anonymity to a juvenile witness or victim/alleged victim in a case, as this chapter explains later.

Case study

The ability of youth courts to lift section 49 'to any specified extent' is illustrated by a 2006 decision of Newbury youth court, which held it was in the public interest to allow media reports to name a 14-year-old girl convicted of drink-driving. But it refused to permit publication of recent photographs of her or to allow her school to be named. Shortly after the court decided this, the girl, who was first convicted of drink-driving when she was 12, threw a punch at the prosecutor and hurled a 2 litre jug of water at the magistrates (*Media Lawyer*, 28 March 2006).

Juveniles in adult courts

A juvenile may appear in the (adult) magistrates' court if jointly charged with an adult. The juvenile may be tried there as a co-accused, or the magistrates can remit the juvenile's case to the youth court for trial or sentencing. If the adult's case is sent for trial to the Crown court, the juvenile's case may be sent there too if the magistrates think a joint trial is in the interests of justice—for example, to avoid making witnesses testify in two trials. Also, a juvenile defendant's case can be sent by a youth court to a Crown court for trial or committed there for sentence.

Section 45 reporting restrictions in adult criminal courts

There is no automatic ban on identifying any juvenile 'concerned in the proceedings' of an adult criminal court—magistrates', Crown or higher court—whether as a defendant, witness or victim/alleged victim.

But these adult courts have discretion to impose anonymity under section 45 of the Youth Justice and Criminal Evidence Act 1999 for any such juvenile.

A section 45 order should specify the individual it covers. Its scope normally is that (here summarised):

- no matter relating to the juvenile shall be included in any publication while he/she is under the age of 18 if it is likely to lead members of the public to identify him/her as someone concerned in the proceedings.

Section 45 says that the following matters in particular should not be included if likely to identify the juvenile:

- his/her name;
- his/her address;

- the identity of any school or other educational establishment he/she attends;
- the identity of any place of work; and
- any still or moving picture of him/her.

A section 45 anonymity order covering a juvenile defendant, witness or victim/alleged victim may well mean that some details in the charge(s) or some details of evidence cannot be published and, possibly, that an adult defendant or adult witness in the case also cannot be identified.

For example, if a father is charged with assaulting his child, whose identity is protected by a section 45 order, the relationship cannot be included in any report which names the father as the defendant, because reporting it would identify the child. Even mentioning the child's age in such reports could inadvertently reveal a familial relationship and so illegally identify the child.

see also
pp. 103– 104,
Cases of
abuse within
a family

The types of detail which could breach section 45 anonymity provided under the 1999 Act are the same as those which could breach the automatic anonymity provided in respect of youth court cases under section 49 of the Children and Young Persons Act 1993.

see
pp. 94–95,
No identify-
ing detail
should be
published

✳ Remember

A section 45 order can apply to a juvenile 'in respect of whom the proceedings are taken'. It can be used to prevent a media report of a truancy case from identifying a child whose parent is prosecuted in the (adult) magistrates' court for failing to ensure the child attends school. The effect would be that the report could not identify the parent either and should not identify the school if there is any likelihood of this identifying the child.

'Publication' and liability for breach

Liability for breach of a section 45 order made under the 1999 Act is the same as for breach of section 49 anonymity under the Children and Young Persons Act 1933, and the definition of 'publication' is the same in both Acts—see pp. 93–96, Section 49 automatic restrictions on identifying juveniles. See also p. 96, Readers' comments which breach anonymity.

See p. 102, Invalid anonymity orders, later in the chapter and see also ch. 15, pp. 190–197, Court orders giving juveniles anonymity, for circumstances in which a court can revoke or relax a section 45 order, and for case law which a media organisation wanting to report a court hearing or trial fully can cite to challenge the provision or continuation of section 45 anonymity for a juvenile.

When section 45 anonymity ceases to apply

Anonymity provided by a section 45 order automatically expires when the juvenile turns 18. The section's wording makes this clear.

The 2015 changes

Section 45 of the 1999 Act was brought into force on 13 April 2015. In the criminal courts, it replaced—as the discretionary power to provide anonymity for juveniles—section 39 of the Children and Young Persons Act 1933. Use of section 39 is now restricted to non-criminal proceedings, as explained later in the chapter. But a section 39 order made before 13 April 2015, unless specifically revoked, remains in force, whichever court made it, until the juvenile turns 18.

� Lifetime anonymity for a juvenile witness or victim/alleged victim

Since 13 April 2015, any criminal court—youth court, magistrates' courts and Crown court—can make an order under section 45A of the Youth Justice and Criminal Evidence Act 1999 to provide:

- lifetime anonymity for a juvenile witness or a juvenile victim/alleged victim so that he/she is not identified as having been 'concerned in the proceedings' (that is, involved in that court case).

The scope of this anonymity is the same as that set out in section 45, except that a section 45A order means the anonymity does *not* expire when the juvenile reaches 18. The circumstances in which a court can make such an order are, in essence, that the juvenile is in 'fear or distress' about being publicly identified as being concerned in the case and that granting anonymity is likely to improve the quality of his/her evidence or level of cooperation. These circumstances are set out in detail in ch. 15, pp. 199–201, Lifetime anonymity for witnesses and juvenile victims, which also explains grounds on which the order can be challenged by the media, as such anonymity may substantially restrict what can be reported. A section 45A order cannot protect the identity of a juvenile defendant. Liability for breach of a section 45A order made under the 1999 Act is the same as for breach of section 49 anonymity under the Children and Young Persons Act 1933, and the definition of 'publication' is the same in both—see pp. 93–96, Section 49 automatic restrictions on identifying juveniles.

see too p. 96, Readers' comments which breach anonymity

▸ Section 39 reporting restrictions in civil proceedings and coroners' courts

ch. 12 explains civil courts and ch. 16 explains coroners' courts

When juveniles are 'concerned' in civil law proceedings—for example, in the High Court or a county court as claimants, defendants or witnesses—or in a coroner's court as a witness, they *can* be identified in the media as being involved in the case unless the court specifically forbids it.

A court which wants, 'in relation' to any such proceedings, to ban the media from identifying such a juvenile can make an order under section 39 of the Children and Young Persons' Act 1933.

The scope of a section 39 order is normally that no publication referring to the case shall reveal:

- the juvenile's name;
- his/her address;
- his/her school;
- any particulars 'calculated' (that is, likely) to lead to his/her identification as being concerned in the proceedings;
- a picture of or including the juvenile.

The wording of section 39 has yet to be fully standardised with that of the other reporting restrictions explained earlier.

As with the section 49 automatic restriction in respect of youth court cases, a journalist must take care not to breach a section 39 order made by a civil or coroner's court by including too much detail about any juvenile protected by it.

see pp. 94–95, No identifying detail should be published

The wording of section 39 means that, unless the court decides otherwise, in any publication referring to the case there is a blanket ban on identifying the juvenile's school, irrespective of whether identifying the school is likely to identify the juvenile, and a blanket ban on using a picture of the juvenile, irrespective of whether it identifies him/her.

Section 39 says that 'any person' who includes in a publication matter which breaches the anonymity is liable for the breach. The definition of 'publication' is the same as in section 49 of the Act and there is the same punishment for breach—see p. 96, Breaches of section 49 and who is liable.

👁 Case study

In 2014 Brian Aitken, then the editor of the *Newcastle Journal*, was fined £1,600 by a district judge after admitting it breached a section 39 order by naming a juvenile's school. Publisher NCJ Media Ltd, part of Trinity Mirror plc, also admitted breaching the order and was fined £2,160 on that charge and a further £2,160 for a similar publication in sister title the *Chronicle*, and ordered to pay £5,000 costs. The charges arose out of a report of the case of a woman teaching assistant at a school who appeared in a magistrates' court charged with a sexual offence involving a female pupil. As the charge was a sexual offence, the alleged victim was automatically entitled to lifelong anonymity under the Sexual Offences (Amendment) Act 1992.

ch. 10 explains sexual offence law

However, the magistrates also gave the pupil anonymity with an order under section 39 of the Children and Young Persons Act 1933—which was at that time used in criminal courts. But Aitken did not know the section 39 order had been made. The *Journal* felt that, with 1,000 pupils, the school was big enough to allow it to be named without identifying the pupil, who was not identified in the reports. But Aitken and NCJ Media were ruled to have breached the section 39 order by naming the school. The High Court later dismissed Aitken's appeal against the district judge's ruling on the liability of editors, a ruling which had led to Aitken changing his plea to guilty (*Press Gazette*, 20 November 2014; *Media Lawyer*, 20 November 2014 and 23 April 2015; *Brian Aitken v DPP* [2015] EWHC 1079 (Admin)).

When does section 39 cease to apply to a juvenile?

In 2014 the Court of Appeal, upholding previous case law, ruled that section 39 anonymity automatically expires when the juvenile reaches the age of 18 (*R (on the application of JC & RT) v Central Criminal Court* [2014] EWCA Civ 1777).

A civil court wanting to extend the juvenile's anonymity provision beyond this age—that is, into adulthood—would need to make an order drawing directly on powers derived from the European Convention on Human Rights. Civil courts also have a specific power in the Civil Procedure Rules (CPR) to order that the identity of a witness or party should not be disclosed.

 See ch. 11, pp. 133–134, Other anonymity orders, on the CPR and ch. 15, pp. 181–182, Convention rights of anonymity for defendants or witnesses.

▶ Invalid anonymity orders

- A court, to pay proper heed to the principle of open justice, should not make a section 45 order under the 1999 Act or a section 39 order under the 1933 Act merely because of the juvenile's age or as an order arbitrarily covering all juveniles in the case. It should consider for each whether there is good reason for anonymity.

- These sections can only provide anonymity for a living juvenile, not one who is dead—for example, a murder victim.

- A court cannot use either type of order to specifically give anonymity to an adult.

 Ch. 15, pp. 190–197 gives guidance and cites law on how the media can challenge section 45 or section 39 orders which are invalid or unnecessary.

▶ Jigsaw identification

- The term 'jigsaw identification' describes the effect when someone to whom the law has given anonymity is nevertheless identifiable to the public because of a combination or accumulation of detail published.

It can occur when two or more media organisations cover the same case. Each may publish a report which in itself preserves the anonymity. But jigsaw identification will occur if someone who reads, views or hears the reports of more than one organisation can, by combining the different detail in each, recognise the person who should be anonymous.

Jigsaw identification can also occur through publication of a series of sequential reports which allow too much detail gradually to accumulate. The term is also used to describe such an accumulation in a *single* report.

The examples given below relate to anonymity for juveniles. But jigsaw identification can also destroy anonymity granted in law to others—for example, victims and alleged victims of sexual offences.

 Sexual offences law is explained in ch. 10. Other law giving anonymity is explained in chs. 11, 12, 13, 16 and 17.

Example 1 A juvenile in a youth court, who should have anonymity under section 49 of the Children and Young Persons Act 1933, admits causing criminal damage to a sports car owned by local millionaire John Doe. One local paper reports: 'A 15-year-old boy vandalised a sports car owned by London tycoon John Doe, costing him £5,000 in repairs.' Another local paper reports: 'A 15-year-old boy vandalised his rich neighbour's sports car, causing £5,000 damage.' Neither paper names the boy. The second paper does not name Doe. But anyone reading both will know the boy is Doe's neighbour, which will identify the boy locally.

Example 2 A juvenile, who should have anonymity after a section 45 order was made under the Youth Justice and Criminal Evidence Act 1999, gives evidence at Crown court in a murder trial. A local radio station describes her as 'a 16-year-old who works as a shop assistant in London'. Another radio station does not mention her job but describes her routine as 'commuting each morning to work in Charing Cross'. A newspaper reports that she lives in Islington. This accumulation of detail could lead those who know her, and who listen to both stations and read that newspaper, to realise that she is the witness.

Cases of abuse within a family

There is a particular danger of jigsaw identification in reporting court cases concerning violence or sexual abuse allegedly inflicted on a child by a relative or family 'friend'—for example, when a father, stepfather or a mother's live-in partner is the adult defendant. In such cases, when the abuse is physical but not sexual, it is standard practice for magistrates or the Crown court judge to make a section 45 order. In cases where the charge is of sexual abuse, the child has automatic anonymity under other law—see ch. 10.

When covering such abuse cases in courts, a media organisation has two options.

(a) *The report can name the adult defendant*—but if the defendant is a relative, the report must not include any detail of his/her relationship to the child, to protect the child's anonymity. This can severely restrict what is published—for example, about how the defendant had opportunity to abuse the child, or even the child's age. Lord Justice Maurice Kay made this comment in the Court of Appeal in 2005, alluding to a case in which a father was convicted of conspiracy to rape a child and of distributing indecent photographs of her: 'Offences of the kind established in this case are frequently committed by fathers and step-fathers. ... If the offender is named and the victim is described as "an 11-year old schoolgirl", in circumstances in which the offender has an 11-year old daughter, it is at least arguable that the composite picture presented embraces "particulars calculated (likely) to lead to the identification" of the victim' (*R v Teesside Crown Court, ex p Gazette Media Company Ltd and others* [2005] All ER (D) 367 (Jul)).

(b) *If the report does not identify the adult defendant in any way,* it can therefore refer to the familial or household relationship between the defendant and child, can definitely refer to the child's age and can include greater detail of evidence, while preserving the child's anonymity.

An editor's instinct is usually that it is in the public's best interests for people charged with crime—and particularly those convicted of it—to be named, as a deterrent and so that a community can be wary of that individual. This is achieved by the approach in (a), if it is possible to construct a meaningful report without revealing the family relationship. But another editor may feel that the public interest is best served by the approach in (b), which can make clear that the alleged abuse was, for example, by a relative. Approach (b) allows publication of more material and more questions to be raised about why the community, social services or the police remained unaware of the abuse within the household.

Jigsaw identification may occur if two media organisations covering the case adopt different approaches. If one follows policy (a), naming the adult defendant but obscuring his relationship to the child victim, and the other follows approach (b), not identifying the defendant but reporting, for example, that he was the child's father, anyone reading both reports will be able to identify the child even though neither report names him/her. To avoid jigsaw identification of the child, all the newsrooms involved need to adopt the same approach.

 See ch. 10, pp. 118–119, Ethical considerations, on the ethical ban on identifying children in sexual cases.

◗ Anti-social behaviour injunctions

Law creating a new type of injunction banning anti-social behaviour came into force on 23 March 2015. These injunctions, created by Part 1 of the Anti-social Behaviour, Crime and Policing Act 2014, replace the 'stand-alone' version of the anti-social behaviour orders known as ASBOs. The new type is 'stand-alone' because, as was the case with an ASBO, it can be imposed on a person even though his/her anti-social behaviour has not led to a criminal conviction. This type is referred to officially as an 'anti-social behaviour injunction' (ASBI), though it seems likely that colloquially they may still be referred to as ASBOs.

In the context of housing—for example, to deter anti-social behaviour in a residential street or on an estate—a county court or (if at least one of the trouble-makers is a juvenile) the youth court may impose an ASBI banning conduct which has caused or is likely to cause 'nuisance and annoyance'. Various bodies, including police and local authorities, can apply for an ASBI to ban, for example, juveniles from residential streets where they have been creating a nuisance. But in non-housing contexts—for example, where an individual is consistently behaving badly in a shopping mall—the threshold for imposing an ASBI is higher, in that the behaviour must have caused or be likely to cause 'harassment, alarm or distress'.

These injunctions are, as ASBOs were, civil orders. Breaching the injunction is a contempt of court—and the maximum punishment for a juvenile aged 14–17 is three months' detention.

Can a juvenile in ASBI proceedings be identified?

- The default position in law is that any juvenile concerned in youth court proceedings which consider an application for an ASBI—which are civil proceedings—will *not* have automatic anonymity in any publication referring to the proceedings, whether or not the ASBI is granted.

This position is set out in section 17 of the 2014 Act, which for these injunction proceedings disapplies the anonymity in section 49 of the 1933 Act that would—as this chapter has explained—normally apply to youth court proceedings.

But a youth court, or any other court, dealing with injunction applications may give anonymity to any juvenile 'concerned in the proceedings' (see earlier), by making an order under section 39 of the Children and Young Persons Act 1933.

Ch. 15 explains how a journalist can argue in courts against reporting restrictions, and ch. 15, pp. 198–199, Anti-social behaviour cases—arguments for identifying juveniles, provides arguments he/she can make that a juvenile made subject to an injunction should be identified in a report of the hearing.

▌ Criminal behaviour orders

A 'criminal behaviour order' (CBO), which can only be imposed on an individual after he/she has been convicted of a crime, has replaced another type of ASBO. The law creating CBOs, in Part 2 of the 2014 Act, came into force on 20 October 2014.

An application for a CBO may only be made by the prosecution after a conviction. A CBO may be imposed on a juvenile after—for example—he/she is convicted of shoplifting or taking a car without the owner's consent ('joy-riding'), to

ch. 5, p. 53, Taking a vehicle without authority, explains the 'joy-riding' offence ban him/her from entering shops or interfering with cars. Breaching a CBO is a criminal offence. A juvenile convicted of a serious breach could be given a training and detention order.

Anonymity in reports of hearings to decide whether to impose a CBO

Any criminal court can impose a CBO, but for juveniles this is most likely to be the youth court. Section 23 of the 2014 Act provides that:

- if—and only if—the youth court makes a CBO against the juvenile, the automatic anonymity in section 49 of the 1933 Act automatically lapses as regards that juvenile, allowing media reports of the CBO hearing to identify him/her;
- but the youth court has discretion to preserve the anonymity by making an order under section 39 of the 1933 Act.

The section 49 anonymity will continue to apply to any juvenile witnesses in the CBO hearing and may still apply to the juvenile defendant in respect of the earlier hearing in the youth court, in which he/she was convicted of an offence. The court should—if section 49 anonymity remains in place for the earlier hearing—say enough in the CBO hearing to explain the behaviour which led to it being imposed.

   The journalist could remind the court clerk that the Justices' Clerks' Society issued guidance to its members that when a court draws up an ASBO it should include details of the anti-social behaviour which led to the order being made, so this guidance should hold good for CBO cases.

 See Useful Websites at the end of this chapter for this guidance.

   A journalist could argue that it would be for the good of the community for the section 49 anonymity to be lifted 'in the public interest' in respect of the criminal conviction—and that for the same reason section 39 anonymity should not be imposed in relation to the juvenile made subject to the CBO.

 See pp. 97–98, When section 49 anonymity ceases to apply, on the youth court's power to consider 'the public interest' and ch. 15, pp. 198–199, Anti-social behaviour cases—arguments for identifying juveniles, which details specific arguments that can be made against the juvenile having section 39 anonymity.

No automatic anonymity for alleged breaches of CBOs

A juvenile alleged to have breached a CBO may be charged with this as a criminal offence, which will normally be dealt with at a youth court. Section 30 of the 2014 Act says that the usual anonymity under section 49 of the 1933 Act for juveniles appearing in a youth court does not apply to a juvenile accused of breaching a CBO.

- So the media *can* identify a juvenile defendant when reporting a youth court's proceedings for alleged breach of a CBO, whether or not it convicts him/her. But any juvenile witness retains the automatic anonymity under section 49.
- The youth court can decide to give the juvenile defendant anonymity. Section 30 of the 2014 Act gives youth courts the discretionary power to give anonymity to a juvenile defendant accused of breaching a CBO by using section 45 of the Youth Justice and Criminal Evidence Act 1999, a power explained earlier in this chapter.

Section 30 of the 2014 Act says that if a court does give such a juvenile anonymity under section 45, it must give its reasons for doing so. Again, a journalist covering the hearing could argue that the juvenile should be named—see ch. 15, pp. 198–199, Anti-social behaviour cases—arguments for identifying juveniles.

➡ Recap of major points

- Most juveniles charged with a crime are dealt with by youth courts. The public cannot attend these courts, but journalists can.
- Section 49 of the Children and Young Persons Act 1933 bans media reports from identifying anyone aged under 18 involved in youth court cases, whether as defendant, witness or crime victim/alleged victim.
- This anonymity can be lifted, in the case of a convicted juvenile, to allow the media to identify him/her in the public interest—for example, after persistent offending.
- There is no automatic anonymity for a juvenile involved in adult court proceedings. But an adult court can make an order under section 45 of the Youth Justice and Criminal Evidence Act 1999 to give the juvenile anonymity.
- There is no automatic anonymity for a juvenile involved in civil proceedings or inquests at coroners' courts. But these courts can make an order under section 39 of the Children and Young Persons Act 1933 to give the juvenile anonymity.
- Courts can impose injunctions or criminal behaviour orders (CBOs) to ban anti-social behaviour. The default position in law is that a juvenile against whom such an injunction is sought, or a juvenile made subject to a CBO or accused of breaching one, can be identified by the media unless an anonymity order is made.

((•)) Useful Websites

www.gov.uk/browse/justice/young-people
   Government guidance on the youth justice system

www.judiciary.gov.uk/publications/reporting-restrictions-in-the-criminal-courts-2/
   Guidance on reporting restrictions, published by the Judicial College, the News
   Media Association, the Media Lawyers Association, the Society of Editors and
   Times Newspapers Ltd, including supplementary guidance about juvenile cases

http://webarchive.nationalarchives.gov.uk/20100418065544/http:/asb.homeoffice.gov.
uk/uploadedFiles/Members_site/Documents_and_images/Evidence_and_court/JCS_
ASBOGuide_May06_0041.PDF
   Justices' Clerks' Society, *Good Practice Guide on ASBOs*

Sexual offences, human trafficking and female genital mutilation

Chapter summary

The law gives victims and alleged victims of sexual offences, including rape, lifetime anonymity in media reports of these crimes and any subsequent prosecutions. Several media organisations have been fined for publishing detail which breached this anonymity and so caused considerable distress to those identified. As this chapter explains, the anonymity may be removed in some circumstances, allowing the media to identify the individual, but a journalist should consider if this would be ethical. The law also gives anonymity to victims/alleged victims of female genital mutilation, and of human trafficking for sexual and non-sexual exploitation, including slavery or forced labour.

▶ The scope of automatic, lifelong anonymity for complainants of sexual or trafficking offences

Section 1 of the Sexual Offences (Amendment) Act 1992 says that after an allegation of a sexual or human trafficking offence is made:

- no matter relating to that victim/alleged victim shall, during his/her lifetime, be included in any publication if it is likely to lead members of the public to identify him/her as the victim/alleged victim of the offence.

see Late News section about *The Sun* error identifying a teenage victim

It says the ban includes in particular, if likely to identify that person:

- his/her name;
- his/her address;
- the identity of any school or other educational establishment he/she attends;

- the identity of any place of work
- any still or moving picture of him/her.

Section 6 of the Act defines publication as any speech, writing, relevant programme or other communication in whatever form addressed to the public at large or to any section of the public, and a 'picture' as 'a likeness however produced'.

The anonymity is automatic and lifelong, and applies from the time an allegation is made by the alleged victim or anyone else—for example, when a parent complains to police, or to a journalist, that a child has been sexually abused—and remains in place regardless of whether the allegation is later withdrawn, or the police are told, or an alleged offender is prosecuted, or anyone is convicted.

The anonymity also applies to anyone who is the target of any attempt or conspiracy to commit a sexual or human trafficking offence.

In rare circumstances a court may lift the anonymity or the individual concerned may waive it. But it usually applies.

 See Additional Material for ch. 10 on www.mcnaes.com, Newspaper breached anonymity after the rape charge was dropped.

The wide application of the anonymity

for detail of the 2015 Act, see pp. 114–118, Trafficking offences for which victims/ alleged victims have anonymity

Parliament decided in 1976 that the violation of rape, and the potential for victims to suffer embarrassment and further trauma when testifying in court, justified giving them anonymity. This anonymity, now provided by the 1992 Act, has since been extended to victims/alleged victims of other sexual offences, and recently to victims/alleged victims of offences of 'human trafficking for exploitation'—including non-sexual offences—in section 2 of the Modern Slavery Act 2015. The anonymity applies to crime stories as well as court reports—for example, in the case of a news website report that police are investigating a rape. Nothing should be published which suggests the identity of the victim/alleged victim, such as a picture of the house where the sexual offence is said to have taken place or the victim/alleged victim of human trafficking lived.

The anonymity also applies to reports of the trials of those accused of these offences, although the defendant can be named, as well as to reports of courts martial and civil cases. So, if a woman who alleges she was raped or subject to trafficking sues the alleged perpetrator in a civil court, she must remain anonymous in reports of that lawsuit.

ch. 17 explains employment tribunals

Similarly, anyone who claims at an employment tribunal that he/she was the victim of a sexual or a trafficking offence must be anonymous in reports of the case.

A person who says, when being interviewed for a biographical feature, that he/she was at some time sexually attacked or molested, or trafficked for exploitation, cannot legally be identified in it as being a victim/alleged victim of this crime, unless he/she gives valid written consent for such identification, as this chapter explains later. Similar anonymity under other law applies for anyone who says she is a victim of female genital mutilation, as this chapter also explains.

👁 Case study

Trinity Mirror Southern Ltd was fined a total of £10,000 in 2011 after it admitted that the *Aldershot News and Mail*, *Farnborough News and Mail*, *Fleet News and Mail* and the *Yateley News and Mail* had published in a report of a court case the names of two women who were victims of sexual assault. It was also ordered to pay each of them £5,000 compensation. Human error was blamed for this breach of the Sexual Offences (Amendment) Act 1992. A Crown Prosecution Service lawyer said: 'The disregard by the newspapers of these women's automatic right to anonymity proved traumatic to those involved and required extensive extra police and victim support' (Hampshire Constabulary's *Frontline* magazine, issue 163, July 2011).

� Care needed with detail

Section 1 of the 1992 Act prohibits publication of matter 'likely to lead' to identification. A report of a sexual or trafficking offence which refers to the alleged victim's school or workplace and gives his/her age could prompt speculation likely to lead to identification. Although saying the victim is a student at a specific university is unlikely to identify him/her, giving further detail, such as that the victim is a 25-year-old music student, is likely to do so. In 1983 the then Solicitor General said that a report of a rape case could be illegal if the detail included were sufficient to identify the victim in the minds of some people even though not in the minds of the community generally.

Jigsaw identification

Jigsaw identification must be avoided whenever the media refer to an offence for which the law gives the victim/alleged victim anonymity. It may occur if in reports of a rape trial a town's newspaper describes the alleged victim as 'a mother of three' who lives and works locally, a TV station describes her as 'a nurse', and a radio station describes her as 'a woman in her 30s' who works nights. This accumulation of detail could identify her to colleagues and acquaintances— see also ch. 9, pp. 102–103, Jigsaw identification.

Media organisations covering cases involving sexual abuse of a child by an adult in the same family or household should agree whether their reports (a) name the adult defendant, but omit any detail of any relationship to the child, or (b) do not identify the adult defendant and report that the alleged abuse was familial or within the household.

see also
ch. 9,
pp. 103–104,
Cases
of abuse
within a
family

Journalists should also pay heed to relevant parts of the Editors' Code or the Broadcasting Code, which are explained later in this chapter.

👁 Case study

The *Luton Herald and Post* was fined £1,000 in 2013 for publishing detail which identified a woman victim of a sexual offence. In a report of a man's trial on rape and sexual assault charges, the newspaper included the victim's age and home country, said she had come to the UK to study, and gave the approximate date and location of her arrival, named the placement agency she used, said where she was studying and how she had met her attacker, and referred to her living arrangements and professional aspirations (*Media Lawyer*, 8 October 2013).

▌ Invalid orders purporting to give an adult defendant anonymity

see ch. 15, pp. 201–202, Sexual offence law does not give anonymity to defendants

The media may decide, when covering a court case involving alleged sexual abuse within a family, that the only way to preserve anonymity for the alleged victim(s) is not to publish anything identifying the adult defendant. But occasionally magistrates' courts and Crown court judges have sought to make that choice for the media by passing an order, purportedly under the Sexual Offences (Amendment) Act 1992, stating that the adult defendant should not be identified. The reason usually given is that the order is needed to protect the anonymity of the alleged victim(s). The Act gives courts no power to make such orders.

▌ Sexual offences for which victims/alleged victims have anonymity

→ glossary

The 1992 Act, as amended by the Sexual Offences Act 2003, applies the anonymity for victims and alleged victims to virtually all offences with a sexual element. The most serious are indictable-only, with a maximum sentence of life imprisonment. These include:

- *rape*—penetration of vagina, anus, or mouth without consent, by penis—if the victim is aged under 13, any such conduct is defined as rape, even if the victim says there was no compulsion, because the victim is so young (and noting that males and females can be rape victims but only males can be rapists; females can be guilty of inciting or aiding rape);

- *assault by penetration*—of vagina or anus, without consent and otherwise than by penis—for example, by finger or object;
- *causing or inciting a child under 13 or a person who has 'a mental disorder impeding choice' to engage in sexual activity* in which the activity caused or incited involves penetration by penis or otherwise;
- *an attempt, conspiracy, or incitement* to commit any of the above offences;
- *aiding, abetting, counselling, or procuring* the commission of any of them.

Some sexual crimes are either-way charges. For some, an offender can be sentenced to a jail term of up to 14 years. Either-way charges include: → glossary

- *sexual assault*—intentional sexual touching, without consent;
- *administering a substance with intent to engage a person in sexual activity*—for example, spiking someone's drink with a drug;
- *trespass with intent to commit a sexual offence*;
- *sexual intercourse with a girl who has reached the age of 13 but who is under 16*—this offending is not classed as rape if there is no compulsion, but could be very serious and exploitative if the perpetrator is much older;
- *abuse of a position of trust, through sexual activity with someone aged under 18*—so, for example, a male teacher having consensual sex with a 17-year-old girl who is not a school pupil is not committing a crime as she is over 16, the age of sexual consent, but if she is a pupil at the school where he works, the sexual relationship is criminal abuse of his position of trust as a teacher;
- *sexual activity by a care worker*—for example, in a hospital—if it involved such activity with a person in his/her care who has a mental disorder and not involving penetration (which would be indictable-only);
- *engaging in sexual activity in the presence of a child*, or causing a child to watch a sexual act, for the perpetrator's sexual gratification;
- *arranging or facilitating commission of a sexual offence against a child*, anywhere in the world;
- *meeting or intending to meet a child following sexual grooming*—for example, an adult contacting a child over the Internet—in which case the child has anonymity even if no meeting takes place;
- *sexual activity by an adult with a child family member* (noting that it is incorrect to describe such an offence as incest, because incest is a consensual relationship);
- *taking an indecent photograph of a child; paying for the sexual services of a child; causing, inciting, arranging or facilitating the sexual exploitation of a child or controlling a child for this purpose*;
- *causing or inciting or controlling prostitution for gain*—some journalists may not realise that anonymity has been extended to cover adults who are or have allegedly been, for example, 'controlled' prostitutes;
- *exposure* (colloquially called 'flashing') of genitals with the intent to cause alarm or distress;

- *voyeurism*—observing for sexual gratification someone else or people doing something private (for example, taking a shower, or having sex), knowing they did not consent to being observed because, for example, a hidden camera was used.

Buggery is no longer illegal between consenting adults, but is an offence if perpetrated on someone aged under 16—who is a victim and therefore has anonymity.

A sexual offence which allegedly occurred before 1 May 2004 will be charged according to older definitions, but anonymity applies. One such older offence is 'indecent assault'.

The anonymity does not apply to two adult relatives who are charged with consensual, illegal sexual activity with each other—which would have been charged as 'incest' under the old law—or to adults accused of consensual sexual activity in a public lavatory. But if only one of them is charged, the other retains anonymity. It also does not apply in cases involving a person accused of sexual activity with an animal.

▌Trafficking offences for which victims/ alleged victims have anonymity

The Modern Slavery Act 2015 was created to clarify and consolidate the law on slavery, forced labour and human trafficking, and to increase the penalties for such offences—which for some is a life sentence. The Act's Explanatory Notes say: 'Modern slavery takes a number of forms, including sexual exploitation, forced labour and domestic servitude, and victims come from all walks of life.'

The 2015 Act amended section 1 of the Sexual Offences (Amendment) Act 1992 so that the lifelong automatic anonymity given to victims of sexual offences in general, explained earlier, now covers all victims/alleged victims of 'human trafficking for exploitation' offences in section 2 of the 2015 Act. These—defined in section 3 of the 2015 Act—are (summarised):

- the arranging or facilitating of the travel of another person with a view to that person being exploited
  - by being held in slavery or servitude, or
  - by being required to perform forced or compulsory labour, or
  - because something is done to or in respect of the person which involves or would involve the commission of an offence listed in Part 1 of the Sexual Offences Act 2003, or in section 1(1)(a) of the Protection of Children Act 1978 (indecent photographs of children), or
  - by being encouraged, required or expected to donate or sell an organ from his/her body, or
  - when the person being exploited is a child, or is mentally or physically ill or disabled, or has a family relationship, being subject to force, threats

or deception designed to induce him/her to provide any kind of service, or to provide or enable someone else to obtain benefits of any kind, in circumstances when an adult who was not ill or disabled or did not have that family relationship would be likely to refuse to be thus exploited.

Sexual offences listed earlier in this chapter are in section 1 of the 2003 Act, so the trafficking could include travel being arranged to control people for prostitution or to sexually exploit children, and the anonymity would apply even if, as events turned out, the victims did not suffer the sexual offences—because, for example, police intervened.

For there to be a trafficking offence, there must be the element of 'arranging or facilitating of travel'. This covers arranged or actual travel within the UK, another country or from one country to another, or merely recruiting someone for such travel. For a journalist, recognising that a person is the victim/alleged victim of such a 'trafficking' offence—and therefore should have anonymity—should be straightforward if police say this or after the alleged perpetrator is charged. And if the person is also the victim/alleged victim of a sexual offence, it should be clear that anonymity applies. But otherwise a journalist learning of or interviewing an exploited person, or one for whom exploitation was planned, will need to understand how such 'trafficking' offences are defined, and that an element may be forced labour or another form of exploitation and that there may not be a sexual element.

The anonymity will cover, for example, a 'trafficked' woman forced to work as a household maid, or 'trafficked' immigrants or mentally vulnerable people being compelled to work by threats of violence, or anyone for whom such a destiny was knowingly planned, irrespective of whether anyone was prosecuted for the offence. If the journalist suspects anonymity may apply, yet the person is willing to be identified in an account of such an ordeal or plan, the best course will be to obtain his/her written consent to be identified—see p. 117, If the victim/alleged victim gives written consent.

▶ Liability for breach of the anonymity provision

Section 5 of the 1992 Act says that those who can be prosecuted if a publication/broadcast breaches the anonymity are the newspaper or periodical's proprietor, editor and publisher, or any 'body corporate' (for example, a company) providing the programme service and any person whose functions in relation to the programme correspond to those of an editor of a newspaper, or as regards any other form of publication, any person publishing it.

It is a defence for the person accused to show that he/she was not aware, and neither suspected nor had reason to suspect, that the material published would be likely to identify the victim/alleged victim of the sexual or trafficking offence.

The punishment is an unlimited fine—see ch. 6, p. 63, Fines and the removal of the £5,000 limit.

 See Additional Material for ch. 10 on www.mcnaes.com for other case studies of media organisations being fined for breaching the anonymity of victims of sexual offences. For a defence if a reader's online comment breaches anonymity, see ch. 21, p. 297, General protection in regulation 19.

▌ When does the anonymity cease to apply for victims/alleged victims of a sexual or trafficking offence?

The anonymity does not apply to dead people—for example, a murdered rape victim.

By court order, at the request of a defendant

- A court due to try someone for a sexual or trafficking offence can, on the application of a defendant or a co-defendant, remove an alleged victim's anonymity if it is satisfied that:
  - it should be lifted to induce people likely to be needed as witnesses to come forward; and
  - otherwise the conduct of the applicant's defence at the trial is likely to be substantially prejudiced.

→ glossary   A defendant may argue that he/she needs witnesses to come forward to support an alibi. For example, allowing the media to identify the alleged victim of a sexual offence when reporting the alibi defence could jog the memories of members of the public about where and when he/she was seen, and who, if anyone, was with him/her at the time of the alleged offence.

Courts are rarely asked to lift anonymity on this ground, specified in section 3 of the 1992 Act. If the alleged offence is indictable-only—for example, rape—a Crown court has power to waive the anonymity. A magistrates' court does not because it cannot try the case.

By court order, to lift 'a substantial and unreasonable' restriction on reporting

- The court trying a sexual or trafficking offence can lift an alleged victim's anonymity if it is satisfied that:
  - the anonymity would impose a substantial and unreasonable restriction on media reporting of the trial; and
  - it is in the public interest to remove or relax it.

Again, if the alleged offence is indictable-only, only a Crown court has power to waive the anonymity. Cases in which courts are asked to lift anonymity on the above ground, specified in section 3, are very rare.

For an example of this power being used, see the Hutchinson case study in the Additional Material for ch. 10 on www.mcnaes.com.

If the victim/alleged victim gives written consent

The media may identify someone as being the victim/alleged victim of a sexual or trafficking offence if he/she consents. But section 5 of the 1992 Act specifies that:

- the consent must be in writing;
- the person waiving his/her anonymity must be aged 16 or over; and
- the consent will not be valid if it is proved that anyone 'interfered unreasonably with the peace and comfort' of the individual with the intention of obtaining it.

The law guards against anyone being pressured into giving consent and makes clear that anyone under 16 is too young to consent. Parents of victims/alleged victims under 16 cannot consent on their behalf.

A court's permission is not needed for this consent to be given. Victims of sexual offences have often given written consent, particularly after the offender is jailed. For example, a woman who has been raped may feel that letting the media identify her sends a powerful signal to other rape victims that they can find the courage to seek justice and that there is no stigma in being a victim. Some trafficked victims may feel the same.

If the case is 'other than' the sexual or trafficking offence alleged

People alleged to have falsely claimed to police that they have been victims of sexual or trafficking offences may be charged with wasting police time, or perjury, or perverting the course of justice.

- A person appearing in court on such a charge—for example, perjury—in relation to what is said to be a false allegation of a sexual or trafficking offence can be identified in reports of those proceedings as someone who was previously said to be the victim of that offence.

ch. 5, p. 54, Other noteworthy crimes, gives definitions of these offences

This is because section 1(4) of the 1992 Act says an alleged victim of a sexual or trafficking offence can be identified in articles which consist 'only of a report of criminal proceedings other than' proceedings for that offence. This would also allow the media covering a burglary case to report that the woman home owner had asserted in court that the burglar raped her or, in a case involving a woman defendant accused of attacking a man, that the defendant claimed that her alleged victim had in fact raped her. But there would still need to be ethical consideration of whether the report should identify her as regards such statements.

> Courts can make prevention orders to restrict the activity of sexual or trafficking offenders. For detail, including how the media may oppose anonymity provision for the offender in respect of the order, see ch. 15, p. 186, Civil orders imposed on sexual or trafficking offenders and the Additional Material for ch. 10 on www.mcnaes.com, which also covers sexual risk orders.

▌ Ethical considerations

ch. 2 intro-
duces the
Code and
Appendix 2,
pp. 463–468
gives it in
full

The Editors' Code overseen by the Independent Press Standards Organisation (Ipso), states in clause 11 that the press must not identify victims of sexual assault or publish material likely to contribute to such identification 'unless there is adequate justification and they are legally free to do so'.

The term 'sexual assault' here includes all sexual attacks, eg rape.

Clause 7 (Children in sex cases) says: 'The press must not, even if legally free to do so, identify children under 16 who are victims or witnesses in cases involving sex offences.'

It adds that in any press report of a case involving a sexual offence against a child:

- the child must not be identified;
- the adult may be identified;
- the word 'incest' must not be used where a child victim might be identified;
- care must be taken that nothing in the report implies the relationship between the accused and the child.

for the
Codebook,
see Useful
Websites at
the end of
this chapter

Clause 7 is subject to the Code's public interest exceptions, but clause 11 is not, though the term 'adequate justification' arguably embraces the idea of the public interest. The Code says there would have to be 'exceptional public interest' to override the normally paramount interests of a child under 16—but the Editors' Codebook says a girl can be identified as an under-age mother if her parents consent.

In the three-year period from 2011 to 2013 Ipso's predecessor, the Press Complaints Commission issued 11 adjudications censuring media organisations for publishing material which identified or could have identified child or adult victims of sexual offences—see the *Luton Herald and Post* case discussed earlier. In 2011 the PCC issued guidance—see Useful Websites at the end of this chapter—stressing that 'editors should err on the side of caution' on what detail is published. In 2015 Ipso adjudicated against a newspaper for breach of Clause 7.

> For case studies on PCC and Ipso adjudications, see the Additional Material for ch. 10 on www.mcnaes.com, which also covers ethical guidance about referring to relatives and friends of people accused of sexual offences.

Rule 1.8 of the Broadcasting Code says broadcasters should 'be particularly careful not to provide clues' which may lead to the identification of children when by law they should have anonymity 'as a victim, witness, defendant or other perpetrator in the case of sexual offences featured in criminal, civil or family court proceedings'. This rule also warns against jigsaw identification and that inadvertent use of the term 'incest' may identify such a child—see ch. 3 for an introduction to the Broadcasting Code.

▶ Lifetime anonymity for victims/alleged victims of female genital mutilation

Part of the Serious Crime Act 2015 amended the Female Genital Mutilation Act 2003, making it a criminal offence, punishable by an unlimited fine, to publish anything likely to lead members of the public to identify someone as a victim/alleged victim of female genital mutilation (FGM).

This lifetime anonymity provision, in section 4A and Schedule 1 of the 2003 Act, has in effect the same scope as the anonymity provision in the Sexual Offences (Amendment) Act 1992 for victims/alleged victims of sexual or trafficking offences.

A journalist covering an actual or alleged case of FGM must take the same care about what detail is published, and to avoid jigsaw identification, as when covering those other offences detailed earlier in this chapter.

The anonymity also covers victims/alleged victims of offences of aiding, abetting, counselling and procuring the main FGM offence, as well as victims/alleged victims of the new offence of failing to protect a girl from the risk of FGM. It also covers a victim who agreed to undergo FGM.

FGM is a cultural tradition in some East African and Middle East nations—for example, Somalia and Yemen. There is evidence that it is inflicted on girls and young women from ethnic communities in the UK which share that culture.

FGM is usually arranged by the victim's parents or other adult relatives, so a report which can identify a defendant without identifying the victim may well be rare. FGM has been illegal in the UK since 1985, but by late 2015 there had not been any successful prosecutions. It is hoped that the anonymity provision will encourage victims to report FGM and help lead to more prosecutions.

Paragraph 1(4)–(8) of Schedule 1 to the Act allows a trial judge to lift the anonymity on what are, in essence, the same grounds on which a judge can lift the anonymity in proceedings for sexual and trafficking offences. One ground is that the judge is satisfied that the anonymity should be lifted to avoid the conduct of a person's defence at the trial of an FGM offence being substantially prejudiced—for example, the judge may accept that such publicity is needed for alibi witnesses for the defence to come forward. The other ground is to enable the media to produce a full report of a particular trial because this would be 'in the public interest'—see pp. 116–117, By court order, to lift a 'substantial and unreasonable'

see pp. 109–110, The scope of automatic lifelong anonymity for complainants of sexual or trafficking offences

see Useful Websites at the end of this chapter for information about FGM restriction on reporting. But it will be very rare for the anonymity to be lifted for such reasons.

The victim herself may consent to waive her anonymity. For that consent to be legally valid, she must be aged 16 or over, give written consent, and not have consented as a result of unreasonable interference with her peace and comfort.

Those who can be prosecuted for breaching a victim's anonymity are the same as for breach of anonymity of a victim/alleged victim of a sexual or trafficking offence—see pp. 115–116, Liability for breach of the anonymity provision—but could also include in some circumstances a 'senior officer' (for example, a director) of a media company, as well as the company.

It is a defence for a person to prove that he/she did not know or suspect the publication included 'the matter in question' or to prove there was valid waiver of the anonymity.

▌ Victims of 'revenge porn'

The new offence of publishing so-called revenge porn came into force in April 2015. The offence, under section 33 of the Criminal Justice and Courts Act 2015, consists of disclosing a 'private sexual photograph or film' without the consent of the person depicted in the content and with the intent to cause him/her distress. The victims of the offence do not have anonymity under the law—but many editors have decided against naming them, taking the view that it is not the media's job to achieve the offender's objective by adding to the victim's embarrassment and humiliation. There is a defence for publishing such a photo or film within 'journalistic material' if done with a reasonable belief that this was in the public interest—a defence which is a safeguard for investigative journalism.

➡ Recap of major points

- It is illegal for the media to identify the victims/alleged victims of sexual offences—including rape and sexual assault—in reports of these crimes or of court cases which follow.

- The same anonymity applies for the victims/alleged victims of offences of 'human trafficking for exploitation' and, under other law, for the victims/alleged victims of female genital mutilation.

- A court can remove the anonymity in certain circumstances, but this rarely happens.

- There is a danger of 'jigsaw identification', particularly when several media organisations are covering a case of alleged sex abuse within a family.

- A victim/alleged victim who is aged 16 or over can waive the anonymity by giving a media organisation written consent to being identified.

((•)) Useful Websites

www.cps.gov.uk/legal/p_to_r/rape_and_sexual_offences/index.html
Crown Prosecution Service guidance on prosecution of sexual offences

www.legislation.gov.uk/ukpga/2015/30/notes/contents
Explanatory Notes to the Modern Slavery Act 2015

www.gov.uk/government/uploads/system/uploads/attachment_data/file/300167/FGM_leaflet_v4.pdf
Guidance on female genital mutilation, published by the Home Office

www.editorscode.org.uk/
The Editors' Codebook provides detailed advice on clauses 7 and 11 of the Editors' Code, covering reporting of sexual offence cases

www.pcc.org.uk/advice/editorials-detail.html?article=NzM0Nw==
PCC guidance on reporting court cases involving sexual offences

http://stakeholders.ofcom.org.uk/broadcasting/broadcast-codes/broadcast-code/
Ofcom Broadcasting Code

11

Court reporting— other restrictions

Chapter summary

Earlier chapters have shown that reporting crime and courts is not a job for an untrained amateur. Reporting restrictions can dictate what is published; breaching them is an offence. This chapter details more restrictions, including permanent bans on using cameras and audio-recording devices in any court. Revealing how individual jurors voted in verdicts is also illegal. Reporting what a court has heard in private can be punished as contempt of court. The chapter also outlines how courts can stop the media identifying some adult witnesses and blackmail victims, or postpone reporting of a case. Chapter 15 shows how to challenge a reporting restriction as invalid or unnecessary. Chapter 21 deals with defamation dangers in court reporting.

▌ Ban on photography, filming and sketching in courts and precincts

In 1925 Parliament banned photography in courts. Case law means the ban includes filming in courts. A primary reason for the ban is that photography and filming, and any publication of images gained, would put added strain on witnesses, defendants and jurors.

Section 41 of the Criminal Justice Act 1925 makes it illegal to:

- take or try to take any photograph or film; or
- make or try to make—with a view to publication—any portrait or sketch of:
  - any person in any court, its building, or within its precincts;
  - any person 'entering or leaving' a court building or its precincts;
- publish such a photo, film, portrait or sketch.

Section 41 applies to criminal and civil courts and inquests. 'Any person' includes judges, magistrates, coroners, jurors, witnesses, defendants and any other party.

- The Act does not define 'precincts', which causes practical difficulties. The term includes rooms, foyers or corridors within the courthouse building, but it is unclear to what extent it includes areas immediately outside. If unsure, check with the particular court.

Journalists standing on the public pavement frequently photograph and film judges, lawyers, defendants and witnesses entering or leaving court buildings—for example, the Royal Courts of Justice in London. Where this practice has become customary, it is rare for a court to object, though it would seem to breach the section 41 ban on showing people 'entering or leaving'. Jurors should not be photographed, as this might be regarded as a contempt in common law, as explained later in this chapter.

see Late News section about a TV pilot scheme for Crown courts

Breaches of section 41 can be punished with fines of up to £1,000. Criminal Practice Direction 6C.4 says that in court 'any equipment which has photographic capability must not have that function activated'.

Artists' sketches of court cases

The media publish artists' sketches of scenes in court, including the face of the defendant, to illustrate newsworthy cases. To comply with section 41, these artists visit the court's public gallery or press bench, memorise the scene and characters, but do the actual sketching elsewhere. A government Consultation Paper made no objection to sketching in a courthouse press room.

Jury visits to the scene of crime or death

If a judge or coroner decides that jurors should visit an outside location such as a crime or accident scene to help them understand evidence, the visit should not be filmed, photographed or sketched without the court's permission. The judge or coroner may allow this, as long as no juror can be identified through what is published. The visit means the court has moved temporarily to that location.

Photography and filming could be contempt of court

- Despite the existence of the 1925 Act, a court may deem photography or filming in court or in its precincts or even elsewhere—for example, on the pavement outside—to be a contempt of court in common law.

see also ch. 18, pp. 231–233, Contempt in common law

A photographer's conduct could be regarded as contempt if it amounts to 'molestation'—interference with the administration of justice. Case law suggests that running after a defendant for a short while in order to photograph him/her would not usually be seen as molestation. But stalking a defendant or witnesses further, or jostling them, could be contempt as it might deter them or other witnesses from giving evidence.

Case study

In 2009 Mr Justice Keith warned photographers to stop taking pictures of two young brothers as they arrived at Sheffield Crown court in cars, under blankets, saying he would take action if he thought a contempt had taken place. The brothers had admitted inflicting, when aged 10 and 11, horrific violence on two boys in a village near Doncaster (*Press Gazette*, 7 September 2009).

The fine or prison sentence to punish such a contempt is at the judge's discretion. Some members of the public have been jailed for taking photos in court.

Case study

In 2014 a 24-year-old man was jailed for four months for using a mobile phone to take a photo of a defendant in the dock in Gloucester Crown court, and for posting it and comments about the case on Facebook (*Gloucestershire Echo*, 12 February 2014).

---

ch. 8 explains the work of the Court of Appeal and the Supreme Court

Broadcasting allowed in highest courts

Provisions in other statutes mean the Supreme Court and Court of Appeal can allow broadcasting of their proceedings which, being concerned with points of law, are argued from documentary evidence, are unlikely to involve witnesses in person and do not have jurors.

> See Additional Material for ch. 11 on www.mcnaes.com for law which permits broadcasting of these courts' proceedings.

▌ Ban on audio-recording in court

It is illegal to use any audio-recording device in a court, including a tape-recorder, or a mobile phone's recording facility, without the court's permission.

- One aim of this ban is to prevent witness testimony being broadcast, which for some witnesses would increase the strain of giving evidence.
- It is also to stop secret recordings being made in the public gallery by, for example, a defendant's criminal associates, who could use it to intimidate or humiliate a prosecution witness, or to help dishonest witnesses collude in false corroboration.

For example, a witness could listen to a recording of another's evidence and repeat the same information in his/her own evidence, but claim to have recalled it independently.

The ban is in section 9 of the Contempt of Court Act 1981, which makes it a contempt to:

- use a tape-recorder or any other audio-recording device in court, or take one into a court for use, unless the court gives permission;
- broadcast any audio-recording of court proceedings, or play any of it in the hearing of any section of the public;
- make any unauthorised use of a recording, if recording has been allowed.

The penalty for breaching section 9 of the 1981 Act is a jail term of up to two years and/or an unlimited fine.

Rule on permission to audio-record

A court has discretion to allow audio-recording, including by a journalist—for example, for note-taking—and to allow publication of the sound recording. Rule 6.9 of the Criminal Procedure Rules says that anyone who wants permission to record must apply to the court as soon as reasonably practicable, and notify the parties in the case and anyone else the court specifies that permission is being sought. An applicant must explain why the court should permit the use of an audio-recorder and why publication of the recording should be permitted, if this is proposed. Criminal Practice Direction 6A.2 says that a relevant factor in a criminal court's decision on whether to permit audio-recording may be 'the existence of any reasonable need' on the part of the applicant, whether a litigant or person connected with the media, for the recording to be made, and 6C.5 says this factor is likely to be relevant when a civil or family court considers such an application.

ch. 14, pp. 162–163, Procedural rules and open justice, explains what the Rules and Directions are

▌ Tweeting, emailing and texting 'live' reports from court

Reporters should not make or receive calls on mobile phones during court hearings—doing so could be punished as a contempt because it is disrespectful, and potentially disruptive and damaging to the administration of justice. A judge might fine or jail a reporter whose mobile phone ringtone interrupts a witness's testimony, particularly if the witness is already finding it difficult to testify. The normal rule is that mobile phones must be turned off in court. The rule derives from the **inherent jurisdiction** courts have to govern their own proceedings.

→ glossary

Since 2011 journalists and legal commentators who want to use 'live, text-based communications' to report court cases have not needed to ask the court's permission. This general permission, now set out in Criminal Practice Directions 6C.1–3, 6C.6, 6C.8 and 6C.11–14, means that the default position in law is that journalists can use internet-connected laptops or mobile phones in courts to email or text court reports, or to post them directly on the internet, including on Twitter. The Directions say the devices must be silent and unobstrusive. This general permission applies only for 'journalistic purposes' and does not extend to members of the public, although they can apply for permission. A court can decide 'at any time' to forbid all use of such devices—for example, if there is concern that a witness due to testify could be coached or briefed on what to say by reference to tweets of earlier evidence. The Supreme Court has a general rule allowing the use of live text-based communications, though not in some types of case.

> See Useful Websites at the end of this chapter for the Criminal Procedure Rules, the Criminal Practice Directions and the Supreme Court's rule.

▶ Confidentiality of jury deliberations

It is a contempt of court to breach the confidentiality of a jury's deliberations, whether the jury is in a Crown court, an inquest or a civil case. Juries arrive at their verdicts in secret discussions, in rooms guarded against intrusion. The secrecy helps jurors to be frank in discussions, without fear of a public backlash for an unpopular decision or retribution from a vengeful defendant they convict. For the role of juries in criminal trials, civil cases and inquests, see chs. 8, 12 and 16.

- Section 20D of the Juries Act 1974, which applies for Crown courts, the High Court and county courts, makes it contempt of court to intentionally obtain, solicit or disclose (for example, by publication) any detail of
  - statements made,
  - opinions expressed,
  - arguments advanced, or
  - votes cast

  by members of a jury during its deliberations.

for similar law for inquest juries, see ch. 16, p. 212, Reporting restrictions

This ban was, until 13 April 2015, in section 8 of the Contempt of Court Act 1981, but was then inserted by other legislation into the 1974 Act as part of changes to that statute. Jurors too breach this law if they disclose such detail.

The ban can be breached even if what is published does not identify an individual juror or even a particular trial. The penalty for a contempt by breaching section 20D is a jail term of up to two years and/or an unlimited fine.

After a trial the media is safe to publish a juror's general impressions of his/her experience of jury service, provided the individual is willing to volunteer these and is not asked about statements made, opinions expressed, arguments advanced or votes cast in the course of the deliberations, and does not refer to such issues in what is published. A juror could be interviewed, for example, on whether he/she felt that evidence was clearly presented. Journalistic investigations of alleged miscarriages of justice such as a controversial murder conviction sometimes prompt jurors from the trial to speak up months or years later. Some have contacted journalists to say that, in the light of new evidence which has emerged, they are no longer certain of the accused's guilt. The safest course is to seek legal advice before conducting or publishing such an interview.

👁 Case study

In 2009 the High Court fined *The Times* £15,000 and ordered it to pay £27,426 costs for breaching the law protecting the confidentiality of jury deliberations. The newspaper had published an article about the 10–2 majority verdict with which a Crown court jury convicted a childminder of a child's manslaughter. It did not name the jury foreman, who had approached the newspaper, but quoted him expressing doubt about the medical evidence, and as saying that, early in its deliberations, the jury voted 10–2 in an initial indication of its consensus and that the majority of jurors—because of what he called 'common sense' rather than 'logical thinking'—held to their initial view that the defendant was guilty. *The Times* denied contempt. But the High Court ruled that *The Times* had, by using these quotes, breached the law against disclosure of 'votes cast', 'opinions expressed' and 'statements made' during the jury's deliberations, even though jurors' identities were not disclosed, and the foreman's descriptions of the jury's deliberations were brief and possibly inaccurate (*Attorney General v Michael Alexander Seckerson and Times Newspapers Ltd* [2009] EWHC 1023 (Admin)). The jury foreman was fined £5,000 for his part in the breach (*Media Lawyer*, 20 December 2009).

▮ Contempt risk in identifying or approaching jurors

There is a risk of a media organisation being accused of common law contempt if it identifies a juror against his/her wishes, even after a trial. The disclosure could be held to interfere with the judicial process by putting the juror at risk of harm from anyone unhappy with a verdict. A reporter deemed to have harassed a juror for an interview might be held to be in contempt, because harassment could discourage people from serving as jurors.

👁 Case study

In 2013 a judge at Oxford Crown court held a hearing to consider an explanation for why Lucy Ford, of the *Banbury Guardian*, photographed two jurors outside the courthouse and asked them to help her identify a defendant. The judge accepted that their being photographed was an accident because they had walked into her picture and that there was no attempt to intimidate them (*Holdthefrontpage*, 12 February 2013).

See ch. 18 about common law contempt. See also ch. 37, p. 453, Identifying jurors, on the statutory ban on identifying jurors who have served in trials in Northern Ireland.

A juror discharged during a case for late attendance or being drunk may well be named in court and could be punished by the judge. In the absence of any court order to the contrary, the media can safely identify him/her, if named, and say how he/she was dealt with.

▌ Section 11 orders—blackmail, secrets, personal safety

A court can ban the media from reporting a person's name, or other information, in coverage of a case.

Section 11 of the Contempt of Court Act 1981 says:

- A court can ban the publication of a name or other information in connection with the proceedings as long as it has first allowed that information to be withheld from the public.

ch. 5, p. 53, Crimes against property or involving gain, gives the definition of blackmail

Section 11 orders are not used routinely, but typical uses are as follows.

To protect the identity of victims/alleged victims of blackmail The target of blackmail involving a threat to reveal an embarrassing secret will be less likely to report the threat to police, or be a witness, if it is likely that his/her identity will be given in open court and be reported by the media when the secret emerges in evidence. In blackmail trials, the alleged victim is usually referred to in open court simply by a letter of the alphabet, for example, 'Ms X'. This protects the administration of justice as a continuing process, as identifying any alleged victim of blackmail publicly in court reports makes it less likely that other blackmail victims will contact police.

→ glossary

To protect commercially sensitive information, secret processes For example, a company may sue another for damages over breach of confidence about valuable research data. The court may hear evidence about the data **in private** to preserve its confidentiality—if it does not stay confidential, the case would be pointless. A section 11 order could ban reports of the case publishing leaks of the data.

ch. 33 explains official secrets law

To protect national security, state secrets For example, a defendant prosecuted under the Official Secrets Act 1911 may be accused of betraying UK military secrets to a foreign power. The court may well go into private session to hear evidence about those secrets. A section 11 order could be used to ban publication of such material, should it leak out. It could also ban the media from identifying intelligence officers who are witnesses, as identification would end their usefulness as undercover agents and put them at risk.

To protect a person from the risk of harm A court might be persuaded that the name and address of a witness, or the address of a defendant—for example, a sexual offender—should not be published, to prevent an attack on that person by criminals or vigilantes. But the media can oppose such orders on the grounds that they are unnecessary—see ch. 15, pp. 187–188, Anonymity and risk of attack?

Two-stage process

A section 11 order is the second step in a two-stage process. The court first has to rule that a name or other information should not be given in proceedings held in public. Only then it can impose a section 11 order. If the name or information then slips out by mistake in a public session—for example, in what a witness or lawyer says—or if the media have discovered it by other means, the order makes it illegal to publish it in any context which connects it to the case. A section 11 order remains in force indefinitely, unless a court revokes it.

When a section 11 order is in force to ban publication of a person's identity, journalists need to guard against 'jigsaw identification'.

ch. 9, pp. 102–103, Jigsaw identification, explains this term

Breaching a section 11 order is an offence of contempt of court punishable by a jail term of up to two years and/or an unlimited fine.

But section 11 only bans the reporting of the name or matter 'in connection with the proceedings'.

▌ Ban on reporting a court's private hearing

Courts sit in private, with the public and media excluded, for some cases, including when considering whether mentally ill people should be confined in hospitals and hearings involving state secrets. The media is automatically banned from publishing what is said in some categories of cases heard by a court in private—that is, **in chambers** or **in camera**.

→ glossary

Section 12 of the Administration of Justice Act 1960 makes it a contempt of court to publish, without the court's permission, a report of proceedings it has heard in private and which:

ch. 13 explains children cases in family courts, and ch. 17 explains tribunals

- relate to the exercise of the inherent jurisdiction of the High Court with respect to children;
- fall under the Children Act 1989 or the Adoption and Children Act 2002, or otherwise relate wholly or mainly to the maintenance or upbringing of a child;
- fall under the Mental Capacity Act 2005, or under any provision of the Mental Health Act 1983 authorising an application or reference to be made to the First-tier Tribunal, to the Mental Health Review Tribunal for Wales or to a county court;

- involve national security;
- involve a secret process, discovery or invention;
- are those, of any kind, where the court expressly bans publication of all or specified information relating to the private hearing.

A reporter may be told what has happened in a private hearing by one of the parties. But in these particular types of case, section 12 automatically prohibits the publication of anything heard by a court in private, to protect the welfare, including the privacy, of children and the mentally ill or incapacitated, and state or commercial secrets.

A breach of section 12, if proved as contempt, is punishable by a jail term of up to two years and/or an unlimited fine.

- Any document 'prepared for use' in a court's private hearing is deemed to be part of those proceedings. If a case falls into the section 12 categories, the court will regard publication by the media of information or quotations from such a document, such as a psychiatric report or a report on a couple's fitness as parents, as a contempt.

Some detail can be published about a private hearing

Some material about a private hearing in these types of case can be published. Section 12 makes clear that publishing the text, or a summary, of any order made in such a hearing is not contempt unless the court has specifically prohibited its publication.

In *Re B (A Child)* [2004] EWHC 411 (Fam), Mr Justice Munby stated that section 12 did not itself ban publishing a reference to 'the nature of the dispute' being heard in the private hearing. He added that what could be published without breaching section 12 included:

- the names, addresses or photographs of parties and witnesses involved in the private proceedings;
- the date, time or place of hearings in the case; and
- 'anything which has been seen or heard by a person conducting himself lawfully in the public corridor or other public precincts outside the court'.

But he added that a court could ban publication of even these details, or that automatic restrictions under other law could apply.

ch. 18 explains contempt law and ch. 21 explains privilege

If the court hearing in private does not fall into the section 12 categories, a media organisation may safely be able to publish an account of it, for example, if guided by a person who was in it. But a media report of a case heard in private is not protected by any statutory privilege in relation to defamation law and will not be protected by section 4 of the Contempt of Court Act 1981 if it creates a substantial risk of serious prejudice or impediment to an 'active' case.

▎ Ban on publishing material from court documents

Even if a case is heard in public, a journalist should exercise care before quoting from a document used in it if the material has not been read out in court.

As explained in ch. 12, civil cases are conducted mainly by reference to documents.

In a civil case, it is safe to quote from any document the journalist obtains with the court's permission or from any case document he/she is able to inspect by right. For example, if the civil case is heard in public, it will be safe to quote from any **skeleton argument** provided to a journalist by lawyers involved unless the court forbids this.

Any reporting restriction—for example, protecting the identity of a child or alleged victim of a sexual offence—must be observed when reporting from such documents.

In criminal cases, the media has a qualified right to see case material, to aid reporting—see ch. 14, pp. 169–172, Access to material in criminal cases.

Journalists should beware of the risk of contempt incurred by publishing material from a document they have obtained irregularly from one side or the other in criminal or civil proceedings, which one party was compelled or had a duty to produce as part of the **disclosure** process and which has not been read out in open court. 'Disclosure' is the pre-trial exchange of evidence and information. Contempt law applies because of the danger that parties who fear that material they provide to the other side might be published, even though it was not used in court, may refuse to cooperate fully with the disclosure process. Also, unauthorised use of material disclosed by the prosecution to the defendant in a criminal case is a specific offence under the Criminal Procedure and Investigations Act 1996. Again, publishing material not aired in open court is not protected by statutory privilege in defamation law or by section 4 of the Contempt of Court Act 1981, unless sanctioned by a court or its rules.

ch. 14, pp. 172–175, Access to documents in civil cases, explains inspection rights

→ glossary

→ glossary

▎ Lifetime anonymity for adult witnesses

A criminal court can ban the media from disclosing an adult witness's identity if there is concern that he/she is scared or distressed about testifying. This discretionary power to ban is in section 46 of the Youth Justice and Criminal Evidence Act 1999 (the 1999 Act).

- Section 46 empowers a court to give an adult witness lifetime anonymity in any published reference to or report of the case if it is satisfied that:
  - the quality of his/her evidence, or of his/her level of cooperation in preparations for the case, is likely to be diminished by fear or distress in

connection with being identified by members of the public as a witness in that case; and

- granting anonymity is likely to improve the quality of the witness's evidence or the level of his/her cooperation.

A main purpose of this law is to provide better protection for witnesses who fear that the fact that they have given evidence, or are due to testify, will provoke hostility from criminal elements in their communities.

Section 46 says a party in the proceedings in a criminal court—including the defence, though it is usually the prosecution—can ask the court to make the anonymity order, called a 'reporting direction', to cover a witness aged 18 or over. The court may hear this request in camera.

The scope of a section 46 order

If a section 46 order is made:

- no matter relating to the witness should, during his/her lifetime, be included in any publication if it is likely to lead members of the public to identify him/her as being a witness in the proceedings.

Section 46 says that the following matters in particular should not be included if likely to identity the person as being a witness;

- the witness's name
- his/her address;
- the identity of any educational establishment he/she attends;
- the identity of any place of work; and
- any still or moving picture of him/her.

Any detail which risks revealing the witness's identity should be left out. The witness may be the alleged victim of the offence(s) being tried. If so, the effect on reports will be major and similar to that of the lifetime anonymity automatically given by other law to victims/alleged victims of sexual or trafficking offences, who therefore do not need section 46 anonymity as witnesses. When a section 46 order is made, journalists should ensure they avoid jigsaw identification.

A section 46 order *cannot* be used to give a defendant anonymity.

 See ch. 9, pp. 102–103, Jigsaw identification, for an explanation of this term. Ch. 10 explains anonymity for victims/alleged victims of sexual or trafficking offences.

Factors a court must consider

When deciding whether to grant section 46 anonymity, the court must take into account: the witness's view about anonymity; the nature and circumstances of the alleged offence(s) being tried; the witness's age, social and cultural background, and ethnic origins; his/her domestic and employment circumstances, religious beliefs, or political opinions; and any behaviour towards the witness on the part of the defendant, or the defendant's family or associates, or anyone else likely to be a defendant or witness in the proceedings.

The court must also consider:

- whether it would be in the interests of justice to make the anonymity order; and
- the public interest in avoiding imposing a substantial and unreasonable restriction on reporting the proceedings.

Breaches of section 46 orders

Publishing material which breaches the section 46 anonymity incurs the same liability as breaching a sexual or trafficking offence victim's anonymity.

 See ch. 10, pp. 115–116, Liability for breach of the anonymity provision.

Anyone prosecuted for breach of section 46 has a defence if he/she can prove that:

- he/she was not aware, and neither suspected nor had reason to suspect, that the publication included the matter or report in question; or
- the witness concerned gave written consent for the matter to be published.

This 'written consent' defence will fail if it is proved that the consent was obtained by interfering with the witness's 'peace or comfort'.

The court which bestowed the section 46 anonymity, or a higher court, can make 'an excepting direction' to remove the anonymity entirely or relax it to some extent, if satisfied that doing so is necessary in the interests of justice, or that the restriction imposes a substantial and unreasonable restriction on reporting the proceedings, and that it is in the public interest to remove or relax the restriction.

 See ch. 15, pp. 199–201, Lifetime anonymity for witnesses, on challenging section 46 orders.

▌ Other anonymity orders

The High Court has power to ban publication of the identities of people concerned in its proceedings and uses it to give anonymity to children involved in high-profile cases or news stories. The court also usually gives anonymity to mentally incapacitated adults when protecting their interests in civil cases. A media organisation which publishes information identifying such people in breach of such an order could be punished for contempt of court. The High Court's powers derive from its inherent jurisdiction and from Article 8 of the European Convention on Human Rights, concerning privacy.

 For further detail of use of such orders in family law, see ch. 13, p. 153, Anti-publicity injunctions in family cases. For their use in privacy cases, see ch. 26.

see Useful
Websites at
the end of
this chapter
for these
Rules

The Civil Procedure Rules apply in civil cases in county courts and the High Court. Rule 39.2(4) states: 'The court may order that the identity of any party or witness must not be disclosed if it considers non-disclosure necessary in order to protect the interests of that party or witness.' The Court of Appeal has ruled that courts dealing with applications to approve settlements in personal injury claims brought by children should normally make anonymity orders, though they should hear representations from a media organisation wishing to argue against such an order being made (*JXMX (by her mother and litigation friend, AXMX) v Dartford and Gravesham NHS Trust, with the Personal Injury Bar Association and the Press Association as interveners* [2015] EWCA Civ 96). But mere embarrassment does not justify anonymity for adults—see ch. 15, p. 187.

See Additional Material for ch. 4 on www.mcnaes.com about anonymity for police informants. For information on anonymity for persons subject, as suspected terrorists, to a 'terrorism prevention and investigation measure', see the chapter on www.mcnaes.com, 'Terrorism and the effect of counter-terrorism law'.

▌ Indefinite anonymity for convicted defendants

In exceptional instances, the High Court has banned the media from publishing the new identities and whereabouts of people who became notorious after committing, or being associated with, horrific crimes. The aim was to help rehabilitate them after their release from prison, and to protect them from public hostility and possible vengeance attacks.

Mary Bell The first such case concerned Mary Bell. In 1968, when she was 11, she was convicted of the manslaughter of two young boys and sentenced to detention for life. When released on licence in 1980, the Home Office gave her a new identity to help her rehabilitation.

Venables and Thompson In 2001 Dame Elizabeth Butler-Sloss granted indefinite anonymity to Jon Venables and Robert Thompson. In 1993 when they were 11, they were convicted of the murder of 2-year-old James Bulger in Merseyside.

Maxine Carr Similar anonymity was given to Maxine Carr, former girlfriend of school caretaker Ian Huntley. In 2003 Huntley was convicted of murdering two schoolgirls in Soham. Carr was convicted of conspiring to pervert the course of justice by giving him a false **alibi**. She was acquitted of knowing, when she gave it, that he had murdered the girls.

→ glossary

Kenneth Callaghan In 2009 Mr Justice Stephen in the High Court in Belfast banned the media from publishing any photograph which would identify Kenneth Henry Callaghan, then aged 39, and any information identifying his address, place of work or anywhere he stayed or frequented. He had become eligible for parole after serving 21 years for raping and murdering a woman. The judge also banned publication of any photo which identified any serving prisoner being assessed for release at a unit run by the Northern Ireland Office unless the Office was first given 48 hours' notice of the intention to publish.

 See Additional Material for ch. 11 on www.mcnaes.com for more detail of these cases, and see there too Additional Material for ch. 37, 'Bans on identifying defendants'.

 See ch. 21, p. 297, General Protection in regulation 19, for law which may protect website operators if a reader posts a comment breaching anonymity law.

▌ Ban on publishing 'indecent' matter

Section 1 of the Judicial Proceedings (Regulation of Reports) Act 1926 prohibits publication in any court report of any 'indecent matter or indecent medical, surgical or physiological details ... the publication of which is calculated to injure public morals'. It is unlikely that mainstream media organisations would be prosecuted today under this legislation.

▌ Section 4(2) of the Contempt of Court Act 1981

Section 4(2) of the Contempt of Court Act 1981 gives courts the power to order the postponement of publication of reports of a court case, or any part of a case, where doing so appears necessary to avoid a substantial risk of prejudice to the administration of justice in that case or any other case which is pending or imminent.

This restriction is best understood in the context of contempt law, so is explained in ch. 18—see pp. 246–249, Section 4(2) orders. See also ch. 15, pp. 188–190, Section 4(2) orders, for grounds on which a section 4(2) order may be challenged.

▌ Postponed reporting of 'special measures' and section 36 orders

Courts can make a 'special measure' direction (order) under the Youth Justice and Criminal Evidence Act 1999 to help a 'vulnerable' or 'intimidated' witness give evidence. For example, the witness may be allowed to give evidence from behind a screen or by live video link, or most reporters present may be asked to leave the court during his/her testimony. Also, section 36 of the same Act allows a court to bar a defendant representing himself/herself from cross-examining a witness.

The Act automatically bans the media from reporting during the trial that a 'special measure' direction or a section 36 order has been proposed or made, and why, because in some cases a jury might be influenced in its verdict if it were to know why such a direction or order was made, or that one was proposed. But what the jury can see—for example, that the witness is giving evidence from behind a screen—or is told by the judge may be reported.

> For more details about these reporting restrictions, see Additional Material for ch. 11 on www.mcnaes.com.

✳ Remember

Decisions on 'special measures' and cross-examination issues are likely to be taken at pre-trial hearings, or when a jury is out of the court, so other statute, or contempt law, will probably also be in effect to restrict contemporaneous reporting of what is decided about such measures and issues—see chs. 6–8 and 18.

▌ Postponing reports of 'derogatory' mitigation

Section 58 of the Criminal Procedure and Investigations Act 1996 allows a court to postpone a media report of a derogatory allegation which is made in a 'speech in mitigation', but has not been given in evidence, if it feels that someone's reputation may have been unfairly besmirched. This restriction is rarely used.

> Chs. 6 and 8 explain when mitigation is heard in magistrates' and Crown courts. More detail on section 58 is in the Additional Material for ch. 11 on www.mcnaes.com.

▌ Extradition hearings

Media coverage of hearings in the UK on whether a person should be extradited to another country are not affected by any automatic reporting restriction. These hearings usually take place in Westminster Magistrates' Court.

➡ Recap of major points

- It is illegal to take photographs of, film or sketch people in a court or its precincts.
- It is also illegal to make an audio-recording of a court hearing without permission.

- Journalists have a general permission to tweet, email or text from the courtroom when reporting, but other use of mobile phones there is punishable as a contempt of court.

- It is illegal to seek to discover, or to publish, what a jury discussed in deliberating on a verdict or how an individual juror voted in the verdict.

- Publication of material identifying a juror may be held to be a contempt of court.

- In certain categories of case it is contempt of court to publish material heard by a court in private.

- An order under section 11 of the Contempt of Court Act 1981 prohibits publication of a name or information which has been withheld from the public proceedings of the court—for example, the name of a blackmail victim.

- Section 46 of the Youth Justice and Criminal Evidence Act 1999 allows a court to give an adult witness in a criminal case lifelong anonymity in media reports.

- In exceptional cases, the High Court has given convicted offenders indefinite anonymity, so the media cannot reveal their whereabouts after they are released.

((•)) Useful Websites

www.judiciary.gov.uk/publications/reporting-restrictions-in-the-criminal-courts/
Guidance on reporting restrictions, published by the Judicial College, the News Media Association, the Media Lawyers Association, the Society of Editors and Times Newspapers Ltd

www.justice.gov.uk/courts/procedure-rules/criminal/rulesmenu-2015
Criminal Procedure Rules and Criminal Practice Directions

www.justice.gov.uk/courts/procedure-rules/civil
Civil Procedure Rules and Practice Directions

12

Civil courts

Chapter summary

Civil law cases are a rich source of news. Civil courts deal with private disputes and wrongs. Some cases involve companies or individuals suing for damages. Some are brought against the state and public bodies—for example, when a patient sues a hospital trust for medical negligence. County courts deal with most civil litigation. The High Court deals with complex or high-value claims. Few civil cases involve juries. Bankruptcies and company liquidations are civil law matters. Magistrates have some civil law functions.

▌ Types of civil litigation

Most civil litigation is concerned with:

- breaches of contract, including recovery of debt;
- torts—civil wrongs for which monetary damages can be awarded (torts include negligence, trespass and defamation);
- breach of statutory duty;
- proceedings by financial institutions against mortgagors;
- possession proceedings by landlords against tenants, usually for failure to pay rent;
- 'Chancery' matters, discussed later;
- insolvency, including bankruptcy and the winding up of companies;
- family law cases, including divorce and disputes between estranged parents over residence arrangements for and contact with their children;
- applications by local authorities to take into care children considered at significant risk of violence or neglect, which are also family law cases.

family law is explained in ch. 13

County courts

County courts deal with most civil cases. In 2015 they were based in about 170 courthouses in England and Wales, but that year the government began consultations about the possible closure of 19 to save costs.

The High Court

The High Court deals with the most complex or serious civil cases and those of highest value. The administrative centre of the High Court is at the Royal Courts of Justice in London. Outside London it is divided administratively into 'district registries', which have offices and courtrooms, mostly in cities, and share buildings with the larger county court centres.

The High Court comprises three divisions:

- the *Queen's Bench Division* (QBD), within which there are also specialist courts, including the Admiralty Court, the Commercial Court, and the Technology and Construction Court;
- the *Chancery Division*, which deals primarily with company work, trusts, estates, insolvency, and intellectual property (county courts also have limited jurisdiction in this area);
- the *Family Division*—see ch. 13.

High Court judges normally sit singly to try cases. The High Court is also an appeal court in civil law. In appeals and for some other functions, two or three judges hear the case, and it is then known as the 'Divisional Court'. A QBD court carrying out certain functions is referred to as the 'Administrative Court'. It handles judicial review of the administrative actions of government departments and other public authorities, and of the decisions of some tribunals.

 Ch. 8, p. 88, The High Court, explains its role as a criminal court. Ch. 17 explains tribunals.

The Court of Appeal

The Court of Appeal, Civil Division, is for most cases the court of final appeal in civil law. It hears appeals from the county courts and the High Court. Some are heard by three judges, but usually by two. When there are three, each may give a judgment but the decision is that of the majority. In a limited number of cases, appeals can be made to the Supreme Court. The Court of Appeal's procedures in civil cases are similar to those in its criminal cases—see ch. 8, p. 86, The Court of Appeal.

the hierarchy of the civil and criminal courts is shown in Figure 1 on p. 5

▌ Types of judge in civil courts

Three types of judge preside in the county courts and High Court.

- *District judges*—These are appointed from among practising solicitors and barristers. Their casework includes many of the fast-track and small claims cases, discussed later, family disputes and insolvency. They may be referred to in media reports as, for example, 'District Judge John Smith', but are increasingly being referred to as, in this instance, 'Judge John Smith'. Deputy district judges are part-time appointments.
- *Circuit judges*—In the busier county courts there may be two or more senior judges known as 'circuit judges'; in some regions they travel round a circuit of several towns or cities to hear cases, hence the origin of the title. Circuit judges may also sit in Crown courts in criminal cases. Recorders are barristers and solicitors who sit part-time with the jurisdiction of a circuit judge. Retired circuit judges who sit part-time are known as 'deputies'. Circuit judges hear some fast-track and most multi-track trials, discussed later, and may also hear appeals against the decisions of district judges. Appeals from a circuit judge lie direct to the Court of Appeal.
- *High Court judges*—These are more experienced, and so more senior, than circuit judges.

▌ Legal terms for parties in civil cases

ch. 13
explains
divorce law

In most civil actions, the party, whether a person or organisation, who initiates the action—for example, claims damages for a tort—is called the 'claimant'. The party against whom the action is taken is the 'defendant'. In some actions—for example, bankruptcy and divorce cases—the person making the claim is the petitioner and the other party is the respondent.

▌ Media coverage of civil cases

ch. 21
explains
privilege

The media have privilege against defamation actions for reports of what is said in open court. In civil cases, there is also privilege for media reports based on case documents made available by the court.

Open justice and case documents

p. 143, Small
claims
hearings,
explains
that track

The general rule is that hearings in civil cases should be heard in public—see ch. 14 for details of Part 39(2) of the Civil Procedure Rules and case law.

Practice Direction 27, supplementing the rule, says a judge may decide to hold a small claims hearing in private if the parties agree. But a journalist could argue against this, citing the general rule and—from case law—the benefits of open justice.

! Remember your rights

Journalists have rights to see case documents in civil proceedings as it might otherwise be impossible to report cases, particularly trials, meaningfully, because evidence is presented in documents and may not be aired orally in court. These rights are explained in ch. 14. pp. 172–175, Access to documents in civil cases.

Settlements

A case in which one party sues another may well be settled before trial, usually by one side paying the other a sum of money. The settlement means there will be no court judgment on the facts.

- A media report of a settlement should not suggest that the side paying the money has admitted liability—that is, blame—for the wrong allegedly suffered by the other unless liability *is* admitted. Wrongly suggesting that a settlement indicates an admission of liability could be defamatory.

For example, a private health clinic might sue for libel if a report wrongly suggests it has admitted liability for medical complications after cosmetic surgery even though it *has* paid out to settle the case.

Reporting restrictions and contempt law

Judges in civil cases have some of the same powers to impose reporting restrictions as those in criminal courts, outlined in earlier chapters. A judge in a civil court can, under section 39 of the Children and Young Persons Act 1933, ban the media from identifying a juvenile concerned in the case as a claimant, defendant or victim. Judges in civil cases can also use their inherent **jurisdiction** to order that certain people, especially children, are given anonymity in reports.

→ glossary

The bans on taking photographs, sketching, filming or audio-recording in court apply to civil courts, as do other statutory and common law protections of the confidentiality of jury deliberations, and of jurors and witnesses generally.

chs. 9–11 explain reporting restrictions

The Contempt of Court Act 1981 applies to media reports of civil cases—once a case is active nothing must be published which creates a substantial risk of serious prejudice or impediment to the course of justice in it. But as juries are rarely used in civil cases, the Act is generally much less restrictive of pre-trial coverage than it is for criminal cases.

ch. 18 explains contempt law, and see in particular pp. 250–251, Contempt of civil proceedings under the 1981 Act

'Payments into court'

The defendant in certain types of civil action—for example, a contract dispute or a defamation case—may make a 'payment into court' before or during the trial. This can be a formal offer of payment to the claimant to settle the case. Journalists who discover such an offer has been made should not report it unless and until it is referred to in open court at the end of the trial, if there is one. Disclosing at any earlier stage that an offer has been made will probably be regarded as contempt of court as it could prejudice the court's decision. The judge in the case (or jury, if there is one) is not told of the offer before reaching a judgment or verdict. If at the end of the trial the court finds for the claimant, but awards less than the defendant has offered, the claimant will have to pay all of the costs he/she incurred after the first date on which the offer could have been accepted.

▌ Starting civil proceedings

→ glossary

Most civil actions in the High Court and county courts are begun by the court issuing a claim form, which is prepared by the claimant. It details the claim against the defendant and the remedy or remedies sought. The remedy sought might be an **injunction**—an order compelling the other party to do something or stop doing something—or an order for the defendant to pay a debt or to pay damages. The claim form is served on the defendant.

The vast majority of money claims—for example, for debts—do not proceed to trial as the defendant usually does not file any defence. The claimant simply writes to the court asking for judgment to be entered 'in default'. If damages are claimed, there might be a hearing to decide the sum. Once a judgment is entered in the court's records the claimant can enforce it, seeking the money from the defendant. The court's enforcement procedures could include bailiffs taking the defendant's goods to sell to pay the money owed.

▌ Trials in civil cases

The general rule is that a defendant who wants to dispute a civil claim must file a defence within 14 days of service of the particulars of the claim (which can be served with the claim form) or, if the defendant files 'an acknowledgment of service', 28 days after service of the particulars of claim.

→ glossary

see ch. 14, pp. 172–175, Access to documents in civil cases

A civil trial is confined to issues which the parties set out in their **statements of case** which include the claim form, the 'particulars of claim', the defence to the claim, any counter-claims or reply to the defence and 'further information documents'. As a general rule, the public, including journalists, have the right to see these documents.

Each case is allocated to an appropriate 'track' based upon various factors including the value of the claim and its complexity.

The three tracks are the:

- small claims track;
- fast track;
- multi-track.

While the money value of the claim is not necessarily the most important factor, the general approach is that claims for more than £10,000 (£1,000 for personal injury) but less than £25,000 are allocated to the fast track. Claims below these levels—but not possession claims—are allocated to the small claims track.

Cases allocated to the fast track are intended to be heard within 30 weeks and to be concluded in a hearing lasting no more than one day.

Many multi-track claims are only a little more complicated than those on the fast track. Courts encourage negotiated (or mediated) settlements.

Most civil cases are resolved without reaching trial.

Small claims hearings

Cases on the small claims track are decided at a county court by a district judge and are intended to be heard within a few months. The procedure is designed to allow litigants to present their own case, without the need for a lawyer. Proceedings are informal. The judge must give reasons for the final decision. A public hearing may be in a courtroom but will usually be in the district judge's 'chambers' (that is, a private room) with access allowed. If all parties agree, the judge can deal with the case without a hearing.

Full trials

In fast-track and multi-track claims there is, if necessary, a formal trial. This is by a judge sitting alone, unless the case is in the few categories in which there may be a jury—see later in the chapter.

see ch. 1, pp. 8–9, The legal profession

Most parties involved in trials at county courts and the High Court instruct solicitors to prepare their cases. Solicitors either brief counsel (that is, instruct a barrister to advise and to argue the case in court) or represent the client themselves in a county court trial. Solicitor-advocates can appear for their clients in the higher courts without needing to brief a barrister.

Claimants and defendants may represent themselves in court and can be assisted by some other layperson (often called a 'McKenzie friend').

Full trial procedure

Unless there is a jury, civil trials are now largely based on documents, read beforehand by the judge, with each party disclosing its documents to the other side before trial. The documents are those listed earlier, plus witness statements. Each party may also supply a 'skeleton argument' setting out its case. In the trial, witnesses may do no more than confirm that their written statement is true, although usually the judge allows some supplementary questions.

ch. 14. pp. 172–175, explains journalists' rights to see case documents

The claimant and his/her witnesses testify first, and are cross-examined by the defendant or his/her advocate, then his/her witnesses face the same process.

Expert evidence may be admitted only with the court's permission. Often the court appoints a single expert, who is jointly instructed by the parties.

After all the evidence, the parties or their advocates make their submissions on the evidence and law. Finally, the judge gives his/her judgment and the reasons for it.

see ch. 4, p. 41, Standard of proof in criminal law

- In civil law, the standard of proof—the test used by a judge (or jury—see later) to decide which of any competing pieces of evidence will be accepted as the truth—is 'the balance of probabilities'. This is a lower standard of proof than that needed for criminal convictions.

A judge may 'reserve'—delay—giving judgment, to have more time to weigh evidence and check the law. The judge may read the judgment out in court at a later date or have it printed and 'hand it down' at a subsequent hearing. Court reporters are usually provided with copies of printed judgments. After the judgment (or, in jury trials, the verdict, discussed later) there is usually argument about costs, an issue on which the judge must make an appropriate order, as it is not simply a question of the loser paying the winner's costs, though the loser can expect to pay a major part of these.

 Ch. 14, p. 174, Judgments and orders, explains what rights journalists have to see judgments.

Trials with juries

In civil law, there is a right to apply for trial by a jury if the claim involves:

- an allegation of fraud; or
- false imprisonment; or
- malicious prosecution.

As ch. 19 explains, the Defamation Act 2013 removed the presumption of jury trial in defamation cases, but left the court the discretion to call a jury.

The reasons why juries can be used in these categories of case were described in a House of Lords judgment as 'historical rather than logical'. They include the notion that fraud claims particularly concern allegations against someone's honour and that false imprisonment or malicious prosecution cases usually involve allegations against an arm of the state such as the police, and so a jury is needed to give the public confidence that the case has been independently decided as a judge alone might be seen as another arm of the state.

A judge has discretion to allow jury trial in other types of civil case, but such instances are exceptional.

If there is a jury trial, the judge will sum up the case after each side has made final submissions. In some cases the judge may ask the jury for a general verdict, but in more complicated cases the judge will give the jury a series of questions to answer in the verdict. Juries decide the level of damages if the verdict is for the claimant. Juries in civil cases, like those in criminal trials, are selected at random from the electoral role. A county court jury consists of eight people and a High Court jury of 12.

Civil functions of magistrates

The role of magistrates' courts in family law cases—a branch of civil law—is outlined in ch. 13. Magistrates also hear appeals from decisions of local authority committees on licensing public houses, hotels, off-licences and betting shops.

Bankruptcy

The civil courts deal with bankruptcy cases. Some yield news stories of wild extravagance at the expense of creditors or HM Customs & Revenue. In law the term 'bankruptcy' only applies to people. Companies go into liquidation—see below.

Company liquidation

Care should be taken, when reporting that a limited company has gone into liquidation, to make the circumstances clear. There are different types of liquidation. Misuse of terms could create a libel problem.

 Additional Material for this chapter on www.mcnaes.com explains: bankruptcy procedures; what being bankrupt means; the defamation danger in wrongly stating someone is bankrupt; that court documents in a bankruptcy case can be inspected by a journalist; and the different types of company liquidation.

➡ Recap of major points

- County courts handle most civil litigation. The High Court deals with the more serious or high-value claims.
- Civil case hearings are mainly conducted by reference to documents. A journalist has rights to see the key documents of cases heard in public.
- Civil courts can impose reporting restrictions. Contempt law applies to media coverage reports of their cases, but is less restrictive if no jury is involved.
- Journalists need to take care before suggesting a person is bankrupt or a company is insolvent, because this could be defamatory if untrue.

((•)) Useful Websites

www.citizensadvice.org.uk/law-and-rights/legal-system/taking-legal-action/small-claims/
Citizens' Advice guide to small claims

www.judiciary.gov.uk/you-and-the-judiciary/going-to-court/county-court/
Judiciary webpage about the county courts

www.judiciary.gov.uk/you-and-the-judiciary/going-to-court/high-court/
Judiciary webpage about the High Court

13

Family courts

Chapter summary

Family law, a branch of civil law, includes cases involving disputes between estranged parents after marital breakdown—for example, about contact with a child—and those brought by local authorities seeking to protect children. A court can remove a child from his/her parents because of suspected abuse or neglect. Reporting restrictions and contempt of court law severely limit what the media can publish about most family cases, to protect those involved, particularly children, who in most instances must not be identified. This chapter examines the main restrictions. But because of the complexity of court rules and the restrictions, a fuller version of this chapter is provided on www.mcnaes.com.

▌ Introduction

The term 'family cases' covers a range of matters in civil law.

A new unified Family Court began operating in 2014, amalgamating the previously complex and piecemeal system. But the Family Court continues to operate from existing courthouses throughout England and Wales, with a role for magistrates and with judges continuing to preside in the most complex cases, including in the Family Division of the High Court.

see ch. 12 for an overview of the civil court system

▌ Types of case in family courts

Two major categories in family court proceedings are 'private' and 'public' law cases.

Private law cases include:

- matrimonial cases—proceedings for divorce, judicial separation or nullity, or to end a civil partnership;
- enforcement of financial arrangements between estranged or divorced couples;
- disputes between estranged parents about their children—for example, over which parent the children live with or the other parent's rights to contact with them, leading to the courts making 'child arrangement orders' under the Children Act 1989;
- applications for court orders—for example, to enforce the return of a child abducted by one parent in defiance of the other's rights;
- paternity disputes;
- applications in domestic violence cases for 'non-molestation' orders;
- applications to protect a person from a 'forced marriage'.

'Public law' cases include:

- applications, mainly by local authorities, for court orders allowing social workers to intervene to protect a child they suspect is being neglected or abused in his/her home, which intervention could be supervision if parental neglect makes the child behave badly—such orders are made under the Children Act 1989, and courts can also make emergency protection orders allowing police or social workers to remove children including babies if there is immediate concern for their safety;
- adoption cases—a court can sanction adoptions of children who have been removed from their birth parents by a local authority in public law cases. Other adoptions may formalise existing relationships, and therefore are private law cases.

◗ Reporting family law cases

Rules—currently the Family Procedure Rules 2010—bar the public from family cases involving children but allow journalists to attend these and most types of family case. But reporting family law cases is fraught with difficulties because of anonymity provisions under the Children Act 1989, contempt of court provisions in section 12 of the Administration of Justice Act 1960 and other extremely tight restrictions. The result is that much of what reporting there is consists of anonymised articles involving, for example, parents' claims that they have suffered a miscarriage of justice at the hands of social workers, medical experts or the courts.

 See the longer version of this chapter on www.mcnaes.com for more about the Rules.

Disputes between parents over where a child lives are almost invariably shrouded in anonymity almost as soon as they arise, because of the 1989 Act's restrictions.

This complex net of restrictions has led to criticism that family courts operate in 'secret'.

Reforms

In 2013 Sir James Munby became President of the Family Division. He pledged to 'improve access to and reporting of' cases in the family court while preserving the privacy of families involved. He said that court rules would change. In January 2014 he issued guidance to judges to increase the number of judgments published by family courts.

see Useful Websites at the end of this chapter for this guidance

✳ Remember

Ethically journalists should not normally interview children aged under 16 on matters concerning their welfare without the consent of a parent or responsible adult—see ch. 27, pp. 350–352, Protecting children's privacy and welfare.

▷ Anonymity under the Children Act 1989

Section 97 of the Children Act 1989 restricts media coverage of family law cases by making it an offence to publish:

- a name or other material intended or likely to identify a child—anyone under the age of 18—involved in any current case in a court in which any power under the Act has or may be exercised with respect to that or any other child;
- an address, as being that of a child involved in such an ongoing case;
- detail identifying the child's school.

Section 97 anonymity automatically applies to children in unresolved disputes between parents and those who are the subject of intervention by social workers. It applies to any report of what is said in court or a written judgment, as well as to any wider feature about a child who is involved in an ongoing case. Clearly, it also means the child's family cannot be identified. Avoid jigsaw identification.

ch. 9, pp. 102–104, Jigsaw identification, explains this term

- Breaching section 97 by publishing material identifying a child covered is punishable by a fine of up to £2,500. It is a defence for an accused person to prove that he/she did not know, and had no reason to suspect, that the published material was intended or likely to identify the child.

Adoptions

Section 97 also bans reports of adoption proceedings—journalists cannot attend them—from identifying the child concerned while he/she is under the age of 18.

When does anonymity under the Children Act 1989 cease?

- Section 97 (4) of the Children Act 1989 says that, if a child's welfare requires it, a court may waive to any specified extent the anonymity otherwise automatically bestowed on a child. The Lord Chancellor may also do so, with the Lord Chief Justice's agreement.

Judges have waived the anonymity to allow the media to identify and show pictures of children abducted by a parent or hidden from social workers, in the hope—usually borne out—that the public will help find them.

Anonymity ends when the case concludes

The Court of Appeal held that section 97 anonymity only applies while Children Act proceedings are going on and ends with the case (*Clayton v Clayton* [2006] EWCA Civ 878). The then President of the Family Division said that if a court feels that anonymity should continue beyond a case's conclusion to protect a child's welfare or privacy, it should issue an **injunction** to continue it. The High Court or a county court can order that the anonymity continue until the child is 18.

→ glossary

✳ Remember

A journalist who wants to identify a child as having been involved in a case under the 1989 Act—for example, in a story about a mother's battle with social workers or a parent's account of the break-up of a marriage—should be sure that the proceedings have ended and that no order has been made to continue a child's anonymity.

Wards of court

Children who are made wards of court by the High Court, or are the subject of proceedings to make them wards, are automatically protected by section 97 anonymity while the case is ongoing (*Kelly v British Broadcasting Corporation* [2001] Fam 59).

see Useful
Websites at
the end of
this chapter
for the
Bobby Kelly
story

👁 Case study

In 2001 Bobby Kelly, aged 16, ran away from home and joined the 'Jesus Christians' cult. His family made him a ward of court. A BBC reporter traced and interviewed him. Mr Justice Munby ruled in the High Court that the media did not require the court's permission to interview a ward of court or to publish the interview. But he warned that the media should observe reporting restrictions (*Kelly v British Broadcasting Corporation*). Anonymity might apply, and a published interview should not breach contempt law in respect of matter heard by a court in private (as this chapter explains). The BBC was allowed to identify Bobby. He was homesick but said 'you have to give everything up to work for God'.

Anonymised judgments

The texts of family case judgments, if published, are usually anonymised to prevent a child or adult being identified. It is an offence to report an anonymised judgment in a way which identifies any protected person.

Contempt danger in reporting on private hearings

Section 12 of the Administration of Justice Act 1960 makes it a contempt of court to publish, without a court's permission, a report of a private hearing if the case falls into certain categories, including those which:

- relate to the exercise of the inherent jurisdiction of the High Court with respect to children;
- are under the Children Act 1989 or the Adoption and Children Act 2002 or which otherwise relate wholly or mainly to the maintenance or upbringing of a child;
- are under the Mental Capacity Act 2005, or any provision of the Mental Health Act 1983 authorising an application or reference to be made to the First-tier Tribunal, the Mental Health Review Tribunal for Wales or to a county court;
- are of any kind where the court expressly bans publication of all or specified information relating to the private hearing.

ch. 17 explains the tribunal system

The section 12 prohibition applies broadly across family cases heard in private, including wardship cases. The definition of 'private'—see below—includes some cases which journalists may attend. It could also be a contempt to publish information from a document prepared for use in a private hearing (*Re F (A Minor) (Publication of Information)* [1977] Fam 58, [1977] 1 All ER 114). This would include a witness statement in a dispute between parents over contact arrangements regarding children, or a social worker's report for a court about a child, irrespective of whether the information published was anonymised.

It might also be a contempt to publish any of the judgment unless the judge authorises publication.

- But section 12 does allow publication of any order a court makes in private proceedings unless the court specifically bans publication of the order.

Also, section 12 does not stop the media making basic reference to a case being heard in private, although anonymity provision may be in place under the Children Act 1989 or court order, making it illegal for any report to identify the family involved.

 For more detail on section 12 of the 1960 Act, see ch. 11, pp. 129–130, Ban on reporting a court's private hearing.

for con-
text, see
President's
guidance
in Useful
Websites at
the end of
this chapter

The definition of 'private'

Section 12 reporting restrictions apply if a family case is heard in private. The position by early 2016 remained that if a Family Court or the Family Division of the High Court excluded the public from a family case, it was classed as private, even if journalists were able to attend. The section 12 restrictions apply unless the judge lifts them. If they are not lifted, a journalist can only report limited detail about the hearing.

Following the creation of the unified Family Court, the only access right for the media in any family case involving children are in the 2010 Rules. This means that the reporting restrictions in section 12 of the 1960 Act apply to cases in which magistrates preside, as the restrictions will in all tiers of the Family Court, unless the court lifts them or new rules are introduced. Check www.mcnaes.com for updates.

▌ Disclosure restrictions

Part 12.73 of the Family Procedure Rules, reflecting section 12 of the 1960 Act, says no information 'relating to' court proceedings concerning children and held in private, whether or not the information is in documents filed with the court, may be communicated to the public, or to anyone other than lawyers, officials or other specified categories of people, without the court's permission. There is a similar ban for adoption cases. These rules therefore implicitly forbid, for example, a parent of a child taken into local authority care, or a lawyer, giving a journalist information about the proceedings (other than the few details permitted by section 12 of the 1960 Act), unless the court authorises it. The ban applies whether or not journalists attend the private hearing.

 See the longer version of this chapter on www.mcnaes.com for courts' powers to authorise journalists to see case documents: 'Can journalists see documents?'

The ban does not stop a parent telling in general terms how he/she feels about the court case or of the wider experience of, for example, a child being removed from him/her—though any anonymity applying under the Children Act 1989, or through a court order, must be preserved in any report.

▌ Other reporting restrictions in family cases

The reporting restrictions of the Children Act 1989 and those in the Administration of Justice Act 1960 were referred to earlier. Other restrictions can apply in family cases, depending on the type of case.

Automatic reporting restrictions under section 2 of the Domestic and Appellate Proceedings (Restriction of Publicity) Act 1968 cover some types of family case—for example, about neglect to pay maintenance—in any court which hears such a case or an appeal.

Divorce cases, referred to later in this chapter, have their own reporting restrictions.

✳ Remember

A full explanation of reporting restrictions and journalists' rights to attend family cases is provided in the longer version of this chapter on www.mcnaes.com. Also, the High Court Family Division has published a detailed guide to reporting family proceedings—see Useful Websites at the end of this chapter.

▶ Anti-publicity injunctions in family cases

The High Court has inherent jurisdiction to order that a person must be anonymous in published reports of its proceedings and judgments. It is a contempt to breach such an injunction. Injunctions can be issued to protect children and mentally or physically incapacitated adults in family cases, and in other types of case in which the court is ruling on their medical treatment or whether they should be kept alive.

> See the longer version of this chapter on www.mcnaes.com for the procedure to alert the media to applications for family law injunctions, and for instances of injunctions restricting media coverage of a criminal trial and an inquest.

News-gathering activity can be banned

An injunction can forbid news-gathering or other activity which is deemed likely to jeopardise a person's welfare or privacy, or could lead to the subjects feeling harassed. Mr Justice McKinnon made such an order in 2008 banning the media from approaching two women whose father was jailed for life at Sheffield Crown court after repeatedly raping them, as children and adults, and fathering children by them. Nobody involved was named in reports of the father's trial, but it was feared that news-gathering activities could lead to their being identified in local communities.

ch. 10 explains anonymity for victims of sexual offences

▶ Coverage of divorce, nullity, judicial separation and civil partnership cases

Divorce, judicial separation or nullity cases, or proceedings to end a civil partnership, have usually been dealt with by Family Courts, although some are transferred to the High Court.

Most divorce proceedings are uncontested. Lists of petitioners granted a decree nisi—the first stage of a divorce—are read out in open court. The decree ends the marriage when it is made absolute, usually after six weeks after being granted. In a contested case, the husband, wife or other witnesses might give evidence in court.

Reporting restrictions, as explained in the longer version of this chapter on www.mcnaes.com, apply to divorce, judicial separation and nullity cases, and proceedings to end a civil partnership—whether the report is of a hearing in a contested case or of case documents open to inspection. Rules on when such cases can be heard in private are also explained in ch. 13 on www.mcnaes.com. In matrimonial cases there may be hearings on financial orders (previously known as 'ancillary relief')—that is, the division of property and other financial arrangements between estranged couples.

Inspection of evidence and copy of decree

Part 7.20 of the Family Procedure Rules 2010 permits anyone, within a period of 14 days after the decree nisi is made, to inspect and make copies of evidence filed with the application for the divorce if it is not contested. Part 7.36 allows anyone to obtain from the court a copy of the decree absolute. For more detail, see the longer version of this chapter on www.mcnaes.com.

▌ The Court of Protection

The Court of Protection is a specialist court established by the Mental Capacity Act 2005 to make decisions for people who lack the mental capability to decide for themselves—for example, on financial or welfare matters or medical treatment. It makes decisions for some elderly people suffering from dementia, for example. It used to sit in private, but a pilot scheme has now been launched to open its proceedings while regulating reporting by the imposition of restrictions to protect the identities of the individuals and families involved. Its judgments are usually anonymised. For more detail, see the longer version of this chapter on www.mcnaes.com.

➡ Recap of major points

- Family courts are difficult to report as reporting restrictions apply in most cases, because the hearings are classed as private.
- A child involved in ongoing proceedings under the Children Act 1989 should not be identified in media reports of such cases unless the court authorises it.

- The High Court has had for decades wide-ranging powers to protect the welfare of children and others, including anonymity orders. The new, unified Family Court—which has a High Court tier—retains these powers.

((•)) Useful Websites

www.judiciary.gov.uk/wp-content/uploads/JCO/Documents/Guidance/family-courts-media-july2011.pdf
  An official guide for journalists, judges and practitioners explaining the law on reporting family courts, endorsed by the President of the Family Division, the Society of Editors and the Judicial College

http://news.bbc.co.uk/1/hi/uk/852109.stm
http://news.bbc.co.uk/1/hi/uk/853876.stm
  BBC reports on Bobby Kelly, when he was a ward of court

www.judiciary.gov.uk/Resources/JCO/Documents/Guidance/transparency-in-the-family-courts-jan2014.pdf
  The President's 2014 guidance to family courts

14

Open justice and access to court information

Chapter summary

Open justice is vital to a democracy. If justice is done in secret, the public can have no confidence in it, because secrecy may hide injustice. Journalists are the public's eyes and ears in courtrooms, so need to know their rights of admission to courts. This chapter explains them, and refers to case law and statute which journalists can cite to oppose attempts to exclude them from courts. But the law does allow courts to sit in private on occasion. This chapter also explains journalists' rights to see court documents needed to report criminal and civil cases. Other chapters refer to admission rights for particular types of court—youth courts in ch. 9, family courts in ch. 13, coroners' courts in ch. 16 and employment tribunals in ch. 17.

▶ Open courts—a fundamental rule in common law

In 1913, the House of Lords in *Scott v Scott* [1913] AC 417 affirmed the common law rule that normally courts must administer justice in public. One law lord, Lord Atkinson, said:

❝ The hearing of a case in public may be, and often is, no doubt, painful, humiliating, or deterrent both to parties and witnesses, and in many cases, especially those of a criminal nature, the details may be so indecent as to tend to injure public morals, but all this is tolerated and endured, because it is felt that in public trial is to be found, on the whole, the best security for the pure, impartial, and efficient administration of justice, the best means for winning for it public confidence and respect. ❞

Additional Material for ch. 14 on www.mcnaes.com gives more detail of *Scott v Scott.*

A major benefit of open justice is that a witness who testifies in public is less likely to lie. A public lie is more likely to be exposed than one told behind closed doors. Other benefits of open justice were categorised by Lord Woolf in the Court of Appeal judgment in *R v Legal Aid Board ex p Kaim Todner* [1998] 3 All ER 541:

> It is necessary because the public nature of proceedings deters inappropriate behaviour on the part of the court. It also maintains the public's confidence in the administration of justice. It enables the public to know that justice is being administered impartially. It can result in evidence becoming available which would not become available if the proceedings were conducted behind closed doors or with one or more of the parties' or witnesses' identity concealed. It makes uninformed and inaccurate comment about the proceedings less likely.

As Lord Woolf noted, any reporting restriction is a departure from the open justice principle and so must have an overriding justification. Ch. 15 provides specific grounds on which journalists can challenge reporting restrictions or decisions to exclude them from hearings. The foundation of such challenges is that general benefits always flow to society from open justice.

In private, in chambers and in camera

- The term **in chambers** refers to occasions when a hearing, usually a preliminary one in a case, is held in the judge's chambers or another room rather than a formal courtroom.   →glossary
- The term **in camera** is used when the public and media are excluded from all or part of the main hearing in a case—such as a criminal trial. The hearing is effectively being held in secret.   →glossary
- The term **in private** is used to cover both the above terms. But a hearing may be held in chambers for administrative convenience, rather than because of a decision or rule that it should be private—see later in the chapter.   →glossary

The limited scope of common law exceptions to open justice

It is generally acknowledged that excluding the press and public from a court case is only justified in common law in three sets of circumstances:

- *when their presence would frustrate the process of justice*—for example, when a woman or child cannot be persuaded to give evidence of intimate sexual matters in the presence of many strangers;

- *when unchecked publicity would defeat the whole object of the proceedings*—for example,
  - when a case concerns a trade secret and publicity would reveal the secret to commercial rivals, or
  - when a case concerns a matter relating to national security which could be damaged by publicity, or
  - when the court is considering granting an order to one party that another party must produce evidence which it might destroy, before the order is served on it, if it were to be tipped off by reports of an open court hearing that such an order was being sought;

ch. 13 explains family law

- *when the court is exercising a parental role to protect the interests of vulnerable people*—mainly:
  - children, for example, in family law cases, or
  - people with mental incapacity or mental illness—
  and unchecked publicity could harm the welfare of those involved.

Statutes and procedural rules allow courts to exclude the public and, in some instances, journalists in specified circumstances, as this chapter explains. These statutory powers cover, to an extent, the same kinds of occasion for which common law justifies exclusion. Common law can be used if no statutory power covers the occasion, but does not give courts a general licence to sit in private.

Lord Diplock, emphasising that common law departs from its open justice principle only in rare circumstances, said in a 1979 House of Lords judgment that the rule should only be set aside when:

> ... the nature or circumstances of the particular proceeding are such that the application of the general rule in its entirety would frustrate or render impracticable the administration of justice or would damage some other public interest for whose protection Parliament has made some statutory derogation from the rule. (*Attorney General v Leveller Magazine Ltd* [1979] AC 440)

 Additional Material for ch. 14 on www.mcnaes.com provides more detail of this case.

▌ Contempt and libel issues in reports of private hearings

If a case being heard in private falls into certain categories—for example, it is about national security or the upbringing of children—it is a contempt for anyone, including a journalist, who discovers what has been said in its private hearing to publish such information or material from documents prepared for use in the case—see the explanation of section 12 of the Administration of Justice Act 1960 in ch. 11, pp. 129–130, Ban on reporting a court's private hearing.

Publishing information from a private hearing in any court case:

- is not protected by section 4 of the Contempt of Court Act 1981 if the publication creates a substantial risk of serious prejudice or impediment to an 'active' case—see ch. 18, p. 246, Court reporting—the section 4 defence;
- is not protected by privilege if someone defamed by it sues for libel—see ch. 21, pp. 283 and 286, Privilege.

▌ The media's role

A journalist's vital role in reporting court cases as trustee for the wider public has been recognised in many judgments. In *R v Felixstowe Justices ex p Leigh* [1987] QB 582, [1987] 1 All ER 551, Lord Justice Watkins said:

> ❝ The role of the journalist and his importance for the public interest in the administration of justice has been commented upon on many occasions. No-one nowadays surely can doubt that his presence in court for the purpose of reporting proceedings conducted therein is indispensable. Without him, how is the public to be informed of how justice is being administered in our courts? ❞

for challenge procedure, see ch. 15

Scott v Scott, Attorney General v Leveller Magazine Ltd and other cases referred to in this chapter—rulings which upheld the open justice principle and referred to its societal benefits—can also be cited by a journalist when challenging exclusion from a court hearing.

Journalists can also direct the court to guidance issued by the Judicial College, *Reporting Restrictions in the Criminal Courts*—see Useful Websites at the end of the chapter. This guidance, drawn up by media organisations and the judiciary, states: 'The test is one of necessity. The fact, for example, that hearing evidence in open court will cause embarrassment to witnesses does not meet the test for necessity.' It also reminds courts that imposing a reporting restriction to stop some detail being published might avoid the need for exclusion.

A defendant's embarrassment is insufficient reason to exclude the media

A High Court judge criticised Malvern magistrates' decision to sit in camera to hear mitigation for a woman who admitted driving with excess alcohol. Her solicitor had asked the court to sit in private because she would refer to embarrassing details of her pending divorce which—the court was told—had made her suicidal and drink to excess. He said her emotional state meant she could not speak about this in open court. The High Court agreed that magistrates did have power to sit in camera but Lord Justice Watkins said that in this case their reason for doing so was 'wholly unsustainable and out of accord with [the open justice] principle' (*R v Malvern Justices, ex p Evans* [1988] QB 540, [1988] 1 All ER 371).

Journalists can sometimes stay when the public is excluded

If the public are lawfully excluded, it does not follow that journalists must necessarily go too.

Rowdy supporters of a defendant may be banned or ejected from a court's public gallery. But journalists are not going to be rowdy, so should be let into the court. In 1989 a Court of Appeal judgment acknowledged that there might be cases during which the press should not be excluded with the other members of the public (*R v Crook (Tim)* (1989) 139 NLJ 1633).

The public and press should not be excluded for longer than necessary

If a court rules that a journalist should be excluded, he/she should point out that the Court of Appeal said in 1989 that a judge should be alive to the importance of adjourning into open court as soon as exclusion of the public was not plainly necessary (*Re Crook (Tim)* (1991) 93 Cr App R 17).

Criminal courts cannot sit in private to protect a defendant's business interests

The risk that publicity might severely damage a defendant's business does not justify a criminal court sitting in private (*R v Dover Justices, ex p Dover District Council and Wells* (1991) 156 JP 433).

▶ Articles 6 and 10

Article 6 of the European Convention on Human Rights says everyone is entitled to a fair and public hearing. The rights which Article 6 primarily protects are those of parties in civil litigation and defendants in criminal cases rather than those of the media or wider public. A journalist challenging exclusion from a court should cite Article 10 which, by protecting the right to impart information (in this context, to report the court case) and the public's right to receive it (to know what happened in the case), can safeguard the benefits of open justice.

 Ch. 1 explains the Convention's effect, and Articles 6 and 10 are set out in Appendix 1, pp. 461–462. Ch. 15 too refers to the media's and public's Article 10 rights in the context of open justice.

▌ Statute law on open and private hearings

Magistrates' cases Section 121 of the Magistrates' Courts Act 1980 says magistrates must sit in open court when trying a case or considering jailing someone, or hearing a civil law complaint, unless other enactment (statute law) permits them to sit in private. There is now such an exception in the 1980 Act itself— inserted there as sections 16A–16F by the Criminal Justice and Courts Act 2015—which is known as the 'trial by single justice on the papers' procedure. In some circumstances—if the offence is not punishable by a jail sentence—this allows a case to be tried in private, in the defendant's absence, and fines to be imposed in private if he/she is convicted. In 2015 the procedure was being trialled in parts of London.

 See also ch. 6, pp. 64–65, Trial by a single justice 'on the papers' about this controversial measure, and pp. 166–167, Getting information about 'trial by single justice on the papers' cases.

Indecent evidence Section 37 of the Children and Young Persons Act 1933 gives any court the power to exclude the public—but not journalists—when a witness aged under 18 is giving evidence in a case involving indecency.

Sexual history Section 43 of the Youth Justice and Criminal Evidence Act 1999 requires a court hearing an application to introduce evidence or questions about a complainant's sexual history—for example, in a rape case—to sit in private. This reflects the sensitivity of someone who may have suffered rape being questioned about her/his sex life. The court must give its decision on whether such evidence will be allowed, and its reasons, in open court.

One journalist can stay Section 25 of the 1999 Act allows a court to make a 'special measures direction' to exclude the public and some journalists when, for example, a witness is due to testify in a sexual offence case or one brought under the Modern Slavery Act 2015 involving alleged slavery, servitude, forced or compulsory labour, or human trafficking for exploitation, or when there are reasonable grounds for believing that someone other than the defendant wants to intimidate the witness. But one journalist must be allowed to stay in court.

 Ch. 11, pp. 135–136, Postponed reporting of 'special measures' and section 36 orders, outlines the law, with more detail in Additional Material for ch. 11 on www.mcnaes.com.

The 1999 Act says that even if, under section 25, some journalists and the public are excluded from a courtroom, the proceedings are still deemed to be held in public 'for the purposes of any privilege or exemption from liability available in respect of fair, accurate and contemporaneous reports'. This is a reference to contempt and defamation law, explained in chs. 18 and 21.

Official secrets trials If a defendant is accused of spying for a foreign power or disclosing state secrets, journalists and members of the public may be excluded on national security grounds when some evidence is given or discussed—see ch. 33, p. 417, The public and media may be excluded from secrets trials.

Sentence review for informants Section 75 of the Serious Organised Crime and Police Act 2005 says a Crown court may exclude the public and press when reviewing a sentence previously imposed on a defendant who pleaded guilty, and who has given or offered assistance—for example, information about a crime—to a prosecuting or investigating agency such as the police. But the public and press can only be excluded if the judge considers it to be in the interests of justice and necessary to protect someone's safety—for example, because the informant would be at risk of retaliation if the fact that he/she gave such assistance were to be publicised. In the review, the original sentence could be reduced as a reward for the assistance offered. If the original sentence was lenient because the defendant had already offered such assistance but knowingly failed to give it, the review can increase it. If a defendant has failed to honour a pledge of assistance, a journalist has strong grounds for arguing that a lenient sentence should be reviewed in open court as the public should be confident that the defendant received an appropriate sentence. The Act allows the court to ban publication of anything about the proceedings 'as it thinks appropriate'.

 See Additional Material for ch. 14 on www.mcnaes.com for guidance which the Crown Prosecution Service gives to prosecutors about the need for 'great caution' in use of this power in the 2005 Act to exclude the public and journalists, and see the case study there.

Closed material procedure Controversial provisions for 'closed material procedure' were enacted in Part 2 of Justice and Security Act 2013 to allow a court considering a civil claim to hear evidence in private—and without the claimant having access to it—if it accepts that disclosing the evidence would damage national security. The government said this would allow it to contest compensation claims from terror suspects without the security services having to reveal sensitive evidence in open court.

 Detail about Part 2 of the Justice and Security Act 2013, and events which led to this legislation being created, can be read in Additional Material for ch. 14 on www.mcnaes.com.

▌ Procedural rules and open justice

Courts have procedural rules which add detail to statute. The wording of some rules gives courts wide discretion to sit in private. A journalist facing exclusion because of a procedural rule should argue that the court's interpretation of it must fully recognise the common law protection of open justice and Article 10, and cite *Scott v Scott*, in which Lord Shaw stressed that judges must be vigilant to ensure that the open justice principle is not usurped.

- Lord Shaw said: 'There is no greater danger of usurpation than that which proceeds little by little, under cover of rules of procedure, and at the instance of judges themselves.'

Criminal cases—rules on open and private hearings

Procedure for criminal cases in magistrates' courts, Crown courts and the Court of Appeal (Criminal Division) is governed by the Criminal Procedure Rules and the Criminal Practice Directions, which explain and supplement the Rules. Both Rules and Directions are regularly updated and amended.

((•)) See Useful Websites at the end of this chapter for these Rules and the Directions.

Rule 6.2 says a court must have regard to the importance of dealing with criminal cases in public and allowing them to be reported. Rule 24.2 states specifically that the general rule is that a trial or sentencing in a magistrates' court must be in public.

Rule 6.6, for magistrates' and Crown courts, says that if the prosecution or defence want to argue that a trial or part of it should be heard in private (that is, in the limited circumstances when a court has power to waive the open justice rule), they must apply in writing to the court not less than five business days before the trial is due to begin—though rule 6.3 allows a court to hear an application sent later than this—and that the court officer must at once display notice of the application prominently in the courtroom's vicinity and give the media notice of it. The application itself will be heard in private, unless the court orders otherwise, and if in a Crown court will be heard after the **arraignment** but before the jury   → glossary
is sworn. The rule adds that if a court orders that a trial will be heard wholly or partly in private, it must not begin until the day after the application was granted, giving the media some time to challenge the decision.

 Ch. 15 explains how a journalist can in any court oppose or challenge an access restriction.

The Criminal Procedure Rules allow courts to conduct some procedures in private—for example, an application to a Crown court judge for bail after magistrates have refused it. But the presumption in law is that a journalist can be allowed into a bail hearing—see Additional Material for ch. 14 on www.mcnaes.com.

ch. 8 explains Crown court procedure

Civil cases—rules on open and private hearings

The Civil Procedure Rules (CPR) cover civil proceedings in the Queen's Bench and Chancery divisions of the High Court and the county courts.

Part 39(2) of the CPR says that the general rule is that a hearing is to be in public but that a hearing, or part of it, may be in private if:

- publicity would defeat the object of the hearing;
- it involves matters relating to national security;
- it involves confidential information (including information relating to personal financial matters) and publicity would damage that confidentiality;
- this is necessary to protect the interests of any child or protected party;
→ glossary
- it is an *ex parte* application (one made **without notice**)—that is, one party in the case is not yet aware of the proceedings—and it would be unjust to any respondent for there to be a public hearing;
- it involves uncontentious matters arising in the administration of trusts or of a deceased's estate;
- the court considers a private hearing necessary in the interests of justice.

The Practice Direction which supplements this rule lists types of case which shall, 'in the first instance', be listed as private. These include a claim by a mortgagee for possession of land, landlords' applications for possession of residential property because rent is owed, and proceedings under the Consumer Credit Act 1974 and the Protection from Harassment Act 1997 (the latter would include some domestic violence cases).

❗ Remember your rights

A journalist can try to persuade the judge that cases in these categories should be heard in public. The Practice Direction states that the judge should have regard to 'any representations' made. The CPR also provide that other types of hearing may be held in private. A journalist excluded from a civil court should ask which rule applies, and can remind the judge that the fact that a rule or Practice Direction indicates a hearing may be held in private does not mean that he/she should automatically exclude the public and press. The judge must consider the facts of the particular case before deciding about exclusion, and the party requesting such exclusion must have clear and cogent evidence to justify the request (*Registrar of Companies v Swarbrick and others* [2014] EWHC 1466 (Ch)).

> Additional Material for ch. 14 in www.mcnaes.com provides summaries of civil cases in which media organisations, by referring to Part 39(2) of the Civil Procedure Rules, have successfully argued for their rights to attend the hearings, even when a party asserted this would expose 'confidential' information. See Useful Websites at the end of this chapter for these Rules. For general information on civil courts, including when small claims cases can be in private, see ch. 12. Other rules apply to the family courts—see ch. 13.

▶ Hearings in chambers are not always private

A hearing may be in chambers—for example, a judge's office—rather than in public in a courtroom, because of routine administrative convenience. Lord Woolf (later Lord Chief Justice) said in the Court of Appeal in 1998 that members of the public and journalists who ask should be allowed to attend a hearing in chambers if this is practical and the case is not in a category listed in section 12 of the Administration of Justice Act 1960 (*Hodgson v Imperial Tobacco* [1998] 2 All ER 673, [1998] 1 WLR 1056).

ch. 11, pp. 129–130, Ban on reporting a court's private hearing, explains the 1960 Act

▶ What information and help must criminal courts provide?

Many court clerks are helpful in giving reporters in court basic detail about a case, such as how to spell the defendant's name. But since 2011 the Criminal Procedure Rules have set out when court officers must provide certain information on request.

Rule 5.8

Rule 5.8 gives members of the public, including reporters—whether in the courtroom or phoning—the right to obtain certain details of a case. This applies if the 'court officer' has the details, if the case is ongoing or the verdict was not more than six months ago, and if no reporting restriction prohibits supply of the details. The 'court officer' must in these circumstances supply the details verbally or by other arrangements prescribed by the Lord Chancellor

The details are: the date of any public hearing in the case, unless any party has yet to be notified of that date; each alleged offence and any plea entered; the court's decision at any public hearing, including any decision about bail or the sending of the case to another court; whether the case is under appeal; the outcome of any trial and any appeal; and the identity of the prosecutor, the defendant, the 'parties' representatives'—normally lawyers—including their addresses, and name of the judge, magistrate or magistrates, or justices' legal adviser by whom a decision at a hearing in public was made.

Rule 5.8 says a request for these details may be made orally, makes clear that no reasons for the request need to be stated and requires the court officer to supply details of any reporting or access restriction ordered by the court.

The person asking must pay 'any fee prescribed'. But as yet there has been no announcement that journalists are expected to pay for these basic details.

But rule 5.8 says that a request for such detail about any other case—which would include an older case—must be in writing, unless the court otherwise permits, must explain why the information is required, and should state if a request for the information has already been made under a protocol, and if so, the reason for refusal. It adds that if any other information about a case is requested or a request is made to see a document containing information about the case, the court may decide this at a hearing, public or private, or without a hearing.

> See also p. 171, The 'Publicity and the Criminal Justice System' protocol. Data protection law must not be used by court staff as a blanket excuse for withholding information from journalists—see ch. 28, p. 360, Getting information from courts.

Protocol on court lists and registers

see Useful Websites at the end of this chapter for the protocol

Under a protocol agreed between the News Media Association, the Society of Editors, and Her Majesty's Courts and Tribunals Service (HMCTS), the Service sends free of charge and by email to local newspapers copies of the daily lists of defendants due to appear in magistrates' courts and copies of these courts' 'registers', which briefly record each day's details of convicted defendants and punishments.

Home Office Circular no. 80/1989 said the lists should contain each defendant's name, age, address, the charge he/she faces and, where known, his/her occupation.

see ch. 21 on privilege and ch. 9 on youth courts

It is likely that qualified privilege protects a fair and accurate media report of court lists and registers should anyone sue for a defamatory error published by the media but which was in the document when supplied by HMCTS. But a journalist at a court hearing should quote the defendant's details and charge(s) as given at the hearing, and not rely on the list or register. A fair, accurate and contemporaneous report of the hearing will be protected by absolute privilege.

If the register includes details of juvenile defendants, check whether they were dealt with by the youth court, in which case usually they must not be identified.

Crown court lists can be accessed from an internet service, www.courtserve.net/homepage.htm, as well as seen at the courts, but give less information than those for magistrates' courts.

The protocol agreed between media organisations and the Courts and Tribunals Service says: 'Crown court staff are encouraged to cooperate with local newspapers when they make enquiries.'

> See Additional Material for ch. 14 on www.mcnaes.com for a case in which a reporter secured such cooperation by citing the protocol.

see also ch. 6, pp. 64–65, Trial by a single justice 'on the papers'

Getting information about 'trial by single justice on the papers' cases

As this chapter has explained, new law in 2015 created, to save costs, the 'trial by single justice on the papers' procedure in which a single magistrate can deal with some types of criminal case in private (and possibly in an office, not a court-room), which—as the Magistrates Association and others pointed out—breaches the open justice principle. Such cases could include TV licence evasion, speeding or driving without insurance.

Shailesh Vara, Under-Secretary of State for Justice, said in 2014 that a local ad-vance list of such cases would only be able to state the date by which they were due to have been heard. This is because under the procedure cases are not allocated specific hearing dates. Also, casework can be transferred from one courthouse to another if the first is too busy. But Mr Vara insisted that local registers made available to the media could include the outcome of such cases. Justice Minister Lord Faulks said that journalists and others would be able to get information about such cases under the Criminal Procedure Rules.

 See p. 65, Rule 5.8, about these information rights.

! Remember your rights

Journalists who learn of a newsworthy case dealt with in the 'trial by single justice on the papers' procedure could apply under the 2005 protocol—explained on p. 171, 'The 'Publicity and the Criminal Justice System' protocol—for material to help report the case—for example, police footage of a politician's traffic offence—as well as ask under the Rules for information about it. Check www.mcnaes.com for updates on whether the new procedure proves to be as 'transparent' as the government claims.

Magistrates' names

As well as Criminal Procedure Rule 5.8, case law says a court *must* give the press and public the names of magistrates—also known as 'justices of the peace' (JPs)—dealing with a case. The High Court made this clear in 1987 in *R v Felixstowe Justices, ex p Leigh*, cited earlier, in which Lord Justice Watkins said: 'There is, in my view, no such person known to the law as the anonymous JP.'

A defendant's details should be given in court

The Home Office said, in Circular no. 78/1967 and a similar circular in 1969, that defendants' names and addresses should be stated orally in magistrates' courts. The 1967 Circular said: 'A person's address is as much part of his description as his name. There is, therefore, a strong public interest in facilitating press reports that correctly describe persons involved.' The High Court ruled in 1988 that a defendant's address should normally be stated in court (*R v Evesham Justices, ex p McDonagh* [1988] QB 553, [1988] 1 All ER 371).

The Judicial College guidance says: 'Announcement in open court of names and addresses enables the precise identification vital to distinguish a defendant from someone in the locality who bears the same name and avoids inadvertent defamation.'

((•))
see Useful Websites at the end of this chapter for this guidance

see Useful
Websites at
the end of
this chapter
for the
Directions

Facts of an admitted case should be stated

If a defendant pleads guilty to a charge, the prosecution should state in open court the facts of the offence, before any sentence is imposed, so that the public and media know the circumstances. This requirement is imposed by Criminal Practice Direction VII Sentencing D.

Documents which must be read aloud in court

Rules 24.5 and 24.15 of Criminal Procedure Rules say that in a magistrates' court the following documents must, unless the court directs (formally decides) otherwise, be read aloud or summarised aloud if any member of the public, including any reporter, is present:

- any written statement by a witness which is admitted as evidence in a trial—including evidence from an expert witness;
- if the defendant has pleaded guilty in writing (and so is not there), the material on which the prosecutor relies to set out the facts of the offence and to provide information relevant to sentence, and any written representations by the defendant.

Rules 25.12 says that if a member of the public or reporter is at a Crown court trial, each relevant part of any written statement by a witness which is admitted as evidence must be read or summarised aloud.

Rule 50.15, which applies to extradition hearings, says that any such written statement by a witness must be read aloud or summarised aloud.

Details of witnesses in criminal cases

Ministry of Justice guidance issued in 2011 says a witness should not be asked to give his/her address aloud in court unless for a specific reason.

 A public register shows if a fine imposed by a criminal court is unpaid—see p. 175.

▌ Journalists' access to case material in court proceedings

Journalists can safely report information from documents as read out in a court's public proceedings or officially provided by the court, if any reporting restriction in place is obeyed. But there are contempt risks in publishing information gleaned from case documents in other circumstances, as explained in ch. 11.

A media organisation may face a libel action if it publishes defamatory material from a document not read out in open court, unless the document was officially made available.

ch. 21 explains defamation defences for court reporting

Access to material in criminal cases

In 2012 the Court of Appeal ruled that *The Guardian* newspaper should have been given access to documents used in an extradition hearing (*R (on the application of Guardian News and Media Ltd) v City of Westminster Magistrates' Court* [2012] EWCA Civ 420). The ruling, a landmark victory for the media, established a presumption in law that journalists covering hearings in courts should be able to see case material to aid that coverage. Provisions in Part 5B of the Criminal Practice Directions, which first came into force in October 2013, reflect this.

Practice Direction Part 5B

Part 5B says that the opening notes, written submissions and **skeleton arguments** used by counsel in criminal courts should normally be provided to journalists who want them. Skeleton arguments are documents in which each side sets out the basis of its case. Part 5B says other documents and information can also be provided to the public or journalists at the discretion of the courts.

→ glossary

A request for access to documents should first be addressed to the party who presented them to the court. If the party—for example, the prosecution—refuses, the request can be made to the court, the Direction says.

It adds that in the case of requests for information by reporters or lawyers acting for media organisations 'there is a greater presumption in favour of providing the requested material, in recognition of the press' role as "public watchdog" in a democratic society', adding: 'The general principle in those circumstances is that the court should supply documents and information unless there is a good reason not to in order to protect the rights or legitimate interests of others and the request will not place an undue burden on the court.'

It goes on:

> Opening notes and skeleton arguments or written submissions, once they have been placed before the court, should usually be provided to the media.
>
> It may be convenient for copies to be provided electronically by counsel, provided that the documents are kept suitably secure.
>
> If there is no opening note, permission for the media to obtain a transcript of the prosecution opening should usually be given—[although a transcript will have to be paid for].

see also ch. 18, pp. 248–249, Proceedings in court in the absence of the jury

The Practice Direction stresses that the media are expected to be aware of the limitations on the use to which such material can be put—for example, that legal argument in the absence of the jury should not be reported before the trial ends.

It also says some information should be given when sought by a member of the public or a journalist, who could simply ask court staff for it and need give no reason for wanting it. This class of information is detailed in rule 5.8 of the Criminal Procedure Rules, explained earlier.

Applications to the court for other information or material—which includes evidential documents, photographs, DVD recordings and closed-circuit television (CCTV) footage—must be made in writing and be notified to the other parties.

Skeleton arguments and written submissions are likely to fall into the category of documents which a court treats as having been read aloud in their entirety, even if they were neither read aloud nor summarised aloud, and 'should generally be made available on request', the Practice Direction says.

Documents which *have* been read aloud in their entirety—such as opening notes or statements, including experts' reports and admissions—should usually be provided on request unless doing so would disrupt the court proceedings or place an undue burden on the court, advocates or others, it adds.

In the case of documents which are read aloud in part, or summarised aloud, the Direction says:

> " Open justice requires only access to the part of the document that has been read aloud.
>
> If a member of the public requests a copy of such a document, the court should consider whether it is proportionate to order one of the parties to produce a suitably redacted version. If not, access to the document is unlikely to be granted; however open justice will generally have been satisfied by the document having been read out in court.
>
> If the request comes from an accredited member of the press ... there may be circumstances in which the court orders that a copy of the whole document be shown to the reporter, or provided, subject to the condition that those matters that had not been read out to the court may not be used or reported. A breach of such an order would be treated as a contempt of court. " "

✱ Remember

for the Authority, see Useful Websites at the end of this chapter

The term 'accredited' here refers to journalists able to produce a press card recognised by the UK Press Card Authority.

The Direction says courts considering applications for material will take account of factors including:

- whether a request is for the purpose of contemporaneous reporting—a request after the conclusion of the proceedings will require careful scrutiny;
- the nature of the information or documents sought and the purpose for which they are required;
- the stage of the proceedings when the application is made;

- the value of the documents in advancing the open justice principle, including enabling the media to discharge its public watchdog role by reporting the proceedings effectively;
- any risk of harm which access may cause to the legitimate interests of others;
- any reasons given by the parties for refusing to provide the material sought, as well as any other representations received from the parties.

It states: 'It is not for the judge to exercise an editorial judgment about "the adequacy of the material already available to the paper for its journalistic purpose" but the responsibility for complying with the Contempt of Court Act 1981 and any and all restrictions on the use of the material rests with the recipient.'

ch. 18 explains contempt law

The Practice Direction indicates that journalists should only apply to the court for material covered by existing protocols after first trying to obtain that information under those protocols from the relevant organisation(s), which would be from:

- HM Courts and Tribunals Service, as regards information in lists and registers from magistrates' courts—see earlier;
- the Crown Prosecution Service or police for material covered by the protocol entitled 'Publicity and the Criminal Justice System'.

The 'Publicity and the Criminal Justice System' protocol

The Crown Prosecution Service in 2005 issued a protocol on 'Publicity and the Criminal Justice System' which says that material on which the prosecution relied in a trial and which *should* normally be released to the media includes:

see Useful Websites at the end of this chapter for the protocol

- maps and photographs, including custody photos of defendants, and diagrams produced in court;
- videos showing crime scenes;
- videos of property seized—for example, weapons, drugs, stolen goods;
- sections of transcripts of interviews which were read to the court;
- videos or photographs showing reconstructions of the crime;
- CCTV footage of the defendant, subject to copyright issues.

→ glossary

The protocol also says that material which *might* be released following consideration by the CPS, in consultation with the police, victims, witnesses, and others directly affected by the case, such as family members, includes:

- CCTV footage showing the defendant and victim, or the victim alone, which the jury and public saw in court;
- video and audio tapes of police interviews with defendants, victims and witnesses;
- victim and witness statements.

The protocol also enables the media to ask the CPS head of strategic communications to become involved in the event of a dispute over disclosure.

! Remember your rights

See ch. 29, p. 372, Parliament and the courts, on why copyright is not infringed if material is used to report a court case.

Access to documents in civil cases

see Useful Websites at the end of this chapter for these Rules

The Civil Procedure Rules (CPR) cover county courts, the High Court and the Court of Appeal (Civil Division). These allow non-parties, such as journalists, access to documents filed with the court in civil claims lodged after 2 October 2006, when rule changes took effect.

This access is important, as civil cases are now largely conducted by reference to documents rather than by the systematic taking of oral evidence. A civil trial may be impossible to report meaningfully if a reporter has not read key documents.

Pending and ongoing civil trials

ch. 12 explains how civil courts operate

Rules 5.4 and 5.4C of the CPR say any person who pays the prescribed fee may see a civil court's register of claims—that is, its list of cases—and, as a general rule, can obtain a copy of any 'statement of case' and a copy of any judgment or order made or given in public:

- if the relevant claim has been listed for a hearing and if the sole defendant has, or all defendants have, filed an acknowledgement of service or a defence; or
- if there is more than one defendant, at least one defendant has filed such an acknowledgement or a defence *and* the court specifically permits provision of the copy; or
- if judgment has been entered on the claim (a judgment means the case is concluded).

'Statement of case', which is defined in rule 2.3, means the claim form, particulars of claim (if not in the claim form) and defence, and also any additional claim, counter-claim or reply to the defence. For further detail, see CPR Parts 16 and 20.

'Further information documents' supplied in response to a request under Part 18 of the Rules are also part of a statement of case.

Rule 5.4D says requests for copies of any of the documents referred to earlier must be in writing. In instances when the court's specific permission is needed to obtain them, the requester must give notice to the relevant party in the case in accordance with Part 23 of the CPR.

👁 Case study

The *Journal* newspaper was able to publish the story of a footballer's dispute with his former landlords because reporter Emma King asked Newcastle county court if she could see the claim form. Former Sunderland player

El Hadji Diouf had been taken to court by the landlords. They said he owed them £12,000. But before the case was due to start they reached a settlement with him which included a confidentiality clause. Ms King asked the court if she could see the claim form as it was a public document and argued that it was in the public interest to publish the allegations in it. Diouf's barrister initially opposed her request, citing the confidentiality agreement, but was told by Judge Christopher Walton that a report of the case would be in the public interest as the footballer was a well-known figure (*Holdthefrontpage* website, 13 May 2011).

((•)) See Useful Websites at the end of this chapter for the *Journal* report.

The Court of Appeal has ruled that if a party to a civil court case objects to a document being made available for publication, a court will require 'specific reasons' why the party will be damaged by its publication and that 'simple assertions of confidentiality', even if supported by both parties in the case, should not prevail (*Lilly Icos Ltd v Pfizer Ltd* [2002] EWCA Civ 2).

Rule 5.4C of the CPR says a non-party may obtain a copy of any other document filed with the court if it gives permission. But a party or any person identified in a statement of case may apply to the court for restrictions on access to such documents.

Witness statements

A statement of case does not include witness statements. But rule 32.13 of the CPR says: 'A witness statement which stands as evidence-in-chief is open to inspection during the course of the trial unless the court otherwise directs.' This enables public access during the course of the trial to written evidence relied on in court but not read out. But the court may rule that a witness statement should not be made available because of the interests of justice, the public interest, or the nature of medical evidence or confidential information, or because of the need to protect the interests of any child or protected party. Rule 32.13 does not apply to small claims cases.

Interlocutory hearings and judicial reviews

The CPR rules on access to documents apply to interlocutory hearings and judicial reviews.

 Additional Material for ch. 14 on www.mcnaes.com has case studies of how the media has used the CPR to gain access to case documents in civil cases—for example, in 2014 in a lawsuit brought against Serco by a woman who claimed she was sexually assaulted by one of its employees while she was detained at an immigration removal centre—and how judges have interpreted the Rules. A case study warns too how to avoid libel pitfalls when basing news reports on case documents.

✳ Remember

In defamation law the defence of qualified privilege *will* protect media reports of documents made available to the media as copies, or for public inspection, by a court if the defence's requirements are met and any reporting restriction is obeyed—see ch. 21 on privilege. Family courts have their own procedural rules, which normally mean that no document can be disclosed other than to a limited range of people—see ch. 13.

Skeleton arguments

Each side in a civil case draws up a skeleton argument—a document summarising its arguments in law. It is now established principle that a civil court can allow a journalist to see these and 'written openings' used by counsel (*GIO Personal Investment Services Ltd v Liverpool and London Steamship Protection and Indemnity Association Ltd (FAI General Insurance Co Ltd intervening)* [1999] 1 WLR 984 and the *Guardian v Westminster City Magistrates* case cited earlier).

Judgments and orders

CPR Practice Direction 39A states that when a hearing takes place in open court members of the public can obtain a transcript of any judgment given or a copy of any order made, subject to payment of the appropriate fee. When a judgment is given or an order is made in a private hearing, a non-party wanting a copy will need permission from the judge involved.

👁 Case study

Mr Justice Jacob said in the Chancery Division in January 1998 that, with very rare exceptions and even when a hearing was in private, no judgment could be regarded as a secret document (*Forbes v Smith* [1998] 1 All ER 973).

 See Additional Material for ch. 12 on www.mcnaes.com for information about bankruptcy records and ch. 13 in this book for divorce records.

Access to statements of case and witness statements after a civil case concludes

The High Court ruled in 2004 that anyone, including a journalist, can obtain access to witness statements relating to a case which has concluded—including a case settled without a judgment (*Chan U Seek v Alvis Vehicles Ltd and Guardian Newspapers* [2004] EWHC 3092 (Ch)).

 See Additional Material for ch. 14 on www.mcnaes.com for an outline of this case.

However, a party to the concluded case can object to such access. If a judge holds a hearing to decide the access issue, costs could be awarded against a journalist or media organisation whose application fails.

▶ Public register of monetary judgments, orders and fines

A public register shows whether a person or business has had a county court or High Court monetary judgment made against him/her/it if the sum was not paid within the required timescale. The register also shows if the sum is recorded as having being paid later or as still unpaid. This information stays on the register for six years. It is run by the Registry Trust and can be searched online by name and address. Not all High Court judgments are shown.

see Useful Websites at the end of this chapter

The register has been extended to include records of:

- fines which were not paid quickly, or which remain unpaid, after being imposed in criminal cases by magistrates' courts or Crown courts;
- Child Support Agency liability orders—see Additional Material for ch. 13 on www.mcnaes.com, 'Types of case in family courts';
- tribunals' 'enforced' awards—sums owed after a tribunal has ordered them to be paid, eg after a successful claim at an employment tribunal.

ch. 17 explains tribunals

A fair and accurate report of matter on the register is protected from a libel action by qualified privilege if the requirements of the defence are met—see ch. 21, p. 289, Stories from documents open to public inspection. Take care to understand what the register shows.

➡ Recap of major points

- A journalist arguing against being excluded from a court represents the wider public's interest in open justice.
- Common law, statute and courts' procedural rules enshrine the open justice principle, but do allow courts to sit in private in some circumstances.
- Criminal courts should give reporters basic details of cases, including magistrates' names. Defendants' details should normally be given in open court.
- Reporters covering criminal trials should be allowed to see case material unless a rule prevents this.
- A protocol enables the media to have access to some types of prosecution material—for example, photos and video footage—to help it report a trial.
- The Civil Procedure Rules enable journalists to get copies of and inspect documents in civil cases.

((•)) Useful Websites

www.judiciary.gov.uk/Resources/JCO/Documents/Guidance/crown_court_reporting_restrictions_021009.pdf

Guidance on reporting restrictions, published by the Judicial College, the News Media Association, the Media Lawyers Association, the Society of Editors and Times Newspapers Ltd

www.justice.gov.uk/courts/procedure-rules/criminal/rulesmenu-2015

Criminal Procedure Rules and Criminal Practice Directions

www.justice.gov.uk/courts/procedure-rules/civil

Civil Procedure Rules and Practice Directions

www.newsmediauk.org/write/MediaUploads/PDF%20Docs/Protocol_for_Sharing_Court_Documents.pdf

Protocol agreed by Her Majesty's Courts and Tribunals Service on magistrates' courts lists and registers, and cooperation by Crown courts

www.presscard.uk.com/

UK Press Card Authority

www.cps.gov.uk/publications/agencies/mediaprotocol.html

'Publicity and the Criminal Justice System'—protocol for release of prosecution material to the media, agreed by the Crown Prosecution Service and the Association of Chief Police Officers

www.thejournal.co.uk/news/north-east-news/el-hadji-diouf-agrees-out-of-court-4431319

Journal story on the Newcastle county court case involving footballer El Hadji Diouf

www.trustonline.org.uk/about-us/

Registry Trust public register

15

Challenging the courts

Chapter summary

Courts often restrict media coverage of cases and journalists must be prepared to challenge invalid or overly broad restrictions—they may be the only people in court arguing for the open justice principle (see ch. 14). This chapter explains the case law and rules journalists can cite when opposing reporting restrictions, and how to make challenges.

▶ Why a challenge may be needed

A criminal or civil court may try to restrict reporting of a case when it has no power to do so, or to impose a restriction which is valid but wider than necessary.

The benefits of open justice are best protected by unrestricted reporting. A journalist challenging a proposed or existing reporting restriction, or possible exclusion from a court, should remind the court of those general benefits—explained in ch.14—as well as raise specific points about the particular case.

It is an established principle that any court should only impose the minimum reporting restriction needed to achieve its objective. The 'test' is therefore 'necessity', a point emphasised in *Scott v Scott* [1913] AC 417 and in the Judicial College guidance to courts about reporting restrictions—see later. The Master of the Rolls, Lord Neuberger, said in the Court of Appeal in 2011 that courts *'should ensure that the restrictions on access and reporting are the minimum necessary to enable justice to be done in that case'* (emphasis added) (*Elena Ambrosiadou v Martin Coward* [2011] EWCA (Civ) 409).

A reporting restriction must be obeyed

Reporting restrictions, even if they are invalid or too broad, must be obeyed unless the court amends or lifts them (*Lakah Group and Ramy v Al Jazeera Satellite Channel* [2002] EWHC 2500, [2002] All ER (D) 383 (Nov) (QB)).

The media's right to be heard

A court should hear representations from a media organisation or a journalist opposing or querying a reporting restriction or a proposal or decision that the court should sit in private.

see Useful Websites at the end of this chapter for the Rules and Direction

This principle is recognised in rule 6.2(3) of the Criminal Procedure Rules which cover magistrates' and Crown courts. It says a court should not impose a restriction unless each party and any other person directly affected—which would include the media—is present or has had an opportunity to make representations. This is re-stated in Criminal Practice Direction 6B.4 in which the Lord Chief Justice details how the Rules should be applied.

Notice of applications for restrictions and of opposition to them

Rule 6.4(3) requires that parties applying for a reporting restriction, or for a court hearing to be held partly or entirely in private, should, if the court directs, give the media advance notice. Rule 6.5(3) imposes obligations on media organisations to apply 'as soon as reasonably practicable' if they wish to oppose a reporting or access restriction, and to notify the parties—the defence and prosecution—that such representations are to be made and why the restriction is opposed or should be amended. But rule 6.3 gives the courts discretion to hear applications for restrictions, or media representations against them, made without notice and made verbally rather than in writing. Practice Direction 6B.4 says the order itself should state that any interested party—which would include a journalist—who was not there or represented when it was made has permission to apply to make representations within a limited period, such as 24 hours.

ch. 1, p. 7, Convention rights, explains Article 10 and ch. 11, pp. 135–136, explains 'special measures'

! Remember your rights

Journalists opposing applications for reporting or access restrictions, or their continuation, should tell the court if they were disadvantaged because no notice was given. The court may allow them more time to prepare their argument.

Practice Direction 6B.1 says open justice is 'an essential principle' in criminal courts, and 6B.4 says that a court needs to be satisfied that the purpose of the proposed order to restrict reporting or access cannot be achieved by a lesser measure, such as special measures—for example, allowing a witness to give evidence by a live video link, or clearing the public gallery while allowing media representatives to stay in court. It adds that the terms of any order must be proportionate so as to comply with Article 10 of the European Convention on Human Rights, which covers freedom of expression and the right to impart and receive information.

Practice Direction 6B.4 says an order which restricts reporting must be in writing, must be worded in precise terms and must specify the legal power under which it is made, as well as its precise scope and purpose and, if appropriate, the time at which it will cease to have effect. The order must also state 'in every case, whether or not the making or terms of the order may be reported or whether this itself is prohibited'.

The media should be told of a restriction made

Rule 6.8 of the Criminal Procedure Rules says that if a reporting or access restriction is made, the court officer should record the reason for this. A notice of the restriction should be displayed somewhere prominent in the courtroom's vicinity and communicated to reporters.

Criminal Practice Directions 6B.6 and 6B.7 say a copy of the order should be provided to any local or national media, and court staff should be prepared to answer any inquiry about a specific case. But 6B.7 says it remains the responsibility of those reporting the case to ensure the order is not breached and to make inquiry in case of doubt.

▶ Judicial College guidance for criminal courts

((•))
see Useful Websites at the end of this chapter for this guidance

Guidance entitled *Reporting Restrictions in the Criminal Courts*, published by the Judicial College, has been drawn up by media organisations and the judiciary. It can be cited usefully in challenges to actual or proposed reporting restrictions or threatened exclusions, and is endorsed by the Lord Chief Justice in Criminal Practice Direction 6B.1. The College guidance points courts to the Rules and says, for example (its page numbers given), that the need for a proposed restriction on access or reporting must be 'convincingly established by clear and cogent evidence' by those arguing for it (pp. 6 and 16), that courts which have imposed or are considering imposing a restriction should hear media representations as soon as possible, because contemporaneous court reporting is important and news is perishable (pp. 5 and 16), and that the media have expertise in reporting restrictions and are well placed to represent the wider public interest in open justice (p. 16).

▌ Methods of challenge

Journalists challenging proposed or actual reporting restrictions or exclusion of the media from a court should raise the issue as soon as possible.

An approach to the court by a reporter or editor

In court, the reporter should approach the clerk as the first step—for example, if a hearing is under way, by asking an usher to pass the clerk a note.

Journalists should refer to the Judicial College guidance (discussed earlier).

If an order has already been made, the clerk can be asked to:

- supply it in written form, if this has not already been provided;
- specify in writing why it was made, if the order does not make this clear;
- state in writing the statute and section under which it was made, if the order does not state this.

ch. 1, p. 7, Convention rights, explains Article 10

Such a request might prompt the court to reconsider the order, especially if a reporter—or an editor, by fax, letter or email—quotes case law against it.

Journalists opposing a restriction or exclusion should remind the court of their and the public's Convention rights under Article 10.

- Raising a query or challenge in person in court, or by an editor writing to the court, has the advantages that doing so may resolve the matter quickly and of being the cheapest method as there is no need to involve a lawyer.

A reporter whose argument is being opposed by both the defence and prosecution should remind the court of the warning by Court of Appeal judge Sir Christopher Staughton that '... when both sides agreed that information should be kept from the public, that was when the court had to be most vigilant' (*Ex p P* (1998) The Times, 31 March, quoted with approval by Lord Rodger in the Supreme Court case *Guardian News and Media Ltd's Application* [2010] UKSC 1).

Duty of Crown Prosecution Service (CPS) prosecutors

see Useful Websites at the end of this chapter for this guidance

A journalist may need to refer to guidance to advocates issued by the CPS which says: 'Prosecutors should oppose reporting restrictions that they do not feel are necessary for a fair trial. Prosecutors should not apply for reporting restrictions themselves unless they feel they are essential ...'

Costs

Courts do not normally make costs orders against journalists or a media employer when these informal challenges are made, even if they fail. But it is important to make the challenge as early as possible.

◗ Challenges taken to a higher court

If a challenge by a reporter or an editor fails, the court's decision can be challenged in a higher court.

Judicial review by the High Court of restrictions imposed by magistrates or coroners

A journalist or media organisation can apply to the Queen's Bench Divisional Court, part of the High Court, for **judicial review** of a decision by a magistrates' or coroner's court. 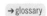 →glossary

- But this normally involves hiring lawyers and there is a court fee, and, if the challenge fails, the journalist or media organisation may have to meet some or all of the costs of any party which opposed the application. An applicant may have to bear its own costs even when successful.

Crown court restrictions can be challenged at the Court of Appeal

Decisions by Crown court judges to impose reporting restrictions or exclude the media can be challenged under section 159 of the Criminal Justice Act 1988, which gives the media a route of appeal to the Court of Appeal.

- The disadvantages are that the appeal may not be considered quickly, so a story may have lost any news value, and the appeal will normally involve hiring lawyers, paying a court fee and, even if it succeeds, costs.

Part 40 of the Criminal Procedure Rules sets out the procedure for appealing to the Court of Appeal against a reporting or access restriction in a criminal case.

 For the Rules, see Useful Websites at the end of this chapter. Also, ch. 8, p. 86, The Court of Appeal, explains that court's role. There are case studies of the Press Association's successful use of the section 159 appeal route on p. 195, Is the juvenile concerned in the proceedings?, and pp. 201–202, Sexual offence law does *not* give anonymity to defendants.

◗ Convention rights of anonymity for defendants or witnesses

Lawyers acting for defendants or arguing on the behalf of witnesses may urge courts to use powers based on Article 2 (the right to life), Article 3 (the right to freedom from degrading treatment including torture) and/or Article 8 (privacy rights) of the European Convention on Human Rights to provide anonymity or otherwise restrict reporting. The statute empowering this is the Human Rights Act 1998.

 ch. 1, p. 7, explains the Human Rights Act 1998

As explained in ch. 11, the High Court has used such powers to ban the media from reporting new identities given to a few notorious defendants after release from prison. But it is exceptionally rare for criminal courts to use any power to ban the media from identifying a defendant and rare too for them to ban publication of a defendant's address or to use Convention powers to protect a witness's identity, bearing in mind that there are other statutory powers to protect witnesses from publicity if this is felt necessary.

Open justice requires that reports should identify the defendant

Case law is that only 'rare circumstances' justify a ban preventing reports identifying the defendant in a criminal trial (*R v Marines A, B, C, D & E* [2013] EWCA Crim 2367).

Lord Steyn said in a judgment in which the House of Lords upheld the media's right to identify a defendant:

> The principle of open justice puts, as has often been said, the judge and all who participate in the trial under intense scrutiny. The glare of contemporaneous publicity ensures that trials are properly conducted. It is a valuable check on the criminal process. Moreover, the public interest may be as much involved in the circumstances of a remarkable acquittal as in a surprising conviction. Informed public debate is necessary about all such matters. (*Re S (a child) (Identification: Restrictions on Publication)* [2004] UKHL 47, [2005] 1 AC 593)

see Late News section about Incedal's trial

In September 2014 the Court of Appeal allowed an appeal by media organisations against an order that two men facing trial on terrorism charges should be anonymous and that all of their trial should be held in secret. The Court named defendants Erol Incedal and Mounir Rarmoul-Bouhadjar, and said only parts of the trial should be held in secret. Lord Justice Gross said: 'We express grave concern as to the cumulative effects of (1) holding a criminal trial in camera and (2) anonymising the Defendants. We find it difficult to conceive of a situation where both departures from open justice will be justified' (*Guardian News and Media Ltd and others v Incedal* [2014] EWCA Crim 1861).

> See also ch. 14, p. 167. A defendant's details should be given in court, for case law that a defendant's address should normally be stated in court, and p. 185, Someone else may be wrongly perceived as the defendant.

see also pp. 187–188, Anonymity and risk of attack?

The Supreme Court said, in *In re Guardian News and Media Ltd and others; HM Treasury v Ahmed and others* [2010] UKSC 1 that, in 'an extreme case', a court has power to ban the media from identifying a witness or 'a party' to a case, such as a defendant, if doing so is necessary to protect that person or his/her family from risks to their lives and safety which could arise, for example, because of what the person had said about 'some powerful criminal organisation'. It said the sources of a court's power to make an anonymity order to protect such a person from 'a threat of violence arising out of its proceedings' were the person's rights under Articles 2 and 3 of the European Convention. But it removed the anonymity lower courts had given four men who were appealing against asset-freezing orders made under anti-terrorism law. The Court said that the men's right to respect for privacy and family life under Article 8 did not override the media's rights under Article 10 as there was a 'powerful, public interest' in identifying them. It dismissed the argument that defendants should be given anonymity when accused of serious, unsubstantiated offences, saying members of the public 'are more than capable of drawing the distinction between mere suspicion and sufficient evidence to prove guilt'.

! Remember your rights

A court considering how the Convention applies must carry out the 'balancing test' if, for example, someone asserts his/her rights under Article 8 against the media's and public's rights under Article 10—see ch. 1, pp. 7–8, Weighing competing rights.

The High Court has used the Convention in the context of family law to ban media reports from identifying a defendant in a criminal case—see ch. 13 on www.mcnaes.com. See also the Additional Material on www.mcnaes.com for ch. 37, 'Bans on identifying defendants'.

▌ Challenging restrictions made under contempt law

Courts have discretionary powers to restrict reports of proceedings. These include those in sections 11 and 4 (2) of the Contempt of Court Act 1981.

Section 11

Courts have common law powers to order that a name or other information should be withheld from the public during proceedings. A court which uses this power can then make an order under section 11 of the Contempt of Court Act 1981 indefinitely banning publication of the name or information—such as a defendant's address—in connection with reports of the proceedings. The media generally accept that blackmail victims should have this anonymity, but have opposed defendants being given it and may object if it is used for witnesses for invalid or insufficient reasons.

see ch. 11, pp. 128–129, Section 11 orders— blackmail, secrets, personal safety

'In connection with the proceedings'

A section 11 order only bans publication of a name or matter 'in connection with the proceedings'—that is, a particular court case. It does not stop the media referring to someone by name in other contexts.

 See the case study in the Additional Material for ch. 10 on www.mcnaes.com, 'Orders to protect the public from risk of sexual offences', about a man who won section 11 protection to stop a newspaper publishing his address in a report of a court proceedings to impose a sexual offences prevention order on him—but the newspaper was able to report from other sources his previous offences and the view that he remained a danger to women. See more detail on such orders on p. 186, Civil orders imposed on sexual or trafficking offenders.

Has the name or matter been withheld from the public?

A section 11 order cannot be made if the name or matter has already been mentioned in public proceedings in the case. In *R v Arundel Justices, ex p Westminster Press* [1985] 2 All ER 390, [1985] 1 WLR 708 magistrates made a section 11 order banning publication of the name and address of a man charged with burglary offences. The High Court ruled in a judicial review that the magistrates had no power to make the order, as the defendant's details had already been given in public—when the clerk routinely checked that information with the defendant in the first hearing.

👁 Case study

In 2012 David Graham, of Blackpool-based Watsons Press Agency, cited the *Arundel* case when he persuaded a district judge to revoke a section 11 order giving anonymity to former professional footballer Alan Burrows, aged 70, who had been made subject to a sexual offences prevention order (SOPO). The order banned Burrows, who once played for Blackpool FC, from contact with children. Mr Graham pointed out that Burrows had already been named in open court when the SOPO proceedings began (*Media Lawyer*, 18 June 2012).

A court which has made a deliberate decision to withhold a name or matter from its public proceedings can use a section 11 order to forbid its publication after it is mentioned by mistake (*Re Times Newspapers Ltd* [2007] EWCA Crim 1925; *Re Trinity Mirror plc and others* [2008] QB 770, [2008] EWCA Crim 50).

Is anonymity necessary for justice to be done?

Section 11 orders may only be made when they are necessary in the interests of the administration of justice. In *Attorney General v Leveller Magazine Ltd* [1979]

AC 440, Lord Diplock said that departure from the open justice rule was only justified:

> … where the nature or circumstances of the particular proceeding are such that the application of the general rule in its entirety would frustrate or render impracticable the administration of justice or would damage some other public interest for whose protection Parliament has made some statutory derogation from the rule.

See the Additional Material for ch. 14 on www.mcnaes.com for this case.

The High Court in Northern Ireland said in 1997: 'The use of the words "some other public interest" indicates that Lord Diplock had in mind the protection of the public interest in the administration of justice rather than the private welfare of those caught up in that administration.' The observation came as it refused to grant anonymity to a man charged with indecent assault. His lawyer had argued that, in the light of incidents involving others facing similar allegations, he was likely to be attacked if it became known in his community that he faced this charge (*R v Newtownabbey Magistrates' Court, ex p Belfast Telegraph Newspapers Ltd* [1997] NI 309).

see also pp. 187–188, Anonymity and risk of attack?

Someone else may be wrongly perceived as the defendant

Page 31 of the Judicial College guidance warns courts that banning publication of a defendant's address creates the risk that the public might think, wrongly, that someone entirely unconnected with the case but with the same name is the defendant.

for this guidance, see Useful Websites at the end of this chapter

Section 11 is not to protect the 'comfort and feelings' of defendants

A section 11 order should not be made for the 'comfort and feelings' of a defendant (*R v Evesham Justices, ex p McDonagh* [1988] QB 553, [1988] 1 All ER 371). Evesham magistrates agreed that a defendant's address should not be given in court, because he feared harassment by his ex-wife, and made a section 11 order banning its publication. But in a judicial review quashing the order Lord Justice Watkins said 'it is well established practice that, save for a justifiable reason', a defendant's address has to be given publicly in court. He said:

> There are undoubtedly many people who find themselves defending criminal charges who for all manner of reasons would like to keep unrevealed their identity, their home address in particular. Indeed, I go so far as to say that in the vast majority of cases, in magistrates' courts anyway, defendants would like their identity to be unrevealed and would be capable of advancing seemingly plausible reasons why that should be so. But section 11 was not enacted for the comfort and feelings of defendants.

It was only in rare circumstances, conforming to those set out in *Attorney General v Leveller* (discussed earlier), that a court would protect a defendant from publicity, he added.

Section 11 is not to protect a defendant's business interests

A section 11 order cannot not be used to protect a defendant's business interests, the High Court held in *R v Dover Justices, ex p Dover District Council and Wells* (1991) 156 JP 433.

Section 11 anonymity is not to protect a defendant's children

A section 11 order cannot be used in a criminal case to shield the children of a defendant from the effects of publicity about a case. The Court of Appeal ruled in 2008 that Croydon Crown court was wrong to use an order to stop the media naming a man who had admitted 20 charges of downloading child pornography from the internet. The judge who made the order justified it by saying the defendant's daughters, aged 6 and 8, who were neither victims nor witnesses in the case, would suffer significant harm if their father were to be identified. The Court of Appeal said the judge was wrong to conclude that the children's privacy rights under Article 8 of the European Convention outweighed those of the media and the public under Article 10. In the Court of Appeal judgment, Sir Igor Judge said 'there is nothing in this case to distinguish the plight of the defendant's children from that of a massive group of children of persons convicted of offences relating to child pornography'. Allowing the defendant anonymity would be 'to the overwhelming disadvantage of public confidence in the criminal justice system' (*In Re Trinity Mirror and others*, cited earlier).

Civil orders imposed on sexual or trafficking offenders

for this Home Office guidance, see Useful Websites at the end of this chapter

Police can apply in civil law for orders restricting the behaviour of convicted sexual offenders if it suggests they may reoffend—for example, banning them from loitering near schools. Home Office guidance says it is normal practice for some police forces to ask magistrates, at the outset of the application hearing, to make a section 11 order to stop the offender being identified in reports and suggests that any disorder arising from public knowledge of his involvement in the hearing would make him more likely to abscond. There is similar Home Office guidance about civil orders restraining the behaviour of people convicted or suspected of slavery or human trafficking offences under the Modern Slavery Act 2015. Both sets of guidance say: 'It is for the court to decide whether such a prohibition [a section 11 order] is necessary.' The media can argue that such a hearing in respect of an offender needs unrestricted reporting because the public should be able to know who such offenders are.

For a case study on media coverage of such an order made against a sexual offender, see the Additional Material for ch. 10 on www.mcnaes.com, Orders to protect the public from risk of sexual offences.

Anonymity should not be used to spare witnesses in criminal cases from embarrassment

A section 11 order made by a Crown court judge giving anonymity to a witness on the grounds that the stress of publicity might cause her to relapse into heroin addiction was criticised in the High Court. Lord Justice Brown said:

> There must be many occasions when witnesses in criminal cases are faced with embarrassment as a result of facts which are elicited in the course of proceedings and of allegations made which are often without any real substance. It is, however, part of the essential nature of British criminal justice that cases shall be tried in public and reported and this consideration must outweigh the individual interests of particular persons. (*R v Central Criminal Court, ex p Crook* (1984) The Times, 8 November)

Section 11 anonymity in civil cases

In *R v Legal Aid Board, ex p Kaim Todner* [1998] 3 All ER 541, Lord Woolf said that, in general, parties and witnesses in civil cases had to accept the embarrassment, damage to their reputation and possible consequential loss which could be inherent in being involved in litigation, and that their protection was that normally a public judgment would refute unfounded allegations.

Anonymity and risk of attack?

Lawyers sometimes urge courts to give a defendant or to witnesses anonymity, or to ban publication of their addresses, on the grounds that they are at risk of violence from criminals or vigilantes.

Case law says:

- a court asked to give a defendant or witness anonymity, or to ban publication of his/her address, on safety grounds must be satisfied that the risk to his/her safety is 'real and immediate'; and
- the risk must have an objective, verifiable basis—be backed by evidence to the court and not be assessed merely on the person's subjective fears.

If allegations against a defendant, and his/her identity, are already public knowledge, there is no justification for restricting media reports,

In the House of Lords in 2007 Lord Carswell referred to the established criterion that there should be 'a real and immediate risk' to life to justify anonymity. A real risk was one which was objectively verified, and an immediate risk was one which was present and continuing, he said, adding: 'It is in my opinion clear that the criterion is and should be one that is not readily satisfied: in other words, the threshold is high' (*Re Officer L* [2007] UKHL 36).

The test is the same whether the person allegedly at risk is a defendant or witness, whether the anonymity is sought for the proceedings—that the person should not be identified in court—or only in respect of media reports, or whether it is sought under section 11 of the Contempt of Court Act 1981 or other law.

see pp. 181–182, Convention rights of anonymity

Police and prison officer defendants—risk of attack

Lawyers defending police or prison officers often argue that their clients should have anonymity or that the media should not publish their home addresses because—it is said—the charges they face or the general nature of their job or duties puts them at risk of attack or harassment from vengeful criminals.

👁 Case study

Two senior police officers were charged in 2010 with misconduct in public office after alleged improper interference in prosecutions for speeding. Aldershot magistrates, after hearing an objection from a reporter, refused the officers' request for a section 11 order banning publication of their home addresses. They sought judicial review, arguing that publication would put them at risk because of their past involvement in investigating serious crime. The High Court, refusing to make an order, noted that the Press Association, which with a regional media group had argued against a ban, had shown that anyone could use internet records of electoral registers, at a cost of £4.95, to discover the officers' addresses within 5 minutes. Any risk to the officers' safety, if it existed, would be from someone who targeted them, who would be not be deterred merely because the media had not published the addresses, it said, adding that the type of charges the officers faced were unlikely to provoke a vigilante attack (*R (on the application of Harper and Johncox) v Aldershot Magistrates' Court and others* [2010] EWHC 1319 (Admin)).

---

see also
the inquest
case study,
ch. 16,
pp. 211–212

Police officers as witnesses—risk of attack

Police firearms officers involved in fatal shootings while on duty have been given anonymity at inquests (*R (on the application of Officer A and another) v HM Coroner for Inner South London* [2004] All ER (D) 288 (Jun)).

Section 4(2) orders

Under section 4(2) of the Contempt of Court Act 1981 courts have power to postpone publication of media reports of all or part of a case if the postponement is necessary to 'avoid a substantial risk of prejudice' to later stages of the same case or to other cases pending or imminent. See also ch. 18, pp. 246–249, Section 4(2) orders.

see ch. 14
on the
benefits of
open justice

Postponement orders frequently mean that when the restriction no longer applies the case receives substantially less coverage than it would otherwise have done, especially if the order means that coverage of a sequence of trials has, because of the practicalities of media production, to be compressed into one day's publication on the day the last trial ends. Many details will never be published and the benefits of open justice will have been eroded.

Risk of prejudice in sequential cases

Lord Justice Farquharson said in *R v Beck, ex p Daily Telegraph* [1993] 2 All ER 177 that the fact that an accused expected to face a second indictment after a trial of the first did not in itself justify making a section 4 (2) order. It depended on all the circumstances, including the nature of the charges, the timing of the second trial and where the second trial would be heard. If substantial prejudice to the accused could be avoided by extending the period between trials, or transferring the case to another court, then that course should be followed.

The risk of prejudice must be substantial

A section 4(2) order should only be made if the risk of prejudice to current or pending proceedings is substantial.

In 1993 in the Court of Appeal the Lord Chief Justice, Lord Taylor, said that, in determining whether publication of information would cause a substantial risk of prejudice to a future trial, a court should credit that trial's jury with the will and ability to abide by the judge's direction to decide the case only on the evidence before it. The court should also bear in mind that the staying power and detail of publicity, even in cases of notoriety, were limited and that the nature of a trial was to focus the jury's minds on the evidence put before them rather than on matters outside the courtroom (*Ex p Telegraph plc and other appeals* [1993] 2 All ER 971).

Risk of prejudice if one defendant is sentenced before others are tried

In 2006 the Court of Appeal overturned a section 4(2) order postponing reporting of the sentencing of terrorist Dhiran Barot. The Crown court judge had made the order on the grounds that reports would prejudice the forthcoming trial of other defendants. But lawyers for the media successfully argued that five months would elapse before that jury trial and so the 'fade factor' would mean that contemporaneous reporting of Barot's sentencing would not create a risk of serious prejudice. Sir Igor Judge said in this Court of Appeal judgment that the right to a fair trial had to be balanced with the hallowed principle that the media had the freedom to act as the eyes and ears of the public. Juries had 'passionate and profound belief in, and a commitment to, the right of a Defendant to be given a fair trial', he said, emphasising the capacity of juries to concentrate on the trial evidence (*R v B* [2006] EWCA Crim 2692).

ch. 18. p. 243, The 'fade factor' and limited publication, explains the term

For more detail of Sir Igor's remarks in this case, see ch. 18, p. 242, Juries are told to put pre-trial publicity out of their minds.

Principles for decisions on section 4(2) orders

In *R v Sherwood, ex p Telegraph Group* [2001] EWCA Crim 1075, [2001] 1 WLR 1983, the Court of Appeal set out three principles on section 4(2) orders:

" (1) Unless the perceived risk of prejudice was demonstrated, no order should be made;

(2) The court had to ask whether an order was necessary under the European Convention on Human Rights. Sometimes wider considerations of public policy would come into play to justify refusing to make a section 4(2) order even though there was no other way of eliminating the prejudice anticipated;

(3) Applications for postponement orders should be approached as follows:

    (i) Would reporting give rise to a substantial risk of prejudice? If not, that would be the end of the matter;

    (ii) if such a risk was perceived to exist, would an order eliminate it? If not, obviously there could be no necessity to impose such a postponement. But even if the judge was satisfied that an order would achieve the objective, he/she would have to consider whether the risk could satisfactorily be overcome by less restrictive means;

    (iii) the judge might still have to ask whether the degree of risk of prejudice contemplated should be regarded as tolerable in the sense of being the lesser of two evils, when compared to the harm which a 4(2) order could cause to the benefits of open justice. 🙶🙶

The possibility of retrial does not mean a hearing is 'pending or imminent'

see ch. 18, p. 235, Proceedings become active again when an appeal is lodged

The mere fact that a defendant has lodged an appeal against a conviction does not mean that a retrial is 'pending or imminent' and so cannot justify use of section 4(2) to postpone the reporting of another case he/she is involved in (*Beggs v The Scottish Ministers* [2006] CSIH 17).

Section 4(2) cannot be used to protect reputation or safety

Magistrates and Crown court judges have occasionally made section 4(2) orders for a purpose other than avoiding a substantial risk of prejudice to a current or future hearing. Such orders are invalid. For example, a section 4(2) order cannot be used to ban publication of a name or material to encourage a witness to give evidence, or to protect anybody's reputation or general welfare or safety. The Court of Appeal made this clear in *Re Trinity Mirror plc and others* and in *Re Times Newspapers Ltd*, cited earlier in this chapter.

((•)) Journalists challenging a section 4(2) order should refer the court to pp. 24–25 of the Judicial College guidance—see Useful Websites at the end of this chapter—and should read the Additional Material for ch. 15 on www.mcnaes.com, including 'Section 4(2) orders cannot restrict reports of events outside the courtroom'.

▌ Court orders giving juveniles anonymity

In April 2015 new law amended the discretionary powers which courts can use to provide anonymity for juveniles 'concerned in the proceedings', while they remain under the age of 18, by restricting what can be published in any reports of or references to such cases. These reporting restrictions are set out in ch. 9. This explains that section 45 of the Youth Justice and Criminal Evidence Act 1999 is now the power which criminal courts can use to bestow such anonymity on a juvenile who is a defendant, witness or the victim/alleged victim, replacing section 39 of the Children and Young Persons Act 1933. Yet section 39 remains the power used by civil courts and coroners' courts to provide such anonymity for a juvenile witness, or—in civil courts—for a juvenile who is a party.

As explained earlier, the Criminal Procedure Rules require criminal courts to hear media challenges to any reporting restriction. Orders made in criminal courts to give juvenile defendants anonymity are probably challenged the most.

Crown court judges tend to protect a juvenile defendant's identity with a section 45 order made pre-trial. They may consider lifting it if the juvenile is convicted and should give the media opportunity to argue for this. For example, in 2014 a Crown court judge revoked a section 39 order to allow the media to identify William Cornick, aged 16, after he admitted murdering a teacher in Leeds by stabbing her in front of the class. It is not unusual for judges and magistrates to remove the anonymity of juvenile defendants convicted of serious offences, particularly if the offending was persistent and/or notorious in the local community. But a court is less likely to revoke an anonymity order after an acquittal.

Challenging section 45 anonymity

As explained later, case law from challenges made before April 2015 in criminal courts to anonymity orders made under section 39 of the Children and Young Persons Act 1933 may well be relevant—and can be cited—when journalists argue against anonymity orders being proposed or already made under the new law in section 45 of the 1999 Act.

see p. 193, Case law on juvenile anonymity

Journalists can also point out that section 45 states that a court which has made such an order can—by making an 'excepting direction' (counter-order)—revoke the order completely or vary the scope of its reporting restrictions to any extent the court chooses to specify, if it is satisfied—

> (a) that the effect of the section 45 order is to impose a substantial and unreasonable restriction on the reporting of the proceedings; *and*
> (b) that it is in the public interest to remove or relax that restriction.

Section 52 of the 1999 Act says that, in considering 'the public interest', the court must have regard, in particular and as relevant, to the interest in the open reporting of crime, the open reporting of matters relating to human health or safety, and the prevention and exposure of miscarriages of justice.

The 1999 Act requires a court considering whether to make an 'excepting direction' to have regard to the welfare of the juvenile and states that no 'excepting direction' shall be made merely because the case before the court has been 'determined in any way' or has been 'abandoned' But, as the Judicial College guidance

see Useful
Websites
at the end
of this
chapter for
the Judicial
College
guidance

points out, if the case outcome has been decided (determined), that 'may be a very relevant consideration'. As indicated earlier, if the outcome is that a juvenile has been convicted of a serious crime, the argument for lifting his/her section 45 anonymity is stronger.

As regards what can be argued to be 'a substantial and unreasonable' restriction in this context, there were—because section 45 was newly in operation—no precedent cases when this book was completed. But—as ch. 14 explains—there is always a public interest argument for court cases to be reported as fully as possible.

> Check www.mcnaes.com for updates to ch. 9 on section 45 cases.

It could be argued that a section 45 order creates 'a substantial and unreasonable' restriction' if—by limiting what detail can be published about a convicted juvenile—it prevents the local community knowing of an ongoing crime problem which needs to be tackled in particular location or school. It is also arguable that identifying in a report of the case a juvenile whose offending has been serious would help maintain public confidence in the justice system and deter him/her or others from offending.

Journalists might also argue that 'a substantial and unreasonable' restriction is created if a section 45 order giving anonymity to a juvenile victim/alleged victim prevents an adult defendant from being identified. As this chapter has explained, for an adult defendant to have anonymity is contrary to the established principle of open justice. But the court will consider how media identification of the juvenile could affect his/her welfare.

On the issue of what is 'unreasonable', a journalist can cite the case law, outlined later in the chapter, that anonymity should not be bestowed merely because of the juvenile's age, or for a baby or toddler too young to need it, and that an anonymity order is invalid if made in respect of a juvenile who is dead or to specify that an adult defendant must not be identified.

Crown Prosecution Service guidance on anonymity for juveniles

Guidance issued in 2015 by the CPS to prosecutors says that they should only ask a court to impose a section 45 order if the public interest and the Article 10 rights to receive and impart information are outweighed by the rights of the juvenile defendant, witness or victim.

see Useful
Websites at
the end of
this chapter
for this CPS
guidance

This guidance accepts that in some cases allowing the media to identify a convicted (and therefore disgraced and punished) juvenile can help deter others from committing crime.

Guidance issued by the CPS in 2011 to prosecutors gave the following examples of types of case in which there is a strong public interest in favour of lifting an anonymity restriction in respect of a convicted juvenile:

- significant public disorder where the public would rightly need to be satisfied that offenders were brought to justice and there was a need to deter others;

- serious offences which undermined the public's confidence in the safety of their communities;
- hate crimes which could have a corrosive impact on the confidence of communities.

 'Hate crimes' include racist attacks. See ch. 38 on www.mcnaes.com on incitement.

Section 45A lifetime anonymity

As ch. 9 explains, in April 2015 the government inserted a new section—section 45A—into the Youth Justice and Criminal Evidence Act 1999. This new law gives criminal courts a discretionary power, in certain circumstances, to ban any publication from identifying a specified juvenile, for their lifetime, as being concerned in a case as a witness or victim/alleged victim. This power cannot be used to provide such anonymity for juvenile defendants, as the Act makes clear. When this book went to press it was unclear how often such courts would use this new power. Because the circumstances in which it can be used are similar as for the power in section 46 of the Act, which can provide lifetime anonymity for adult witnesses, section 45A is discussed later in this chapter with section 46—see p. 201, Section 45A anonymity for juvenile witnesses and juvenile victims.

Case law on juvenile anonymity

Section 39 of the Children and Young Persons Act 1933 can be used in civil law proceedings and coroners' courts. It gives the court the discretionary power to order that the specified juvenile should not be identified in any publication as being 'concerned in the proceedings'. In a civil case it can cover a juvenile who is a claimant, defendant or witness; in a coroner's court, a juvenile who is a witness.

Because until April 2015 section 39 was also used in criminal courts, case law concerning challenges by journalists in those courts to section 39 orders may be relevant to challenges to anonymity orders made under section 45 of the Youth Justice and Criminal Evidence Act 1999, as well as remaining relevant to challenges to use of section 39 orders in civil proceedings and inquests.

The 2015 CPS guidance to prosecutors says case law relating to section 39 orders 'may be cited as good authority' in respect of section 45 orders.

((•))
see Useful Websites at the end of this chapter for this guidance

The seven principles

Lord Justice Simon Brown in *R v Crown Court at Winchester, ex p B* [2000] 1 Cr App R 11 identified seven principles a criminal court deciding whether to make or revoke a section 39 order should consider the following.

(1) In deciding whether to impose or lift the reporting restrictions, the court will consider whether there are good reasons for allowing the juvenile defendant to be named.

(2) It will give considerable weight to the offender's age and the potential damage to this juvenile of public identification as a criminal before he/she has the benefit or burden of adulthood.

(3) It must have regard to the juvenile's welfare.

(4) The prospect of being named with the accompanying disgrace is a powerful deterrent and naming a defendant in the context of his/her punishment serves as a deterrent to others. These deterrents are proper objectives for the court.

(5) There is a strong public interest in open justice and in the public knowing as much as possible about what has happened in court, including the identity of those who have committed crime.

(6) The weight to be attributed to different factors may shift at different stages of the proceedings and, in particular, after the defendant has been found, or pleads, guilty and is sentenced. It may then be appropriate to place greater weight on the interest of the public in knowing the identity of those who have committed crimes, particularly serious and detestable crimes.

(7) The fact that an appeal has been made may be a material consideration.

Is the juvenile concerned in the proceedings?

see Remember, p. 99, which mentions truancy cases

Neither a section 39 order nor a section 45 order is valid if the juvenile is not 'concerned in the proceedings', so criminal courts should not use section 45 to give a juvenile anonymity merely because his/her parent is the defendant, *unless* the juvenile is a witness or the victim/alleged victim of the offence, or is the juvenile 'in respect of whom the proceedings are taken'—for example, in a truancy case in which a parent is prosecuted for failing to ensure a child attends school.

In 2000 Mr Justice Elias said in the High Court:

> Sadly, in any case where someone is caught up in the criminal process other members of the family who are wholly innocent of wrongdoing will be innocent casualties in the drama. They may suffer in all sorts of ways from the publicity given to another family member. But I do not consider that in the normal case that is a relevant factor or a good reason for granting a direction under section 39. (*Chief Constable of Surrey v JHG and DHG* [2002] EWHC 1129 (Admin), [2002] All ER (D) 308 (May))

chs. 2 and 3 introduce these codes

Journalists should heed clause 9 of the Editors' Code, which says that relatives of people convicted or accused of crime should not generally be identified without their consent unless they are genuinely relevant to the story. The Broadcasting Code, section 8, says that children do not lose their right to privacy because of a parent's notoriety, so it may be unethical to name a child in a report.

But sometimes a defendant's children *are* relevant in a court case even when they are not 'concerned in the proceedings'. Moreover, the media—even if they do not intend to publish the name of a child—may have to challenge a section 45 order if its blanket ban on publication of any detail which could identify the child has the effect of preventing reports from identifying the adult defendant.

👁 Case study

The Court of Appeal in 2013 said that Recorder J J Wright had been wrong to impose at Swindon Crown court a section 39 order banning the media from identifying a 15-year-old boy whose father—a former Army officer—was on trial for defrauding taxpayers of more than £180,000 to send his three sons to an independent boarding school. The trial was already well under way—the prosecution having already identified in open court all three sons, including the 15-year-old, and media reports having mentioned them—when the Recorder made the order. The boy was not a witness. The father was convicted on most charges (*R v Robert Jolleys, ex p Press Association* [2013] EWCA Crim 1135).

The High Court made a similar ruling in 2008—that section 39 cannot be used to spare the embarrassment of a defendant's children if they are 'not concerned in the proceedings' (*Crawford v Director of Public Prosecutions*, The Times, 20 February 2008).

The identity of the juvenile is already in the public domain

In *R v Cardiff Crown Court, ex p M (a minor)* (1998) 162 JP 527 (DC) the High Court ruled that if a section 39 order was not made when the case was first listed, publicity identifying the juvenile might make it inappropriate to make an order at a later stage.

Statute created to protect juveniles cannot specifically give adults anonymity

The Court of Appeal ruled in 1991 that section 39 orders could not be used to ban the publication of the identity of an adult defendant (*R v Southwark Crown Court, ex p Godwin* [1992] QB 190, [1991] 3 All ER 818). The same reasoning will apply to orders under section 45 of the Youth Justice and Criminal Evidence Act 1999.

Lord Justice Glidewell said:

> In our view, section 39 as a matter of law does not empower a court to order in terms that the names of [adult] defendants should not be published. ... If the inevitable effect of making an order is that it is apparent that some details, including names of [adult] defendants, may not be published because publication would breach the order, that is the practical application of the order; it is not a part of the terms of the order itself.

see ch. 9,
pp. 103–104,
Cases of
abuse within
a family

In 2005 the Court of Appeal ruled there was no power under section 39 to prohibit identification of adults charged with sexual offences against children. But it warned of the danger of publishing material which might identify the children if the adult's name were published (*R v Teesside Crown Court, ex p Gazette Media Co Ltd* [2005] EWCA Crim 1983).

Which proceedings are covered by an order?

In 1993 Lord Justice Lloyd in the Court of Appeal said the word 'proceedings' in section 39 must mean proceedings in the court making the order and not any proceedings anywhere (*R v Lee* [1993] 2 All ER 170, [1993] 1 WLR 103). So, it can be construed that a section 45 order made in a magistrates' court does not apply to reports of the case when it reaches Crown court—but that the Crown court can make a new section 45 order.

An order must be clear about whom it protects

The child or children covered by an anonymity order should be clearly identified in it, so the media can be clear about who it covers (*R v Central Criminal Court, ex p Godwin and Crook*, cited earlier, which concerned a section 39 order).

There must be a good reason for an anonymity order

A court should not make an anonymity order automatically, merely because of a juvenile's age, or unthinkingly as a 'blanket' order covering all juveniles in the case.

- In *R v Lee*, cited earlier, Lord Justice Lloyd pointed out that the 1933 Act made a distinction between section 49 anonymity, automatic under the Act in the juvenile (now youth) court, and section 39 anonymity, which is not automatic, in the Crown court—'a distinction which Parliament clearly intended to preserve'. This distinction was preserved in the creation of section 45 of the 1999 Act to replace—in criminal courts—section 39 of the 1933 Act.

see Useful
Websites
at the end
of this
chapter for
the Judicial
College
guidance

An anonymity order cannot validly be made in respect of a dead juvenile

Courts sometimes make anonymity orders attempting to ban the identification of dead children. Several High Court judges have said the courts do not have this power. The Judicial College guidance says that for section 39 of the 1933 Act to apply the juvenile 'must be alive' and cites in support *Re S (a child) (Identification: Restrictions on Publication)* [2005] 1 AC 593.

Victim is too young to need anonymity

The Judicial College guidance says: 'Age alone is not sufficient to justify imposing an order as very young children cannot be harmed by publicity of which they will be unaware ...'

Courts have accepted that a baby or a toddler who is the victim/alleged victim of a crime does not need section 39 anonymity, because by the time he/she is old enough to be harmed by the case's publicity it is likely to have been forgotten.

⟨◉⟩ Case study

In 2013 the High Court upheld a refusal by Lowestoft magistrates' court to grant section 39 anonymity for a 3-year-old girl in a case in which her mother, Tess Gandy, aged 35, was convicted of being drunk in a public place while in charge of the girl, having been cautioned previously for a similar offence. Section 39 anonymity would have prevented the media identifying Gandy, a local councillor. Her identity in the case was protected by a temporary injunction until the High Court made its decision. It ruled that the child was too young to be directly affected by publicity about her mother's conviction, and that open justice and the Article 10 rights of the media and public should prevail (*R (on the application of A) v Lowestoft Magistrates' Court, with the Crown Prosecution Service and Archant Community Media Ltd as interested parties* [2013] EWHC 659 (Admin)).

A section 39 order cannot be in force if the juvenile has turned 18

A section 39 order can only be made to give anonymity to a person aged under 18. The order cannot be made simply because a defendant was under the age of 18 when the offence was committed. And case law has made clear that if a section 39 order is made, the anonymity automatically expires when the juvenile turns 18.

 See ch. 9, p. 102, When does section 39 cease to apply to a juvenile?, for this case law, and p. 99, When section 45 anonymity ceases to apply, about how section 45 anonymity expires when the juvenile reaches the age of 18.

▌ Challenges to youth court anonymity

As ch. 9 explains, section 49 of the Children and Young Persons Act 1933 gives all juveniles 'concerned' in youth court proceedings, or in appeals from youth courts, automatic anonymity in media reports.

see ch. 9, pp. 97–98, When section 49 anonymity ceases to apply

A youth court which convicts a juvenile can, by using section 49(4A), lift the anonymity if satisfied that it is 'in the public interest' to do so.

In 1998 the Home Office and Lord Chancellor's Department issued a joint Circular, *Opening up Youth Court Proceedings*, which said that lifting the anonymity would be particularly appropriate in respect of a juvenile defendant:

see Useful Websites at the end of this chapter about the Circular

- whose offending was persistent or serious; or
- whose offending had had an impact on a number of people; or
- in circumstances when alerting people to his/her behaviour would help prevent further offending.

It said occasions when it would not be in the best interests of justice to lift section 49 anonymity included:

- when publicity might put the offender or his/her family at risk of harassment or harm;
- when the offender was particularly young or vulnerable;
- when the offender was contrite and ready to accept responsibility for his/her actions;
- when public identification of the offender would reveal the identity of a vulnerable victim and lead to unwelcome publicity for that victim.

 Case study

In 2001 the High Court upheld a youth court's decision to lift the section 49 anonymity in the case of a 15-year-old offender who had admitted taking a car without the owner's consent. He had previous, similar convictions for 'joy-riding', and the media had been told he had been arrested 130 times (*McKerry v Teesdale and Wear Valley Justices* (2000) 164 JP 355, [2000] Crim LR 594).

The guidance issued in 2011 by the CPS on circumstances in which there is a strong public interest in favour of lifting anonymity also applies to the lifting of section 49 anonymity for a convicted juvenile.

 See p. 192, Crown Prosecution Service guidance on anonymity for juveniles and Useful Websites at the end of this chapter.

▌ Anti-social behaviour cases— arguments for identifying juveniles

Courts have the power to make orders in civil law to curb anti-social behaviour— see ch. 9, pp. 104–107, Anti-social behaviour injunctions and Criminal behaviour orders. This also explains that courts can make orders to provide anonymity for juveniles made subject to such measures and for those accused of breaching them. A journalist who wants a court to permit a report to identify a juvenile in such a case can cite Home Office guidance, *Publicising Anti-social Behaviour Orders*, issued to local authorities in 2005—see Useful Websites at the end of this chapter.

Check www.mcnaes.com for updates on guidance about injunctions and orders.

This 2005 guidance said that orders against anti-social behaviour protect local communities and that: 'Publicity should be expected in most cases.'

The guidance said the benefits of publicity included:

- public reassurance that action was being taken to protect the community's human rights;
- enforcement—local people have the information to identify individuals who breach such orders;
- deterrence—if a person subject to such an order knows people might identify him/her for breaching it, a breach may be less likely, while others who see publicity about such orders might be deterred from anti-social behaviour.

A Home Office factsheet, *Replacing the ASBO*, said in 2013 that allowing the media to identify the juvenile in reports of hearings to decide on whether to impose a criminal behaviour order (CBO) and reports of CBO breach cases 'may be necessary, in some circumstances, to help in enforcing the order and to protect victims and communities'.

((•))
for the
factsheet,
see Useful
Websites at
the end of
this chapter

Case law on ASBOs will be relevant to the new ASBIs and CBOs.

- Mr Justice Wilson said in the High Court in 2001 that in most cases magistrates should not ban identification by the media of a child subject to an ASBO, because the effectiveness of such orders would often depend on the local community knowing that the ASBO applied to that child (*Medway Council v BBC* [2002] 1 FLR 104).

▶ Lifetime anonymity for witnesses and juvenile victims

Section 46 of the Youth Justice and Criminal Evidence Act 1999 gives criminal courts the power to stop the media identifying an adult witness during his/her lifetime as being a witness in the relevant case. The court must be satisfied that the quality of this witness's evidence, or level of cooperation in connection with preparations for the case, is likely to be diminished by reason of his/her fear or distress in connection with being identified as a witness by members of the public. It must also be satisfied that anonymity is likely to improve the quality of his/her evidence or the level of his/her cooperation. Ch. 11, pp. 131–133, Lifetime anonymity for adult witnesses, provides general detail about this power. A court can revoke—or relax the scope of—a section 46 order if satisfied that its effect is to impose 'a substantial and unreasonable restriction' on the reporting of the case *and* that it is in the public interest to revoke or relax it.

A journalist wishing to challenge the imposition or continuation of a section 46 order should follow the rule 6 procedure in the Criminal Procedure Rules, explained earlier in this chapter, and can make the following arguments.

Is there 'fear' or 'distress', and would the quality of evidence really be diminished?

Home Office Explanatory Notes to the 1999 Act state: 'Neither "fear" nor "distress" is seen as covering a disinclination to give evidence on account of simple embarrassment.'

👁 Case studies

In 2010 at the Old Bailey Judge Jeremy Roberts refused to make a section 46 order requested by the prosecution. It wanted anonymity for a 58-year-old woman, a prosecution witness in a case in which two men faced charges relating to possessing unlicensed herbal medicines. The judge, after hearing the Press Association's arguments that such an order would not be justified, said he did not believe that the quality of her evidence was likely to be diminished if he did not make the order, adding: 'She is a responsible, obviously intelligent lady. She has held a very responsible position in the past' (*Media Lawyer*, 10 February 2010).

At Blackpool magistrates' court in 2009 a journalist successfully opposed a prosecution application that section 46 anonymity was needed for a barrister to improve the quality of his evidence. He was a prosecution witness in an assault case in which—the prosecution said—the defendant was expected to make derogatory allegations (*Media Lawyer*, 7 April 2009).

Does the section 46 order serve much purpose?

If a prosecution witness's identity is known to the defendant—almost always the case—the defendant will tell associates who he/she is. In such cases, the only purpose of section 46 anonymity would be to shield the adult witness's identity from the rest of the population. A journalist can ask the court why a witness's identity has to be shielded if the defendant already knows it and can tell others.

👁 Case study

In 2007 a judge at Kingston Crown court made a section 46 order banning identification of witnesses due to testify as the victims of an attempted robbery. But she lifted it after the Newsquest newspaper group and local reporters pointed out that the defendants knew the witnesses, whose identities were already in the public domain as they had previously been named in open court, and that if the order were to remain in force, the media would no longer be able to identify the victims or say where the offence occurred (*Holdthefrontpage* website and *Media Lawyer*, 19 and 20 September 2007).

There have been occasions when a judge has made a section 46 order although it was clear that the person whose identity it protected would not be giving evidence because the defendant had already pleaded guilty—so no trial would take place. Such an order can be challenged as invalid because section 46 was created to safeguard the quality of evidence and level of cooperation provided by a person due to testify in a trial.

Section 45A anonymity for juvenile witnesses and juvenile victims

The Criminal Justice and Courts Act 2015 inserted a new section—section 45A—into the 1999 Act to give criminal courts a discretionary power to provide a juvenile witness or juvenile victim/alleged victim—that is, a person aged under 18—with the lifetime anonymity which a section 46 order can give to adult witnesses. The same circumstances have to apply—that the juvenile is in 'fear' or 'distress', etc: see ch. 9, p. 100, Lifetime anonymity for juvenile witness or victim/alleged victim, for detail of section 45A. The Act's wording means that a court can revoke or relax a section 45A order in the same circumstances as it can revoke or relax a section 46 order. A section 45A order made unnecessarily or invalidly can be challenged on the same grounds as such a section 46 order can be challenged—see earlier.

▌ Sexual offence law does *not* give anonymity to defendants

As ch. 10 explains, the Sexual Offences (Amendment) Act 1992 bans the media from identifying victims and alleged victims of sexual offences. Occasionally magistrates and judges assert that the Act allows them to ban the media from identifying a defendant, insisting that anonymity for a defendant is necessary as an extra precaution to prevent media reports including detail likely to identify a victim/alleged victim. But there is no such power in the Act. The Judicial College guidance states this.

> ((•)) See Useful Websites at the end of this chapter for the College guidance.

👁 Case study

In 2012 the Court of Appeal ruled that a judge at Cambridge Crown court was wrong to ban the media from identifying a convicted rapist, purportedly under section 1 of the 1992 Act. The judge had ruled such a ban was necessary to stop the media, by naming the rapist, inadvertently identifying the victim. The Court of Appeal agreed with Press Association Legal Editor Mike Dodd (who is co-author of *McNae's*) that the Act contains no power to grant anonymity to a defendant. The Court agreed that the responsibility for preserving in reports the lifelong anonymity automatically granted by the Act to sexual offence victims rested with editors and those reporting such a trial, not with the trial court (*R (Press Association) v Cambridge Crown Court* [2012] EWCA Crim 2434).

▌ Postponement of reports of derogatory mitigation

Section 58 of the Criminal Procedure and Investigations Act 1996 allows courts to ban, for 12 months, publication of an assertion which is derogatory of a person's character and which is made during a speech in mitigation. The banning order cannot be made if the assertion was aired during the trial or at any other stage of the proceedings prior to the mitigation speech.

 See the Additional Material for ch. 11 on www.mcnaes.com for more details of this restriction and for grounds of challenge if it is made invalidly.

➡ Recap of major points

- Challenges to reporting restrictions can be made by a reporter addressing the court or by an editor writing to it. If this fails, the challenge can be taken to a higher court.

- An order under section 11 of the Contempt of Court Act 1981 should only be made if the relevant name or matter has already been deliberately withheld by the court from its public proceedings.

- A court order bestowing anonymity on safety grounds is only justified if the risk which publicity would create for that person is 'real and immediate', verified by evidence.

- An order under section 4(2) of the Contempt of Court Act to postpone media reporting of a case should only be made to avoid a substantial risk of prejudice to a pending or imminent hearing.

- A section 45 or section 39 order cannot be made in respect of an adult or a dead juvenile. It can be argued that a baby or toddler is too young to need it.

- Journalists arguing for a youth court, magistrates' court or Crown court to permit reports of a case to identify a juvenile defendant can cite Home Office and CPS guidance on this.

- An anonymity order under sections 45A or 46 of the Youth Justice and Criminal Evidence Act 1999 should only be made if the witness is eligible and if the order is needed to achieve the relevant section's purpose.

((•)) Useful Websites

www.justice.gov.uk/courts/procedure-rules/criminal/rulesmenu-2015#Anchor1
Criminal Procedure Rules

www.judiciary.gov.uk/publications/reporting-restrictions-in-the-criminal-courts-2/
Judicial College guidance, *Reporting Restrictions in the Criminal Courts*, including supplementary guidance

www.cps.gov.uk/legal/p_to_r/prosecuting_advocates_instructions/
Crown Prosecution Service (CPS) general guidance to prosecutors on reporting restrictions

www.gov.uk/government/uploads/system/uploads/attachment_data/file/442151/2015-07-03_FINAL_Guidance_Part_2_SOA_2003.pdf
Home Office guidance on sexual harm prevention and sexual risk orders

www.gov.uk/government/uploads/system/uploads/attachment_data/file/449991/Guidance_on_Slavery_and_Trafficking_Prevention_Orders_and_Slavery_and_Trafficking_Risk_Orders_under_Part_2_of_the_Modern_Slavery_Act_2015.pdf
Home Office guidance on slavery and trafficking prevention and risk orders

www.cps.gov.uk/legal/p_to_r/reporting_restrictions/
CPS guidance to prosecutors on reporting restrictions concerning juveniles

www.holdthefrontpage.co.uk/2011/news/under-18s-involved-in-riots-could-be-named/
Report of CPS 2011 guidance to courts on lifting anonymity for juvenile offenders

http://webarchive.nationalarchives.gov.uk/20100405140447/http:/asb.homeoffice.gov.uk/uploadedFiles/Members_site/Documents_and_images/Enforcement_tools_and_powers/ASBOs_PublicisingGuidance_0031.pdf
Home Office guidance, *Publicising Anti-social Behaviour Orders*

www.gov.uk/government/uploads/system/uploads/attachment_data/file/251312/01_Factsheet_Replacing_the_ASBO_-_updated_for_Lords.pdf
Home Office factsheet, *Replacing the ASBO*

16

Coroners' courts

Chapter summary

Coroners investigate certain types of death to establish the cause. The inquests they hold are court hearings, often newsworthy. This chapter outlines coroners' duties and explains why some inquests have juries. The Contempt of Court Act 1981 affects what can be reported, and coroners can impose reporting restrictions to give witnesses and children anonymity. Media coverage of inquests must be sensitive to the grief of the bereaved. In another role, coroners' courts decide whether a found object should be classed as historical 'treasure'.

▌ Overview of the coroner system

A coroner—the office dates from the twelfth century—is appointed to serve a district. Coroners must have practised as a barrister or solicitor for five years (in 2013 the government agreed that suitably qualified legal executives could also become coroners). There remain some who are not lawyers but practised as doctors. The Coroners and Justice Act 2009 says new coroners must be legally qualified. Coroners investigate the causes and circumstances of certain types of death, in some cases having hearings in their courts to do so. The other role of the coroner system is to decide whether found historical objects should be classed as 'treasure'. Both types of hearing are called 'inquests'.

The 2009 Act, which took effect in 2013, reformed the system. Coroners' districts became known as 'areas', and some have been merged to form larger ones. The former offices of coroner, deputy coroner and assistant deputy coroner became, respectively, senior coroner, area coroner and assistant coroner.

Chief Coroner

The 2009 Act created the national post of Chief Coroner, whose duties include providing leadership for coroners, setting national standards for their work, approving coroner appointments (which are made by local authorities) and reporting annually to the Lord Chancellor on how the coroner system is performing.

▌ Investigations into deaths

Under the 2009 Act a coroner must investigate certain categories of death: those for which he/she has reason to suspect the cause is unknown; those which are 'violent or unnatural'; and those of people in custody or otherwise held in state detention. 'Violent or unnatural' deaths include those caused by crime, accidents, suicide, neglect or lack of care, excessive alcohol, drug abuse or any other form of poisoning. Police and doctors have a duty to report such deaths to the local coroner. Anyone concerned about the circumstances of a death can report it. Those in 'state detention' include people held in police stations, prisons, immigration detention centres and mental hospitals.

A coroner has the right at common law to take possession of a body to make his/her inquiries.

▌ Inquests into deaths

Not all investigations require an inquest. There may be no need if, for example, a post-mortem examination shows that someone died of natural causes. But holding an inquest means a coroner can require witnesses to testify. Inquests help keep communities and institutions vigilant about fatal dangers, and reassure the public that suspicious deaths are investigated. Inquest determinations on how people died are included in national statistics such as those for road accidents.

✳ Remember

An inquest is a fact-finding hearing to establish the reason for a death. It does not decide who, if anyone, might be criminally responsible—that is the role of the criminal courts in, for example, murder cases. The civil courts decide if any party must pay damages to a deceased person's family.

A coroner's jurisdiction to hold an inquest arises from the fact that the body is in his/her district. A coroner must hold an inquest if a body has been brought into his/her district from abroad and he/she has reason to suspect the death was violent or unnatural—which is why the deaths of UK service personnel overseas give rise to inquests in the UK.

Purpose of inquests into deaths

The purpose of a coroner's investigation into a death, and therefore of an inquest if one is held, is:

- to determine who the deceased was;
- to determine how, when and where he/she came by his/her death; and
- to make 'findings' on the particulars about the death which have to be registered according to statute.

Establishing a deceased's identity is usually straightforward, but may require lengthy investigation if, for example, a decomposed body is found. The particulars, which have to be communicated to the Registrar of Births, Marriages and Deaths, include the deceased's name, the date and place of death, and his/her gender, age, address and occupation.

In most inquests the decisions are made by a coroner alone. But juries figure in some inquests to decide on facts, with a coroner presiding to rule on law and procedure.

Inquests which have juries

The practice of having juries in some types of inquest helps safeguard civil liberties and public health—for example, by providing scrutiny other than by officialdom of police, prisons and workplace safety.

Under the 2009 Act, an inquest must be held with a jury if the senior coroner has reason to suspect that the death falls into one of these categories:

- the deceased was in custody or otherwise in state detention *and* the death was either violent or unnatural or the cause is unknown;
- the death resulted from an act or omission of a police officer or member of a police force of the armed services in the execution of his/her duty;
- the death was caused by those types of accident, poisoning or disease which by law must be notified to a government department or inspector, such as workplace fatalities.

An inquest into any other type of death may also be held with a jury if the senior coroner thinks there is 'sufficient reason'. An inquest jury, selected randomly from electoral rolls, comprises at least seven and not more than 11 people.

see Useful Websites at the end of this chapter for the Rules

▶ Rules

Section 45 of the 2009 Act enables the Lord Chancellor to make rules to govern coroners' work. The Coroners (Inquests) Rules 2013 govern inquest procedure.

Information about inquests

Rule 9 of the 2013 Rules says a coroner must notify the dead person's next of kin and any 'interested person who have made themselves known' to the coroner of the date, time and place of the inquest hearing within one week of setting the date, and must make such details publicly available before the inquest commences. Guidance from the Chief Coroner makes clear that this is to ensure that the media can attend if they wish.

see Useful Websites at the end of this chapter for this guidance

---

👁 Case study

Lincolnshire coroner Stuart Fisher showed in 2006 how helpful coroners can be. After being called by a Press Association reporter about an inquest he had held the previous day into a baby's death, Mr Fisher fetched the file on the hearing from the boot of his car and proceeded to read his conclusions, as well as evidence from witnesses (*Media Lawyer*, 13 April 2006).

Admission to inquests

A coroner investigating a death by means of an inquest may hold three types of hearing—'a pre-inquest review hearing' (rule 6), the opening of the inquest and the full hearing.

The 'opening' is usually an initial, brief hearing for the coroner formally to ascertain the deceased's identity. The inquest can then be adjourned—there having already been a post-mortem examination and possibly burial or cremation—and is usually resumed after a period of weeks or months to hear evidence gathered about the circumstances of the death.

Rule 11 says that generally any pre-inquest hearing and the inquest hearings must be held in public but that:

see also pp. 210–211, Defamation and contempt issues in media coverage

- a coroner may direct that the public be excluded from a pre-inquest review hearing if he/she considers it would be in the interests of justice to do so;

- a coroner who does not have immediate access to a courtroom or other appropriate place in which to open the inquest may open it privately and then announce that it has been opened at the next hearing held in public;

- as regards a pre-inquest review hearing or any inquest hearing, a coroner can direct that the public (a term which here would include journalists) should be excluded from all or part of it because he/she considers it would be in the interests of national security to do so.

There is nothing in the Rules to stop a coroner allowing journalists to attend a pre-inquest review if the only reason the public has been excluded is to avoid noisy disruption to the process of justice.

The airing of evidence

Unlike the criminal courts, where the process is accusatorial, adversarial and subject to strict rules on how evidence is given, an inquest is inquisitorial. The coroner can 'lead' witnesses through their evidence.

Rule 23 allows a coroner to take written rather than oral evidence from any witness if satisfied that this evidence is unlikely to be disputed, or that it is not possible for the witness to attend at all or within a reasonable time, or that there is a 'good and sufficient reason' why he/she should not attend or to believe he/she will not attend. So, the coroner may decide, for example, that a busy hospital doctor has no need to attend an inquest to testify in person.

But the rule says that the coroner must, in any circumstance in which he/she accepts written evidence, announce the nature of the evidence and the witness's full name at the inquest hearing, and that any 'interested person' is entitled to see a copy of any written evidence.

It adds that: 'A coroner may direct that all or parts only of any written evidence submitted under this rule may be read aloud at the inquest hearing.'

Coroners generally read written evidence aloud. But if it is not read out, a journalist would have a strong argument to be allowed to see it, because of Article 10 rights, the open justice principle and the decision of the Court of Appeal in *R (Guardian News and Media) v City of Westminster Magistrates' Court* [2011] 1 WLR 3253, [2011] EWCA Civ 1188.

 Ch. 14, p. 169, Access to material in criminal cases, gives more detail on this appeal case and ch. 1, p. 7, Convention rights, explains Article 10 rights.

Coroners do not usually read suicide notes aloud, to spare the bereaved further anguish.

Access to documents

The 2009 Act was intended to increase transparency in inquests. Reflecting this, the 2013 Rules require coroners to keep a recording of every inquest hearing, including 'pre-inquest reviews', and formalise when a coroner must disclose documents. Rule 13 says a coroner must provide to anyone who is an 'interested person' in the case—for example, the deceased's next of kin—any document in the case or a copy of it, including the post-mortem report and where available the recording of the inquest hearing, or must make the document available for inspection by that person as soon as is reasonably practical. 'Document' means any medium in which information is recorded. It is unlikely that a journalist would be classed as an 'interested person' under rule 13. But the recent creation of rules for criminal courts giving journalists qualified access to case documents and the Court of Appeal decision in the *Guardian News and Media* case mean there are strong arguments that journalists should have similar access to inquest documents.

 ch. 14 covers these criminal court rules

Rules 14 and 15 permit a coroner to redact a document before disclosure or to refuse to disclose it in some circumstances—for example, when it relates to commenced criminal proceedings. A coroner may also restrict how a disclosed document can be used—a next of kin or journalist who ignores that restriction could be punished for contempt of court. If a coroner discloses a document before or during an inquest, no fee can be charged for it.

▶ Inquest determinations and conclusions—formerly 'verdicts'

An inquest produces a decision on what caused a death, determined by the coroner, or the jury if there is one. These decisions, announced at inquests, are traditionally referred to as 'verdicts'. It has become the journalistic convention to report that a coroner's jury *returns* a verdict and that a coroner sitting without a jury *records* a verdict. The 2009 Act uses the term 'determination' to denote a decision as to the identity of the deceased, and how, when and where he/she died. But it seems likely that 'verdict' will continue to be used colloquially, though the term 'conclusion' is now officially used too.

Determinations can, as was the case with verdicts, be expressed in 'short-form conclusions' comprising single words or short phrases including 'natural causes', 'accident', 'road traffic collision', 'misadventure', 'drug-related', 'industrial disease', 'unlawful killing' or 'suicide'. An 'open' determination is recorded or returned when an inquest decides there is insufficient evidence for any other conclusion.

Narrative conclusions

Recent years have seen increasing use of **narrative verdicts**—brief statements →glossary summing up the coroner's or jury's conclusions on how the deceased came to die, providing some factual detail. These can include the 'short-form' terminology.

The use of such narrative conclusions also fulfils a requirement that a coroner should allow a jury to express a brief conclusion about disputed facts at the centre of the case, so that inquest procedure complies with Article 2 of the European Convention on Human Rights, the right to life, on the principle that a jury must be able to express conclusions in a way which can help avoid similar loss of life. Coroners also usually make concluding remarks to focus public attention on lessons to be learnt from a death and have a legal duty to produce reports for the Chief Coroner if an inquest has revealed circumstances which could continue to place lives at risk.

 Article 2 is set out in Appendix 1, p. 461; ch. 1, pp. 6–8, The European Convention on Human Rights, gives context.

ch. 17 outlines the law on public inquiries

▶ Related criminal proceedings

When someone is suspected of crime in connection with a death, an inquest is usually opened, then adjourned until after any criminal proceedings have ended. The inquest may then be resumed if there is sufficient cause. For example, if someone accused of a murder is acquitted, an inquest may subsequently return a determination of unlawful killing while not attributing blame. If a public inquiry is instigated under the Inquiries Act 2005 to consider why a person or people died—for example, in a rail crash—the Lord Chancellor can direct that any inquest should be adjourned. It will not be reopened unless there is an exceptional reason.

▶ Review of inquest decisions

There is no direct route of appeal against an inquest decision, but an aggrieved person with sufficient legal interest in the case—for example, a deceased's next of kin—can apply to the High Court for judicial review. This could result in that court making an order to quash an inquest determination and to order that a fresh inquest should be held.

▶ Defamation and contempt issues in media coverage

privilege is explained in ch. 21

An inquest is a type of court proceeding, so fair, accurate and contemporaneous reports of an inquest held in public are protected from libel actions by absolute privilege. Non-contemporaneous reports are protected by qualified privilege if the requirements of that defence are met.

Publication of material heard in any part of an inquest held in private will not be protected by privilege in libel law and—if the inquest is being conducted in private on national security grounds—could be deemed a contempt of court as a breach of section 12 of the Administration of Justice Act 1960, which is explained in ch. 11.

An inquest is covered by the Contempt of Court Act 1981 (the 1981 Act). As explained in ch. 18, it is a contempt to publish material which creates 'a substantial risk of serious prejudice or impediment' to an active case. The Court of Appeal has ruled that an inquest becomes 'active' when it is opened (*Peacock v London Weekend Television* (1986) 150 JP 71). It seems unlikely that a coroner, being an experienced professional, could be prejudiced in his/her considerations by media coverage. But the media should take care, in an inquest case in which a jury is or could be involved, not to publish material which creates a substantial risk of serious prejudice or impediment to its deliberations. The media should also avoid publishing material which could breach the Act by affecting a witness's testimony.

An inquest may precede a hearing in a criminal court into the same events—for example, an inquest might be opened, then adjourned, because someone is charged with murder. The media can safely report that inquest hearing contemporaneously if it is held in public, because the report—provided it is fair, accurate and published in good faith—will be protected by section 4 of the 1981 Act unless the coroner has made an order under section 4(2) postponing reporting of the hearing.

▌Reporting restrictions

Coroners can make orders restricting media reports of inquests—for example, by using section 39 of the Children and Young Persons Act 1933 to give a juvenile witness anonymity, a power explained in ch. 9.

Coroners also have **inherent jurisdiction** in common law and under Article 2 of the European Convention on Human Rights to order that a witness should have anonymity in inquest proceedings—for example, to prevent a real and immediate risk to his/her life (*R (on the application of Officer A) v HM Coroner for Inner South London and others* [2004] EWHC Admin 1592). Article 8 rights—for example, for the protection of family life—may also be cited in favour of anonymity.

→glossary

 See also ch. 15, pp. 187–188, Anonymity and risk of attack?, on anonymity for police officers.

👁 Case study

The media successfully opposed an attempt by the Greater Manchester police force to preserve anonymity for five policemen due to give evidence at an inquest in 2015. It concerned the death of factory worker Jordon Begley, aged 23. He died in hospital from a cardiac arrest about two hours after one of the officers shot him with a police-issue 50,000 volt Taser electric stun gun for nine seconds, leading to him being restrained. Manchester coroner Nigel Meadows lifted a temporary anonymity order, agreeing with media organisations that there was no specific evidence of any 'real and immediate' risk to the officers' safety if they were identified in reports of the inquest.

Up to 11 officers had gone to Mr Begley's home after his mother rang 999 because he had threatened to take a knife outside following a row with a neighbour. She told the inquest that her son, who had a history of alcohol and drug abuse, had nothing in his hands and had begun to obey police instructions before being Tasered. But the police officer who fired the Taser said he feared Begley had a concealed weapon, and Begley began to walk towards him despite being told to stand still. The inquest jury concluded that the restraint methods and use of the Taser 'more than materially contributed' to a 'package' of stress factors which caused Mr Begley's death (*Media Lawyer*, 3 February 2015; *BBC*, 2 June 2015; *The Guardian*, 6 July 2015).

Common law and statutory protections of witnesses and jurors apply to inquest proceedings, as does the ban on photography, filming and audio-recording in courts. Ch. 11 explains these laws.

Part 1A of Schedule 6 to the Coroners and Justice Act 2009, inserted by the Criminal Justice and Courts Act 2015, protects the confidentiality of an inquest's jury's deliberations. This law is, in essence, the same as law in the Juries Act 1974, which covers other courts—see ch. 11, pp. 126–127, Confidentiality of jury deliberations.

▷ Media challenges to reporting restrictions or lack of access

judicial review is explained in ch. 15, p. 181

Any media challenge to a reporting restriction imposed by a coroner, or to a decision to exclude the media from an inquest, must—if the coroner will not reconsider—be made to the High Court as an application for judicial review.

▷ Ethical considerations when covering deaths

chs. 2 and 3 introduce the codes

The Editors' Code and the Broadcasting Code set out ethical standards, explained in ch. 27, to minimise media intrusion into bereaved people's grief or shock. These are particularly pertinent to coverage of inquests. The Editors' Code and Broadcasting Code also say that excessive detail about suicide methods should not be published.

see Useful Websites at the end of this chapter

Samaritans has published media guidance on reporting suicides.

▷ Treasure inquests

Historically, coroners' courts have decided whether historical objects found on or buried in the ground should be classed as 'treasure'. The Crown or a franchisee has legal rights to take possession of valuable objects ruled to have been treasure deliberately hidden by a past generation—for example, buried for safety during warfare. The Treasure Act 1996 amended this ancient law to encourage those who use metal-detectors to declare discoveries so that museums can decide if they want the found objects. The Act has various definitions of treasure, including:

- a found object which is not a single coin, which contains at least 10 per cent of gold or silver and which is at least 300 years old, and any other object found with it.

Anyone with reasonable grounds for believing an object they have found might be classed as treasure is required to notify a coroner within 14 days of the discovery or the realisation. Failure to do so is punishable by a fine or a jail term of up to three months.

The coroner, once notified or if he/she has reason to suspect any other found object is treasure, must hold an investigation, which could involve an inquest with a jury if there is 'sufficient reason'.

If the find is ruled to be treasure, the British Museum or National Museum of Wales is given the opportunity to acquire it. The finder can be paid a reward, based on the treasure's market value, from public funds, and some money may be awarded to the owner of the land on which the treasure was found.

The reward may be reduced, or not even offered, if the finder was trespassing or illegally disturbing an archaeological site. If the object is not classed as treasure or no museum wants it, the finder can keep or sell it, subject to the rights of the land-owner or occupier.

((•)) see Useful Websites at the end of this chapter for treasure definitions

➡ Recap of major points

- The purpose of an inquest is to find out who a deceased person was and how he/she died.
- A coroner can exclude the public and journalists from an inquest on grounds of national security.
- Coroners can impose reporting restrictions.
- Inquests are court hearings and so are covered by the law of contempt of court, which can affect media coverage.
- A treasure inquest decides if a found historical object should be classed as 'treasure', in which case a museum is given the opportunity to acquire it.

((•)) Useful Websites

www.legislation.gov.uk/uksi/2013/1616/article/34/made
    Coroners (Inquests) Rules 2013

www.gov.uk/after-a-death/
    Government guidance on inquests into deaths

www.judiciary.gov.uk/publications/
the-chief-coroners-guide-to-the-coroners-and-justice-act-2009/
   Chief Coroner's guidance on the Coroners and Justice Act 2009—see paragraphs
   110–116

www.judiciary.gov.uk/related-offices-and-bodies/office-chief-coroner/
   Information about the Chief Coroner

www.coronersociety.org.uk/
   The Coroners' Society of England and Wales

www.courtsni.gov.uk/en-GB/Services/Coroners/Pages/default.aspx
   Coroners Service for Northern Ireland

www.inquest.org.uk/
   Inquest—a charity providing free advice to the bereaved on contentious deaths

www.samaritans.org/media-centre/media-guidelines-reporting-suicide
   Samaritans' media guidelines on reporting suicides

www.gov.uk/treasure
   Government guidance on treasure, including definitions

Tribunals and public inquiries

Chapter summary

Tribunals are specialist judicial bodies which decide disputes in particular areas of law. The UK has a wide range of tribunals with a huge annual caseload which can yield news and human interest stories. Tribunals adjudicate issues such as asylum and immigration cases, the rents tenants can be charged, whether a patient in a secure mental health hospital is safe to return to the outside world, benefit entitlements and employment disputes. Some tribunals are termed a 'commission' or 'panel'. Some regulate professions and decide, for example, whether doctors or lawyers should be banned from practising because of misconduct. The term 'public inquiry' denotes other kinds of legal investigatory process.

▌ Tribunals in the administrative justice system

Most tribunals are official bodies which make decisions determining someone's legal rights. There are more than 70 types of tribunal. The majority rule on disputes between an individual, or a private organisation, and a state agency—for example, about tax obligations, benefit entitlements or immigration status. The annual workload of tribunals in the UK's 'administrative justice' system can exceed 700,000 cases.

Tribunals listed here are among those which may be of particular interest to journalists.

Immigration and Asylum Chamber of the First-tier Tribunal This hears appeals against decisions made by the Home Secretary and his/her officials in asylum, immigration and nationality matters.

Health, Education and Social Care Chamber of the First-tier Tribunal This hears, for example, appeals from people who have been banned from working for organisations concerned with children and vulnerable adults, and includes the First-tier Tribunal (Mental Health) for England, which hears appeals from patients detained under the Mental Health Act 1983 for release from secure mental hospitals. Wales has a separate Mental Health Review Tribunal.

Property Chamber (Residential Property) of the First-tier Tribunal This hears, for example, appeals against rent levels fixed by a rent officer for regulated tenancies.

The First-tier Tribunal is a generic tribunal created to merge the administration of most tribunals dealing with appeals against decisions made by state officials. First-tier Tribunal decisions may, in some instances, be appealed to, or be reviewed by, the next tier of the administrative justice system, known as the Upper Tribunal.

Special Immigration Appeals Commission (SIAC) This hears appeals against Home Office decisions to deport, or exclude, people from the UK on national security or public interest grounds and appeals against decisions to deprive people of UK citizenship.

ch. 34 warns about police surveillance of journalists

Investigatory Powers Tribunal Created by the Regulation of Investigatory Powers Act 2000 (RIPA), this investigates and rules on complaints that public authorities—including intelligence, police or other law enforcement agencies—have unlawfully used covert surveillance techniques, breaching people's rights to privacy or other human rights. RIPA stipulates that the tribunal hears cases in secret but it has held some public hearings.

 The Additional Material for ch. 17 on www.mcnaes.com gives an outline of the procedural rules of these tribunals, which say who can attend them and specify when they can prohibit the disclosure or publication of specified documents or information relating to their proceedings.

▌ Examples of disciplinary tribunals

The disciplinary tribunals listed below, being those of regulated professions, are not part of the 'administrative justice' system.

Medical Practitioners Tribunal Service This tribunal of the General Medical Council hears complaints against doctors in its fitness to practise panels. These normally sit in public, but can sit in private—for example, when considering confidential information concerning a doctor's health.

Solicitors Disciplinary Tribunal This must, in general, sit in public to hear allegations of professional misconduct against solicitors. But it can in some circumstances exclude the public from all or any part of a hearing.

✳ Remember

Amendment in 2015 to the Police (Conduct) Regulations 2012 means that the default position is now that a police force disciplinary panel should sit in public when considering alleged gross misconduct by a police officer or a special constable, or when the force believes there are grounds for him/her to be sacked without delay. But these Regulations are weak in promoting transparency, because they allow the panel chair, as he/she sees fit, to exclude any person from the hearing—so that it can sit in private—and there is no duty to notify the public or media of when and where the hearing will take place.

 For more detail on these disciplinary tribunals, and those for barristers and nurses, see the Additional Material for ch. 17 on www.mcnaes.com.

▶ Defamation and contempt issues in reporting tribunals

A tribunal is classed as a court if it exercises 'the judicial power of the State'—a definition in section 14 of the Defamation Act 1996 and section 19 of the Contempt of Court Act 1981.

Tribunals which are courts

The Upper Tribunal, the Special Immigration Appeals Commission and the Employment Appeal Tribunal were each created by statute to be a 'superior court of record', and so are courts under the 1996 and 1981 Acts. There is case law that employment tribunals and First-tier Tribunals in the administrative justice system run by HM Courts and Tribunals Service, including mental health review tribunals, also meet this definition. The Investigatory Powers Tribunal says it is a type of court (but not required by law to have public hearings). If a tribunal is classed as a court, this determines how defamation and contempt laws apply to journalists covering its cases.

Privilege in coverage of tribunals

If a tribunal is classed as a court, then under the Defamation Act 1996 a fair and accurate media report of its proceedings held in public, if published contemporaneously, is protected by absolute privilege, and if non-contemporaneous, such a report is protected by qualified privilege under Part 1 of the Act's Schedule 1, with no requirement to publish 'explanation or contradiction'. These defamation defences are explained in ch. 21.

In 2009 the High Court ruled that a media account of the proceedings of the Solicitors Disciplinary Tribunal enjoyed absolute privilege (*Imran Karim v Newsquest* [2009] EWHC 3205 (QB)), which means that the High Court classed it as a court. But such case law does not exist or is not conclusive for some tribunals.

ch. 21, pp. 286–288, The requirements of qualified privilege, explains the defence

However, the disciplinary tribunals of some other professions and other types of tribunal derive their powers from an Act of Parliament. In the case of any tribunal constituted by or under, or exercising functions under, statutory provision, a media report of its public proceedings will be protected by qualified privilege bestowed by paragraph 11 of Part 2 of Schedule 1 to the Defamation Act 1996 if all the requirements of that defence are met. Again, these include that the report fairly and accurately reflects the proceedings. Also, a requirement is that, at the request of anyone defamed by the published report, a reasonable letter or statement of explanation or contradiction must be published.

✳ Remember

This type of qualified privilege also protects fair and accurate reports of the findings (but not of the proceedings) of the disciplinary committees of certain private associations—for example, in the field of sport, business and learning. See ch. 21, p. 291, Disciplinary actions by private associations.

Proceedings are not always formal

The proceedings of many tribunals are not as formal as those in an ordinary court of law. An appellant might not be represented by a lawyer. Journalists should remember that qualified privilege does not extend to any published matter which is not 'of public interest' and the publication of which is not 'for the public benefit'—so a flare-up at a hearing of irrelevant, personal abuse may well be such matter.

Contempt issues in coverage of tribunals which are courts

If a tribunal is classed as a court, the Contempt of Court Act 1981 applies, which means that the media should not publish material which could create 'a substantial risk of serious prejudice or impediment' to any of the tribunal's 'active' cases. Contempt law is explained generally in ch. 18. Under the 1981 Act's Schedule 1, a tribunal case is 'active' 'when arrangements for the hearing are made or, if no such arrangements are previously made, from the time the hearing begins. It remains 'active' until 'the proceedings are disposed of or discontinued or withdrawn'.

In many instances, it would be unlikely that media stories about an 'active' tribunal case—for example, published before its full hearing—could create a substantial risk of serious prejudice or impediment, in that judges and/or professionals such as doctors or lawyers preside in tribunals and are unlikely to be influenced by media reports. But there is a possibility that such media reports could affect witnesses in their testimony. Media contact with a witness prior to such a hearing could be punished as contempt in common law if it were ruled to amount to interference with him/her.

Other restrictions

Unauthorised use of cameras or audio-recorders at a tribunal classed as a court could be punished as common law contempt or a breach of the 1981 Act or the Criminal Justice Act 1925. If such a tribunal holds a hearing in private, it may be held to be contempt under section 12 of the Administration of Justice Act 1960 to report what was said in that hearing in a case concerning mental health, national security, the welfare or upbringing of children, or secret processes and in any other case in which the tribunal expressly prohibited publication of information.

Ch. 11 explains these restrictions.

 See the Additional Material for ch. 17 on www.mcnaes.com, 'Tribunals which are courts', for further detail of relevant law.

▌ Employment tribunals

Employment tribunals adjudicate on complaints against employers—for example, of unfair dismissal or of 'constructive dismissal' in which a person claims that he/she had to quit the job because of improper conduct by another/others in the workplace. They also adjudicate on complaints that employers discriminated on grounds of gender, race or age.

Employment tribunals are based in regional centres. For some types of case an employment tribunal has three members: a lawyer—appointed to be an 'employment judge'—who is chair and two lay members, one with experience as an employer and one with a background as an employee—for example, a trade unionist. Unfair dismissal claims are now among those which can be decided by an employment judge sitting alone.

Procedure

Employment tribunal hearings in England, Wales and Scotland are governed by rules set out in the Employment Tribunals (Constitution and Rules of Procedure) Regulations 2013.

Northern Ireland has its own system of employment tribunals.

Hearings in employment tribunal cases tend to be informal. A case may have more than one 'preliminary hearing' for rulings by an employment judge on whether the case can proceed or on case management. If it proceeds, there is a further hearing, referred to in the rules as the 'final' hearing. This may last several days. In it the tribunal first decides on *liability*—whether the complaint

((•))
see Useful Websites at the end of this chapter for these rules

against the employer is justified. This decision may be announced in summary on the same day it is made but may not be revealed until sent out later in a written judgment. If the employer is held liable, subsequently—often after an adjournment of some weeks—there is another 'final hearing' in which the tribunal decides the *remedy*—for example, requiring the employer to pay compensation to someone sacked unfairly. If the tribunal finds employment law has been breached, it can also impose a financial penalty on the employer.

Rule 46 of Schedule 1 to the 2013 Regulations permits all or part of a tribunal hearing to be conducted 'by use of electronic communication', including by telephone, provided that members of the public attending the hearing are able to hear what the tribunal hears and see any witness as seen by the tribunal.

Appeals on points of law from employment tribunal decisions can be made to the Employment Appeal Tribunal (EAT).

Information about pending cases and judgments

for these sites, see Useful Websites at the end of this chapter

Employment tribunal staff are instructed to provide journalists with the details of the parties in a case and the nature of the claim once it is listed for a hearing. Lists of hearings due to take place can also be obtained a week in advance through the *CourtServe* website. Journalists wanting a copy of a judgment can, if a regional tribunal office refuses to supply it, get it from the public register of judgments which keeps them for at least six years.

EAT judgments can be read online at its website.

Admission to employment tribunal cases

Rule 56 of Schedule 1 to the 2013 Regulations states that a preliminary hearing shall be conducted in public if it involves a ruling on a 'preliminary issue', or is considering if all or part of a claim or response should be struck out—for example, because it has no reasonable prospect of success. A preliminary hearing can be held in private if dealing with case management or exploring if there can be a settlement. Rule 59 says final hearings shall be in public. But rules 56 and 59 are subject to other rules which empower a tribunal to sit in private.

see ch. 1, pp. 6–8, The European Convention on Human Rights, and ch. 26 on privacy

Rule 50 says that a tribunal can sit in private if it considers this necessary 'in the interests of justice', or in circumstances set out in section 10A of the Employment Tribunals Act 1996, or to protect a person's rights under the European Convention on Human Rights—for example, the right to privacy.

Section 10A of the 1996 Act says an employment tribunal can sit in private:

- when a witness's evidence is likely to contain:
  - information which he/she cannot disclose without breaking statutory law or without breaking an obligation of confidence; or
  - information which would cause substantial injury to any undertaking of his/her, or his/her employer's, interests other than interests in collective negotiations over pay, conditions, trade union membership or representation.

! Remember your rights

The rule 50 provision—that an employment tribunal can exclude the public (and therefore journalists too) from a hearing in order to protect a person's Convention rights—reflects **case law** developments in recent years. This rule could lead to more instances of people or companies arguing that cases should be heard in private. Journalists wishing to argue against an order to exclude them should remember that, according to rule 50, a tribunal deciding whether to sit in private 'shall give full weight to the principle of open justice' and to the right to freedom of expression (in the Convention's Article 10).

→ glossary

see also ch. 14 on open justice

Rule 50 adds that any person with a legitimate interest (which would include a journalist wanting to cover the case) who has not had a reasonable opportunity to make representations against an exclusion order 'may apply to the tribunal in writing for the order to be revoked or discharged, either on the basis of written representations or, if requested, at a hearing'.

A Minister of the Crown, under the 1996 Act's section 10 and rule 94 of the 2013 Regulations can direct an employment tribunal to hear a case in private in the interests of national security—if the tribunal has not already decided to do so.

👁 Case study

The High Court has ruled that an employment tribunal is not empowered to sit in private merely because there is to be evidence of a sensitive or salacious nature when sexual misconduct is alleged (*R v Southampton Industrial Tribunal, ex p INS News Group Ltd and Express Newspapers plc* [1995] IRLR 247).

Witness statements

In an employment tribunal, as in a civil court, usually a witness's written statement is his/her **evidence-in-chief**. The witness may give oral evidence too, but a journalist will probably need to see the written statement to understand the case.

→ glossary

see ch. 12, p. 143, Full trial procedure, for civil court procedure

! Remember your rights

Rule 44 of Schedule 1 to the 2013 Regulations says that any witness statement which stands as evidence-in-chief shall be available for inspection during the hearing by members of the public (and therefore journalists) attending it unless the tribunal decides that all or any part of the statement is not to be admitted as evidence. But the tribunal has the power under rules 50 (for example, on privacy grounds) or 94 (national security grounds) to revoke this inspection right.

Reporting and disclosure restrictions

Rule 50 empowers employment tribunals, on their own initiative or at the request of a party, to make an order 'with a view to preventing or restricting the public disclosure of any aspect of those proceedings' if the tribunal considers this necessary 'in the interests of justice' or in order to protect the Convention rights—including the privacy—of any person, or in the circumstances described in section 10A of the 1996 Act (which are set out earlier).

Such an order can ban indefinitely the disclosure of parts of the evidence and/or the identities of 'specified parties, witnesses or other persons referred to in the proceedings' or in any documents 'forming part of the public record' of the case, including its listing and judgment.

see ch. 9, pp. 102–103, Jigsaw identification

Such an order can, then, permanently prevent a media report of the case from identifying the complainant and/or respondent—for example, the employer. The order could make it illegal to publish any identifying detail—not just a person's name—so care must be taken by journalists to avoid 'jigsaw identification'.

This power in rule 50 to protect people's Convention rights co-exists with older powers to restrict reporting, explained in the next section, which are set out in the 1996 Act's section 11, relating to cases in which sexual misconduct is alleged, and in section 12, relating to cases in which discrimination on grounds of disability is alleged. These older powers allow employment tribunals to ban temporarily any media report of these types of case from identifying people involved in them. It seems likely that anyone arguing in such cases to be granted anonymity will now seek it under rule 50 in respect of Convention rights, under which it may be indefinite, not temporary. But the media can argue that principles laid down in judgments about these older types of reporting restriction should apply too when tribunals decide if rule 50 restrictions are justified.

Anonymity in sexual misconduct and disability cases

Section 11 of the 1996 Act and Rule 50 of Schedule 1 to the 2013 Regulations give employment tribunals discretionary power to make temporary anonymity orders, known as 'restricted reporting orders', in cases involving allegations of sexual misconduct—for example, that a woman was forced to leave her job because her boss sexually harassed her. Sexual misconduct is defined as a sexual offence or sexual harassment or other adverse conduct (of whatever nature) related to sex, or to the sexual orientation of the person at whom the conduct is directed.

In a restricted reporting order, an employment tribunal can prohibit the inclusion in reports of any matter likely to lead members of the public to identify:

- the person making the allegation of sexual misconduct; and/or
- anyone 'affected' by it—for example, the person(s) accused of such misconduct or any witness due to give evidence in such proceedings.

The tribunal can decide in each such case who should have such anonymity, if anyone. It may, for example, decide not to grant anonymity for the accuser, but order it in respect of the person accused to safeguard his/her reputation until judgment on whether the accusation is proved. Such an order cannot specifically bestow such anonymity on an employer that is a company or institution, so its corporate name can be published if this does not identify a person named in the order (*Leicester University v A* [1999] IRLR 352). But in a case where the employing organisation is small—for example, a small firm—it may be that to preserve anonymity for the person the firm itself cannot be identified in media reports while the order remains in force, because reference to the person's gender or age or job description would in itself be enough to identify him/her to people who know he/she works there.

👁 Case study

In 1997 the Court of Appeal said it was important that tribunals should recognise that their power to make these orders in cases of sexual misconduct was not to be exercised automatically and that the public interest in the media's ability to communicate information should be considered (*Kearney v Smith New Court Securities* [1997] EWCA Civ 1211).

Section 12 of the 1996 Act and rule 50 of Schedule 1 to the 2013 Regulations allow employment tribunals to make restricted reporting orders when considering claims that an employer unlawfully discriminated on disability grounds if evidence 'of a personal nature' is likely to be heard and is likely to cause significant embarrassment if published.

Rule 50 says a restricted reporting order made under sections 11 or 12 of the Act shall specify the person whose identity is protected and may specify particular matters of which publication is prohibited as likely to lead to that person's identification, and that the order should also specify the duration of the restriction. The rule adds that a notice that such an order has been made should be displayed on the notice board of the tribunal with any list of cases taking place and on the door of the room in which the case affected by the order is being heard.

✳ Remember

The automatic reporting restrictions in the Sexual Offences (Amendment) Act 1992 mean that anyone in employment tribunal proceedings who states that he/she is, or who is alleged to be, a victim of a sexual offence—for example, rape or sexual assault—must not be identified in media reports of the case in his/her lifetime, unless he/she has given valid written consent for this. This law is explained in ch. 10. It applies irrespective of whether a restricted reporting order under the Employment Tribunals Act 1996 has been imposed or expired.

Revocation or lapse of section 11 and 12 anonymity

The 1996 Act says that once the employment tribunal has made a restricted reporting order under sections 11 or 12:

- it can revoke (that is, cancel) the order at any stage—for example, while the case is ongoing or when it makes a verbal announcement of its decision on *liability*—to permit media reports to immediately identify the person formerly covered by the order; but

- anyway, if not revoked, the order only has effect 'until the promulgation of the decision of the tribunal', according to the Act. Under regulations published in 2004, this meant the date when the ruling on *liability* was sent to the parties or, in cases where there needed to be a ruling on *remedy*, the date on which that ruling was sent to them—see the earlier explanation of these terms. The 2013 Regulations replaced those of 2004 and, as explained earlier, require the tribunal to state the duration of a section 11 or 12 order when making it. Under the Act it can only last until 'promulgation'.

see ch. 6, p. 63, Fines and the removal of the £5,000 limit

Penalty for breach of anonymity

Publishing material which breaches a restricted reporting order made under the Act's section 11 or 12 is a summary offence punishable by a fine. The maximum fine was formerly £5,000 but there is now no specified limit. Any proprietor, editor or publisher held responsible will be liable to pay it. It is a defence for the person or company prosecuted to show that he/she/it was not aware, and neither suspected nor had reason to suspect, that what was published breached the order.

National security reporting restrictions

Rule 94 of Schedule 1 to the 2013 Regulations, reflecting section 10 of the 1996 Act, says a Minister of the Crown can order an employment tribunal to conceal the identity of a witness in a case concerning national security issues and order it to keep secret all or part of the reasons for its decision in such a case, or the tribunal can, on its own initiative, take either of these courses of action. When the tribunal has taken such steps, it is an offence to publish anything likely to lead to the identification of the witness or to publish any part of a decision the tribunal intended to keep secret. Again, there is no limit on the fine imposed for this offence.

Challenging reporting restrictions

A journalist covering an employment tribunal case may wish to challenge the imposition or continuation of a reporting restriction made under rule 50 or under the 1996 Act's sections 11 or 12, or the restriction's scope or duration. Rule 50(4) gives anyone 'with a legitimate interest' the right to make a challenge by written or verbal representations, just as it does in the case of an order that a hearing should be in private—see earlier. Again, rule 50 (4) requires the tribunal considering imposing a restriction, or deciding on a challenge to it, to give full weight to the open justice principle and Article 10 rights.

👁 Case study

In 2015 the BBC successfully challenged an anonymity order granted under rule 50 by an employment tribunal judge to a man who had allegedly committed serious sexual assaults. D Roden was claiming he was unfairly and wrongfully dismissed by the BBC from his contract job as a development producer. By the time this contract ended in 2013 the BBC had been told that serious allegations of a sexual nature had been made against him in Glasgow. Police later told the BBC they had information suggesting he posed a risk to young men with whom he came into contact during his BBC work. During the tribunal proceedings it emerged he had not told the BBC that he had been dismissed for gross misconduct from a previous job—with a theatre attached to a college—following distribution of a photo that showed him simulating oral sex with a student in fancy dress. Employment judge Andrew Glennie ruled that Mr Roden should have permanent anonymity in respect of the proceedings because the allegations of sexual assaults were not directly an issue in them and so he would not have any opportunity of gaining a finding which disproved the allegations. In the Employment Appeal Tribunal Mrs Justice Simler heard the BBC's appeal against the anonymity order, which she revoked. She said that the principle of open justice was of paramount importance, and that Judge Glennie was wrong to think that it and the strong public interest in full publication were outweighed by the risk of the public not understanding that the sexual assault allegations against Mr Roden were unproven. She said there was no evidence to support the claim that if a report of the case were to identify Mr Roden, this could have 'devasting consequences' for him. She added that he had chosen to bring a claim against the BBC in a public tribunal while knowing he had not been honest about the circumstances of his dismissal from a previous job, and the tribunal had dismissed most of his claim. 'The mere publication of embarrassing or damaging material is not a good reason for restricting the reporting of a judgment', Mrs Justice Simler said (*BBC v D Roden*, UKEAT/0385/14/DA).

 For further case studies on tribunal anonymity orders, see Additional Material for ch. 17 on www.mcnaes.com.

Where a restricted reporting order is imposed under the Act's section 11 or 12, but a settlement is reached without the case proceeding to judgment, the restriction remains in place indefinitely (*Fiona Davidson v Dallas McMillan* [2009] CSIH 70). However, it can be lifted if there is a change in circumstances—for example, if a person who wanted anonymity originally now wishes the media to be able to iden-tify him/her (*Tradition Securities & Futures SA and another v Times Newspapers Ltd and others*, UKEATPA/1415/08/JOJ; UKEATPA/1417/08/JOJ).

Contempt and defamation law affecting coverage of employment tribunals

Employment tribunals and the Employment Appeal Tribunal are classed as courts. Therefore, as explained earlier in this chapter about all such tribunals, media reports of their hearings can enjoy privilege against libel actions, and the Contempt of Court Act 1981 and other contempt law apply to their proceedings. This includes the ban in section 9 of the 1981 Act on unauthorised use in their hearings of audio-recording devices (*Neckles v Yorkshire Rider Ltd* [2002] All ER (D) 111 (Jan)).

▌ Public inquiries

Public inquiries can be broadly categorised either as local inquiries, set up rou-tinely in certain circumstances, or those which are set up ad hoc to consider a matter of national concern.

Local public inquiries

Some Acts of Parliament provide that an inquiry hearing must be held before cer-tain decisions are made affecting the rights of individuals or of public authorities. An inquiry might be held, for example, before planning schemes are approved. In some cases, an 'Inspector' appointed by a Minister to chair the inquiry decides the matter at issue. In others, he/she must report to the Minister, who subse-quently announces a decision and the reasons for it. Some statutes under which inquiries are held stipulate that they must be held in public. In others, this is dis-cretionary. Local authorities and health trusts also have general statutory powers under which they can fund an ad hoc inquiry into a matter of local (or national) concern, though it will be at their discretion whether it is held in public.

Public inquiries into matters of national concern

Public inquiries initiated ad hoc by government Ministers have in recent years included:

ch. 2 gives context about the Leveson inquiry

- the inquiry chaired by Sir Brian Leveson into the culture, practices and ethics of the press, which was established under the Inquiries Act 2005 (the 2005 Act)—see www.levesoninquiry.org.uk/;
- the Hutton inquiry set up in 2003 into the death of Dr David Kelly, who com-mitted suicide after investigation by his employer, the Ministry of Defence,

into his contact with BBC journalists about the government's stated justi-fication for the Iraq war. This inquiry was held on a non-statutory basis by a chair appointed by the Secretary of State for Constitutional Affairs—see Useful Websites at the end of this chapter.

If an inquiry is held on a non-statutory basis, it has no legal powers to compel witnesses to give evidence, but is seen as a flexible option when full cooperation is anticipated.

If the inquiry is established under the 2005 Act, under section 19 a Minister or an inquiry's chair can decide on various grounds—for example, national se-curity or to protect the 'efficiency' of the inquiry—that it should hear evidence in private.

The Additional Material for ch. 17 on www.mcnaes.com sets out the reporting restrictions which can be imposed under the Act, including by the chair of such an inquiry. It also outlines the powers of the chair to compel production of evidence—including from a journalist—and explains how section 18 of the Act gives journalists some rights to obtain or view a record of an inquiry's evidence and documents, but says that audio recording and televising of the proceedings need the chair's permission.

Coverage of public inquiries—defamation law

Reports of public inquiries held under the Inquiries Act 2005 have, under its section 37, the same privilege 'as would be the case if those proceedings were pro-ceedings before a court'. This means that, as regards proceedings held in public, absolute privilege applies under section 14 of the Defamation Act 1996 to con-temporaneous reports and qualified privilege applies under Part 1 of Schedule 1 to the 1996 Act to non-contemporaneous reports if the respective requirements of these defences are met, including that the reports fairly and accurately reflect the proceedings.

ch. 21 explains ab-solute and qualified privilege

The Schedule is set out in this book's Appendix 3. Part 1 of the Schedule also applies qualified privilege, subject to the same requirements, to media reports of the proceedings in public 'of a person appointed to hold a public in-quiry by a government or legislature anywhere in the world'. Media reports of public inquiries of the type defined in paragraph 11 in Part 2 of the Schedule enjoy qualified privilege subject to the additional requirement to publish 'ex-planation or contradiction' if this is requested. The 1996 Act does not make clear in Part 2 of the Schedule how what it describes as a person appointed by 'a Minister of the Crown' to run an inquiry differs from what Part 1 of the Schedule describes as a person appointed to do this 'by a government'. But it is an established legal principle that when an event/circumstance is described both generally and specifically in a statute, the part which is most specific applies.

Privilege will not apply to media reports of anything aired in a private session of an inquiry. As is the case with administrative tribunals, proceedings of public inquiries are not as formal as those in an ordinary court of law, so some extra care must be exercised in what is reported if qualified privilege under the 1996 Act is relied on—see p. 218, Proceedings are not always formal.

The findings of a public inquiry are usually published by a government department, by Parliament or by the relevant local authority. Under the Defamation Act 1996:

- a fair and accurate media report of such findings, when they have been officially published by a government or legislature anywhere in the world, is protected by qualified privilege under Part 1 of the Act's Schedule 1 (paragraph 7);

- a fair and accurate media report of findings officially published by a local authority anywhere in the world is protected by qualified privilege under Part 2 of the Schedule (paragraph 9).

➡ Recap of major points

- Most types of tribunal adjudicate in disputes in specialist areas of law. Some are regulatory tribunals for professions—for example, doctors or lawyers.

- Employment tribunals can make permanent anonymity orders in some circumstances, but some anonymity orders are temporary.

- Media reports of the public proceedings of tribunals are protected by qualified privilege and, as regards those classed as courts, by absolute privilege when reports are contemporaneous.

- For any tribunal classed as a court, contempt law applies.

- Media reports of the public proceedings of public inquiries are, as regards defamation actions, protected by either qualified privilege or absolute privilege.

((•)) Useful Websites

www.gov.uk/government/publications?departments%5B%5D=tribunal-procedure-committee
Procedural rules for the First-tier Tribunal and the Upper Tribunal

www.justice.gov.uk/tribunals/employment
Government guidance on employment tribunals

www.gov.uk/government/publications/employment-tribunal-procedure-rules
Procedural rules for employment tribunals

www.gov.uk/appeal-employment-appeal-tribunal
Government guidance on the Employment Appeal Tribunal

http://biallpr.pbworks.com/w/page/5259170/Employment%20Tribunal%20cases
Details of the register of employment tribunal judgments

www.employmenttribunalsni.co.uk/
Northern Ireland's industrial tribunal service

www.courtserve.net/
CourtServe website

www.legislation.gov.uk/ukpga/2005/12/notes/contents
Government's Explanatory Notes to the Inquiries Act 2005

http://webarchive.nationalarchives.gov.uk/20051219094446/the-hutton-inquiry.org.uk/
Hutton Inquiry home page on National Archives site

18

Contempt of court

Chapter summary

The law of contempt protects the integrity of the administration of justice and the fundamental principle that a defendant is presumed innocent until proven guilty. Contempt law most affects journalists when they publish material which might affect a trial by making a jury more likely to find a defendant guilty—or innocent— or by influencing a witness's evidence. Publications might also 'impede' the course of justice by creating a risk that witnesses will refuse to come forward to help the prosecution or defence. Media organisations which have committed contempt by publishing prejudicial material have been fined heavily. The law of contempt applies as much to material on the internet as to other coverage.

▌ What does contempt of court law protect?

The law of contempt of court protects the judicial process. Anyone who is disruptive or threatening in a courtroom can be punished immediately for contempt by being sent by the magistrates or judge to the court's cells, and in some cases subsequently to jail, as contempt is a criminal offence.

The greatest risk of the media committing contempt is by publishing material which could prejudice a fair trial by:

- giving the impression that a defendant or suspect is the sort of person who is likely to have committed the crime, or vilifying a suspect to the extent that witnesses might refuse to come forward to help his/her defence or the prosecution case;

- seeking to discover or publishing information from the jury's confidential discussions about a verdict—see ch. 11, pp. 126–127, Confidentiality of jury deliberations;

- publishing material which breaches the **common law** of contempt—for example, by 'vilifying' a person for being a witness at a trial—see later in this chapter; → glossary
- contaminating a witness's evidence by interviewing him/her in detail or offering payment for his/her story before a trial—see later in this chapter;
- publishing material in breach of a court order—for example, by naming a blackmail victim in reports of a trial—see ch. 11, pp. 128–129, Section 11 orders—blackmail, secrets, personal safety.

✳ Remember

The Court of Appeal has ruled that the punishment for publishing material in breach of an order made under a statute other than the 1981 Act—for example, under the Youth Justice and Criminal Evidence Act 1999 explained in ch. 9—should be that specified by that statute, rather than as a contempt (*R v Tyne Tees Television* [1997] EWCA Crim 2395, The Times, 20 October 1997).

▌ Types of contempt

There are two types of contempt—common law contempt and strict liability contempt. Common law contempt consists of publishing material which creates a substantial risk of serious prejudice to proceedings which are pending or imminent with the intention of creating that risk, or of behaviour or conduct which interferes with the administration of justice.

Strict liability contempt, which is governed by the Contempt of Court Act 1981, consists simply of publishing material which creates a substantial risk of serious prejudice or impediment to 'active' proceedings—the court decides whether the publication has created the risk and the writer or publisher's motives are irrelevant. In March 2011, the Attorney General, Dominic Grieve QC, expressed alarm about the media's approach to crime reporting, saying there was 'frenzied interest' in high-profile arrests which stopped only when a suspect was charged or released, and warned that arrested people might have to be given anonymity until they were charged.

see p. 237, What type of material can cause a substantial risk of serious prejudice or impediment

▌ Contempt in common law

Common law contempt makes it an offence to publish material which creates a substantial risk of serious prejudice to legal proceedings which are imminent or pending if it can be proved that there was intent to create such a risk.

- The term 'intent' could mean either deliberate intention to create such a risk or recklessness in publishing material which the person responsible for the publication should have foreseen would create such a risk.

The Contempt of Court Act 1981 largely superseded the common law by creating the strict liability rule in respect of a case which is 'active' under the Act. Common law contempt still applies to material published before proceedings become active (and arguably may apply to material published at later stages in the proceedings). Prosecutions of the media for common law contempt are extremely rare as the prosecution must prove that the journalist or editor intended to create a serious risk of prejudice.

👁 Case study

In 2010 the Police Service of Northern Ireland sought a High Court injunction to stop the BBC broadcasting a documentary about the 1972 bombings in the village of Claudy in which nine people died and 30 were injured. Police argued that even though no proceedings were active, the programme—which the BBC refused to allow an officer to see before it was broadcast—was a contempt, would interfere with the administration of justice or could breach confidentiality. Mr Justice Seamus Treacy rejected the 'unprecedented' application, saying it was based on pure speculation, was not supported by any legal authority and, if allowed, would significantly extend the boundaries of the law (*Media Lawyer*, 3 November 2010).

Witness interviews and 'molestation'

Publishing detailed accounts of a witness's evidence while a case is active could breach the 1981 Act. But even if the intention was not to publish any interview with a witness until after the trial, a reporter who interviews a witness about a case before he/she testifies might be held guilty of common law contempt for having contaminated the witness's memory—for example, by telling him/her what other witnesses said, or by influencing what the witness remembered or otherwise affecting his/her testimony.

It could also be a contempt by 'molestation' for a journalist to pester a witness so much for a pre-trial interview, or by photographing him/her, that he/she is deterred from testifying. A media organisation's offer to 'buy up' a witness who has yet to give evidence to tell his/her story after the trial could amount to common law contempt if it were held to have influenced how the witness testified.

 Ch. 2, p. 20, Payments to witnesses, shows how clause 15 of the Editors' Code governs this practice. There is similar provision in the Broadcasting Code—see ch. 3, p. 24, Ofcom—its role and sanctions.

Vilifying a witness

Media organisations which publish, after the end of a trial, criticism of a witness which was so abusive that a judge could rule that it was likely to deter others from being witnesses in future could be punished for common law contempt for 'vilifying' the witness.

 Ch. 11 explains that publishing information from some types of court document, photography or filming in a courtroom, or harassment of a defendant or witness by photographers or film crews, could be ruled to be a contempt in common law.

▶ The Contempt of Court Act 1981— strict liability

A primary purpose of the Contempt of Court Act 1981 was to replace some aspects of common law contempt and to give greater certainty about what constitutes a contempt. Section 1 of the Act made contempt by publication a strict liability offence in the case of 'active' criminal or civil proceedings.

* The Act makes it a contempt to publish material which creates a substantial risk of serious prejudice or impediment to 'active' legal proceedings.

The strict liability rule means that the prosecution, when seeking to prove that a contempt was committed, does not have to prove that the editor or media organisation responsible intended to create the risk. The court simply judges the actual or potential prejudicial effect of what was published. Prosecutions for contempt are usually of the relevant publishing company.

* The Act defines publication as any writing, speech, broadcast or other communication addressed to any section of the public—and includes material on websites.

Breaching the Act is punishable by an unlimited fine and/or a maximum of two years' in jail.

 Ch. 1, p. 9, High offices in law, explains the Attorney General's role.

Who can prosecute for contempt of court?

Proceedings for contempt caused by a publication can be initiated only by a Crown court or higher court, or by or with the consent of the Attorney General. Crown court judges usually refer such matters to the Attorney General to decide if the case should be referred to the High Court.

Magistrates cannot punish a contempt of their courts caused by a publication. It would have to be dealt with by the High Court (although no such case concerning their courts has yet been recorded).

When are criminal proceedings active?

The strict liability rule applies only if proceedings are 'active'.

The Act says a criminal case becomes active when:

ch. 4 explains these early stages of a criminal case

- a person is arrested;
- an arrest warrant is issued;
- a summons is issued;
- a person is charged orally; or
- a document specifying the charge is served on the accused.

These steps all mean that there is a definite prospect of an individual facing trial.

A potential problem for the media is that the police may not make clear, after a crime is committed, if a person is under arrest or simply 'helping police with their inquiries'. Journalists must seek clarification.

When do criminal proceedings cease to be active?

Criminal proceedings cease to be active when any of these events occurs:

ch. 4 explains police bail

- the arrested person is released without being charged (except when released on police bail);
- no arrest is made within 12 months of the issue of an arrest warrant;
- the case is discontinued;
- the defendant is acquitted or sentenced; or
- the defendant is found unfit to be tried or unfit to plead, or the court orders the charge to lie on file.

A defendant can be ruled to be unfit to be tried or unfit to plead if he/she suffers acute physical or mental illness. An order that a charge should 'lie on file' means that the defendant has not been acquitted or convicted, but the court agrees that the charge is no longer worth pursuing. For example, if after a lengthy trial a defendant is convicted of four charges but the jury cannot agree on the fifth, the judge may order that charge to 'lie on file' because the expense of a re-trial for that charge would be excessive or a conviction would not lead to a longer prison sentence.

Period between verdict and sentence at Crown court

A Crown court case remains active, even though all the verdicts have been reached, until the defendant is sentenced. It is technically possible for a media organisation to publish material during this period which breaches the 1981 Act even though the jury's involvement has ended. But Crown court judges are regarded as too experienced to be influenced by media coverage, so it is thought unlikely that there can be any substantial risk of serious prejudice, whatever is published, after all verdicts but before an adjourned sentencing. Media organisations are therefore generally safe in publishing background features about such a case, including material which did not feature in the trial, as soon as the last verdict is given, although judges have been known to order the postponement of publication of such material until after sentencing.

Proceedings become active again when an appeal is lodged

The 1981 Act states that:

- when an appeal is lodged, the case becomes active again, so strict liability contempt resumes;
- the case ceases to be active when the hearing of any appeal is completed—unless in that appeal a new trial is ordered or the case is remitted to a lower court.

Lawyers often announce at the end of a criminal or civil case that their clients will appeal, but it usually takes some weeks for an appeal to be prepared and lodged, so there is a time when the case is not active between, in a criminal case, the sentence and the lodging of an appeal.

- Even if an appeal is lodged against a Crown court conviction, the media still have considerable freedom on what can be published about such a case, although it has become active again, as the appeal will be heard by the judges of the Court of Appeal.

see ch. 8, p. 86, Court of Appeal

It can safely be assumed that nothing the media publishes will create a substantial risk of serious prejudice to the way these experienced judges approach the case. But if they order a re-trial—that is, another jury trial—the media must be wary of publishing anything which creates a risk of serious prejudice to the re-trial, as witnesses and potential jurors will be considered susceptible to publicity about the case before and during the retrial.

Where to check if an appeal has been lodged

Appeals to the Court of Appeal from Crown courts may be lodged at the Crown court office. Appeals on a point of law to the Queen's Bench Divisional Court (the High Court) from a Crown court appeal hearing must be lodged at the Royal Courts of Justice in London. Appeals from magistrates' court summary trials may be lodged at a local Crown court office.

see ch. 15, p. 190, The possibility of retrial, and the ruling in the *Beggs* case

◗ Police appeals for media assistance

Sometimes, after obtaining a warrant for someone's arrest, police seek media help in tracing him/her. The warrant makes the case active under the 1981 Act. Police may supply the suspect's photograph and/or description for publication, even though visual identification evidence may figure in the case. If the person is armed or likely to be violent, police may say so, to warn the public.

- Technically, a media organisation publishing such a photograph, description or warning about the person's character could be accused of creating a substantial risk of serious prejudice or impediment to such an active case— see explanations below.
- But the then Attorney General said in the House of Commons during the debate on the Contempt of Court Bill in 1981:

> ❝ The press has nothing whatever to fear from publishing in reasoned terms anything which may assist in the apprehension of a wanted man and I hope that it will continue to perform this public service. ❞

- There is no known case of a media organisation being held in contempt for publishing such a police appeal. But there is no defence in the 1981 Act for assisting the police in this way.

The Attorney General's comments would not apply to information supplied by police which was published or repeated after the person's arrest.

❙ Section 3 defence of not knowing proceedings were active

Section 3 of the 1981 Act provides a defence for an alleged breach of the Act by what has been published. The defence applies if:

- the person responsible for the publication, having taken all reasonable care, did not know and had no reason to suspect when the material was published that relevant proceedings were active.

The person accused of contempt must prove that all reasonable care was taken. So, to be sure that the section 3 defence can be used, a journalist reporting a crime story must check regularly with police, especially before a deadline, about whether someone has been arrested or charged, as either event would make the case active and the story would need to be re-edited to remove any detail likely to breach the strict liability rule. For some news stories journalists might need to check with magistrates' courts whether arrest warrants or summonses have been issued.

If the police or court spokesperson says the case is not active, the journalist should keep a note of what was said, by whom and when, to show that he/she took reasonable care to establish if the case was active.

See p. 250, Contempt of civil proceedings, for detail of when a civil case is active. See ch. 16, p. 210, Defamation and contempt issues, for when an inquest is active, and ch. 17, p. 217, Contempt issues in coverage of tribunals, for detail of when cases before certain types of tribunal are active.

What type of material can cause a substantial risk of serious prejudice or impediment?

The 1981 Act does not define what creates a substantial risk of serious prejudice or impediment to an active case. But cases in which editors and media organisations have been convicted of contempt show that material which could be held to be a contempt in active cases includes:

- references to a suspect or defendant's previous convictions;
- information suggesting he/she is dishonest or of bad character in other ways;
- any evidence seeming to link him/her directly to the crime of which he/she is suspected or accused;
- any other suggestion that he/she is guilty.

ch. 6 explains when 'bad character' evidence is admissible

If the person is tried, the magistrates or jury will probably not be told of his/her previous convictions, while character evidence may be admissible only in certain circumstances.

As this chapter explains, it could also be strict liability contempt in an active case to publish:

- a witness's detailed account of a relevant event after a case becomes active;
- a photograph or footage or physical description of a suspect when visual identification of the alleged perpetrator is or is likely to be an evidential issue because:
  - a police identity parade is to be held; and/or
  - a witness is expected to testify at the trial on such identification.

✳ Remember

Contempt law is enforced more strictly in Scotland. This means particular care must be taken in cross-border publication, including on the internet. See the chapter on Scotland on www.mcnaes.com.

References to a defendant's previous convictions

Coverage in *The Times* of a knife attack in which one woman died and another was injured which reported the attacker's previous conviction for the manslaughter of her own mother did not amount to a breach of the Act, the High Court ruled in February 2013. But it was 'deeply regrettable' that the newspaper had detailed Nicola Edgington's previous conviction, said Sir John Thomas, the then President of the Queen's Bench Division, sitting with Mr Justice Eady. The court stressed that those who reported crime should recognise that they published articles making assumptions about the extent of the issues likely to be disputed in forthcoming criminal trials at their peril. Sir John added: 'If there is created a substantial risk of serious prejudice, the danger is that those most immediately concerned in the case, not only any accused person but also the victims and their families, may unnecessarily be deprived of access to justice. That should be a danger no editor wants to create.' The court said it had 'narrowly reached the conclusion' that Attorney General Dominic Grieve QC had failed to prove that *The Times* breached the Act with its coverage of the incident in Bexleyheath in which Nicola Edgington attacked and injured Kerry Clark before stabbing and killing grandmother Sally Hodkin nearby. Edgington was convicted on 7 February 2013 of having murdered Mrs Hodkin and attempting to murder Ms Clark on Monday 10 October 2011 (*Attorney General v Times Newspapers Ltd* [2012] EWHC 3195 (Admin)).

Information suggesting a suspect or defendant is dishonest or of bad character

The *Daily Mirror* and *The Sun* were fined £50,000 and £18,000 respectively in July 2011 over their coverage the previous December of the arrest of former teacher Chris Jefferies, the landlord of murdered landscape architect Joanna Yeates. The court heard that one *Daily Mirror* front page carried the headline 'Jo Suspect is Peeping Tom' beneath a photograph of Mr Jefferies, and another front-page headline read 'Was Killer Waiting in Jo's Flat?', with sub-headings below reading 'Police seize bedding for tests' and 'Landlord held until Tuesday'. *The Sun's* front-page headline read 'Obsessed by Death' next to a photograph of Mr Jefferies and below the words 'Jo suspect "scared kids"'. Attorney General Dominic Grieve QC said material in the articles gave an 'overall impression' that Mr Jefferies had a 'propensity' to commit the kind of offences for which he had been arrested. The Lord Chief Justice, Lord Judge, said section 2(2) of the Contempt of Court Act 1981 provided that the strict liability contempt rule applied only to a publication which created a substantial risk that the course of justice in the proceedings in question 'will be seriously impeded or prejudiced' and went on: 'Dealing with it briefly, impeding the course of justice and prejudicing the course of justice are not synonymous concepts. If they were, they would not have been identified as distinct features of the strict liability rule.' The issue of impeding the course of justice outside the trial process was 'less well trodden'. Vilification of a suspect under arrest was a potential impediment to the course of justice, he said, adding:

> At the simplest level publication of such material may deter or discourage witnesses from coming forward and providing information helpful to the suspect, which may, (depending on the circumstances) help immediately to clear him of suspicion or enable his defence to be fully developed at trial.

It was not an answer, he said, to argue that, on the evidence actually available, the combination of the judge's directions and the integrity of the jury would ensure a fair trial—the evidence at trial might be incomplete 'because its existence may never be known, or indeed may only come to light after conviction' (*Attorney-General v MGN Ltd and another* [2011] All ER (D) 06 (Aug)). Mr Jefferies was released without charge after his arrest. Another man was convicted of murdering Ms Yeates.

 Mr Jefferies won damages from newspapers for libel—see ch 4, p. 45, The risk of libel in media identification of crime suspects.

👁 Case study

In 2011 the *Daily Mail* and *The Sun* were found guilty of strict liability contempt after both mistakenly published on their websites a photograph, taken from a social networking website page, showing a man who was on trial for murder posing with an automatic pistol. The case was the first time website operators in the UK had been found guilty of contempt. Lord Justice Moses, sitting with Mr Justice Owen in the Queen's Bench Divisional Court, said: 'The criminal courts have been troubled by the dangers to the integrity and fairness of a criminal trial, where juries can obtain such easy access to the internet and to other forms of instant communication. This case demonstrates the need to recognise that instant news requires instant and effective protection for the integrity of a criminal trial.' The newspapers were found to have created a 'a substantial risk' of prejudicing the trial of Ryan Ward, who was eventually convicted of murdering father-of-two Craig Wass by hitting him on the head with a brick when he intervened in a row to protect Ward's girlfriend. The offending photograph of Ward appeared on the two newspapers' websites alongside their reports of the first day of the trial. They were removed immediately the newspapers were alerted to the risk—the *Daily Mail* had used the picture uncut, but *The Sun* had cropped it, although part of the barrel of the gun could still be seen. No juror saw the pictures. The Divisional Court said that although the jury was warned against researching material on the internet, a juror would not have understood the trial judge's instructions to have prohibited reading online news reports of the case (*Attorney General v Associated Newspapers Ltd and Another* [2011] All ER (D) 45 (Mar)). The court fined each paper £15,000 and ordered them to pay the Attorney General's costs of £28,117 (*Media Lawyer*, 19 July 2011).

Publishing a witness's detailed account

Publishing a witness's detailed account of a relevant event after a case becomes active may be deemed a contempt because of the risk that:

- the witness may, because such a detailed account has been published, feel obliged to stick to it and therefore less able honestly to retract or vary some detail after further reflection; or
- the witness's evidence may not figure in the trial at all, because it is ruled inadmissible or has been retracted—but if it has already been published, other witnesses or jurors in the case may have read or heard it and been influenced by it.

Visual identification evidence

Publishing a photo or footage or description could influence or confuse a witness who gives identification evidence so that the court might not be sure if the witness's evidence—for example, from an 'identity parade'—is based on what was seen during the crime or on recollection of a subsequently published photograph or footage or description.

Police investigating crimes often ask the media to publish a sketch or computer-generated image of an alleged offender's face as described by one witness—for example, the alleged victim—or to issue a physical description in an attempt to get members of the public to give information about who the alleged offender might be, or whether they too witnessed such a person being at or near the crime scene.

The need to avoid breaching 1981 Act—that is, to avoid creating a substantial risk of serious prejudice—means that the image and description must usually not be published again after the case becomes active, to protect the validity of the provision, particularly by other witnesses, of visual identification evidence in respect of the arrested or charged person, if it is necessary in the case.

👁 Case study

In 1994 *The Sun* was fined £80,000 and its editor Kelvin MacKenzie, £20,000, after it published a photograph of a man charged with murder. The picture was published before an identity parade in which he was picked out by witnesses (*The Independent*, 6 July 1994).

✳ Remember

The examples of prejudicial material in this chapter relate mainly to the contempt risk of saying or suggesting that a suspect or defendant is guilty—but the Act can be breached by publishing material suggesting or asserting a suspect's innocence.

The High Court and Crown courts can grant injunctions to prevent the media publishing material deemed capable of creating a substantial risk of serious prejudice or impediment to a criminal case, or to restrain reporters' attempts to interview witnesses before a trial—see Additional Material for ch. 18 on www.mcnaes.com.

What can be published after a criminal case becomes active?

Contempt law does not mean that the media cannot publish anything about a crime after a case becomes active.

Non-prejudicial basic information about the crime can be published—for example, the media can report that there was a robbery, where it took place and that later someone was arrested. They should not report that 'the robber was later arrested' as this says the arrested person is guilty of the offence. Note the Attorney General's concern about 'frenzied interest' in high-profile cases.

In most cases, it will not be contempt to name the arrested person, because he/she will be named at the trial. But it may be unsafe in defamation law to name an arrested person before he/she is charged. Ch. 4 explains that risk and other law which gives pre-charge anonymity to teachers accused by pupils.

In contempt law it is safe to identify the alleged victim(s) of crime before any prosecution begins. But a reporting restriction may apply to media reports of the court case, as chs. 9 and 11 explain. Victims/alleged victims of sexual offences and slavery and trafficking offences have automatic anonymity from the time the offence is alleged—see ch. 10.

Common ground

It is not prejudicial to publish material which will be common ground between the defence and prosecution at the trial, such as non-prejudicial background material about a defendant and any alleged victim. Also, in a murder case, there will rarely be dispute about where the body was found. In contested cases, the nature and extent of a victim's injuries will probably be common ground because much of the forensic or medical evidence will be beyond dispute—the trial issue will be how the injuries were caused or who caused them.

How the courts interpret the 1981 Act

In *A-G v MGN Ltd* [1997] 1 All ER 456 Lord Justice Schiemann set out the principles a court should follow when deciding whether published material created a substantial risk of serious prejudice in cases with a potential for jury trial. The court, he said, should consider what risk occurred at the time the material was published. The mere fact that by reason of earlier publications there was already some risk of prejudice did not in itself prevent a court finding that the later publication had created a further risk. The court should consider:

- the likelihood of the publication coming to a potential juror's attention;
- its likely impact on an ordinary reader; and
- crucially, the residual impact on a notional juror at the time of the trial.

The court will also consider whether the publication would have given rise to a seriously arguable ground of appeal if the trial had been allowed to continue and ended with a conviction.

Juries are told to put pre-trial publicity out of their minds

At the start of Crown court trials judges tell juries to reach verdicts only on the evidence presented to them and to put pre-trial publicity about the case, or media coverage of the trial, out of their minds. They are also warned not to research the internet for material.

Judges have made clear that juries must be trusted and more recently have firmly re-stated the view that jurors given directions by a judge are capable of looking at the evidence fairly. In *Re B* [2007] EMLR 5, The Times, 6 November 2006, Sir Igor Judge, as he then was, presiding at the Court of Appeal, stressed the robustness and independence of juries in a case in which the Court lifted an order postponing reporting of a hearing at which Dhiren Barot, self-confessed terrorist, was to be sentenced.

He said, at paragraphs 31 and 32 of the judgment, that 'juries up and down the country have a passionate and profound belief in and a commitment to' the defendant's right to a fair trial and went on:

" They know that it is integral to their responsibility. It is, when all is said and done, their birthright; it is shared by each one of them with the defendant. They guard it faithfully. The integrity of the jury is an essential feature of our trial process. Juries follow the directions which the judge will give them to focus exclusively on the evidence and to ignore anything they may have heard or read out of court. "

The judge at the trial would give the jury appropriate directions, he said, adding:

" We cannot too strongly emphasise that the jury will follow them, not only because they will loyally abide by the directions of law which they will be given by the judge, but also because the directions themselves will appeal directly to their own instinctive and fundamental belief in the need for the trial process to be fair. "

There were, he added, at least two safeguards against the risk of prejudice—the media's responsibility to avoid inappropriate comment, which might interfere with the administration of justice, and the trial process, including the integrity of the jury.

The 'fade factor' and limited publication

The 'fade factor' recognises that the public will probably have forgotten detail in reports published in the early stages of a criminal case—for example, soon after the crime, or about the time that someone is arrested or charged—by the time a jury is selected. Others factors a court takes into account include the area where the material was published and the likely extent to which it was read—or, if broadcast, seen or heard—in that area.

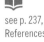

see p. 237, References to a defendant's previous convictions

But some material may be so striking, even when published some time before a trial, as to create a substantial risk of serious prejudice or impediment to the trial. This has been said to include, especially, disclosure of a defendant's criminal record.

👁 Case study

The lapse of time was a factor in assessing the substantial risk of serious prejudice in a contempt case in 1997. The *Daily Mail* and *Manchester Evening News*, which reported how a home help was caught on video film stealing from an 82-year-old widow, were found not guilty of contempt of court by the High Court. Mr Justice Owen said his initial view was that the stories were a plain contempt of court as they carried the clearest statements that the accused was guilty at a time when proceedings against her were active. The key issue was whether the stories created a substantial risk that the criminal proceedings against her would be seriously prejudiced. But the stories were several months old by the time of the trial, and Mr Justice Owen had concluded that the contempt allegation was not made good. But Lord Justice Simon Brown warned the media against thinking that when someone was apparently caught red-handed there was no possibility of a not guilty plea at trial (*A-G v Unger* [1998] 1 Cr App R 308).

✳ Remember

The 'fade factor' alone might not be enough to avoid liability for contempt if the court holds that published material has created an impediment to the course of justice—see the Jefferies case on pp. 238–239, Information suggesting a suspect or defendant is dishonest or of bad character.

Publishing material shortly before or during a trial

The 'fade factor' offers no protection if the material concerned is published shortly before a trial begins or after it has started. In 2008 ITV Central was fined £25,000 for contempt for broadcasting an item on the morning on which the trial of five men was due to start which reported that one defendant was in jail serving a sentence for murder.

Case studies

The *Sunday Mirror* was fined £75,000 in 2002 over articles which led to the collapse of the first trial of two Leeds United footballers on assault charges. The two-page spread—published while the jury was deliberating and had been sent home for the weekend—contained an interview in which the victim's father said his son was the victim of a racial attack, although the jury had been told that there was no evidence of a racial motive, and a story commenting on a major witness's credibility. In the contempt proceedings, counsel for the Attorney General estimated the cost of the aborted trial at £1,113,000 and the cost of the subsequent re-trial at £1,125,000 (*Attorney General v Mirror Group Newspapers Ltd* [2002] EWHC 907 (Admin)).

see ch. 35 on the hacking allegations

In November 2015 the magazine *GQ* was found to have committed strict liability contempt by publishing an article by New York-based journalist and media commentator Michael Wolff about the trial of former News International chief executive Rebekah Brooks, former *News of the World* editor Andy Coulson and others on charges of conspiracy to hack phones.

The trial started in November 2013 and lasted until June 2014—and the *GQ* piece appeared in March 2014, as some of the defendants were about to give evidence. The Lord Chief Justice, Lord Thomas, said: 'I am left in little doubt that the effect of the article read as a whole was very seriously prejudicial.' The piece 'plainly implied that Mr Rupert Murdoch was a participant in the phone hacking, that the defendants must have been aware of the phone hacking, that the defence was being funded by him and conducted on the defendants' instructions so as to protect his interests, but in a way that might also secure their acquittal'. Lord Thomas pointed out that no such allegations against Mr Murdoch were made in the trial, and added: 'It was in my view unrealistic to expect a member of a jury who read the article to be uninfluenced by or to put out of his or her mind the contents of such an article published as it was during the trial.' *GQ*'s publisher, Conde Nast, said the magazine took legal advice before running the piece—and was told that it was not prejudicial. The company was fined £10,000 for the contempt and ordered to pay the Attorney General's costs of nearly £50,000. Nearly 100,000 copies of the magazine were withdrawn from sale and destroyed after concerns were raised about the article (*Attorney General v The Condé Nast Publications Ltd* [2015] EWHC 3322 (Admin); *Media Lawyer*, 4 February 2016). Coulson was convicted of hacking. Ms Brooks was acquitted and reappointed as chief executive of News UK (formerly News International).

 For more detail of the *GQ* case see the Additional Material for this chapter on www.mcnaes.com.

Archive material on news websites

'Fade factor' protection does not apply to material which, since it was originally published, remains accessible to the public in a media organisation's online archive. Jurors might find stories in news archives referring to a defendant's previous convictions, or accounts of the crime they are trying, which were published before the case became active. They might also find accounts published by foreign media which ignore UK contempt law.

But if a UK media organisation's attention is drawn to archived material which, in the view of the defence or prosecution, creates a substantial risk of serious prejudice or impediment to a particular active case, the safest course to avoid a contempt problem is to remove it or block public access to it until the case is no longer active.

In 2012 a woman juror who used the internet to research the defendant, despite the judge's direction forbidding it, was jailed for six months for contempt. The trial at Luton Crown court had to be halted and the defendant re-tried.

In April 2015 new provisions inserted into the Juries Act 1974 by sections 69–73 of the Criminal Justice and Courts Act 2015 made it a criminal offence, punishable by up to two years in jail and/or an unlimited fine, for jurors to do any kind of research, including on the internet, into a case on which they are sitting.

Readers' comments

Media organisations must be wary of allowing readers to post comments online about an 'active' criminal case, as they might contain facts or allegations—for example, about the character or appearance of an arrested person or a defendant's criminal history—which could create a substantial risk of serious prejudice or impediment, because of the risk of witnesses or jurors reading them.

Best practice includes not providing any place for comments under a report of an arrest or ongoing jury trial. The media might be able to rely on the defence in 'regulation 19'—for example, if a reader posts such a comment elsewhere on the site. See ch. 21, p. 297, General protection in regulation 19.

▶ Media could face huge costs if 'serious misconduct' affects a case

Under the Courts Act 2003 the Lord Chancellor made regulations in 2004 allowing a magistrates' court, a Crown court or the Court of Appeal to order a third party (which could be a media organisation) to pay costs which were incurred in a court case as a consequence of that party's 'serious misconduct'—the Costs in Criminal Cases (General) (Amendment) Regulations 2004. The 'serious misconduct' could be held to have occurred through publication of material or through a reporter's action even if there was no strict liability contempt. The measure was largely inspired by the costly abandonment of the trial in the Leeds footballers case following a *Sunday Mirror* article, referred to earlier. If 'serious misconduct' not amounting to a contempt were held to have occurred in future, the media organisation involved could become liable for huge costs.

Regulation 3F(4) says the court must allow the third party against whom such a costs order is sought to make representations and may hear evidence. An appeal against such an order made by magistrates may be made to the Crown court; an appeal against a Crown court order may be heard in the Court of Appeal. There is no appeal against such an order made in the Court of Appeal.

Court reporting—the section 4 defence

In some circumstances, a media report of a court hearing might create a substantial risk of prejudice to a later stage of the same case or to another case due to be tried.

Before the Contempt of Court Act 1981, even a fair and accurate report of proceedings in open court could be held to create such risk of prejudice and so be contempt. But section 4 of the 1981 Act gives the media a defence, saying a person cannot be found guilty of breaching the strict liability rule in respect of a report of a court hearing which is held in public which is:

see ch. 21, p. 285, Reports must be contemporaneous, for definition of the term

- a fair and accurate report of that hearing;
- published contemporaneously; and
- in good faith.

The Act does not define 'good faith', but the overall effect of section 4 is that courts are expected to make a specific order restricting the media if they do not want all or part of any hearing in public to be reported contemporaneously.

The section 4 defence does not protect reports of a court hearing held in private—see also ch. 11, p. 129, Ban on reporting a court's private hearing.

Inaccurate reporting of a current jury trial

The section 4 defence does not protect an unfair or inaccurate court report. The High Court fined the BBC £5,000 in 1992 for an inaccurate report of a continuing trial before a jury, saying it contained errors which created a substantial risk of serious prejudice since it was foreseeable that publication would delay and obstruct the course of justice (*A-G v BBC* [1992] COD 264).

Section 4(2) orders

In some circumstances, it might be argued that fair, accurate and contemporaneous reporting of a trial could prejudice a later stage of that case or another, linked, case.

If several defendants are to be dealt with in a series of trials, reports of the first in the series could arguably influence people who read or see them and who are then selected as jurors for the next trial or subsequent trials, concerning different allegations against the same defendant(s).

The jury in the second trial, because of the principle of the presumption of innocence for defendants, might well be told nothing about the earlier trial.

But a juror in the second trial who remembers media reports of the first might be more likely to find a defendant guilty, especially if he/she was convicted in the first trial.

To avoid this danger, section 4(2) of the 1981 Act gives a court power to postpone publication of reports of a hearing or trial. In the earlier example, a judge could order that no report of the first trial should be published until the second has finished.

Section 4(2) says a court may order the postponement of the reporting of a case or part of a case:

ch. 4, p. 41, Standard of proof in criminal law, explains this principle

- where this appears to be necessary for avoiding a substantial risk of prejudice to the administration of justice in those proceedings; or
- in any other proceedings, pending or imminent; and
- that the period of postponement may be as long as the court thinks necessary for this purpose.

Note that a court may make a section 4(2) order if there is a substantial risk of any prejudice, not necessarily 'serious' prejudice. Publishing material which breaches a section 4(2) order is punishable as contempt, with an unlimited fine and/or up to two years in jail.

Normally all charges against a defendant can be reported prior to any trial, even under the automatic reporting restrictions of other statutes as described in chs. 6–8. But in cases involving a defendant who faces more than one trial, a Crown court judge may at a stage prior to trial—for example, at the arraignment—make a section 4(2) order postponing publication of the charge(s) the defendant is due to face in any subsequent trial until after the end of the first trial, to stop potential jurors in the first trial knowing that the same defendant is to face another trial.

→ glossary

Ch. 15, pp. 188–190, Section 4(2) orders, explains the grounds on which the media may challenge the imposition of an order.

What if a section 4(2) order is not made?

Sometimes, a defendant facing a number of charges will, when arraigned, plead guilty to some but deny the others, so the jury will try him/her on the charge(s) he/she has denied. If a media organisation carries a report before the end of that trial which mentions that the defendant has admitted, or faces, other charge(s), and if the jury has not been told of other charges and/or any such guilty plea (that is, a previous conviction), the judge might feel obliged, to ensure fairness to the defendant, to stop the trial and order a re-trial before a fresh jury elsewhere. Had the judge made a section 4(2) order before the trial began, postponing reporting of the other charge(s) or guilty plea(s), the media's position would have been clear and they would have obeyed the order. But if the judge did not make such an order, the legal position would be less clear on whether reporting the other charge(s)/ guilty plea(s) during the trial would be a contempt.

Some experts say the section 4 defence should protect the media in such circumstances, arguing that the defence should apply unless the court makes it clear that information aired in open court should not be contemporaneously reported by making a section 4(2) postponement order. But the section 4 defence is subject to 'good faith' in publishing, so it would fail if it could be proved that the person responsible for publication intended to create prejudice to the subsequent trial. Proof of such intent could lead to the offence being regarded not as a breach of the 1981 Act but as a graver contempt at common law.

Proceedings in court in the absence of the jury

During trials judges often have to rule on the admissibility of evidence or other matters after hearing argument from defence and prosecution lawyers in the absence of the jury (which is kept out of the courtroom). The process of making such a ruling is still classed as a public proceeding. But the judge may tell the lawyers not to mention the matters discussed to the jury—for example, if knowledge of them could prejudice its deliberations on the verdict(s). Publishing reports of those discussions and rulings—creating a risk that the jury can quickly become aware of them—before the verdicts are given could lead to the trial being aborted. Judges may not make section 4(2) postponement orders covering such discussions or rulings in the jury's absence, because the expectation is that the media will realise that these should not be published prematurely.

The law is not clear

The application of the law of contempt in both the circumstances outlined earlier—that is, publication before a trial of any guilty plea(s)/other charge(s), or contemporaneous reporting of discussions held or rulings made in a jury's absence during a trial—is unclear if no section 4(2) order has been made.

But specialists suggest that journalists would have a defence by arguing that a court could have made an order under section 4(2), that it should have done so if it wanted material kept from potential jurors and that if it failed to do so, it made that decision on good and sufficient grounds.

Journalists should not, even if no section 4(2) order is made, contemporaneously report things discussed or rulings made in the absence of the jury at a Crown court trial. Even if the publication cannot be held to be contempt, there is a risk—explained earlier in this chapter—that a media organisation might be accused of 'serious misconduct' under section 93 of the Courts Act 2003 and be held liable for the costs of an aborted or delayed trial. The material can be published after all verdicts are reached unless the judge orders otherwise. But judges have been known to make clear on occasion that they have no objection to contemporaneous reporting of what happened in the jury's absence because they did not think it would be prejudicial. Arguably, a cautious approach should be taken to publication of any other charge(s) faced, or guilty plea(s) entered, by a defendant who is shortly to be tried on other matters unless it is clear that the jury will be told about them.

▌ Section 5 defence of discussion of public affairs

Section 5 of the Contempt of Court Act 1981 says:

> " [A] publication made as, or as part of, a discussion in good faith of public affairs will not be treated as contempt of court under the strict liability rule if the risk of impediment or prejudice to particular legal proceedings is merely incidental to the discussion. "

The defence was introduced because of complaints that freedom of expression in the UK was unnecessarily restricted by a ruling in a case in 1973.

👁 Case study

The Sunday Times wanted to publish an article raising important issues of public interest about the way the drug thalidomide was tested and marketed—at a time when civil actions were pending against the manufacturer, Distillers Company (Biochemicals) Ltd, on behalf of children born with deformities because their mothers took the drug during pregnancy. The House of Lords ruled that the proposed article would be contempt in respect of those pending cases. The government-appointed Phillimore Committee said of the decision: 'At any given moment many thousands of legal proceedings are in progress, a number of which may well raise or reflect such issues (matters of general public interest). If, for example, a general public debate about fire precautions in hotels is in progress, the debate clearly ought not to be brought to a halt simply because a particular hotel is prosecuted for breach of the fire regulations.'

The European Court of Human Rights held in 1979 that the Lords' ruling violated the right to freedom of expression under Article 10 of the European Convention on Human Rights.

The government's response was to introduce the section 5 defence. The time of liability for contempt in civil proceedings, explained later in this chapter, was also changed.

👁 Case study

Two newspapers were prosecuted in 1981 for contempt arising from comments published during the trial of Dr Leonard Arthur, a paediatrician accused of murdering a newborn baby with Down's syndrome. It was alleged that the doctor, complying with the parents' wishes, let the infant starve. Dr Arthur was acquitted of murder. The *Sunday Express* admitted that a contempt was committed in a comment article by the editor, John Junor, which said the baby had been drugged instead of being fed and had died 'unloved and unwanted'. The editor was fined £1,000 and Express Newspapers, £10,000.

But the *Daily Mail* denied contempt, arguing that its article was protected by section 5. The House of Lords ruled on appeal that while the article, which trenchantly considered whether or not severely disabled babies should be allowed or encouraged to survive, did create a substantial risk of serious prejudice to Dr Arthur's trial, it was written in good faith and, because it was written in support of a 'pro-life' candidate at a by-election, was a discussion of public affairs. Lord Diplock said the article made no express mention of Dr Arthur's case and the risk of prejudice would be properly described as merely incidental (The Times, 16 and 19 December 1981; *Attorney General v English* [1983] 1 AC 116).

Safest course

To be sure of section 5 protection a media organisation should not, when publishing a general feature or discussion about a social issue, refer in it to any active case in which the issue figures and in particular should not suggest that the defendant in such a case is or is not guilty.

▶ Contempt of civil proceedings under the 1981 Act

Under the strict liability rule:

- civil proceedings are deemed to be active from the time a date for the trial or a hearing is fixed;
- a civil case ceases to be active when it is disposed of, abandoned, discontinued or withdrawn.

ch. 12 explains civil courts and which cases could involve juries

There is generally less possibility of media coverage creating a substantial risk of serious prejudice to active civil cases, as most of them are tried by a judge alone, and judges are regarded as highly unlikely to be affected by media coverage.

But there remains the possibility that witnesses in a civil case could be affected by media coverage if it delves so deeply into the circumstances of the case that witnesses' evidence given in advance of or at the trial could be coloured, or their memories be contaminated, by detail they read or see in reports.

When a jury is involved, particular care must be taken not to breach the strict liability rule, and material aired in court in the jury's absence should not be published while the jury is involved in the case.

 Case study

Mr Justice Poole, in the High Court sitting in Birmingham in 1999, reminded reporters that civil proceedings remained active until a case ended. A jury had decided in favour of a man claiming damages from West Midlands Police for malicious prosecution. Before the jury decided on the amount of damages, the *Birmingham Post* suggested he would get £30,000. The judge said the proceedings were therefore tainted. The claimant abandoned his case rather than go through a re-trial (*Media Lawyer*, Issue 25, January/February 2000).

Sometimes, when a journalist seeks a comment about a civil case, a lawyer involved will insist that little can be published because it is **sub judice**—a term indicating merely that the legal action has begun. But this is not the same as the case being active: a civil case becomes active at what may be a later stage, when a date is fixed for the trial or hearing—and even then, media coverage is not prohibited, provided the strict liability rule is obeyed.

→glossary

> See ch. 12, p. 141, 'Payments into court', for an explanation of the contempt danger of reporting that such an offer has been made in a civil case.

Other contempts under the 1981 Act and other Acts

Section 9 of the 1981 Act says it is a contempt to use or take into court for use any audio-recorder (except with the court's permission), and to broadcast any such recordings.

Section 11 of the Act gives courts powers, when they allow a name or other information to be withheld from the public, to prohibit publication of that name or material in connection with the proceedings. Breach of a section 11 order would be a contempt.

Section 20D of the Juries Act 1974 says it is contempt to seek to discover or to publish how an individual juror voted in a verdict, or what was discussed by a jury to reach a verdict. That law is explained in ch 11, p. 126, Confidentiality of jury deliberations, and ch. 16, p. 211, Reporting restrictions, explains similar law applying to inquest jury deliberations.

 ch. 11 explains these sections in the 1981 Act

Section 12 of the Administration of Justice Act 1960 makes it a contempt for the media to publish an account of what was said or done at a court hearing held in private if the case falls within certain categories. The ban also covers quoting from court documents—see ch. 11, p. 129, Ban on reporting a court's private hearing.

➡ Recap of major points

- For the media, the greatest danger of committing contempt of court lies in publishing material which, under the Contempt of Court Act 1981, could be ruled to have created a substantial risk of serious prejudice or impediment to an 'active' case.

- Certain types of information are more likely than others to be regarded as creating such risk—for example, details of the previous convictions of a defendant awaiting trial.

- Journalists should know when, under the 1981 Act, a criminal or a civil case becomes active and when it ceases to be active—because the 'active period' determines what can be published.

- Juries are rarely used in civil cases, so the media have greater leeway about what can be published about active civil cases than they have in relation to active criminal cases.

- In prosecuting under the Act for strict liability contempt the Attorney General does not have to prove intent to cause prejudice.

- Under section 4(2) a court can order the media to postpone a report of a court case, or part of it, to avoid a substantial risk of prejudice.

- Section 5 provides a defence for a published discussion in good faith of public affairs where the risk of prejudice is merely incidental to the discussion.

- When during a trial there are legal discussions or rulings which occur in the jury's absence, the media should not report such material until all the verdicts are reached.

- Under the Courts Act 2003, any party, including a media organisation, held to have committed 'serious misconduct' affecting a court case could be liable for huge costs.

((•)) Useful Websites

www.judiciary.gov.uk/wp-content/uploads/2015/05/reporting-restrictions-guide-2015-final.pdf
Guidance on reporting restrictions, published by the Judicial College, the News Media Association, the Media Lawyers Association, the Society of Editors and Times Newspapers Ltd

Part 3

Defamation and related law

Defamation—definitions and dangers

Chapter summary

This chapter explains what defamation is, and why it is of such concern to journalists and publishers. It covers the risks of being sued for libel and losing, and so having to pay huge costs and damages. The chapter explains the definitions of what is defamatory. The following chapters explain who can sue for defamation, what the claimant must do to bring an action, the defences and reforms in the Defamation Act 2013, which came into effect in England and Wales on 1 January 2014, meaning that there are now radical differences between libel laws in England and Wales, in Scotland and in Northern Ireland, which rejected the English reforms. Defamation is one of the greatest legal dangers for anyone who earns a living with words and images—so handling a complaint or drafting an apology about something published is not a job for an inexperienced journalist.

▶ Seeking legal advice

Defamation law is complex, so this book can provide nothing more than a rough guide. While media organisations can sometimes safely go further than many journalists suppose, they also need to stop and reflect before taking what might be a dangerous course of action.

The golden rule for the journalist is that if publication seems likely to bring a threat of a defamation action, he/she should take professional advice.

But the media's role in exposing wrongdoing is extremely important. As Lord Justice Lawton (then Mr Justice Lawton) said in a case in 1965:

> It is one of the professional tasks of newspapers to unmask the fraudulent and the scandalous. It is in the public interest to do it. It is a job which newspapers have done time and time again in their long history.

▮ What is defamation?

The law protects an individual's personal and professional reputation from unjustified attack. In civil law a statement making such an attack may be found to be a tort—a civil wrong for which a court may award monetary damages.

Defamatory statements are those published or spoken which affect the reputation of a person, company or organisation. A defamatory statement in written or in any other permanent form—including on the internet—is a libel, for which damages can be awarded. But a statement may be protected by a defence.

A defamatory statement which is spoken is the tort of slander, which may also incur damages unless a defence applies. But defamatory statements spoken in a radio, television, cable or web broadcast, or in the public performance of a play, are classed as libel by the Broadcasting Act 1990 and Theatres Act 1968 respectively. Libel and slander have different requirements in terms of what a claimant must prove, as chs. 20 and 24 explain.

The Defamation Act 2013 abolished the presumption of jury trial for defamation cases, so they are heard by a judge alone unless the court orders otherwise. This means the judge now decides the key issues of what the words mean and whether they have caused serious harm.

Definitions of a defamatory statement

A statement about a person is defamatory if it seriously affects his/her reputation by:

- exposing him/her to hatred, ridicule or contempt, or causing him/her to be shunned or avoided;
- lowering him/her in the estimation of right-thinking members of society generally; or
- disparaging the person in his/her business, trade, office or profession.

Section 1 of the Defamation Act 2013 requires that the claimant—the person suing—must now cross a further threshold by showing that a statement has caused, or is likely to cause, serious harm to his/her reputation.

A company which wishes to sue must show that the statement has caused, or is likely to cause, it serious financial loss.

Lawyers sometimes find it difficult to decide whether a statement is defamatory, and judges sometimes disagree.

Note the phrase 'right-thinking members of society generally' in the second definition—it is not enough for a claimant to show only that the words of which he/she complains have lowered him/her in the estimation of a limited class in the community which may not conform to that standard.

✳ Remember

It is almost always defamatory to say of a person that he/she is a liar, or a cheat, or is insolvent or in financial difficulties; whether the statement is a libel will depend on whether the publisher has a defence—for example, it can be proved true.

Meaning of words

The test in law of what words mean is what a 'reasonable person' would think they mean. In defamation law, a statement is held to have just one meaning—and this will not necessarily be the meaning intended by the author or publisher. Sir Anthony Clarke, Master of the Rolls, detailed the principles of deciding meaning in *Jeynes v News Magazines Ltd* [2008] EWCA Civ 130, saying (at paragraph 14):

> They may be summarised in this way: (1) The governing principle is reasonableness. (2) The hypothetical reasonable reader is not naïve but he is not unduly suspicious. He can read between the lines. He can read in an implication more readily than a lawyer and may indulge in a certain amount of loose thinking but he must be treated as being a man who is not avid for scandal and someone who does not, and should not, select one bad meaning where other non-defamatory meanings are available. (3) Over-elaborate analysis is best avoided. (4) The intention of the publisher is irrelevant. (5) The article must be read as a whole, and any 'bane and antidote' taken together. (6) The hypothetical reader is taken to be representative of those who would read the publication in question. (7) In delimiting the range of permissible defamatory meanings, the court should rule out any meaning which, 'can only emerge as the produce of some strained, or forced, or utterly unreasonable interpretation … ' … (8) It follows that 'it is not enough to say that by some person or another the words might be understood in a defamatory sense' … .

see p. 258, Bane and antidote

The words must be read in full and in their context, because a statement which is innocuous when standing alone can acquire defamatory meaning when juxtaposed with other material. Juxtaposition is a constant danger for journalists, particularly for sub-editors and those dealing with production. Those editing footage must take care how pictures interact with each other and with any commentary—what meanings are being created?

 See also ch. 20, p. 270, Juxtaposition

Inferences

Many statements may carry more than one meaning.

- An inference is a statement with a secondary meaning which can be understood by someone without special knowledge who 'reads between the lines in the light of his general knowledge and experience of worldly affairs'.

For example, an inference is created if someone says: 'I saw the editor leave the pub, and he was swaying and his speech was slurred.' The inference is that the editor was drunk, though the term 'drunk' is not used. But for some statements there may be dispute about whether a defamatory inference was created.

Innuendoes

- An innuendo in the law of libel is a statement which may seem to be innocuous to some people but is defamatory to people with special knowledge.

For example, saying 'I saw our editor go into that house on the corner of Sleep Street' would not in itself be defamatory, unless the communication is to someone who knows that the house is a brothel.

The term *innuendo* comes from a Latin word meaning 'to nod to'.

The libel claimant who says he/she has been defamed by an innuendo must show not only that the special facts or circumstances giving rise to the innuendo exist, but also that they are known to the people to whom the statement was published.

👁 Case study

In 1986 Lord Gowrie, a former Cabinet Minister, received 'substantial' damages over a newspaper article which created the innuendo that he took drugs. He had recently resigned as Minister for the Arts and the *Daily Star* newspaper then asked: 'What expensive habits can he not support on an income of £33,000? I'm sure Gowrie himself would snort at suggestions that he was born with a silver spoon round his neck.' His **counsel** said the reference to expensive habits, the suggestion that he could not support those habits on his ministerial salary, the use of the word 'snort' and the reference to a 'silver spoon around his neck' all bore the plain implication to all those familiar with the relevant terminology that Lord Gowrie took illegal drugs, particularly cocaine, and resigned because his salary was not enough to finance the habit.

→ glossary

A journalist would clearly be mistaken to believe that using inference or innuendo is any safer in libel law than making a direct allegation.

Bane and antidote

Just as a defamatory meaning may be conveyed by a particular context, so too a defamatory meaning may be removed by the context. A judge said in 1835 that if in one part of a publication something disreputable to the claimant was stated that was removed by the conclusion, 'the bane and the antidote must be taken together'.

The House of Lords applied this rule in 1995 (*Charleston v News Group Newspapers Ltd* [1995] 2 AC 65), when it dismissed a case in which Ann Charleston and Ian Smith, two actors from the television serial *Neighbours*, sued the *News of the World* over headlines and photographs in which their faces were superimposed on models in pornographic poses.

The main headline read: 'Strewth! What's Harold up to with our Madge?' The text said: 'What would the Neighbours say ... strait-laced Harold Bishop starring in a bondage session with screen wife Madge. The famous faces from the television soap are the unwitting stars of a sordid computer game that is available to their child fans. The game superimposes stars' heads on near-naked bodies of real porn models. The stars knew nothing about it.'

The actors' counsel conceded that anyone who read the whole of the text would realise the photographs were mock-ups, but said many readers were unlikely to go beyond the photographs and headlines.

Lord Bridge said it was often a debatable question, which the jury must resolve, whether the antidote was effective to neutralise the bane. The answer depended not only on the nature of the libel conveyed by a headline and the language of the text which was relied on to neutralise it, but also on the manner in which all the material was set out and balanced. In this case, no reader who read beyond the first paragraph could possibly have drawn a defamatory inference.

Lord Nicholls warned that words in the text would not always 'cure' a defamatory headline: 'It all depends on the context, one element in which is the layout of the article. Those who print defamatory headlines are playing with fire.' The ordinary reader might not notice words tucked away low down in an article.

Changing standards

Imputations which were defamatory 100 years ago may not be defamatory today, and vice versa. In the reign of Charles II it was held to be actionable to say falsely of a man that he was a papist and went to mass. In the next reign similar statements were held not to be defamatory.

During the First World War a UK court decided that it was a libel to write falsely of a man that he was a German.

Is it defamatory to call someone homosexual? It used to be, but now no 'right-thinking member of society' would think less of someone because he/she is gay. So to state wrongly that someone is gay would not in some circumstances be defamatory. But it could be defamatory if it were to imply the person lied about his/her sexual orientation.

👁 Case study

Singer-songwriter Robbie Williams won 'substantial' damages from publisher Northern and Shell in 2005 after the magazines *Star* and *Hot Star* ran stories alleging that he had omitted from a forthcoming authorised biography details of an alleged sexual encounter with a man in the lavatories of a club in Manchester and that, by disclosing details of his female conquests but not mentioning this episode, he was concealing his true sexuality. But the allegations were completely false—the publisher apologised, and paid damages and the singer's costs (*Robert Peter Williams v Northern and Shell Plc*, statement in High Court, 6 December 2005).

◗ Why media organisations may be reluctant to fight defamation actions

Defamation law tries to strike a balance between the individual's right to a reputation and the right to freedom of speech, and so provides defences for those who make defamatory statements about others for acceptable reasons—see subsequent chapters. But media organisations can be reluctant to fight defamation actions, for a variety of reasons.

Uncertainty of how a judge will interpret meaning

- The first is the uncertainty about how a judge will decide the meaning of what was published—for example, a statement which seems innocuous to one person may equally clearly be defamatory to another.

Difficulty of proving the truth

Even if a journalist and his/her editor are convinced of a story's truth, they may be unable to prove it in court.

ch. 21 explains the defence of truth

- People needed as witnesses to an event may not wish to become involved in a libel case; witnesses' memories may prove unreliable; they may forget detail by the time the trial begins; by the time the case gets to trial they may have moved and cannot be traced.

Huge damages could be awarded if trial lost

ch. 2 explains press regulation

- Media organisations considering contesting a libel action also find it difficult to assess what amount of damages might be awarded should they lose. In addition, damages could now be inflated by aggravated damages as a result of sections 34–42 of the Crime and Courts Act 2013, which allow a court to impose 'exemplary damages' on a publisher which has not signed up to a press regulator recognised under the Royal Charter system created in October 2013. The system was devised as part of the government's response to the Leveson Report on press regulation.

In the past juries have awarded huge sums. In 2000 the magazine *LM* (formerly *Living Marxism*) shut down after a jury awarded a total of £375,000 damages to two television reporters and ITN over a story accusing them of having sensationalised the image of an emaciated Muslim pictured through barbed wire at a Serbrun detention camp in Bosnia (*The Guardian*, 21 March 2000).

In 2002 libel judge Mr Justice Eady said that the ceiling for the most serious defamatory allegations was currently 'reckoned to be of the order of £200,000'—the figure he awarded that year, when trying a case without a jury, to each of two nursery nurses wrongly accused of sexual abuse (*Christopher Lillie and Dawn Reed v Newcastle City Council, Richard Barker, Judith Jones, Jacqui Saradjian and Roy Wardell* [2002] EWHC 1600 (QB)). In 2012 Mr Justice Tugendhat noted that the upper limit would now, taking into account factors including inflation, be around £275,000 (*Cairns v Modi* [2012] EWCA Civ 1382).

Huge costs

- Damages might be high, but they are usually much lower than legal costs in the case.

In one case Mirror Group Newspapers paid £15,000 in settlement of a defamation action but was then presented with a costs bill of £382,000—which was reduced on appeal.

In June 2010 martial arts expert Matthew Fiddes, a former bodyguard to entertainer Michael Jackson, dropped at a very late stage his defamation case against Channel 4 over a documentary about members of the Jackson family. By that time, Channel 4's costs exceeded £1.5 million. Mr Fiddes was operating on a no-win, no-fee conditional fee agreement (CFA).

→ glossary

The Crime and Courts Act 2013 also allows a court to refuse to award costs to a publisher which wins a defamation, privacy or harassment case but is not signed up with recognised press regulator.

It may be better to settle

It is not surprising that, faced with these kinds of figures and risks over costs and damages, even if the case is won at a trial, ardent campaigning editors may decide either not to carry a story or, having carried it, to avoid a trial by apologising and paying damages.

As the vast majority of libel cases settle out of court, with the amounts involved rarely disclosed, the ongoing cost of libel actions to media organisations is often underestimated. A settlement usually involves paying some or all of the other side's costs.

'No win, no fee' legal representation

((•))

The introduction of the CFA, known as 'no win, no fee', for libel cases in 1998 had a serious chilling effect on the media, significantly restricting what the public was able to read and hear, most obviously when articles, books or programmes were changed because of legal considerations.

see Useful Websites at the end of this chapter on 'no win, no fee'

Legal aid was never available for libel actions, so historically the libel courts were beyond the reach of people on modest incomes. But CFAs meant litigants without the means to sue could do so, represented by lawyers who received nothing if they lost a case but could claim a 'success fee' of up to a 100 per cent increase on fees if they won. In January 2010 the European Court of Human Rights held that a 100 per cent success fee claimed by Naomi Campbell's lawyers from Mirror Group Newspapers was a breach of the publisher's right to freedom of expression.

 Campbell was a privacy case—see ch. 26, p. 329, Development of the law.

In 2011 the Coalition government announced that it would implement reforms recommended by Lord Justice Jackson in his report on costs, and stop success fees and premiums for insurance taken out by claimants to cover a winning defendant's costs from being reclaimed from a losing defendant. That reform has been put on hold while the government draws up a new scheme to protect would-be litigants of modest means from having to pay the costs if they sue a publisher and lose.

The media has argued that the CFA system allows an impecunious claimant to hold it to ransom. If the claimant loses, the media defendant is unlikely to recover its costs, while if the claimant wins, the media defendant has to pay not only damages but also the lawyers' 'success fees' and associated insurance premiums. There is also no incentive for a claimant on a CFA to control what his/her solicitor spends, as the defendant will pay. The pressure to settle such cases rather than go to court is considerable.

◗ Freedom of expression

Most journalists believe that defamation law, in attempting to 'strike a balance' between protecting reputation and allowing freedom of speech, has been tilted historically in favour of claimants.

But developments in recent years, particularly the Defamation Act 2013, seem likely to tilt the balance in favour of freedom of expression.

They are as follows.

ch. 1 explains the Convention generally

(1) The Human Rights Act 1998, which took effect on 2 October 2000, requires courts to pay regard to Article 10 of the European Convention on Human Rights, concerned with freedom of expression. The European Court of Human Rights has said that Article 10 does not involve a 'choice between two conflicting principles' but 'a freedom of expression that is subject to a number of exceptions which must be narrowly construed'.

ch. 22 explains the public interest defence

(2) The decision of the House of Lords in *Reynolds v Times Newspapers* [2001] 2 AC 127, greatly extended the ambit of privilege defences and has now taken statutory form in section 4 of the Defamation Act 2013—the defence of 'publication on a matter of public interest'.

(3) The increased willingness of the courts to strike out cases in which a claimant could not show that a substantial tort had been committed has now been given statutory expression in the requirement in section 1 of the Defamation Act 2013 that a claimant must show that a statement has caused, or is likely to cause, serious harm to his/her reputation.

Other reforms aiding freedom of expression include the introduction of qualified privilege for peer-reviewed publications in scientific and academic journals, the widening of qualified privilege in relation to courts and press conferences, and the liberalising of the honest opinion defence, formerly known as 'fair comment'.

ch. 21 explains defences

▌ Errors and apologies

Sometimes publication of a libel is the result of an innocent error. The arrival of a solicitor's letter from a potential claimant which could start the journey to the High Court is the moment to take legal advice. Libel law is not a matter for an inexperienced person, because of the dangers of aggravating a problem by mishandling it. A reporter who receives a complaint about something which has been published should refer the issue to the relevant executive or editor.

Publishing an apology or an inadequate correction can itself, in certain circumstances, create a further libel problem.

ch. 21 explains the danger of ill-considered apologies

Taking the correct legal steps, including, if necessary, publishing a prompt apology or correction, can remove the heat from a libel threat and save thousands of pounds even if the claim is settled. The effect of a prompt apology can now play a significant part in a court's consideration of whether or not a statement caused 'serious harm' to reputation and could prevent a claim from being viable in the first place. Also, as ch. 24 explains, a failure to correct an article which is known to be wrong, especially if it remains visible online, could mean the publisher has to pay damages for malicious falsehood.

✳ Remember

The most common cause of libel actions against media organisations is a journalist's failure to apply professional standards of accuracy and fairness. The best protection against becoming involved in an expensive action is to make every effort to get the story right.

➡ Recap of major points

- A defamatory statement made in permanent form is generally libel, and if in transient form, it is generally slander—if it cannot be defended.
- In a defamation action, the test of what the words actually mean is the test of what a reasonable person would take them to mean.
- Words may carry an innuendo, a 'hidden' meaning clear to people with special knowledge, or create an inference, obvious to everybody.

- The financial implications of losing a defamation action in terms of damages and costs are so punitive that journalists must always consider whether what they are writing or plan to broadcast will be defensible if a defamation action results.

((•)) Useful Websites

www.lawsociety.org.uk/for-the-public/faqs/conditional-fee-agreements/
Law Society explanation of 'no win, no fee' arrangements

http://inforrm.wordpress.com/
Inforrm blog site, which publishes analysis of defamation and other law

www.legislation.gov.uk/ukpga/2013/26/contents/enacted
Defamation Act 2013

www.legislation.gov.uk/ukpga/2013/26/notes/contents
Explanatory Notes to the 2013 Act

The claimant and what must be proved

Chapter summary

This chapter details who can sue for libel. A claimant has to prove that the material was published to a third party—a formality in a case against the media—that it is capable of bearing the defamatory meaning complained of, that he/she has been identified in it and that his/her reputation has suffered, or is likely to suffer, serious harm. But the claimant does not have the burden of proving the material is false. A claimant can sue anyone who 'publishes' the libel, including reporters and the publication's distributors. The practical effects of some of the reforms in the Defamation Act 2013 are not yet clear.

▌ Who might sue?

All citizens as individuals have the right to sue for libel—that is, to be a claimant.

The availability of 'no win, no fee' arrangements, described in ch. 19, has opened the libel courts to greater numbers of people. This reinforces the need for journalists to be accurate and approach stories thus:

- Is what I am writing potentially defamatory?
- If so, do I have a defence?

All would-be claimants now have to pass the 'serious harm' test introduced in the Defamation Act 2013—failure to get over this hurdle will stop a claim in its tracks.

Corporations, including companies

A corporation can sue for a publication injurious to its trading reputation. But section 1(2) of the Defamation Act 2013 now requires that any body that 'trades for profit' must show that the serious harm it claims to have suffered 'has caused

see also
p. 267,
Dispar-
aging goods

or is likely to cause the body serious financial loss'. Previously the threat of being sued by a company was significant. Although companies are likely to find it difficult to prove that they have suffered or are likely to suffer serious financial loss, for a smaller company even the loss of one prospective client may help to establish such loss. The mere fact that a company's share price has fallen is insufficient (*Collins Stewart Ltd & another v The Financial Times* [2004] EWHC 2337). But individual directors and managers may be able to sue, if 'identified'—see later.

Local and central government

ch. 24
explains
malicious
falsehood

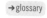→glossary

The House of Lords ruled in *Derbyshire County Council v Times Newspapers* [1993] AC 534 that institutions of local or central government could not sue for defamation in respect of their 'governmental and administrative functions' as this would place an undesirable fetter on freedom of speech. But they can sue as institutions for libels affecting their property, and for malicious falsehood if they can show malice.

A council's individual members or officers *can* sue if what is published is seen as referring to them personally. Lord Keith said in the *Derbyshire County Council* case:

> 66 A publication attacking the activities of the authority will necessarily be an attack on the body of councillors which represents the controlling party, or on the executives who carry on the day-to-day management of its affairs. If the individual reputation of any of these is wrongly impaired by the publication any of these can himself bring proceedings for defamation. 99

An individual can pursue a defamation claim if what is published 'identifies' him/her which can occur even if he/she is not named. The legal test for identification is explained later in the chapter.

As a general rule, an association, such as a club, cannot sue unless it is an incorporated body, but words disparaging an association will almost invariably reflect upon the reputations of one or more of the officials who, as individuals, can sue if 'identified'.

Trade unions

The House of Lords seems to have accepted in the *Derbyshire County Council* case cited earlier that trade unions can sue, even though they are not corporate bodies. A union's officers can sue.

Members of Parliament

Parliamentarians' right to waive their parliamentary privilege in defamation actions and thus sue was repealed by the Deregulation Act 2015, Schedule 23, paragraph 44.

Disparaging goods

Can a publication defame a person or a firm by disparaging goods? This is an important question as product testing becomes commonplace in newspapers, magazines and other media.

The answer is yes. But it is not enough that the statement should simply affect the person adversely in his/her business—it must also impute to him/her discreditable conduct in that business, or tend to show that he/she is ill-suited or ill-qualified to do it *Griffiths v Benn* [1911] 927 TLR 26, CA, applied in *James Morford and others v Nic Rigby and the East Anglian Daily Times Co Ltd* [1998] EWCA Civ 263).

For example, it will be defamatory to write falsely of a businessman that he has been condemned by his trade association, or of a bricklayer that she does not know how to lay bricks properly, if either can show that his/her reputation suffered, or was likely to suffer, serious harm as a result of the publication.

Not all words criticising a person's goods are defamatory—for example, a motoring correspondent could criticise a car's performance without reflecting upon the character of the manufacturer or dealer. But the statement might prompt an action for malicious falsehood—see ch. 24.

The imputations that give most problems in this context are dishonesty, carelessness and incompetence.

In 1994 a jury awarded £1.485 million damages to the manufacturer of a yacht, Walker Wingsail Systems plc, over an article in *Yachting World* which contrasted the manufacturer's striking claims for the yacht's performance with its drastically poorer performance when tested by the journalist.

▌ What the claimant must prove

A claimant suing for libel has to prove that:

- the publication is defamatory and has caused, or is likely to cause, his/her reputation to suffer serious harm;
- it may be reasonably understood to refer to him/her—that is, 'identification'; and
- it has been published to a third person.

This can be remembered as 'defamation, identification, publication'.

Defamation

Legal definitions of defamatory statements are given in ch. 19. Broadly speaking, any allegation or smear which causes, or is likely to cause, serious harm to a person's reputation among honest citizens will be defamatory.

see p. 256, Definitions of a defamatory statement

A claimant does *not* have to prove that the statement is false. If a statement is defamatory, the court assumes it is false. If the statement is true and the journalist can prove it is true, then there is a defence, as the next chapter explains.

The claimant does not have to prove intention: it is no use the journalist saying 'I didn't mean to damage this person's reputation'. However, as explained in ch. 21, intent is relevant in the 'offer of amends' defence. As ch. 22 explains, the public interest defence in section 4 of the Defamation Act 2013 provides protection in some circumstances for publication of untrue statements.

Identification

The claimant must prove that the published material identifies him/her.

Some journalists believe they can play safe by not naming an individual—but omitting the name may prove no defence.

- The test in defamation law of whether the published statement identified the claimant is whether it would reasonably lead people acquainted with him/her to believe that he/she was the person referred to.

A judge said in 1826: 'It is not necessary that all the world should understand the libel; it is sufficient if those who know the claimant can make out that he is the person meant' (*Bourke v Warren* (1826) 2 C&P 307). That is still the law.

During the late 1980s and 1990s the Police Federation, representing junior police officers, brought many actions against newspapers on behalf of their members. During the 33 months to March 1996 it launched 95 libel actions, winning them all and recovering £1,567,000 in damages. Many of the officers were not named in what was published, but it was claimed that acquaintances and/or colleagues would realise who they were. The *Burton Mail* paid £17,500 compensation plus legal costs to a woman constable who featured anonymously in a story following a complaint about an arrest. It was argued that the story's details identified her.

Derogatory comments about an institution can reflect upon the person who heads it—newspapers have had to pay damages to head teachers, who were not named in the paper, for reports criticising schools.

Wrong photos or wrong caption

People are identified by what they look like, so using the wrong photo could identify someone in a defamatory context, even if he/she is not named.

Use of file or 'stock' photographs or film to illustrate news stories or features is fraught with libel risks. A photo of a social function, with people holding drinks, is perfectly acceptable—but if it is later used as a stock shot to illustrate the perils of drinking, those pictured may sue, particularly any who are teetotal.

Confusion about who is shown in a photograph can be very costly. In 2014 Thames Valley Police paid 'substantial' damages plus costs to a man whose photograph was wrongly released with a police press release about a rapist (*Media Lawyer*, 23 April 2014).

Importance of ages, addresses and occupations

It can be dangerous to make a half-hearted effort at identification, particularly in reports of court cases.

👁 Case study

In *Newstead v London Express Newspapers Ltd* [1940] 1 KB 377, the *Daily Express* had reported that 'Harold Newstead, a 30-year-old Camberwell man', had been jailed for nine months for bigamy. Another Harold Newstead, who worked in Camberwell, sued the newspaper, claiming that the account was understood to refer to him—and won. He argued that if the words were true of another person, which they were, it was the paper's duty to give a precise and detailed description of that person, but the paper had 'recklessly struck out' the convicted person's occupation and address.

✳ Remember

A defendant's age, address and occupation, if mentioned in court, or provided by the court, should be given with his/her name in reports of the case unless the court directs otherwise. Ch. 14 explains that courts should give reporters such details.

Blurring identity increases risk

The problem with not fully identifying the subject of a story is not only that the person may argue in a libel case that he/she was the person referred to, but also that another person may claim that the words were taken to refer to him/her. A newspaper quoted from a report by the district auditor to a local council, criticising the council's deputy housing manager. The paper did not name him. But a new deputy manager had taken over. He sued, claiming he was thought to be the offending official.

Defamation of a group

If a defamatory statement refers to someone as being a member of a group and includes no other identifying detail of that person, all members of the group, if it is sufficiently small, may be able to sue for defamation, even though the publisher intended to refer to only one of them.

For example, saying 'One of the detectives at Blanktown police station is corrupt' without naming the allegedly corrupt individual will allow all the detectives there to sue because the statement 'identifies' them to their acquaintances and colleagues. Even if the publisher has evidence that one is corrupt, the rest will win damages. But if the group referred to is large, no one in it will be able reasonably to claim to have been identified merely by a reference to the group. Case law does not set a clear figure for when a group is too large for those in it to claim that reference to the group identified them as individuals. In one case, reference to a group of 35 police dog-handlers based in an area of London was ruled to be sufficient to identify them as individuals.

👁 Case study

A case in 1986 concerned a reference published by a newspaper to an allegation that detectives at Banbury CID had raped a woman. The newspaper did not name those allegedly involved. It was successfully sued by members of the group, which comprised only 12 detectives (*Riches and others v News Group Newspapers Ltd* [1985] 2 All ER 845).

Referring to a group may also identify those with particular responsibility for it. Saying 'The supermarket in Blanktown Road is run badly' refers to a small group of managers, each of whom could sue.

Juxtaposition

Placing a photograph incorrectly, or using the wrong picture, can cause expensive problems if it wrongly suggests by juxtaposition that someone shown is a person 'identified' in the accompanying story.

In 2002 motivational therapist and part-time nightclub doorman Shabazz Nelson won 'substantial' damages from *The Sun* after it used his picture with an article in which Oasis star Liam Gallagher alleged he and his girlfriend were assaulted by door attendants—referred to as 'monkeys'—at the Met Bar in London. The piece was illustrated by a picture of Mr Nelson, who was working there that night as a doorman. Mr Nelson had not assaulted Mr Gallagher or his girlfriend, had 'conducted himself in a perfectly proper and responsible manner', and was 'understandably concerned' that *Sun* readers who saw the article 'would have understood that he was the subject of Mr Gallagher's claims', Mr Justice Eady was told at the High Court.

Lack of care in the editing and 'voice-over' of footage can also cause trouble if the commentary is 'juxtaposed' with an unconnected image.

👁 Case study

In 1983 a Metropolitan Police detective constable won £20,000 damages from Granada TV after being shown walking out of West End Central police station during a *World in Action* programme on Operation Countryman, an anti-corruption investigation into the force. As he was shown emerging from the station the voice-over said: 'Since 1969 repeated investigations show that some CID officers take bribes.' The officer was not identified by name and there was no suggestion that he was guilty of such behaviour—he was merely a figure in a background shot. But his recognisable, unexpected guest appearance was enough to earn him healthy damages, because it wrongly 'identified' him as corrupt.

Publication

The claimant must prove that the statement was published. There is no defamation if the words complained of, however offensive or untrue, are addressed, in speech or writing, only to the person to whom they refer. To substantiate defamation, they must have been communicated to at least one other person. In the case of the news media, there is no difficulty in proving this—publication is widespread.

If very few readers see online material

There is an exception to this rule about publication for claimants suing over items published on the internet.

👁 Case study

In 2005 the Court of Appeal rejected a Saudi Arabian businessman's claim for defamation by ruling that it would be an abuse of process for any claimant to bring an action over material on the internet unless 'substantial publication' in England could be shown. In that case, the complained-of material was downloaded by only five people in England—three, including the claimant's lawyers, were in his 'camp' and the other two were unknown. There was no 'real or substantial' **tort** (*Dow Jones and Co Inc. v Yousef Abdul Latif Jameel* [2005] EWCA Civ 75).

→glossary

But a tweet published to 65 people can justify a substantial five-figure award of damages (*Cairns v Modi* [2013] 1 WLR 1015, CA), as can internet publication to 550 people (*Times Newspapers Ltd v Flood* [2014] EWCA Civ 1574).

The court, however, will not assume that internet publication is necessarily substantial publication (*Amoudi v Brisard* [2006] 3 All ER 294).

A court in Canada ruled that hyperlinks to articles containing defamatory material did not amount in that particular case to substantial publication of defamatory statements by the publisher of the article containing the hyperlinks (*Crookes v Wikimedia Foundation Inc.* (2008) BCSC 1424).

Who are the 'publishers'?

A person who has been defamed may sue the reporter, sub-editor, editor, publisher and broadcaster. All have participated in publishing the defamatory statement and are regarded as 'publishers' at common law. Others, such as the printer and distributor, may be protected from an action by section 1 of the Defamation

Act 1996 or section 10 of the Defamation Act 2013—see ch. 21, p. 294, 'Live' broadcasts and readers' online comments.

Repeating statements of others

- Every repetition of a libel is a fresh publication and creates a fresh cause of action. This is called the 'repetition rule'. It is no defence to say that you, the publisher, are not liable because you only repeated the words of others.

The person who originated the statement may be liable, but anyone who repeats the allegation—for example, by publishing material from a defamatory press release—may also be sued. One of the most common causes of libel actions is repeating statements made by interviewees without being able to prove the truth of the words. Also, a publisher who 'lifts' (copies and publishes) material published elsewhere is liable.

In 1993 and 1994 papers paid damages to defendants in the Birmingham Six case, who were jailed for terrorism but later cleared on appeal. Former West Midlands police officers were accused of fabricating evidence in the case, but prosecution of the officers was abandoned. The *Sunday Telegraph* subsequently reported one of the three officers as referring to the Birmingham Six and saying: 'In our eyes, their guilt is beyond doubt.' *The Sun* newspaper published an article based on the *Sunday Telegraph's* interviews. It later carried an apology and reportedly paid £1 million in damages to the six.

Journalists on local newspapers also need to be alert when handling the bygone days column. A doctor received damages for statements published afresh in 1981 in the 'Looking Back' column of the *Evening Star*, Ipswich. The statements, repeated from an article published 25 years previously, went unchallenged when first published—but see p. 273, The 'single publication rule' and online archives.

Online archives and repetition

The repetition rule is particularly relevant to websites containing archive material. It dates from the 1849 case of the Duke of Brunswick, who sued a newspaper for defamation after sending his butler to buy a back copy.

 See www.mcnaes.com ch. 20 for details of this case.

Nowadays the Duke would call up the archive version on the internet.

As ch. 21, explains, the limitation period for a defamation action is one year from the date of publication. But the limitation period for a defamation claim over material which has been placed directly on a website will begin from the date on which it is downloaded.

Under the repetition rule, each time an article or footage or sound recording in an internet archive was accessed by someone it was deemed to amount to a new publication, potentially giving rise to a new action.

It is especially important to remove from an archive any material which has been held to be libellous.

In 2006 a businessman, Jim Carr, won two libel damages payouts from the *Sunday Telegraph* over one story. In April that year he won £12,000 and an apology over an article published in November 2005. The newspaper later paid him a further £5,000 in damages over the same defamatory story, which, by an oversight, it had left on its website.

The 'single publication rule' and online archives

Section 8 of the Defamation Act 2013 introduces the 'single publication rule'. This means that in England and Wales the 12-month limitation period for bringing a defamation action runs from the date of the first publication 'to the public' of the complained-of statement. So if the allegation appears in a story in the print edition of a newspaper late on the evening of 1 January and the same story is then put on the newspaper's website at mid-morning on 2 January, the limitation period for both runs from January 1, as this was the first publication. Or, if the article is only online, the first publication is the first time any member of the public accessed it.

Note that, in exceptional circumstances, courts can extend the 12-month limitation period.

Also, the 2013 Act says that the 'single publication rule' will not apply if the manner of the subsequent publication by the same publisher is 'materially different' from the manner of the first, and that when a court is deciding if there is a material difference, factors it can consider include 'the level of prominence that a statement is given' and 'the extent of the subsequent publication'. The Act's Explanatory Notes, referring to what may be 'materially different', say:

> 66 A possible example of this could be where a story has first appeared relatively obscurely in a section of a website where several clicks need to be gone through to access it, but has subsequently been promoted to a position where it can be directly accessed from the home page of the site, thereby increasing considerably the number of hits it receives. 99

Publication by a *different* publisher of the same allegation will trigger a new limitation period in relation to that specific publication, so creating an opportunity for anyone who claims to have been defamed by the allegation to sue that different publisher for defamation.

➡ Recap of major points

- A claimant suing for libel must prove three things:

  (1) it is defamatory and has caused or is likely to cause his/her reputation serious harm; (2) it may be reasonably understood to refer to him/her; and (3) it has been published to a third person.

- The test of 'identification' is whether the words would reasonably lead people who know the claimant to believe he/she was the person referred to.

- Publication is assumed in the case of traditional media. But this is not always the case with online publication.

- Every repetition is a fresh publication. The journalist is liable for repeating a defamatory statement made by an interviewee or source. But the single publication rule was introduced in the Defamation Act 2013.

Defences

Chapter summary

The law provides defences for media organisations sued for defamation—without them many of the stories published and broadcast each day would be suppressed for fear of a libel action. This chapter explains the main defences and gives practical advice on what a journalist must do when preparing a story to ensure it meets their requirements.

▌ The main defences

Journalists need to know about how defamation defences work, as the steps they take in researching and writing a story will often determine whether a defence is available to avoid a costly defamation action. Some defences are now in the Defamation Act 2013.

The main defences are:

- truth—section 2 of the 2013 Act, replacing the common law defence of justification; →glossary
- honest opinion—section 3 of the 2013 Act, replacing the common law defence of honest comment or fair comment; →glossary
- absolute privilege;
- qualified privilege;
- accord and satisfaction;
- offer of amends.

The fact that new statutory defences in the 2013 Act repeal the common law defences of justification and honest comment means that courts must follow the words of the statute when making rulings. Cases decided before the statute came into force may be a guide to the correct approach, but only after the court has considered the statutory requirements.

◗ Truth—its requirement

The defence requires that the published material complained of can be proved in court to be substantially true. Meeting this requirement gives complete protection against a libel action (the only limited exception arises under the Rehabilitation of Offenders Act 1974—see ch. 23).

The defence applies to statements of fact. If the words complained of are an expression of opinion, they may be defended as honest opinion.

Media organisations sued for defamation often rely on both truth and honest opinion as defences, applying each as appropriate to different elements of what was published.

- The standard of proof needed for a truth defence is that used in civil cases generally—the material must be proved true 'on the balance of probabilities'.

Although this is a lower requirement than 'beyond reasonable doubt', the standard of proof in criminal cases, a media organisation relying on a truth defence must have enough evidence to persuade a judge at trial that its version of the event(s) is correct.

The imputation of the libel must be proved

Section 2(3) of the 2013 Act says that, in a defamation case involving publication of two or more imputations involving the claimant, 'the defence under this section does not fail if, having regard to the imputations which are shown to be substantially true, the imputations which are not shown to be substantially true do not seriously harm the claimant's reputation'.

This means that a defendant does not have to prove the truth of every statement in what was published. But the most damaging imputation must be proved and the damage to reputation it causes must outweigh any damage caused by unproved allegations. So if a newspaper runs a story saying that a politician is cruel to his children and swears at his neighbours, the former allegation is the most damaging. But a media organisation unable to prove the minor allegations might find it harder to persuade a jury of the truth of the major allegation.

Examples

The *Daily Telegraph* was sued by tennis player Robert Dee after reporting that he was 'ranked as the worst professional tennis player in the world after 54 defeats in a row ...'. The newspaper pleaded justification (now truth) and fair comment (now honest opinion). Mrs Justice Sharp held that the facts in the story were sufficient to justify any defamatory meaning the words were capable of bearing (*Robert Dee v Telegraph Media Group Ltd* [2010] EWHC 924 (QB), [2010] EMLR 20).

In July 2015 comedian Freddie Starr sued a woman who said he groped her when she was 15 years old and attending a Jimmy Savile TV show *Clunk Click*. Starr lost, which left him facing a costs bill unofficially estimated at about £1 million.

Starr had told Mr Justice Nicol at the High Court that he did not at first remember appearing on the show in March 1974—41 years ago—until footage showed him in the studio, with Karin Ward in the audience behind him. He rejected her allegation that he groped her and humiliated her in Savile's dressing room by calling her a 't**less wonder'.

Starr, 72, sued over interviews given to the BBC and ITV in October 2012, and statements on a website and in an e-book—and claimed he had lost £300,000 because of shows cancelled as a result of the allegations.

Ms Ward, 56, denied the slander and libel claims, and relied on the defences of justification and public interest.

Mr Justice Nicol ruled that the claim in slander based on Ms Ward's interview with the BBC failed as it was brought outside the limitation period. The claim in libel was based on the broadcast of a clip from the BBC interview in *Panorama* and Ms Ward was not liable for the composite broadcast.

The judge said Starr's slander claim over an interview Ms Ward gave to ITV failed because she had proved that it was true that Starr groped her—an underage schoolgirl—and humiliated her by calling her a 't**less wonder' (*Media Lawyer*, 10 July 2015).

Cases in which the media plead truth can be extremely complex.

👁 Case study

In 1997 *The Guardian* newspaper and Granada TV risked paying huge libel damages and costs when they defended a case brought by former Conservative Cabinet Minister Jonathan Aitken over reports in the newspaper and the *World in Action* programme that he was involved in arms dealings with Saudi businessmen and that he allowed an Arab business associate to pay his bill at the Ritz hotel in Paris, in breach of ministerial guidelines. Aitken resigned from the Cabinet in order, he said, to pursue *The Guardian* and 'cut out the cancer of bent and twisted journalism in our country with the simple sword of truth and the trusty shield of British fair play'. *The Guardian* discovered, at a late stage in the trial, vital evidence of credit card payments found in the records of another hotel. Aitken, who had seemed to be winning, abandoned the case, facing a £2 million costs bill. He was later jailed for perjury (*The Guardian*, 8 June 1999).

Levels of meaning and reporting on police investigations

When considering reports linking a claimant with criminal or wrongful conduct, the courts recognise three levels of meaning:

- the person is guilty of the criminal offence or misconduct (a level 1 meaning)— if the court decides this meaning applies, then a publisher using the truth defence will have to prove that the offence or misconduct occurred; or
- he/she is reasonably suspected of the offence or misconduct (level 2); or
- there are grounds for an investigation—for example, by police (level 3).

These are known as *Chase* level 1, 2 and 3 meanings, having been detailed by Lord Justice Brooke in *Chase v News Group Newspapers* [2002] EWCA Civ 1772, [2003] EMLR 2180.

Proving reasonable suspicion or that there were grounds for an investigation

It may be defamatory to say someone is reasonably suspected of an offence or that there are grounds for investigating his/her conduct, because it implies there was conduct on the person's part which warrants the suspicion. So a successful plea of truth must prove conduct by the individual which gives rise to the suspicion or the grounds. It is no use saying other people told you about their suspicions (*Shah v Standard Chartered Bank* [1999] QB 241).

👁 Case study

In *Chase v News Group Newspapers Ltd* (cited earlier) *The Sun* newspaper paid £100,000 damages to children's nurse Elaine Chase for a story headlined 'Nurse is probed over 18 deaths'. Police were investigating the deaths of a number of terminally ill children she had treated but concluded—after the newspaper's story appeared—that there were no grounds to suspect her of an offence. *The Sun* tried to show there were reasonable grounds for suspicion, but the Court of Appeal said it was relying almost entirely on the fact that a number of allegations against Ms Chase had been made to the hospital trust and police. The only respect in which the newspaper focused upon the nurse's conduct concerned an allegation made after publication, which the Court said could not be taken into consideration.

Avoid implying habitual conduct

The statement that someone 'is a thief' may be true—but if the basis for the statement is just one minor conviction—for example, for stealing a packet of bacon from a shop—a defence of truth would almost certainly fail, as the individual would argue that the words meant he/she was a persistent thief, whereas he/she was essentially an honest person who had had a single lapse.

Inferences and innuendoes must be proved

The truth defence will involve proving not only the truth of each defamatory statement, but also any reasonable interpretation of the words and any innuendoes lying behind them.

 see also
ch. 19 on
meanings
of words

Persisting with a truth defence can be financially risky

Persisting in a defence of truth has financial risks. If it fails, the court may view critically a defendant's persistence in sticking to a story which it has decided was not true, and may award greater damages—see *Cairns v Modi* [2012] EWCA Civ 1382 in which Mr Justice Bean awarded cricketer Chris Cairns £75,000 in damages over match-fixing allegations, adding a further £15,000 in aggravated damages because of the defendant's 'sustained and aggressive assertion of the plea of justification'.

See also ch. 19, p. 260, Why media organisations may be reluctant to fight defamation actions.

The investigative journalist—practical advice on procedure

The Additional Material for ch. 21 on www.mcnaes.com gives tips for journalists beginning to do investigations, to help them be able to prove the truth.

- For example, the journalist should persuade each witness to make a signed statement and date it before the story is published. In some circumstances it may be best to persuade him/her to sign an affidavit.

→ glossary

A media organisation's case is often weakened because a journalist has failed to keep notes or recordings and research in good order to prove what someone said.

Honest opinion

The defence of honest opinion protects published opinion, not any statement put forward as factual. The defence is similar to the defence formerly known as 'fair comment', then as 'honest comment'. But section 3 of the Defamation Act 2013, which created the honest opinion defence, abolished that common law defence.

The requirements of honest opinion

The main requirements of the honest opinion defence, all of which must be met, are:

- the published comment must be the honestly held opinion of the person making it (though it may have been published by another party);

see
pp. 282–292,
Privilege

- it must be recognisable to the reader/viewer/listener as opinion rather than as a factual allegation;
- it must be based on a provably true fact or privileged material—so media organisations relying on the honest opinion defence should be prepared to run another defence, such as truth, absolute privilege or qualified privilege in tandem;
- it must explicitly or implicitly indicate, at least in general terms, the fact or information on which it is based.

Opinion must be 'honestly held', not 'fair'

The law does not require the 'truth' of the comment to be proved—by its nature it cannot be. Comment may be responsible or irresponsible, informed or misinformed—but cannot be true or false. Defendants pleading honest opinion do not need to persuade the court to share their views—but they do need to satisfy it that the opinion on an established fact represents a view that an honest person could hold. Mr Justice Diplock in his summing up to the jury in *Silkin v Beaverbrook Newspapers* [1958] 1 WLR 743 (QB), said:

> The basis of our public life is that the crank and the enthusiast can say what he honestly believes just as much as a reasonable man or woman. It would be a sad day for freedom of speech in this country if a jury were to apply the test of whether it agrees with a comment, instead of applying the true test of whether this opinion, however exaggerated, obstinate, or prejudiced, was honestly held.

The defence will fail if a claimant can show that the person expressing the opinion did not in fact hold that opinion. It will also fail if, for example, the editor of a newspaper which published the comment—for example, in a column—did so when he or she knew, or should have known, that the author did not hold the opinion being expressed.

Only recognisable comment, not facts

A judge gave an example of an opinion protected by the fair comment defence, saying that if one accurately reports what some public man had done, then says 'such conduct is disgraceful', that is merely an expression of one's opinion—a comment on the person's conduct. But if one asserts that the man is guilty of disgraceful conduct without saying what that conduct was, one is making an allegation of fact for which the only defences are justification (now truth) or privilege.

👁 Case study

Sub-editors must take special care if they introduce comment into headlines. In 2003 the *Daily Telegraph* published articles making allegations about left-wing MP George Galloway after a reporter found documents said to refer to him in a ruined government building in Baghdad soon after the invasion of Iraq. One story was headlined 'Telegraph reveals damning new evidence on Labour MP'. When sued, the paper did not claim the allegations were true but said the headline was an expression of opinion. But the judge said 'damning' had a plain meaning—'that is to say, that the evidence goes beyond a **prima facie** case and points to guilt'. The MP won the libel case (*George Galloway MP v Telegraph Group Ltd* [2004] EWHC 2786 (QB)).

→ glossary

 For more detail of this case, see the Additional Material for ch. 22, The public interest defence, on www.mcnaes.com.

The basis on fact or privileged material must be indicated

The requirements of section 3 of the 2013 Act reflect the decision of the Supreme Court in *Spiller and another v Joseph and others* [2010] UKSC 53 that it was incorrect to require that the comment must identify the matters on which it was based with sufficient particularity to enable the reader to judge for himself/herself whether it was well founded. Instead, it said, the requirement was that the comment 'must explicitly or implicitly indicate, at least in general terms, the facts on which it was based'. The new statutory defence provides that an honest person must be able to hold the opinion on the basis of 'any fact' which existed when the statement complained of was published.

The exception to the rule that comment must be based on a true fact is when the comment is based on privileged material, such as a report of judicial proceedings or proceedings in Parliament. A media organisation can safely make scathing comments about a defendant convicted of a crime if based on privileged reports of the trial's evidence. The honest opinion defence will succeed in relation to what was published at the time of the conviction even if the defendant is later acquitted on appeal. The honest opinion defence should also protect publication of criticism of judges, magistrates and coroners, based on privileged reports of their actions in court.

Imputing improper motives

Because the Defamation Act 2013 repeals the common law defence of honest comment, earlier cases cannot be taken to be a definitive guide to how the courts will interpret its replacement, the honest opinion defence. But these cases might provide some indication.

The suggestion that someone has acted from improper motives has in the past been hard to defend as honest comment. But judges in the Court of Appeal took a more helpful view when entrepreneur Richard Branson sued his biographer Tom Bower for libel (*Branson v Bower* [2001] EWCA Civ 791, [2001] EMLR 800). Bower wrote of Branson's attempt to run the National Lottery: 'Sceptics will inevitably whisper that Branson's motive is self-glorification.' Bower said this was fair comment (which at that time was the name of the honest comment defence) but Branson said it was a factual allegation (that he had a questionable intention in bidding for the National Lottery) and was untrue.

Lord Justice Latham, giving the Court of Appeal's judgment, said comment was 'something which is or can reasonably be inferred to be a deduction, inference, conclusion, criticism, remark, observation', and that the judge in the lower court was fully entitled to conclude that Bower was expressing a series of opinions about Branson's motives.

Reviews

The honest opinion defence protects the expressions of opinion contained in reviews of, among other things, performances, books, holidays and restaurants.

Humour, satire and irony

In 2008 Sir Elton John sued *The Guardian* for libel over a spoof article written by Marina Hyde under the headline 'A peek at the diary of … Sir Elton John'—a regular feature in the paper's Weekend section satirising the activities of celebrities and others. Sir Elton claimed the article meant his commitment to the Elton John Aids Foundation was insincere and that, once the costs of his White Tie and Tiara fund-raising ball were met, only a small proportion of the funds raised would go to good causes. *The Guardian's* defence was that the words were clearly comment and could not have the meaning claimed by the claimant.

Mr Justice Tugendhat struck out Sir Elton's claim, accepting *The Guardian's* argument that the words were a form of teasing, and that had it actually unearthed a story about a charity ball's costs leaving nothing for good causes, it would have treated it as a serious story and written it without any attempt at humour (*Sir Elton John v Guardian News and Media Ltd* [2008] EWHC 3066 (QB)).

▌ Privilege

The public interest sometimes demands that there should be complete freedom of speech without any risk of proceedings for defamation, even if the statements are defamatory and even if they turn out to be untrue. These occasions are referred to as 'privileged'. Privilege exists under common law and statute.

▌ Absolute privilege

The defence of absolute privilege, where it is applicable, is a complete answer and bar to any action for defamation. It does not matter if the words are true or false, or if they were spoken or written maliciously.

But while someone may be speaking on an occasion which is protected by absolute privilege, it does not follow that a journalist's report of the comments will also be protected by absolute privilege. Members of Parliament may say whatever they wish in the House of Commons without fear of being sued for defamation. The reports of parliamentary proceedings published on Parliament's behalf in *Hansard*, its official record, are protected by absolute privilege, as are reports published by order of Parliament, such as White Papers. But media reports of the contents of parliamentary publications enjoy only qualified privilege, a defence which, as this chapter explains, depends on there being a proper motive in publication.

The requirements of absolute privilege

The only time journalists enjoy absolute privilege is when they are reporting court cases or the proceedings of certain types of tribunal.

ch. 17 explains tribunals

In this context the requirements of absolute privilege are that what was published was:

- a fair and accurate report of judicial proceedings held in public within the UK, published contemporaneously.

The Defamation Act 2013 extended this protection to reports of proceedings in any court established under the law of a country or territory outside the UK, and any international court or tribunal established by the Security Council of the United Nations or by an international agreement. A 'court' includes 'any tribunal or body exercising the judicial power of the State'.

Privilege for court reports is vital for the media because what is said in court is often highly defamatory, and reporting it would be impossible without this protection.

The law thus recognises that the media help sustain open justice, a principle examined in ch. 14. Privilege does not apply if the court (or tribunal) hearing is in private.

Reports must be fair

For absolute privilege to apply, a report of a court case must be 'fair and accurate'. This does not mean that the proceedings must be reported verbatim—a report will still be 'fair and accurate' if:

- it presents a summary of the cases put by both sides;
- it contains no substantial inaccuracies;
- it avoids giving disproportionate weight to one side or the other.

In a case in 2006 (*Bennett v Newsquest* [2006] EWCA Civ 1149), Mr Justice Eady pointed out that a newspaper report of a criminal case, which was the subject of a defamation action, contained inaccuracies, then said:

   The report must be fair overall and not give a misleading impression. Inaccuracies in themselves will not defeat privilege. Omissions will deprive a report of privilege if they create a false impression of what took place or if they result in the suppression of the case or part of the case of one side, while giving the other. 🟥🟥

A media organisation loses the protection of absolute privilege if its report is held to be unfair or inaccurate in any important respect.

- To be fair, a report of a trial must make clear that the defendant denies the charge(s) and, while it proceeds, that no verdict has been reached—for example, the report can conclude by stating: 'The case continues.'

How much of a court case must be reported to be fair?

In 1993 the *Daily Sport* paid substantial damages to a police officer acquitted of indecent assault. It reported the opening of the case by the prosecution and the alleged victim's main evidence, but did not include her cross-examination by the defence, which began on the same day and undermined her allegation. Later the paper briefly reported the officer's acquittal. He still decided to sue. The settlement in the case means that the issue of how much of a day's proceedings in court must be covered for a report to be fair remains something of a grey area.

Trials may last for days, weeks or months, and the defendant may later show that statements made by the prosecution were wrong. Reports of proceedings may be published each day, but the safest practice is that if the publication has reported allegations that are later rebutted, it should also carry the rebuttals.

Reports must be accurate with quotes attributed

All allegations in court reports must be attributed because a report that presents an allegation as if it were a proved fact is inaccurate. Do not write 'Brown had a gun in his hand' but 'Smith said Brown had a gun in his hand'.

A media organisation is left with no protection at all if it wrongly identifies as the defendant someone who is only a witness or unconnected with the case. A report which gets the charge or charges a defendant faces wrong could prove expensive in libel damages.

 Ch. 20, p. 268, Identification, explains the need for a report to fully identify a defendant.

Journalists must also avoid wrongly reporting that the defendant has been convicted when he/she has in fact been acquitted. One paper paid damages when it reported a man's acquittal on drug charges—but did so in terms which gave the impression that he was in fact guilty.

 See also the Additional Material for ch. 21 on www.mcnaes.com, 'Case study on accuracy'.

The courts do allow some leeway to publications compressing material in reports (*Elizabeth and Peter Crossley v Newsquest (Midlands South Ltd)* [2008] EWHC 3054 (QB)).

Reports must be contemporaneous

To have the protection of absolute privilege, court reports should be published contemporaneously with the proceedings.

- Contemporaneous means 'as soon as practicable'—for example, in the first issue of a newspaper following the day's hearing. For a broadcaster, it can be construed that the report should be aired on the same day of the hearing or early on the next day. For a weekly paper, contemporaneous publication may mean publishing the following week.

chs. 11 and 18 explain postpone-ment orders

Sometimes reports of court proceedings have to be postponed because a court order compels this. Section 14(2) of the Defamation Act 1996 says that in these circumstances a story is treated as if it were published contemporaneously if it is published 'as soon as practicable after publication is permitted'.

Even if the report is not contemporaneous, it will still attract qualified privilege under statute and under common law, explained later in this chapter.

Reports of earlier sections of a hearing published to put later reports in context should still be treated as having absolute privilege (the *Crossley* case, cited earlier).

Privilege is only for reports of proceedings

Suppose a 'court report' in the media contains background matter or comment that did not originate from the court? In the *Bennett* case referred to earlier, the judge said this would not destroy the privilege of the report: 'Extraneous comments can be included or other factual material but it must be severable, in the sense that a reasonable reader could readily appreciate that the material did not purport to be a report of what was said in court.'

But the added material itself is not covered by privilege.

Outbursts from the public gallery

Privilege may not protect defamatory matter shouted out in court—for example, from the public gallery by someone who is not part of the proceedings.

But if the shouted comment is by someone who has given evidence as a witness in that case, privilege would protect its inclusion in a court report, provided all the defence's requirements were met.

If the shouted comment is not defamatory, it can in defamation law be reported safely, no matter who made it.

▌ Qualified privilege

Qualified privilege is available as a defence for the publication of certain types of information. This law, in effect, categorises this information as of importance to society. The defence allows these 'statements'—including media reports of certain documents and events—to be freely published in the public interest, with no requirement for the publisher to be able to prove them as true, though there are some preconditions.

▶ Qualified privilege by statute

see also
ch. 23
on past
convictions

Schedule 1 of the Defamation Act 1996—now amended and expanded by the Defamation Act 2013—lists 'statements' to which the statutory form of qualified privilege applies, if the defence's requirements are met. For example, the defence applies to media reports of press conferences, of parliamentary debates held in public, of public meetings, and of public meetings of councils, their committees and their sub-committees. It also applies to media reports of statements issued for the public by government departments, councils, the police and other governmental agencies. It also protects non-contemporaneous reports of court cases held in public, including references to people's past convictions.

The Schedule is set out in Appendix 3, pp. 469–473.

The requirements of qualified privilege

The defence's requirements differ from those of absolute privilege. For absolute privilege, the publisher's motive is irrelevant. But a qualified privilege defence will fail if the claimant can show malice by the publisher or author.

Fair and accurate, without malice, and in the public interest

The basic requirements of the qualified privilege defence relating to those 'statements' listed by Schedule 1 are that:

- the published report must be fair and accurate, and published without malice.

There is also a general requirement for qualified privilege that:

- the matter published must be a matter of public interest, the publication of which is for the public benefit.

This can be summed up as 'published in the public interest'.

Malice in this context means ill-will or spite towards the claimant, or any indirect or improper motive in the defendant's mind. Lord Nicholls explained in *Tse Wai Chun Paul v Albert Cheng* [2001] EMLR 777, Court of Final Appeal, Hong Kong, that the purpose of the qualified privilege defence was to allow someone with a duty to perform, or an interest to protect, to provide information without the risk of being sued—and if a person's dominant motive was not to perform this duty or protect this interest, he/she could not use the defence.

So a journalist or editor may be denied the protection of qualified privilege if, in a defamation action, the court accepts that the motive for publication was not from a duty to inform the public but was spite—for example, the publisher aired a defamatory allegation merely to settle a private score.

The question of what is in the public interest is approached objectively and does not depend on the journalist or editor's views. If a reasonable person would be aware of facts contradicting those in a report, such as that a defendant to a claim which had been filed at court denied it and was contesting it, a court is unlikely to see publication of the report without including those facts as being in the public interest.

 See the Additional Material for ch. 14 on www.mcnaes.com for a case study of how in 2012 the *Mail on Sunday* lost a defamation action when a judge ruled that its report of a court case was not protected by qualified privilege because it was not sufficiently fair or accurate, and therefore publication was not in the public interest.

Is there a requirement to publish explanation or contradiction?

Schedule 1 to the 1996 Act sets out in Part 1 a list of statements having qualified privilege 'without explanation or contradiction' and in Part 2 a list of statements thus privileged but 'subject to explanation or contradiction'.

This difference is important.

- A publisher relying on qualified privilege under Part 2 to protect a report must, to retain the protection, publish a 'reasonable letter or statement by way of explanation or contradiction' if required to do so by anyone defamed in the report.

This will apply, for example, if a person wants the publisher to publish or broadcast a letter or statement from him/her responding to a report of a council meeting which defamed him/her. Failure to publish such a letter or statement would destroy the qualified privilege defence for what was published earlier. The Act says such a statement must be published 'in a suitable manner', meaning 'in the same manner as the publication complained of or in a manner that is adequate and reasonable in the circumstances'.

✳ Remember

Get legal advice if any statement that the complainant wants published gives rise— because he/she make counter-allegations—to any risk of libelling another person. Publication of a statement of 'explanation or contradiction' is not protected by privilege under the 1996 Act, so the statement must be 'reasonable' in this respect, though common law privilege may apply.

 see also pp. 291–292, Privilege at common law, on replies to attack

A statement listed in Part 1 of Schedule 1—for example, a report of what is said in public in a legislature such as the UK Parliament, or a report of material published by a legislature, including *Hansard*, or by a government department, or a report of what is said in a public register open to inspection, discussed later in this chapter—is not subject to the requirement to publish such a letter/statement by anyone defamed by the report (though an editor may decide it is newsworthy or ethical to do this).

Part I is the means by which the 1996 and 2013 Acts greatly widened the categories of statements protected, by including reports of proceedings held in public in foreign legislatures, foreign courts and of all public inquiries appointed by governments.

Statute only protects a report of the occasion or material specified

The protection of statutory qualified privilege applies only to reports of the actual proceedings, events or material listed in Schedule 1 to the 1996 Act, as amended by the 2013 Act.

- For example, this qualified privilege in Part 2 of the Schedule protects a report of speeches by councillors in a council meeting held in public, but will not protect a report of defamatory allegations a councillor makes after the meeting when asked to expand on statements made during it.

What the councillor says in the meeting—such as that a builder is corrupt—can, if the meeting was held in public, be safely reported. But if the comment is made afterwards, the publisher who airs it would have no privilege and so would need to rely on the truth defence—that is, would have to prove the builder was corrupt, which might be impossible.

Reports of public meetings, press conferences, scientific and academic conferences

Reports of a public meeting on a matter of public interest held anywhere in the world are now protected by qualified privilege, by virtue of the 2013 Act amending Part 2 of Schedule 1 to the 1996 Act, as are reports of press conferences held anywhere in the world for the discussion of a matter of public interest, and reports of scientific or academic conferences held anywhere in the world, or copies of, extracts from or summaries of material published by such conferences.

What is a public meeting?

Paragraph 12 of the Schedule, following amendment by the 2013 Act, defines a 'public meeting' as:

- a lawful meeting held anywhere in the world for the furtherance or discussion of a matter of public interest, whether admission to the meeting is general or restricted.

This definition is fairly wide, covering public meetings about a particular community or those held about national issues. The term 'restricted' means the definition can apply, for example, to a meeting called by residents of one village who exclude from it people from the neighbouring village. Again, the privilege is subject to the 'explanation and contradiction' requirement.

The nature of press conferences

The 2013 Act extended qualified privilege to coverage of press conferences held anywhere in the world on matters of public interest. This codified in statute a decision by the House of Lords in 2000 that a press conference, held after the issuing of a general invitation to the press, is a form of public meeting.

👁 Case study

Law firm McCartan Turkington Breen sued *The Times* over its report of a press conference, called by people campaigning for the release of a soldier convicted of murder, during which defamatory comments were made about the firm. It had represented the soldier. A jury awarded £145,000 damages to the firm, but on appeal Lord Bingham, the senior law lord, said: 'A meeting is public if those who organise it or arrange it open it to the public or, by issuing a general invitation to the press, manifest an intention or desire that the proceedings of the meeting should be communicated to a wider public.' Journalists could be regarded as 'the eyes and ears of the public' (*McCartan Turkington Breen v Times Newspapers Ltd* [2001] 2 AC 277).

In *McCartan*, The House of Lords also ruled that a written press release—handed out at the meeting, but not read aloud, and reported by the media—was in effect part of the press conference proceedings. This means that fair, accurate reports of documents handed out at a press conference also have qualified privilege in the context of coverage of the press conference.

Stories from documents open to public inspection

Paragraph 5 in Part 1 to the Schedule gives privilege for a fair and accurate copy of or extract from a document which the law requires to be open to public inspection.

❗ Remember your rights

Paragraph 5 means, for example, that the media have qualified privilege for material quoted fairly and accurately, etc, from publicly available records such as those at Companies House, the Land Registry or other public registries, even if the records themselves turn out to be inaccurate.

Paragraph 5 also gives qualified privilege to media reports of court documents which court rules say can be inspected—see ch. 14. But it does not apply to reports of documents released under the Freedom of Information Act 2000, though the public interest defence may apply to such reports. This defence is explained in ch. 22.

ch. 30 explains the FoI Act

Reports of statements issued for the public by government agencies

Paragraph 9 in Part 2 of the Schedule gives qualified privilege, subject to explanation or contradiction, to 'a fair and accurate copy of or extract from' a notice or other matter issued for the public by governments anywhere in the world and authorities anywhere in the world which have governmental functions. This includes government departments, councils, and police forces and authorities, so would cover, for example, fair and accurate reports of official police statements, and statements made on behalf of local authorities—for example, press releases about consumer protection or environmental health matters.

- These statements could be defamatory—for example, a police press release might name a man and say police want to trace him to question him about a murder. But the qualified privilege allows the media to report this without fear of being sued by the man, provided, if asked, that they publish his 'reasonable letter or statement of explanation or contradiction'.

There will be many occasions when a reporter will wish to report the misdeeds of a person but may be inhibited by the fear of a defamation action. The answer is often to obtain confirmation of the information in the form of an official statement by a police or local authority spokesman.

✳ Remember

Statutory qualified privilege does not protect reports of information unofficially 'leaked' from such authorities, or of what was said by people who are not official spokespersons.

Not all authorities are covered

Paragraph 9 of the Schedule does not cover reports of all statements by people in authority—it does not cover, for example, reports of statements by the spokespersons of British Telecom, a gas board, a water board, the rail companies, London Regional Transport, British Airport Authority or other bodies created by statute which are involved in providing day-to-day services to the public. But it seems likely that a fair and accurate account of the official statements of such a body would be held to be covered by privilege at common law, referred to later in this chapter.

Verbal comments by press officers

Suppose a reporter telephones a press officer at one of the bodies of the type specified under paragraph 9 of the Schedule. Is the report of the spokesperson's verbal comments protected by qualified privilege under the Act? The general position seems to be 'yes', unless the spokesperson was given no chance to make considered comments.

Case study

In *Blackshaw v Lord* [1984] QB 1, Lord Justice Stephenson, referring to the protection paragraph 9 gives the media, said: 'It may be right to include … the kind of answers to telephoned interrogatories which Mr Lord [a *Daily Telegraph* reporter], quite properly in the discharge of his duty to his newspaper, administered to Mr Smith [a government press officer]. To exclude them in every case might unduly restrict the freedom of the press … But information which is put out on the initiative of a government department falls more easily within the paragraph than information pulled out of the mouth of an unwilling officer of the department.'

Disciplinary actions by private associations

Paragraph 14 in Part 2 of the Schedule bestows qualified privilege on media reports of the findings or decisions of a wide variety of bodies—for example, in the field of sport, business or learning—anywhere in the world which have a constitution empowering them to make disciplinary decisions about members. So, for example, the media can safely report a decision by the British Horseracing Authority disciplinary panel to ban a jockey from racing, the Football Association Independent Regulatory Commission to discipline a player or a scientific association to censure an academic, if the association is of the type listed in paragraph 14. The protection does not apply to a report of the proceedings of such bodies, and is subject to the 'explanation and contradiction' requirement.

Reports about companies

The 1996 and 2013 Acts also greatly extended qualified privilege with respect to reporting company affairs. Earlier, qualified privilege only covered reports relating to proceedings at public companies' general meetings. The Acts extended Part 2 privilege to documents circulated among shareholders of a listed company with the authority of the board or the auditors or by any shareholder 'in pursuance of a right conferred by any statutory provision', and to fair and accurate copies of, extracts from or summaries of any document circulated to members of the company about the appointment, resignation, retirement or dismissal of directors of the company or its auditors.

▌ Privilege at common law

There are some circumstances in which the media can benefit from privilege in common law. This will apply, within certain bounds, to publication of a person's response to an attack on his/her character or conduct. Also, privilege in common law applies to reports of court cases and parliamentary proceedings, if held in public, in addition to statutory privilege. For more detail, see the Additional Material for ch. 21 on www.mcnaes.com.

▶ 'Accord and satisfaction', apologies and corrections

A media organisation can use the defence of 'accord and satisfaction' to halt a defamation case on the ground that the issue has already been disposed of—for example, by publication of a correction and apology which the claimant accepted at the time as settlement of his/her complaint. But negotiating an apology or correction is not a job for an inexperienced journalist.

'Without prejudice'

A solicitor acting for a client demanding a correction and apology will always avoid suggesting that this action by the media organisation will be enough in itself to settle the dispute, and will make it clear that the request is made 'without prejudice' to any other action that might be thought necessary.

What does this mean? The basic principle is that parties attempting to settle their differences before going to law should be encouraged to speak frankly—anything said or written in the course of negotiations to settle and described as 'without prejudice' (that is, off the record) cannot subsequently be used against a party in court if negotiations fail. The rule applies whether or not the phrase 'without prejudice' is expressly used, but it can be good practice for the media organisation to use it too.

Journalists speaking with someone complaining about a story need to distinguish between:

- discussions over an offer to publish a follow-up story or a correction; and
- discussions over settling a claim.

In the former case, which often involves the journalist and the subject themselves, the discussion need not necessarily be 'without prejudice'; the journalist may well want to refer to this discussion in court, to show fairness or lack of malice, or to mitigate damages.

In the latter case, often involving solicitors and mention of money, the discussion should be 'without prejudice'. As a general rule journalists should notify their insurers about potential claims immediately, and, if there are solicitors 'on the other side', the publisher should also involve its own lawyer.

Care needed in apologies and corrections

It is no defence for a media organisation to publish a correction and apology not agreed by the claimant.

Publishing such apology can make matters worse for the publisher, because:

- a court may find that it constitutes an admission that the material which prompted the complaint was defamatory;
- a badly drafted apology or correction might also repeat the original defamatory statement, further angering the person who complained about it, or even unwittingly libel someone else.

For example: 'In our article yesterday we said Mr Red hit Mr Green. But we wish to point out that Mr Red says Mr Green struck him first'. If this is published, Mr Green may sue over the wording of the apology.

 See Additional Material for ch. 21 on www.mcnaes.com, 'Practical advice on waivers'.

On the other hand, if the claimant wins, the fact that the media organisation took prompt and adequate steps to correct the error, and to express regret, will reduce the damages if his/her reputation was seriously harmed despite the apology.

Complainants might also be prepared to sign waivers—statements saying they waive their right to legal redress in exchange for the publication of a correction and apology—which will provide a complete defence of 'accord and satisfaction'.

A practical danger for an editor who asks a complainant to sign a waiver is that the reader may not previously have realised that he/she has a claim for damages and, thus alerted, may consult a lawyer. The waiver is therefore most useful when the complainant has already threatened to consult a lawyer.

Inexperienced reporters sometimes try to avoid the consequences of errors without referring them to the editor, by trying to shrug them off or by incorporating a scarcely recognisable 'correction' (without apology) in a follow-up story—a highly dangerous course of action, which may further aggravate the damage and prompt the potential claimant to take more formal steps to secure satisfaction. Reporters should always tell the editor about a problem immediately so it can be dealt with properly.

▌ Offer of amends

The media can defame a person unintentionally. The classic example was the case of Artemus Jones, in which a journalist introduced a fictitious character into a descriptive account of a factual event in order to provide atmosphere—referring to what he thought of as his fictional character as being at the Dieppe motor festival 'with a woman who is not his wife'.

Unfortunately the name he chose was that of a real person, a barrister—and former journalist—from North Wales. Stung by the comments of his friends the real Artemus Jones sued and recovered substantial damages.

Another example is when a story about one individual is understood to refer to another as in the case of Harold Newstead, explained in ch. 20, p. 269, Importance of ages, addresses and occupations.

The Defamation Act 1996 provides for a defence known as 'offer to make amends'.

To use it, a defendant who is alleged to have published a defamatory statement must make a written offer to make a suitable correction and apology, to publish the correction in a reasonable manner, and to pay the claimant suitable damages and legal costs.

If the offer of amends is rejected, and is not withdrawn, it will be a complete defence unless the claimant can show that the defendant 'knew or had reason to believe' that the published statement was false and was also defamatory of the claimant.

Editors planning to make an offer of amends must not delay. If the resulting compensation is to be assessed by a judge, he/she will start by deciding what would be 'suitable damages' if the editor had made no offer of amends and will then award a 'discount' of perhaps 50 per cent as a 'reward' for making the offer. The *News of the World* received only a 40 per cent discount after it was slow to respond to a complaint and published an apology six months after the original story.

Once an offer is made it is binding.

▌ Leave and licence

The 'leave and licence' defence is that the claimant suing for libel had previously agreed that the material could be published. If it is clear the material is defamatory, a publisher intending to rely on this defence needs to be sure he/she can prove there was such pre-publication agreement. The person who is going to be defamed by the material should be asked to sign a statement agreeing to its publication or be recorded agreeing. Otherwise it might be difficult to prove that consent was given if it was merely verbal.

Sometimes, even without an explicit agreement, the context will be that leave and licence was given—for example, by a pop star who chooses in an arranged interview to speak on the record about false allegations made against him/her, seeking to dispel them.

But in other circumstances—for example, a media investigation into wrongdoing—the leave and licence defence will not be secured merely by the journalist giving the target the opportunity to comment.

▌ 'Live' broadcasts and readers' online comments

Newsagents and booksellers have a defence of innocent dissemination as they are merely the conduit for the passage of the words complained of and are not responsible for them. But the defence was not available to others, such as distributors and broadcasters.

The Defamation Act 1996, in section 1, and section 10 of the Defamation Act 2013 extended the defence, which now applies to anyone who was not the author, editor or publisher (as defined by the Act) of the statement complained of, who took reasonable care in relation to its publication, and who did not know and had no reason to believe that whatever part he/she had in the publication caused or contributed to the publication of a defamatory statement.

A court deciding whether a person took reasonable care, or had reason to believe that what he/she did caused or contributed to the publication of a defamatory statement, must have regard to:

- the extent of his/her responsibility for the content of the statement or the decision to publish it;
- the nature or circumstances of the publication; and
- the previous conduct or character of the author, editor or publisher.

Section 10 of the 2013 Act says a court does not have jurisdiction to hear and determine an action for defamation brought against a person who was not the author, editor or publisher of the statement complained of unless it is satisfied that it is not reasonably practicable for an action to be brought against the author, editor or publisher.

Live broadcasts protected by section 1

The list of categories of people who are not authors, editors or publishers for the purposes of the defence includes broadcasters of live programmes who have no effective control over the maker of the statement complained of.

In 1999 the research firm MORI and its head, Bob Worcester, sued the BBC over defamatory remarks made by controversial politician Sir James Goldsmith during a live radio interview. The BBC said it had a defence under section 1—but could it be said it had taken 'reasonable care'? It was argued it should have known Sir James was likely to say something defamatory and it should at least have used a 'delay button'. The case was settled before the jury reached a verdict.

Broadcasters in 'live' situations need to react quickly to halt or cut off defamatory utterances to be sure of benefitting from section 1.

Internet service providers and website operators

The section 1 defence is also available for internet service providers (ISPs) which provide a service as 'host' to enable people and companies to publish their own content on their websites. ISPs play a merely passive role in the process of transmission of any defamatory matter and are therefore not publishers under section 1. But an ISP may be successfully sued for libel if it fails quickly to take down defamatory material on a site it hosts after receiving a complaint about it. In *Godfrey v Demon Internet Ltd* [2001] QB 201 the ISP was successfully sued for material on a newsgroup it hosted which it left online for about 10 days after receiving a complaint. The claim was for damages for those 10 days.

Section 5 defence

see Useful
Websites at
the end of
this chapter
for the
Regulations

Section 5 of the 2013 Act provides a new defence for website operators who follow the procedures detailed in the Defamation (Operators of Websites) Regulations 2013. The defence protects a website operator from a defamation action over postings from users if they follow the steps intended to allow a would-be claimant to act directly against the individual or individuals who posted the material and ensure that they keep within the specified timetable for doing so.

> See the Additional Material for ch. 21 on www.mcnaes.com for a detailed explanation of this defence.

There is also an additional protection for those who 'host', 'cache' or are 'mere conduits' for internet publication—the Electronic Commerce (EC Directive) Regulations 2002. In outline, they are protected from liability to pay damages or any other financial remedy unless and until they have notice of the defamatory publication. This is why many ISPs operate 'notice and take down' procedures.

It is not yet known how these defences will operate in connection with each other.

The moderation of readers' comments posted on websites

Newspapers, magazines, TV channels and radio stations cannot use the section 1 defence in the 1996 Act in respect of content which staff place on their websites, as they are clearly publishers.

As regards comment posted there by readers, the section 1 defence and that in section 5 of the 2013 Act will, as long as the correct procedural steps are followed, offer some protection. Also, the media organisation might have a defence under regulation 19 of the Electronic Commerce (EC Directive) Regulations 2002 in relation to comments posted directly on to the sites by readers—discussed later.

Section 1 or regulation 19 are unlikely to apply if the media organisation's staff moderate—check—material before it goes online, or subsequently check a comment which is clearly defamatory or attracts complaint, but let it remain online. But the section 5 defence in the 2013 Act may offer some protection, as it specifies that the defence 'is not defeated by reason only of the fact that the operator of the website moderates the statements posted on it by others'.

- The safest course is to remove a reader's comment from the website quickly if there is a complaint that it is defamatory. The material can be re-posted later if, after consideration, it is deemed safe.

👁 **Case study**

In 2009 Mr Justice Eady ruled that the *Croydon Guardian* was not liable as the publisher for comments posted on its website by others. A man had tried to sue for defamation about readers' comments posted about a report of a disciplinary tribunal case in which he was struck off as a solicitor. Mr Justice Eady said the newspaper was protected by the regulation 19 defence because it had not had actual knowledge of the alleged 'unlawful activity or information' until the man complained, and it had then removed the material including the comments, as soon as it became aware of the nature of his complaint (*Karim v Newsquest Media Group Ltd* [2009] EWHC 3205 (QB)).

▌ General protection in regulation 19

Regulation 19 provides a general protection for website operators—including media organisations—in respect of comments posted directly onto the sites by readers. As explained earlier, it can protect against defamation actions, but it can also protect the operator if a reader posts a comment which breaches criminal law—for example, by threatening violence or identifying someone in a context in which by law he/she should have anonymity, such as a juvenile defendant or a rape victim—or breaches the Contempt of Court Act 1981 or is a contempt in some other way.

chs. 9–13, 16 and 17 explain anonymity law, and ch. 18 explains contempt law

For the protection to apply, the operator must act 'expeditiously to remove or to disable access' to the comment as soon as it realises or is made aware that the comment is unlawful. The protection will not be available if such 'user-generated material' is moderated by the site's operator before it appears on the site.

▌ Other defences

Defences which might be available are as follows.

The claimant has died A defamation action is a personal action. A dead person cannot be libelled. Similarly, an action begun by a claimant cannot be continued by his/her heirs and executors if he/she dies.

That proceedings were not started within the limitation period If the person suing did not begin the action within 12 months of the material being published, this should be a complete defence, unless there is a new publication of offending material. A court may extend the limitation period if it is thought to be in the interests of justice to do so. Reporters should date their notebooks, recordings and research material, and store them carefully, in case this proof is needed if someone sues towards the end of the limitation period or there is a possibility of using this material again after that. Journalists must remember that every repetition is a new publication.

See ch. 20, p. 272, Repeating statements of others, for the case of the 'bygone days' column and p. 273, The 'single publication rule' and online archives, on this new defence in the Defamation Act 2013.

→ Recap of major points

- The main defences against an action for libel are truth, honest opinion, and absolute and qualified privilege.

- It is a complete defence (with one exception arising under the Rehabilitation of Offenders Act 1974) to prove that the words complained of are substantially true.

- A defendant can plead that an article expressing comment was an honestly held opinion on a matter of public interest.

- Absolute privilege applies to court reports, but reports must be fair, accurate and contemporaneous.

- Qualified privilege is available on many occasions under statute—for example, for a report of a public meeting. The defence is qualified because it is lost if the motive in publishing is malicious.

- Other defences include 'accord and satisfaction' and 'offer of amends'.

More on www.mcnaes.com

Test whether your story has a defence—see Additional Material for ch. 21 on www.mcnaescom.

((•)) Useful Websites

www.legislation.gov.uk/uksi/2013/3028/pdfs/uksi_20133028_en.pdf
    Defamation (Operators of Websites) Regulations 2013

The public interest defence

Chapter summary

This defence, introduced in the Defamation Act 2013, grew from the common law *Reynolds* defence, which was developed to allow journalists to fulfil their duty to report stories in the public interest, even if they included defamatory material they could not prove to be true, if the publication was the product of responsible journalism. Attempts to use the defence led to the courts closely examining whether a story was truly in the public interest, and the way in which it was researched and written. This chapter reviews the old defence, details the requirements of the new statutory defence and highlights the real difficulties journalists are likely to face in using it. Journalists should never consider using this defence without taking legal advice.

▶ The birth of the defence

The 'public interest' defence created by the Defamation Act 2013 is intended to help liberalise libel law by protecting the publication of defamatory material concerning a matter of public interest, even if at the time the publisher cannot prove the material to be true. Editors hope it will increase the occasions on which responsible investigative journalism can safely be published.

The defence's origins are in the '*Reynolds* defence'. This evolved in common law, taking its name from a 1998 case in which former Irish premier Albert Reynolds sued Times Newspapers, publisher of the *Sunday Times*, over an article he claimed meant he deliberately and dishonestly misled the Irish parliament by suppressing information about the appointment of Ireland's Attorney General as President of its High Court. Times Newspapers argued in its defence that, in keeping with Article 10 of the European Convention on Human Rights, the public interest in media coverage of political issues and in scrutinising the

→ glossary

ch. 1 explains the Convention's effect and see also ch. 21, pp. 285–291, Qualified privilege

conduct of elected politicians should be protected by a common law form of qualified privilege.

Times Newspapers lost in the High Court. But in the Court of Appeal, the Lord Chief Justice, Lord Bingham, said: 'As it is the task of the news media to inform the public and engage in public discussion of matters of public interest, so is that to be recognised as its duty.' In 1999 the case reached the House of Lords. Times Newspapers lost, but the court confirmed the principle that in some circumstances the media have a duty to publish material in the public interest, even if it could not be proved to be true, and that therefore qualified privilege in common law should, in those circumstances, protect that publication—and the *Reynolds* defence was born (*Reynolds v Times Newspapers* [2001] 2 AC 127).

Lord Nicholls, in the leading speech, set out a non-exhaustive list of factors a court should consider when examining whether a publication was the product of responsible journalism and therefore whether it could be protected by the new defence.

Lord Nicholls' list (with summarised explanation added in italics)

'1. The seriousness of the allegation. The more serious the charge, the more the public is misinformed and the individual harmed, if the allegation is not true.' *Therefore, the more serious the allegation, the greater should be the reporter's efforts to ensure that what is published is correct if the story is to be protected by the new defence.*

'2. The nature of the information, and the extent to which the subject matter is a matter of public concern.' *The less the matter is of public concern, the weaker the defence. In some cases, if a judge decides the matter is not of public concern, the defence will fail. Judges often say that what interests the public and what is in the public interest are two different things.*

'3. The source of the information. Some informants have no direct knowledge of the events. Some have their own axes to grind, or are being paid for their stories.' *It is important to note that courts are wary of unidentified informants, although a newspaper or broadcaster will not necessarily be penalised for refusing to identify a source.*

'4. The steps taken to verify the information.' *It is always important to check, whenever possible, to ensure that what you have been told is true or correct. Making no or insufficient checks before publication will be regarded as irresponsible journalism and the defence will not apply.*

'5. The status of the information. The allegation may have already been the subject of an investigation which commands respect.' *For example, if a reputable agency—such as the police—has already decided the relevant allegations are not true, then the media must have sufficient reason to air them if the defence is to apply.*

'6. The urgency of the matter. News is often a perishable commodity.' *That is, the courts, when deciding if the defence applies, must take into consideration that journalists need to work and publish quickly.*

'7. Whether comment was sought before publication from the claimant [*that is, the person who claims he/she was defamed*]. He may have information others do not possess or have not disclosed. An approach to the claimant will not always be necessary.' *But generally the person who is the subject of an allegation should be approached. It is also important to make it clear in a story that, if the person about whom allegations have been made cannot be contacted, efforts have been made to reach him/her. Only rarely will an approach to the subject not be necessary.*

'8. Whether the article contained the gist of the plaintiff's [*now claimant's*] side of the story.' *That is, the journalism must be fair to benefit from the defence. Leaving out the claimant's side is a recipe for disaster.*

'9. The tone of the article. A newspaper can raise queries or call for an investigation. It need not adopt allegations as statements of fact.' *For example, the defence may not apply to material which brashly and unfairly suggests that unproven allegations are true. It is important to mind your phrasing. Make sure that what you write is what you mean—and that your meaning is clear to anyone who reads your copy, including the man on the Clapham omnibus. Sloppy writing will almost undoubtedly prove expensive.*

'10. The circumstances of the publication, including the timing.' *That is, was it really so urgent that the story had to be published when it was? Could it have waited an hour or two, or a day or so?*

▌ The *Jameel* case

The *Reynolds* defence developed further in *Jameel v Wall Street Journal Europe* [2006] UKHL 44 in which Lord Bingham, then the senior judge in the House of Lords, said the material published had to be of public interest and the product of responsible journalism, adding: 'The publisher is protected if he has taken such steps as a responsible journalist would take to try and ensure that what is published is accurate and fit for publication.' He recalled that in *Reynolds* Lord Nicholls had 'listed certain matters which might be taken into account in deciding whether the test of responsible journalism was satisfied'—which he said were 'pointers', not 'hurdles'—and added that the rationale of the test was that 'there is no duty to publish, and the public has no interest to read, material which the publisher has not taken reasonable steps to verify'.

In the *Jameel* case the *Wall Street Journal* reported that, at the request of US authorities, Saudi Arabia's central bank was monitoring a number of accounts to stop them from being used, 'wittingly or unwittingly', to funnel funds to terrorist groups, and that millionaire Saudi Arabian businessman Mohammed Jameel and his companies were among those being tracked.

Mr Jameel sued for defamation, and a jury found that the article was defamatory of him and his companies, and awarded them damages.

The Court of Appeal rejected the newspaper's appeal against the trial judge's denial of *Reynolds* privilege, because the newspaper had refused to give Mr Jameel's spokesman 24 hours to produce a response.

But the newspaper won on appeal to the House of Lords (which has now been replaced by the Supreme Court). There Lord Bingham said that denying the *Reynolds* privilege just because the newspaper failed to delay publication of the claimants' names and did not wait long enough for them to comment was a very narrow ground—Mr Jameel could only have issued a denial, and Saudi Arabia's central bank would not have admitted to monitoring accounts.

❚ The Act's public interest defence

Section 4 of the Defamation Act 2013 created the new defence of publication on a matter of public interest. It abolishes and replaces the *Reynolds* defence, because Parliament's intention was to clarify this area of law. The Explanatory Notes published when the Act was passed say the new defence is intended to reflect the principles established in the *Reynolds* case and subsequent case law. The previous cases are therefore not binding authority for the statutory defence, although they might be a 'helpful' guide to interpreting how it should be applied.

Section 4(1) says the defence is available if the defendant can show that the statement complained of was, or formed part of, a statement on a matter of public interest and that he/she reasonably believed that publishing it was in the public interest.

This provision, say the Explanatory Notes, is intended to reflect the common law *Reynolds* defence as it was detailed in *Flood v Times Newspapers* [2012] 2 AC 273.

The Act reflects the two elements of the common law test. Section 4(1)(a) requires that the words complained of were about a matter of public interest. If the publication passes this test, it then has to meet the requirements of section 4(1)(b), which has subjective and objective elements.

First comes the subjective element, which is the defendant's belief that publication was in the public interest; then comes the objective element, which is the question of whether it was reasonable, in all the circumstances, for the defendant to hold that belief.

❚ The *Flood* case

In the *Flood* case, the *Sunday Times* ran a story saying that Detective Sergeant Gary Flood of the Metropolitan Police extradition unit was being investigated following an allegation of corruption. Det. Sgt Flood—who was later completely exonerated by an inquiry—sued for defamation. Mr Justice Tugendhat at first instance ruled that the newspaper report was protected by the *Reynolds* defence. But the Court of Appeal, taking an extremely narrow view of the defence, said it was not available because the journalists responsible for the article had failed to act responsibly, by failing adequately to verify the allegations in it.

The Supreme Court reversed that decision, saying that the newspaper was entitled to use the *Reynolds* defence. Lord Brown said:

> ❝ In deciding whether *Reynolds* privilege attaches (whether the *Reynolds* public interest defence lies) the judge, on true analysis, is deciding but a single question: could whoever published the defamation, given whatever they knew (and did not know) and whatever they had done (and had not done) to guard so far as possible against the publication of untrue defamatory material, properly have considered the publication in question to be in the public interest? ❞

This, said Lord Brown, involved a host of different considerations, starting with the non-exhaustive list of 10 factors identified by Lord Nicholls in the original *Reynolds* case but also including other considerations.

▶ The court must consider all the circumstances

Section 4(2) of the 2013 Act says that, in determining whether the public interest defence is made out, the court must have regard to all the circumstances of the case.

Courts will doubtless examine whether the journalism was conducted responsibly—and might be expected to have in mind, at least, the non-exhaustive list of 10 factors detailed by Lord Nicholls in the original *Reynolds* case. The Act itself places no requirement on a publisher to demonstrate that what was published was the result of 'responsible journalism', and the abolition of the common law defence means that the *Reynolds* case is no longer a binding authority. But the old cases showing the approach judges have taken to responsible journalism might give some indication of factors which might be taken into account in deciding whether the defendant's belief—that publishing it was in the public interest—*is* reasonable.

▶ Audit trails to justify the public interest element and belief

Sir Brian Leveson suggested in his 2012 report into the press that any new regulator should require investigative journalists and their editors to produce an 'audit trail' of the development of a story, the investigation itself, and the issues considered and factors discussed when deciding whether to publish and whether the story was in the public interest.

ch 2, pp. 12–14, outlines the context of the report

Whether the courts will require this as part of the public interest defence should become clearer when cases on the new defence have been decided. Some editors are already familiar with such 'audit trail' practices, because, for example, the BBC Editorial Guidelines require that use of undercover tactics must be approved by senior managers as being in the public interest and because in 2012 the Editors' Code was changed to require press editors, in the event of a relevant complaint about what was published and/or reporters' methods, to be able to demonstrate fully that they—the editors —held a reasonable belief that 'public interest' considerations applied. Chs. 2 and 3 explain these codes.

Section 4(4) of the 2013 Act states that, when deciding whether it was reasonable for a defendant to believe that publication was in the public interest, the court 'must make such allowance for editorial judgement as it considers appropriate'.

▌ Defining the public interest

Both the Broadcasting Code and Editors' Code include some definitions of what journalism can be considered to be 'in the public interest'—for example, exposing crime, or showing that someone is misleading or endangering the public. The wording of those definitions was influenced by legal judgments in breach of confidence cases about the circumstances when the public interest justifies confidential or private material being published against someone's wishes. But the 2013 Act does not define the public interest. The Explanatory Notes say simply that 'this is a concept which is well-established in the English common law'.

The publication must be, or form part of, a statement on a matter of public interest, meaning that the court can either deal solely with the words complained of or take a holistic view of them in the wider context of the document or article in which they appear when deciding if overall this is a matter of public interest.

It was held that the *Reynolds* defence was available to anyone who publishes material in the public interest, including in a book. The same seems to apply to the new statutory defence.

In *Charman v Orion Publishing Group Ltd and others* [2007] EWCA Civ 972, [2008] 1 All ER 750 the Court of Appeal allowed the use of the defence to defeat a libel claim by a former police officer over Graeme McLagan's book, *Bent Coppers—The Inside Story of Scotland Yard's Battle against Police Corruption.*

It seems from rulings so far that judges will consider material to be in the public interest if it is of 'real public concern'—but the test is not as strict as saying the public needs to know. The concept is also flexible—the degree of public interest required will vary according to the publication and market, as in the *GKR Karate* case (cited below) in 2000, in which a judge found in favour of *Leeds Weekly News*, a free newspaper which was sued over a front-page article warning readers about the activities of doorstep salesmen selling karate club membership.

The judge said the fundamental question was one of public interest and the people of Leeds clearly had an interest in receiving this information (*GKR Karate Ltd v Yorkshire Post Newspapers Ltd* [2001] 1 WLR 2571).

▌ The responsible journalism test

The courts examined the issue of 'responsible journalism' in a number of cases, which might throw light on the approach they will take in future.

Reynolds Although the House of Lords in *Reynolds* established the *Reynolds* defence, it also decided, by a majority, that the *Sunday Times* could not take advantage of it as it had conspicuously failed to 'give the gist of the subject's response' (point 8—see pp. 300–301, Lord Nicholl's list). Asked at the trial why his account contained no reference to Mr Reynolds' explanation, the reporter said: 'There was not a word of Mr Reynolds' defence because I had decided that his defence ... there was no defence.' Mr Reynolds had addressed the Irish parliament on the issue, but the paper did not report his statement.

On the steps taken to verify the story (Lord Nicholls' point 4), the reporter, asked why he took no notes during his inquiries, said: 'I was not in note-taking mode.'

Loutchansky In 1999 *The Times* published articles alleging that international businessman Grigori Loutchansky controlled a major Russian criminal organisation involved in money-laundering and smuggling nuclear weapons.

The High Court judge rejected its claim to a *Reynolds* defence. The case went to the Court of Appeal, which agreed that the articles dealt with matters of public concern (Lord Nicholls' point 2), but made the following points.

- Implicating Mr Loutchansky in misconduct of the utmost gravity was manifestly likely to be highly damaging to his reputation, so a proportionate degree of responsibility was required of both journalist and editor (Lord Nicholls' point 1). *The Times* had failed to show this—the allegations were vague, the sources were unreliable, insufficient steps were taken to verify the information and no comment was obtained from Mr Loutchansky before publication.

- The High Court judge was entitled to find that 'such steps as were taken' by the reporter in his unsuccessful attempts to contact either Mr Loutchansky or his company, Nordex, or its lawyers were far less diligent than required by the standards of responsible journalism (Lord Nicholls' point 7).

- On the question whether the coverage contained the gist of Mr Loutchansky's side of the story (Lord Nicholls' point 8), it only contained the bare statement that he had 'repeatedly denied any wrongdoing or links to criminal activity', which was insufficient, given the seriousness of the unproven allegations published.

Both the *Reynolds* and *Loutchansky* cases demonstrate the importance of journalists having a good shorthand note to support what they write. Asked in court in the *Loutchansky* case to produce the note he made of a vital conversation he said he had had with his most important source, the reporter replied that he thought he must have made the note on a scrap of paper which he had subsequently thrown away (Lord Nicholls' point 4).

The Court of Appeal rejected the newspaper's appeal (*Loutchansky v Times Newspapers Ltd* [2001] EWCA Civ 1805).

The source of the information and the steps taken to verify it—Lord Nicholls' points 3 and 4—require more than a journalist making a number of calls which do not actually yield useful information or verification. In *Lord Ashcroft v Stephen Foley, Independent News and Media and Roger Alton* [2011] EWCA 292 (QB) Mr Justice Eady agreed with the claimant's argument that if sources provided no relevant information or none that was relied upon, the fact that they had been contacted was irrelevant. He added: 'Journalists, in other words, cannot collect "brownie points" for having rung round a number of people who had no relevant information to give.'

Seeking comment from the claimant

A key point in many cases involving the *Reynolds* defence was whether the publisher sought comment from the claimant (Lord Nicholls' point 7).

Any damaging story should be put to the subject before publication. As Lord Nicholls said: 'He [the subject] may have information others do not possess or have not disclosed.' The courts regard observance of the practice as one indication of responsible journalism. But point 7 also states: 'An approach to the claimant will not always be necessary'—the view the court took in the *Jameel* case because of its special circumstances.

Journalists should always try to put defamatory or damaging allegations to the subject if they intend to report them in the public interest.

Websites

The new defence is available to anyone who publishes material—so will cover bloggers, Twitter users and everyone else with access to the World-Wide Web.

But in the *Flood* case—discussed earlier—the Court held that the *Sunday Times* was protected by the *Reynolds* defence in relation to the copy of the story in its internet archive only until the date on which it was told that Det. Sgt Flood had been exonerated. Mr Justice Tugendhat held that its failure to make clear that Flood was innocent—for example, by adding an indication to this effect to the online story—could not be said to be responsible journalism.

All journalists should keep the internet in mind when dealing with investigative stories—and ensure that archive material is updated to reflect changes in circumstances.

A delicate balance

This new defence in the 2013 Act is extremely important to the media, journalists and editors but also to those who might seek to sue. It seeks to strike a balance between the right to reputation and a free press—but when it succeeds it means that a would-be claimant is deprived of any remedy for what might be a defamatory publication which severely damages his/her reputation. So the journalist's activities and professionalism will be closely scrutinised—in effect, the journalist's conduct will be on trial rather than that of the claimant.

Neutral reportage

The 'public interest' defence created in the 2013 Act includes protection of neutral reportage—that is, when a dispute or issue is being reported even-handedly in instances in which the fact that allegations are being made by one person against another, or that something is a matter of controversy, is itself a matter of public interest, even though the publisher cannot prove which people in a dispute or opposed in the controversy are telling the truth.

Section 4(3) says that if the complained-of statement (the reportage) was 'an accurate and impartial report of a dispute to which the claimant is a party', a court must, when determining whether it was reasonable for the publisher to believe that publishing the statement was in the public interest, disregard any omission by the publisher 'to take steps to verify the truth of the imputation conveyed by it'. But publishers should be wary of reporting disagreements which have been generated artificially so as to give the impression of a 'dispute' which can reasonably be reported in the public interest.

Again, when considering if the defence applies, judges can be guided, but not bound, by case law, outlined below, on a variant of the *Reynolds* defence which became known as the 'neutral reportage' defence.

The *Al-Fagih* case

In *Al-Fagih v HH Saudi Research & Marketing (UK) Ltd* [2001] EWCA Civ 1634 the Court of Appeal ruled that a newspaper could rely on the *Reynolds* defence where it reported, in an entirely objective manner, an allegation about someone made by an opponent during a political dispute. The defence was not lost merely because the newspaper had not verified the allegation. The newspaper had argued that, where two politicians made serious allegations against each other, it was a matter of public importance to report the dispute, provided that this was done fairly and accurately, and that the parties were given the opportunity to explain or contradict.

The *BNP* case (*Roberts v Searchlight*)

Another case showed that a 'neutral reportage' defence could be used even when, by contrast with *Al-Fagih*, the journal and its staff are clearly not neutral. The test was whether the journalist has reported the matter neutrally. The anti-fascist magazine *Searchlight* reported a dispute between British National Party (BNP) factions, repeating defamatory allegations made in the BNP's own bulletin. The magazine, its editor and a journalist successfully argued that they had a defence of qualified privilege in common law as they were merely reporting the allegations, not adopting or endorsing them (*Christopher Roberts and Barry Roberts v Gerry Gable, Steve Silver and Searchlight Magazine Ltd* [2006] EWHC 1025 (QB)).

➡ Recap of major points

- The *Reynolds* defence protected publication of material if it could be shown to be a matter of public interest, responsibly reported.

- The new statutory 'public interest' defence, which has its origins in the *Reynolds* defence, has two principle elements—the publication must be a statement on a matter of public interest, and the defendant's belief that it was reasonable.

- Judges will be guided to an extent by case law on the *Reynolds* defence, and the new defence can protect 'neutral reportage'—accurate and impartial reports—of a dispute in which the claimant is involved.

((•)) Useful Websites

www.legislation.gov.uk/ukpga/2013/26/contents/enacted
   Defamation Act 2013

www.legislation.gov.uk/ukpga/2013/26/notes/contents
   Explanatory Notes to the Act

www.bailii.org/uk/cases/UKSC/2012/11.html
   Supreme Court's decision in *Flood v Times Newspapers Ltd*

www.bailii.org/uk/cases/UKHL/2006/44.html
   House of Lords' decision in *Jameel*

www.publications.parliament.uk/pa/ld199899/ldjudgmt/jd991028/rey01.htm
   House of Lords' decision in *Reynolds*

The Rehabilitation of Offenders Act 1974

Chapter summary

The Rehabilitation of Offenders Act 1974 allows people to live down previous criminal convictions after specified periods, which vary with the sentence they receive. It limits the defences journalists have against libel claims over a published reference to a 'spent' conviction if the claimant can prove it was published maliciously. The Act presents no problem for journalists if disclosing someone's criminal record is in the public interest.

▶ Rehabilitation periods

The 1974 Act created the concept of spent convictions. Convictions become 'spent' after a 'rehabilitation period', which varies according to the sentence imposed, and includes a so-called Buffer period which runs from the end of the sentence. Some convictions, such as murder which carries an automatic life sentence, are never spent. → glossary

The aim was to allow people convicted of less serious offences to live down previous convictions and get a fresh start. There is no legal obligation to declare a 'spent' conviction when applying for most jobs, whatever the application form says, although there is for some occupations, such as working with children.

The Act also seeks to stop the media referring to someone's spent conviction without good reason.

Rehabilitation depends on the length of an offender's sentence. Serious crimes for which convictions never become spent are those for which an offender receives a jail sentence, or a term of detention in a young offender institution, of more than four years, whether the sentence is immediate or suspended, or an extended sentence for public protection, which is given for violent or sexual offences.

> Various types of sentence are explained in ch. 6, pp. 62–64, Sentencing by magistrates, and ch. 8, pp. 85–86, Sentencing at Crown court.

The rehabilitation periods determining when less serious convictions become spent vary from two years, for a prison sentence of six months or less, to seven years for a jail sentence of between 30 months and four years. But a further conviction during the rehabilitation period can extend it. Cautions and absolute discharges become spent immediately. Rehabilitation periods for many convictions are halved for those under 18, and in some cases are even shorter for those aged 12–14. Suspended sentences are treated as if they were put into effect.

> See Useful Websites at the end of this chapter and the Additional Material for this chapter on www.mcnaes.com for a detailed breakdown, issued by Nacro, the crime reduction charity, of rehabilitation periods arising from particular sentences.

see ch. 21 for explanation of all these defences

▌ The Act's effect on the media

The 1974 Act limits the defences available for a media organisation sued for libel for publishing reference to a person's spent conviction.

(1) A defence of truth—that the report of the previous conviction was true—will fail if the claimant can prove that the conviction was spent and the publication was malicious. This breaches the principle that truth is a complete defence to a defamation action, because the Act aims to deter the media from referring to a spent conviction without good reason.

(2) The defences of absolute or qualified privilege are not available for reporting a spent conviction which is mentioned in court proceedings but is then ruled inadmissible by the court.

Example A man sues a newspaper for defamation after it publishes an accurate reference to his previous criminal conviction. Three defences are available.

- *Truth*—because there was a conviction, defamation law accepts that the conviction is proof that the person committed that crime. So a media organisation, once it proves the conviction—for example, from a court record—is not required to re-prove that the claimant committed the offence.

- *Qualified privilege* protects non-contemporaneous reports of court cases if the defence's requirements are met. Mention of a conviction is, in effect, a report of the court case in which the conviction occurred when the defendant pleaded guilty, or when magistrates or a jury announced the guilty verdict. The defence also protects quotations from the case, such as the judge calling the convicted defendant 'a scoundrel'.

- *Honest opinion* protects opinion expressed about the person based on the fact of the conviction, if the defence's requirements are met. If a council election candidate has a criminal conviction, an editorial comment column could safely publish the author's honestly held opinion that the conviction made the person unfit for public office. Similar comments from others could also be safely published if they were their honestly held opinions. Even if no such comment is made explicitly, a media organisation publishing the conviction in this context creates an inference that the person could be regarded as unfit for public office. The honest opinion defence should protect the media organisation over that inference.

ch. 19, p. 257, Inferences, explains this term

Even if the conviction referred to is 'spent', the above defences apply unless the publication was malicious—for example, there was no public interest in referring to it.

But a claimant would win if it were proved at a defamation trial that there was malice. There will be malice if a journalist or editor publishes a reference to a spent conviction merely to further some interest of his/her own or in spite. In such a case the Act stops use of the truth defence, even though the conviction is a fact. Proof of malice also destroys the qualified privilege defence.

✳ Remember

In most news stories the media can refer to and comment on spent convictions—disclosing a council candidate's previous conviction or the criminal record of a dodgy businessperson—with no fear of libel consequences because the disclosures are in the public interest and no malice is involved.

Spent convictions revealed in court proceedings

A person giving evidence in any civil proceedings should not, generally, be asked questions about spent convictions.

But rehabilitated people who appear before criminal courts again, after their convictions have become spent, can still be asked about them.

Absolute or qualified privilege applies to media reports of a spent conviction mentioned in a court case unless the court ruled that the fact that the conviction exists was inadmissible.

Judges have been directed that spent convictions should never be referred to in criminal courts, unless this is unavoidable, and that no one should refer in open court to a spent conviction without the judge's authority.

Criminal penalties

There is no criminal penalty for journalists who mention a spent conviction. But it may well be an offence for a public servant to disclose details of spent convictions other than in the course of official duties.

It is a criminal offence to get information of spent convictions from official records by fraud, dishonesty or bribery.

 Ch. 28 explains data protection, and ch. 35 explains 'misconduct' law and bribery law.

➡ **Recap of major points**

- Convictions become spent at the end of the rehabilitation period.
- A conviction which led to a jail term of more than four years is never spent.
- The rehabilitation period varies between seven years (in respect of a jail sentence of between 30 months and four years) and three months, although some offences become spent immediately.
- The Rehabilitation of Offenders Act 1974 restricts the libel defences available to journalists who maliciously refer to spent convictions.

((•)) **Useful Websites**

www.nacro.org.uk/wp-content/uploads/2014/05/rehabilitation-of-offenders-act-1974-guide.pdf
Nacro guide to the Rehabilitation of Offenders Act 1974, with charts showing rehabilitation periods

Slander, malicious falsehood and obscenity

Chapter summary

Defamation in its spoken form is slander—and can present journalists with problems. This chapter examines those problems and looks at malicious falsehood, which occurs with the publication of a statement which is not defamatory but is false and can be shown to have caused financial loss. It also briefly examines law banning publication of obscene material.

▌ Slander

The most obvious difference between the torts of libel and slander is, as ch. 19 explains, that libel is in permanent form (eg written words, a drawing or a photograph), while slander is spoken or in some other transient form.

→glossary

But:

- defamatory statements broadcast on radio or television, or in a cable programme are treated as libel—Broadcasting Act 1990;
- as are defamatory statements in a public performance of a play—Theatres Act 1968.

For there to be slander, as with libel, the statement must be published to a third person and must refer to the claimant.

ch. 20 explains what a libel claimant must prove

A claimant in a slander case must prove the financial damage suffered, except in the case of:

- an imputation that he/she has committed a crime punishable by death or imprisonment; or
- any statement calculated to disparage him/her in his office, profession, calling, trade or business.

Journalists are less likely to become involved personally in a slander action than a libel action, but must be aware of the dangers.

Suppose X says that Y, a borough councillor, used his position to secure building contracts—actionable because it disparages Y in his office of councillor. A reporter checking the story will have to interview people to reach the truth and must be wary of being sued for slander over questions asked during interviews in which the original slander might be repeated to a third party. There is also a risk that a message left on an answering machine could spark an action for slander if it is heard or re-played by someone other than the claimant. There is also a risk if broadcasters shout allegations, in public, at people who have refused to be interviewed about them—the broadcast itself could spark a libel action, while the fact that the shouted question was heard by members of the public at the scene might tempt the subject to sue for slander as well.

The limitation period for bringing a slander action is one year.

▐ Malicious falsehoods

Publication of a false statement may cause a person financial damage even though it does not cast aspersions on his/her character or fitness to hold a certain office or to follow a particular calling. For example, a false statement that a solicitor had retired from practice would doubtless cause loss as the lawyer's clients would seek other solicitors to do their work. But it is clearly not defamatory to be considered retired.

The wronged person cannot sue for libel or slander if a published statement is not defamatory—but might be able to sue for malicious falsehood.

The claimant must prove the statement is untrue—in contrast with a libel action, where the court assumes that a defamatory statement is false unless the defendant can prove it to be true.

The claimant in a malicious falsehood action must also prove that the statement was published maliciously.

As with the defence of qualified privilege in libel law, malice means a statement made by someone who knows it is false, or is reckless as to its truth. But a defendant who believes a statement is true but publishes it with the aim of injuring the claimant will also be viewed as motivated by malice (*Spring v Guardian Assurance plc* [1993] 2 All ER 273, CA). Negligence—that is, wrongly believing a statement to be true, and so failing to check it, when there is no aim to injure—is not malice.

The claimant in a malicious falsehood case does not have to prove that he/she has suffered actual damage if the words are in permanent form, such as printed words, and calculated—likely—to cause financial damage, or they are spoken or written and likely to cause him/her financial damage in his/her office, profession, calling, trade or business.

But once a claimant has proved financial damage, he/she can also claim damages for emotional distress, hurt feelings and so on—and these damages could be substantial because the defendant will be shown to have acted maliciously.

The limitation for bringing a malicious falsehood action is one year.

Meaning

Claims for malicious falsehood also differ from those for defamation because they are not based on the notion that a statement has only one meaning (*Ajinomoto Sweeteners Europe SAS v Asda Stores Ltd (No 2)* [2010] EWCA Civ 609, [2011] QB 497).

 See ch. 19, p. 257, Meaning of words, for this rule in defamation cases.

Journalists must therefore be aware of the need for clear and concise writing, and the risk that, in a malicious falsehood claim, a court will take account of a range of possible meanings for a statement, one or more of which could leave them liable to pay damages.

👁 Case study

Former Conservative Party Co-Treasurer Peter Cruddas was initially awarded £180,000 in damages when he sued the *Sunday Times* for libel and malicious falsehood. The case arose from articles—published in 2012 after he met undercover journalists masquerading as potential donors to the Party—saying he asked for £250,000 in such donations for them to meet David Cameron. But in 2015 the Court of Appeal cut the damages to £50,000, ruling that the trial judge was wrong in one of his findings that the meanings in the articles did not give a true account of what Mr Cruddas told the journalists. In the appeal judgment, Lord Justice Jackson said Mr Cruddas was effectively saying to the journalists that if they were to donate large sums to the Conservative Party, they would have an opportunity to influence government policy and to gain unfair commercial advantage through confidential meetings with the Prime Minister and other senior Ministers. Lord Justice Jackson said it was 'unacceptable, inappropriate and wrong' for Mr Cruddas to do this, and therefore this meaning of the articles was 'substantially true'. But the Court of Appeal upheld findings of libel and malicious falsehood over two other pleaded meanings which it said the journalists knew were false—that Mr Cruddas made the offer even though he knew the money offered for meetings would come, in breach of the ban under UK electoral law, from Middle Eastern investors in a Liechtenstein fund, and that to evade that law he was happy that the foreign donors should use deceptive devices to conceal the true source of the donation. The *Sunday Times* said it did not think it had accused him of these meanings (*Cruddas v Calvert, Blake and Times Newspapers Ltd* [2015] EWCA Civ 171; *Media Lawyer*, 17 March 2015).

((•))
see Useful Websites at the end of this chapter for the full judgment

Corrections

see ch. 19
p. 263,
Errors and
apologies

An editor may realise that the facts of a story are wrong, but they were not defamatory and it was an honest mistake. If so, he/she should act quickly to publish an adequate correction. A failure to correct a story which is known to be wrong, especially if it remains visible online, could be held to be malicious.

Slander of goods and title

Two types of malicious falsehood are known as 'slander of goods' (false and malicious statements disparaging the claimant's goods) and 'slander of title' (false and malicious denial of the claimant's title to property). The word 'slander' is misleading in both cases. The damaging statement can be in permanent form or spoken.

▌ Obscenity

It is an offence to publish obscene material—the test is whether the words or material published would tend to deprave and corrupt those likely to read them/it.

The Obscene Publications Act 1959 introduced a defence that the publication was 'for the public good ... in the interests of science, literature, art, or learning, or of other objects of public concern'. The Obscene Publications Act 1964 made it an offence to possess an obscene article for publication for gain.

➡ Recap of major points

- Slander, a civil wrong (like libel), concerns defamatory words which (unlike libel) are spoken or in some other transient form.

- In slander (unlike libel), actual damage may need to be proved.

- Malicious falsehoods are false statements that, though not defamatory, may still be damaging. The claimant must prove that the statement is untrue and was published maliciously.

((•)) Useful Websites

www.bailii.org/cgi-bin/markup.cgi?doc=/ew/cases/EWCA/Civ/2015/171.html
  Court of Appeal judgment in *Cruddas*

Part 4

Confidentiality, privacy and copyright

Breach of confidence

Chapter summary

The law of breach of confidence is based upon the principle that a person who has been given information in confidence should not take unfair advantage of it. This chapter explains the kind of information and relationships considered confidential. If a media organisation publishes this type of information, it needs a legal defence to avoid having to pay damages. Governments, businesses and individuals use this law to protect information they regard as officially or commercially secret, or private. The main means of preventing a breach of confidence is an injunction banning publication of confidential information. This area of law was also the foundation of the law of privacy, the focus of the next chapter.

▶ Development of the law

The law on breach of confidence is at its most straightforward in protecting commercial secrets. An employee has a duty to protect commercially sensitive information he/she creates or gains in the course of employment—for example, data on market research or plans for new products. That duty arises from the employment relationship. If an employee disloyally passes that information to the employer's commercial rival, that is a breach of confidence. In most instances the betrayed employer could, apart from sacking the employee, successfully sue him/her and the rival in the civil courts for damages to compensate for any financial loss suffered, because breach of confidence is a tort, a civil wrong. The duty to preserve confidentiality can automatically pass to anyone else who receives the material and realises its confidential nature. So, a media organisation to which a business's commercial secrets are leaked may also be successfully sued if it publishes these, unless it has a defence.

→glossary

The law of breach of confidence can also protect material which is personally private. Queen Victoria's husband Prince Albert used it in 1848 to prevent commercial publication of private family etchings depicting their children and pets after copies were purloined from the printers to which they were sent by the Royal household to be printed merely as a personal collection (*Prince Albert v Strange* (1848) 1 Mac. & G. 25).

But what is now the wide scope of this law is a comparatively recent development.

Development of privacy law

Until 2000 UK law recognised no general right to privacy. So in previous decades people who believed their privacy was about to be infringed sought to use the law of breach of confidence to prevent intrusions. Their main difficulty lay in the different nature of the two kinds of right. An obligation of confidence, by definition, arises, first, from the circumstances in which the information is given—a relationship which gives rise to one party owing a duty of confidence to another.

In contrast, a right of privacy relating to information arises from the nature of the information itself and the principle that certain kinds of information are private and for that reason alone should not be disclosed. Many cases involving invasions of privacy did not result from breaches of confidence.

p. 322, Breach of confidence and official secrets, explains *Spycatcher*

Privacy law evolved as judges began to abandon their strict view on the circumstances in which an obligation of confidence could occur. In the *Spycatcher* case in the House of Lords in 1988 (*A-G v Times Newspapers* (1992) 1 AC 191) Lord Goff of Chieveley said:

> **“** A duty of confidence arises when confidential information comes to the knowledge of a person (the confidant) in circumstances where he has notice, or is ruled to have agreed, that the information is confidential, with the effect that it would be just in all the circumstances that he should be precluded from disclosing the information to others. **”**

Lord Goff said he had expressed the duty in wide terms to include the situation where 'an obviously confidential document was wafted by an electric fan out of a window into a crowded street, or when an obviously confidential document such as a diary was dropped in a public place and then picked up by a passer-by'.

In this scenario the passer-by has no relationship with the person whose information he/she has picked up—but, because it is obviously confidential, in law the passer-by should not, for example, give or sell it to a media organisation for publication, unless there is a legal defence.

In 2000 the Human Rights Act 1998 came into force, incorporating into UK law the European Convention on Human Rights, Article 8 of which guarantees the right to respect for privacy and family life, as ch. 1 explains. In cases involving alleged breach of personal privacy, the courts started abandoning the legal contrivance of implying a confidential relationship where none existed, and so a separate type of tort—misuse of private information—developed. That is the focus of the next chapter.

▌ Elements of a breach of confidence

There are three elements in a breach of confidence.

The information:

- must have 'the necessary quality of confidence';
- must have been imparted in circumstances imposing an obligation of confidence; and
- there must be an unauthorised use of that information to the detriment of the party communicating it (*Coco v AN Clark (Engineers) Ltd* [1969] RPC 41).

The phrase 'the party communicating it' means the person who originally communicates the information—that is, the person to whom the confidence is owed. For example, a company allows its employees to access commercially sensitive information about its products and finances—in effect, it communicates such information to them, and so they owe it a duty of confidence. A patient who tells a doctor about an ailment, or allows him/her to take blood tests or conduct a pregnancy test, is communicating information. The doctor and any other staff at the surgery or hospital owe the patient a duty of confidence in respect of that information.

But, again, it should be remembered that a court enforcing the law of confidentiality does not require a direct relationship between the person who wishes to protect the information and the person who wishes to disclose it. This is because the law of equity operates on the consciences of the parties, so the legal criterion is whether a reasonable person would understand from the nature and circumstances of a disclosure that he/she was receiving information or material in confidence. Thus, a journalist who receives a leak of a company's commercially sensitive data or someone's medical records usually has a duty not to reveal it to others, just as an employee of that company or the patient's doctor has.

The quality of confidence

The law of breach of confidence safeguards ideas and information imparted or obtained in confidential circumstances. Generally, information is not confidential if it is trivial—for example, a company's canteen menu—or is already in the public domain.

Obligation of confidence

An obligation of confidence can arise in a variety of ways.

Contractual relationship Employees might have signed agreements not to disclose an employer's secrets. This applies as much to a celebrity's chauffeur, who wants to sell to the media tales of what he saw and heard in his employment, as it does to scientists employed in commercial research. Even if the written contract does not make this clear, there is an implied term in every employment relationship that an employee will not do anything detrimental to an employer's interests.

ch. 26, p. 335, Relation- ships, gives context

see too ch. 26, p. 339, Information obtained covertly

Personal relationship In 1967 the Duchess of Argyll prevented the *People* newspaper, and her former husband, from publishing marital secrets (*Argyll v Argyll* [1967] Ch 302). This was an early example of the courts accepting that a couple in a relationship owe a duty of confidence to each other about intimate matters, which still applies after they split up. By the 1980s the courts had extended the protection to prevent the publication of kiss-and-tell stories originating from less formal relationships. Disputes about whether such stories can be or should have been published are now generally dealt with in privacy law.

Unethical behaviour It now seems to be established by case law that journalists who obtain confidential information by unethical means such as trespass, theft, listening devices or long-range cameras are usually in breach of an obligation of confidence owed to the targets of this activity—an obligation created and breached by the tactics used.

If not, the case will probably be covered in privacy law. Electronic snooping will be covered by criminal law.

Detriment

The confiding party must suffer, or be at risk of suffering, a detriment of some sort to be able to claim a breach of confidence, such as financial loss from exposure of commercially sensitive information. But in the *Spycatcher* case in the House of Lords, Lord Keith of Kinkel said it would be a sufficient detriment to an individual that information he/she gave in confidence was to be disclosed to people he/she would prefer not to know it. The detriment could be the adverse effect on someone's mental well-being or physical health, caused by unauthorised publication of his/her confidential, personal information—for example, if it causes people to ridicule or shun him/her.

▶ Breach of confidence and official secrets

In 1985 the UK government used the law of breach of confidence when attempting to stop publication of information acquired by Peter Wright during his former job as a senior officer of its internal security service, MI5. He planned to make money by selling his memoirs—a book called *Spycatcher*. The Attorney General, on behalf of the UK government, sought an injunction to stop the book's publication, arguing that former members of the security services had an absolute and lifelong duty not to reveal any details of their employment.

In June 1986 the *Observer* and *The Guardian* newspapers carried stories giving brief details of some allegations Wright, who had retired to Australia, planned to publish. An English court then gave the Attorney General interim injunctions preventing both newspapers from disclosing any information Wright had obtained as a member of MI5. In 1988, after many legal actions involving the government and newspapers, in the UK and abroad, the House of Lords ruled: that the original articles in the *Observer* and *The Guardian* in 1986 were not published in breach of confidence; that the government was not entitled to a permanent injunction preventing the newspapers from making further comments on the book and using extracts from it; and that the government was not entitled to a general injunction restraining the media from future publication of information derived from Wright.

The *Spycatcher* case showed that the government was prepared to use the civil law of breach of confidence rather than rely on prosecutions under (controversial) official secrets law. The case also established the principle that an injunction granted against one media organisation, to stop it publishing material, could cover all of them.

ch. 33 explains official secrets law

 For more details of *Spycatcher*, see ch. 33 on www.mcnaes.com on official secrets law, and see Useful Websites at the end of this chapter for a BBC report of the House of Lords' judgment.

▌ Injunctions

A person or an organisation who discovers that the media intends to publish confidential information without his/her/its consent can apply to the High Court for a temporary injunction to stop it.

Such an order is intended to 'hold the ring' until the case is fully heard. As a condition for obtaining an interim injunction the party which applies for it has to undertake to pay the other side damages if, at the trial, it is ruled that the order should not have been made.

But a media organisation, having been injuncted, may decide the cost of fighting the injunction or the case in a full trial is not worth it.

Disobeying an injunction can result in an action for contempt of court which could lead to an unlimited fine.

Section 12 of the Human Rights Act 1998 is intended to provide some protection against injunctions in matters involving freedom of expression.

Claimants applying to the High Court for injunctions should only obtain them if they persuade the judge that they are 'likely' to establish at the trial that publication should not be allowed.

Before the 1998 Act was implemented, the application might be without notice, which meant that only one party—the claimant—was represented and a media organisation, as the defendant, would only learn of the proceedings when it was told that an injunction had been granted. That can and still does happen—for example, injunctions have sometimes been granted when a newspaper has been printed and ready to go on sale.

Section 12 says that if the defendant is not present when the application is made, the court must not grant an injunction unless satisfied either that the claimant seeking the injunction has taken all practicable steps to notify the defendant or that there are compelling reasons for not giving notice.

The journalist's dilemma

The law of confidentiality regularly presents journalists with a dilemma. Suppose a reporter learns about some newsworthy misconduct from a source who received the information confidentially. The journalist should, as a matter of ethical conduct and because of the law of libel, approach the person alleged to have mis-behaved to get his/her side of the story and to check facts.

For example, the BBC Editorial Guidelines tells broadcasters:

> **"** When our output makes allegations of wrongdoing, iniquity or incompetence or lays out a strong and damaging critique of an individual or institution the presumption is that those criticised should be given a 'right of reply', that is, given a fair opportunity to respond to the allegations. **"**

But a journalist who does make such an approach runs the risk that, as explained later, the subject will immediately obtain an injunction banning use of the information, killing the story before it can be published.

((•)) See Useful Websites at the end of this chapter for this part of the BBC Editorial Guidelines.

✳ Remember

You should certainly check a story if it might be defamatory—but, if possible, phrase your questions so that you do not reveal that you have confidential material, to avoid laying yourself open to the risk of an injunction.

Injunction against one is against all

In 1987 the Court of Appeal ruled that when an interim injunction is in force preventing a media organisation from publishing confidential information, other media organisations in England and Wales which know of it can be guilty of contempt of court if they publish that information, even if they are not named in the injunction.

In 1989 two papers were fined £50,000 each for publishing extracts from *Spycatcher* because at the time of publication they knew that interim injunctions were in force against the *Observer* and *The Guardian* preventing them from publishing this material. The fines were later discharged, but the convictions were upheld and the ruling on the law was confirmed by the House of Lords in 1991.

This legal device for silencing the media might be phrased in such a way that journalists are banned even from mentioning the existence of the proceedings—a so-called super-injunction. Super-injunctions are discussed in the next chapter.

An injunction issued by an English court does not prevent publication in another country. In particular, it does not prevent publication in Scotland—though Scottish judges may be asked to impose their own injunction, known as an 'interdict'.

 See the www.mcnaes.com chapter on Scotland.

Legal remedies for breach of confidence

People or organisations who say their confidential information has been unlawfully published can, as claimants in legal action:

- ask a judge to impose an injunction to stop it being published again by that publisher or by others;
- seek an order for the confidential material, such as documents or pictures, to be 'delivered up'—that is, given back to the claimant or destroyed;
- sue the publisher for damages or 'an account of profits';
- ask a judge to order the publisher to reveal the source of the information, if this is not known, so that the source can be sued for damages and/or to stop disclosure of more confidential information.

Damages

These are likely to be higher in a case where the breach of confidence caused commercial loss—for example, the £1 million damages which *Hello!* magazine had to pay to *OK!* magazine in the *Douglas* case—rather than loss of personal privacy.

In the *Douglas* case it was ruled that the law of confidence protected what should have been the value of the exclusive, commercial deal which *OK!* had struck with Hollywood couple Michael Douglas and Catherine Zeta-Jones to take and publish photographs of their 'private' wedding reception, an arrangement which *Hello!* had undermined by publishing 'spoiler' photos of the occasion, secretly taken by an undercover paparazzo—see Additional Material for ch. 25 on www.mcnaes.com for details of the case.

In 2008 Max Mosley, then president of the Fédération Internationale de l'Automobile (FIA), which runs Formula 1 grand prix racing, was awarded £60,000 against the *News of the World* in an action alleging breach of confidence and unauthorised disclosure of personal information for its exposure of his participation in a sado-masochistic orgy with prostitutes. One of the prostitutes had breached the confidence of her arrangement with Mosley by telling the newspaper about and filming the orgy, and the newspaper was ruled to be liable for the damages.

Account of profits

A person misusing confidential information to make money may be asked to account for the profits to the person or organisation whose confidence was betrayed. A court may rule, after seeing this account, that the person who misused the information should pay some or all of these ill-gotten profits to the party betrayed. But for a media organisation, the order is more likely to be for damages, because of the difficulty a judge would face in deciding which story in its output at that time led to what profit.

Order to reveal source

ch. 34
explains the
ethics of
protecting
sources

A court can order a journalist to reveal the name of the informant who provided the confidential information. If the journalist promised the source anonymity, the ethical position is that he/she must keep that promise—which means facing the consequences of disobeying the court. The defiance could be deemed a contempt of court which could lead to a fine or, conceivably, to the journalist being jailed, though he/she may have some protection from Article 10 of the European Convention on Human Rights and the 'shield law' in section 10 of the Contempt of Court Act 1981.

👁 Case study

→ glossary

In 1989 an engineering company, Tetra Ltd, obtained injunctions against *The Engineer* magazine and its trainee reporter Bill Goodwin. The company, which was in financial difficulties, had prepared a business plan for the purpose of negotiating a substantial bank loan. A copy of the draft plan 'disappeared' from the company's offices, and the next day an unidentified source telephoned Mr Goodwin and gave him information about the company, including the amount of the projected loan and the company's forecast results. Mr Goodwin phoned the company and its bankers to check the information. The company obtained a **without notice** injunction restraining the magazine from publishing information derived from the draft plan, and later obtained an order requiring Mr Goodwin and *The Engineer* to hand over notes that would disclose the source of the information. Mr Goodwin refused to comply and was fined £5,000. In 1996 the European Court of Human Rights ruled that the court order and the fine violated his right to freedom of expression under Article 10. Mr Goodwin was supported by the National Union of Journalists (*Goodwin v United Kingdom*, Application no. 17488/90 (1996) 22 EHRR 123).

▌ Defences

A media organisation sued for an alleged breach of confidence might have a defence. Defences include:

- the information did not have 'the necessary quality of confidence' because:
  - of its nature—for example, it was trivial and/or unlikely to cause much detriment; or
  - it was already in the public domain;
- it was in the public interest to publish the information—for example, to expose wrongdoing, negligence or hypocrisy.

The same arguments can be used against an application for an injunction.

Information already in the public domain

If a media organisation publishes commercially sensitive information leaked from a business, or information leaked from a public institution, a court is unlikely to grant an injunction or award damages for breach of confidence if the material was already widely in the public domain—for example, already published by other media outlets or by members of the public on internet sites and other social media.

Judges, as some have said, do not wish to make pointless orders like King Canute ordering the tide to recede.

But the scope for the public domain defence may be more limited if personal privacy has been infringed—for example, a judge might rule that embarrassing private footage improperly copied by a maid from a celebrity's computer should not, to spare the celebrity any further distress, be published by the mainstream media, even if thousands of copies are already visible on the internet.

 The issue of what was already in the public domain was a feature of the *Watford Observer* case, which is outlined in Additional Material for this chapter on www.mcnaes.com.

Publication in the public interest

Section 12 of the Human Rights Act 1998 says a court considering imposing an injunction in a matter affecting freedom of expression in which journalistic material is involved must have particular regard to the extent to which it is, or would be, in the public interest for the material to be published.

But even before the Act was implemented, journalists had successfully argued that disclosing confidential information would be in the public interest.

👁 Case study

The Court of Appeal ruled in 1984 that it was in the public interest for the *Daily Express* to publish information from an internal memo, leaked from a company making breathalyser equipment, which cast doubt on its accuracy at a time when police were using it to clamp down on drink-driving (*Lion Laboratories v Evans* [1985] QB 526).

Correcting 'a false public image'

In 2005 celebrities David Beckham and Victoria Beckham failed to get an injunction against the *News of the World* concerning information about the state of their marriage. The paper argued that the Beckhams had portrayed a false image about their private life, and so it was in the public interest for it to publish information from their former nanny that she had witnessed blazing rows between the couple (*Media Lawyer*, 25 April 2005).

▌ Relevance of ethical codes

see ch. 26, p. 340, Relevance of ethical codes, and ch. 27

As the next chapter explains, in a case involving a claim of breach of privacy, which may include a claim of breach of confidence, the judge will—if the defendant is a media organisation—take into account what the relevant ethical code says and whether the organisation conformed to it. This could be the Editors' Code or the Broadcasting Code.

➡ Recap of major points

- The law says that a person who has obtained information in confidence must not take unfair advantage of it.
- The person who believes his/her confidence is to be breached can get an injunction preventing this.
- Disobeying an injunction can result in an action for contempt of court.
- If confidential matter is published, the person whose confidences have been breached may be able to claim damages.

((•)) Useful Websites

http://news.bbc.co.uk/onthisday/hi/dates/stories/october/13/newsid_2532000/2532583.stm
   BBC news archive story in the *Spycatcher* saga

www.bbc.co.uk/editorialguidelines/guidelines/fairness/right-of-reply
   BBC Editorial Guidelines on fairness and right of reply

Privacy

Chapter summary

The law of privacy—misuse of private information—has been used by celebrities and others to prevent publication of information about their lives and activities. Increasing numbers of sportsmen and celebrities have sought injunctions to stop the media reporting on their activities. This chapter explains privacy law—and warns that journalists who electronically snoop on people or hack into their phone messages will probably be committing a crime.

▌ Development of the law

As ch. 1 explains, the Human Rights Act 1998 came into force on 2 October 2000, incorporating the European Convention on Human Rights—Article 8 of which guarantees the right to respect for privacy and family life—into UK law. This gave it what it previously lacked—a specific law of privacy.

As the legislation went through Parliament, journalists and media organisations expressed concerns about the potential effect of the right to privacy on their freedom to publish true information of public interest.

Section 12 of the Act requires courts considering granting any order or injunction banning publication of information to have 'particular regard' to the importance of freedom of expression, guaranteed by Article 10 of the Convention. But in the *Douglas* case, Lord Justice Sedley rejected the view that section 12 gave greater weight to freedom of expression than to privacy, saying: 'Everything will ultimately depend on the proper balance between privacy and publicity in the situation facing the court.'

In the House of Lords, in *In Re S (FC) (a child) (Appellant)* [2004] UKHL 47, [2005] 1 AC 593 Lord Steyn made it clear that neither Article 8, guaranteeing the right to respect for privacy and family life, nor the Article 10 right to freedom of

→ glossary

see Additional Material for ch. 25 on www. mcnaes.com for more on *Douglas* expression 'has as such precedence over the other'. This is also the view of the European Court of Human Rights (ECtHR).

ch. 28
explains the
1998 Act

see p. 339,
The public
interest,
for more on
Campbell

👁 Case studies

In 2004 supermodel Naomi Campbell won a privacy claim in the House of Lords after suing Mirror Group Newspapers for breach of her Article 8 privacy rights, breach of confidence and infringement of the Data Protection Act 1998.

The *Daily Mirror* had published detail about her receiving therapy from Narcotics Anonymous for drug addiction, including photos of her emerging into the street after leaving a session. Although she was only awarded a total of £3,500 damages for distress and injury to her feelings, her victory in law—which infuriated the *Mirror*—showed how Article 8 had changed the UK's legal landscape (*Campbell v Mirror Group Newspapers* [2004] UKHL 22).

Another landmark ruling in 2004 was the European Court of Human Rights' judgment that Princess Caroline of Monaco's privacy was breached by the publication of photographs of scenes from her daily life, shopping or on holiday with her family, in public places. Important considerations in the decision was that she was not an elected politician, and had suffered years of being stalked and photographed by paparazzi, which had interfered with her human right, protected by Article 8, to enjoy social interaction with people (*Von Hannover v Germany*, Application no. 59320/00, 24 June 2004, ECtHR). But the Grand Chamber of the ECtHR has since stepped back from the position established in that case, as explained later in this chapter.

▌ The scope of Article 8

Article 8 of the European Convention on Human Rights says:

> 1. Everyone has the right to respect for his private and family life, his home and his correspondence.
> 2. There shall be no interference by a public authority with the exercise of this right except such as is in accordance with the law and is necessary in a democratic society in the interests of national security, public safety or the economic well-being of the country, for the prevention of disorder or crime, for the protection of health or morals, or for the protection of the rights and freedoms of others.

Article 8 gives protection for privacy against a 'public authority', the media or anyone else, such as bloggers.

Remedies for breach of privacy

The remedies which courts will provide for a breach of privacy include damages and permanent injunctions to prevent material being published.

Damages

In May 2015 Mr Justice Mann awarded damages totalling more than £1.2 million to eight claimants whose phones were hacked by journalists at Mirror Group Newspapers (MGN), publisher of the *Daily Mirror, Sunday Mirror* and *Sunday People*. The highest sum—£260,250—went to actress and businesswoman Sadie Frost, while former footballer Paul Gascoigne was awarded £188,250. The case set a new high for damages for invasions of privacy. MGN has appealed against the level of damages.

ch. 35 outlines the hacking scandal

 See the Late News section for the appeal decision.

Injunctions and super-injunctions

If a person is told or learns that a media organisation intends to publish material he/she considers private, he/she can seek an injunction to ban its publication. Initially, a judge may grant an interim (temporary) injunction to hold the position until the court can rule after a full trial hearing—which will be costly for the losing party—on whether the injunction should be permanent or lifted to allow publication.

The issue of injunctions and so-called super-injunctions—orders which include a clause banning the media or anyone from even publicising the fact that they have been made—attracted considerable media coverage in April and May 2011. Concern was expressed that freedom of expression, including that of the media, and the public's right to receive information was being irrevocably damaged by such bans. Footballers, actors and business people facing allegations—for example, of adultery—were granted orders giving them anonymity in these cases, to block publication of information about their private lives, while bloggers and Twitter users sought to undermine orders by naming those whom they claimed—sometimes incorrectly—had obtained them. The uproar led Lord Neuberger, then the Master of the Rolls, to issue useful Practice Guidance tightening up the rules on non-publication injunctions and requiring that, once an interim injunction was made, the case should normally proceed to a trial. The number of applications for privacy injunctions against the media subsequently dropped sharply.

ch. 25, p. 323, Injunctions, gives more context

The permanent injunction *contra mundum*

ch. 25
explains the
Spycatcher
case

→ glossary

see ch. 11,
p. 134,
Indefinite
anonymity
for
convicted
defendants

ch. 10
explains
automatic
anonymity
for sexual
offence
victims

An interim injunction is held, under the *Spycatcher* principle, to bind all those on whom it is served or who are aware of it. But an injunction made permanent after a full hearing (trial), binds only the particular parties—for example, media organisation(s)—against whom it was obtained. This means that another media organisation could then publish the information covered. The response of the courts in these circumstances has been to issue so-called *contra mundum* ('against the world') orders—orders of general effect which bind anyone who knows about them, including all media organisations made aware of them.

This was the power used in 2000 by Dame Elizabeth Butler-Sloss, the then President of the Family Division of the High Court, in a ground-breaking injunction banning the media from revealing the new identities and whereabouts of Robert Thompson and Jon Venables, juveniles who murdered 2-year-old James Bulger. One reason that injunction was granted was to protect their Article 8 privacy rights.

In April 2011 Mr Justice Eady said the court's jurisdiction to grant an injunction *contra mundum* was available, wherever necessary and proportionate, for the protection of Convention rights whether of children or adults (*OPQ v BJM and CJM* [2011] EWHC 1059 (QB)).

In June 2015, Mr Justice Keehan, sitting in the Family Division of the High Court, issued a *contra mundum* injunction giving lifelong anonymity to a teenage girl who had been the victim of sexual exploitation by a group of Asian men in the Birmingham area, one of whom had fathered her child. There were, he said, 'compelling reasons' why the teenager, known only as AB, should be protected, and why her history as a victim of child sexual exploitation should remain confidential and private to her. The injunction was granted because the girl was not automatically entitled to lifelong anonymity under the Sexual Offences (Amendment) Act 1992 as no complaint was ever made that any sexual offence had been committed (*Birmingham City Council v Safraz Riaz and others* [2015] EWHC 1857 (Fam)).

▶ A shift in the law

see also
p. 339,
The public
interest

At one point it seemed clear that, in a privacy case, unless there was a strong public interest justification—the material in question had to contribute to a debate of general public importance—the courts would issue injunctions to prevent publication of the sort of kiss-and-tell stories which were once the standard fare of tabloid journalism. But in February 2012 the ECtHR eased the position somewhat, saying that media coverage of celebrities' private lives was 'acceptable if in the general interest and if in reasonable balance with the right to respect for private life' (*Axel Springer AG v Germany*, Application no. 39954/08 (2012) 55 EHRR 66; *Von Hannover v Germany No. 2*, Applications nos 40660/08 and 60641/08).

The factors a court will consider in deciding on injunctions include the degree to which the material makes a contribution to a debate of general interest—which does not just cover politics—how well-known the person concerned is, the subject of the report itself, the prior conduct of the person concerned, the method of obtaining the information and its truth, and the content, form and consequences of the publication.

▌ Privacy versus freedom of expression

In a privacy case, what factors will persuade a judge that material which a media organisation seeks to publish *will* contribute to a 'debate of general interest to society'?

Decisions by the ECtHR indicate that it sees freedom of expression as having various levels of value to society, with political expression about the conduct of politicians in public office, at the top of the table. This means that an elected politician who conceals his/her improper behaviour from the electorate is unlikely to persuade a court that the media should be banned from exposing it. The higher up the hierarchy, the greater the protection the courts should give freedom of expression, and vice versa, although each case will, as the ECtHR and UK courts consistently stress, depend on its specific facts.

But, as outlined earlier, in the *Axel Springer* and *Von Hannover No. 2* cases the ECtHR acknowledged that society had a 'general interest' in debating matters other than politics. It quoted Resolution 1165 (1998) of the Parliamentary Assembly of the Council of Europe on the right to privacy, including paragraph 7, which said:

> 66 Public figures are persons holding public office and/or using public resources and, more broadly speaking, all those who play a role in public life, whether in politics, the economy, the arts, the social sphere, sport or in any other domain. 99

In these cases the ECtHR adopted a wider approach to what could legitimately be published than it did in the first *Von Hannover* case (the *Princess Caroline* case, discussed earlier).

👁 Case study

In February 2012 Mr Justice Tugendhat declined to continue an interim injunction obtained by then Environment Secretary Caroline Spelman and her husband Mark which banned the *Daily Star Sunday* from reporting that their teenage son, Jonathan, an international rugby player, had, after being injured, taken drugs to aid his recovery which, while legal, were banned under anti-doping rules. Keeping the order in place was neither proportionate nor necessary, said the judge, who also quoted Resolution 1165. In effect, he held that, as Jonathan Spelman was an international rugby player, he was a public figure (*Spelman v Express Newspapers* [2012] EWHC 355 (QB)).

■ 'Reasonable expectation of privacy'

A claimant seeking an injunction to stop the media publishing information about his/her private life and activities must first demonstrate that he/she has a 'reasonable expectation of privacy' in relation to the information. Only after that will the court go to the second stage, balancing the rights to privacy in Article 8 against the rights to freedom of expression in Article 10, and considering the proportionality of any interference with either right in a process called the 'parallel analysis', before conducting the 'ultimate balancing test' to reach a decision. This is the test set out in the *In Re S* judgment, referred to earlier in this chapter, and in ch. 1, p. 7, Weighing competing rights.

A court deciding if the expectation of privacy is reasonable may take into account the location of the event(s)—because the expectation may not be reasonable, for example, in respect of something done in a public place. But location may not be a key consideration. Someone who falls ill or suffers an accident in a public street has a reasonable expectation that this vulnerability gives them a right of privacy—for example, filming them in their distress would infringe it.

👁 Case study

In 2003 the ECtHR ruled that a British man's privacy was infringed when the media broadcast footage of his suicide attempt in the centre of Brentwood in 1994. The council released the footage to show that its installation of CCTV cameras helped save his life because police, alerted by the camera operators, took a knife from him. But the man, who was mentally ill at the time, was recognisable in images broadcast, despite the council's request that he should not be (*Peck v United Kingdom,* Application no. 44647/98 (2003) 36 EHRR 41). His complaints about this were upheld in 1996 by the broadcast regulators but he took a case to the ECtHR, because in 1996 the UK courts did not recognise a specific right of privacy.

 Ch. 27 gives examples of how the Independent Press Standards Organisation and its predecessor, the Press Complaints Commission, have viewed 'reasonable expectation'.

Information concerning health

Information about health is normally treated as being of the highest confidentiality—people usually have 'a reasonable expectation' that information about their health is private.

In 2002 the Court of Appeal banned the *Mail on Sunday* from naming a local health authority where a healthcare worker, referred to as H, had quit his job after being diagnosed HIV positive. The High Court had earlier said it could name the authority, but not the healthcare worker.

Lord Phillips, then Master of the Rolls, said there was a public interest in preserving the confidentiality of healthcare workers who might otherwise be discouraged from reporting they were HIV positive. While the *Mail on Sunday* believed H's patients were entitled to know they had been treated by someone who was HIV positive, naming the authority would inevitably lead to the disclosure of H's identity, as only his patients would be offered HIV tests and counselling, the judge said. But the paper could say the healthcare worker was a dentist.

There are exceptions—in 2006 murderer Michael Stone failed to ban the press and public from seeing an independent inquiry report into the treatment he had received from mental health, probation and social workers before he killed. A judge said the report would assist public debate about treatment of the mentally ill and those with disturbed personalities (*Michael Stone v South East SH* [2006] EWHC 1668).

 Health—treatment for drug addiction—figured in the *Campbell* case—see p. 329, Development of the law, and p. 339, The public interest.

Relationships

The courts also recognise that people have a reasonable expectation that what they say and do intimately within a personal relationship is private—whether the relationship is a marriage, co-habitation, love affair or friendship. If, after the relationship ends, one person wants (often to earn money) the media to publish secrets from the relationship, the courts may injunct to protect the other person's Article 8 rights, or—if the information is already published—award damages for the infringement. It is now rare for a media organisation to be able to demonstrate that a claimant in such a case did not have a reasonable expectation of privacy, not only in relation to what happened within the relationship, but also over the fact that there was a relationship at all.

The privacy of sexual relationships

In the years immediately after the Human Rights Act 1998 came into force, courts took the view that not all sexual conduct was entitled to be viewed as confidential or, indeed, deserved legal protection. But the courts have become more willing to rule that adulterous or casual sexual affairs are matters in which one or both of the people involved have a reasonable expectation of privacy and will issue gagging orders—injunctions—unless the defendant (the party from the relationship who wishes to reveal the intimate matters) or the media can persuade the judge that there is a strong public interest in publishing the information.

If such material is published, damages could be awarded. For example, in 2008 Max Mosley, then president of the Fédération Internationale de l'Automobile (FIA), which runs Formula 1 grand prix racing, won £60,000 from the *News of the World* for breach of privacy and—as ch. 25 explains—for breach of confidence over stories, photos and video footage it published about his participation in

see also ch. 25, p. 325, Damages, for *Mosley*

sado-masochistic activities with prostitutes (*Mosley v News Group Newspapers Ltd* [2008] EWHC 1777).

In 2011 one footballer was known to have obtained two privacy injunctions banning the media from reporting on his sexual liaisons with two different prostitutes, with the court agreeing that the material was not in the public interest and that the player had a reasonable expectation that the information would remain private.

But another player, former England football captain John Terry obtained and then lost an interim injunction which had banned the media from reporting on his alleged relationship with a former team-mate's ex- partner. Mr Justice Tugendhat concluded that the injunction had been sought to protect Terry's reputation, and sponsorship and commercial deals relying on it, rather than his privacy. This, the judge said, meant that the injunction was in reality a way of circumventing the rule in libel law from *Bonnard v Perryman* [1891] 2 Ch 269 that a prior restraint injunction would not be granted to stop publication of an alleged libel if the defendant intended to plead that what was published was true (*LNS v Persons Unknown* [2010] EWHC 119 (QB)).

👁 Case study

In March 2015, Mr Justice Warby discharged an interim injunction granted to Manchester United defender Marcos Rojo which had banned the media from running a kiss-and-tell story involving a fitness instructor with whom the player had cheated on his wife. The judge, who noted that Rojo had not given evidence to support his case, said it was claimed that the woman was blackmailing the player for £100,000—but in fact that was an offer made to her to buy her silence, with the blackmail claim being made only after she turned it down. What was left of the footballer's claim was 'relatively weak' (*YXB v TNO (No. 2)* [2015] EWHC 826 (QB)).

The claimant's family

The way in which the privacy or other rights of those linked to a claimant, such as family members or, in particular, children, will also influence the outcome of an application for an injunction was illustrated in a decision by the Court of Appeal.

👁 Case study

The Court of Appeal said a judge was wrong to refuse to grant an interim injunction to stop a newspaper publishing information about a married man in the entertainment industry who had had an affair with a woman with whom he was working. The man's wife found out about the relationship. The woman, who was also married, subsequently lost her job. The Court of Appeal held that a sexual relationship was essentially a private matter—the fact that the pair's work colleagues knew of it did not put the information into the public domain. But it said weight also had to be given not only to the man's right to respect for his privacy, but to the same rights in respect of his wife and children. Lord Justice Ward said of the children's position: 'They are bound to be harmed by immediate publicity, both because it would undermine the family as a whole and because the playground is a cruel place where the bullies feed on personal discomfort and embarrassment' (*ETK v News Group Newspapers Ltd* [2011] EWCA Civ 439, The Times, 22 April 2011).

The likelihood now is that anyone with a spouse or partner and children will seek to put their rights into the balance when applying for a privacy injunction banning publication of stories of extra-marital affairs or other questionable behaviour.

see Late News section, Celebrity wins privacy injunction

▶ Children's own privacy rights

The media must be careful about children, especially the children of celebrities and others in the public eye. Their age makes them more vulnerable than adults to the effects of media intrusion, and case law reflects this.

Using paparazzi pictures taken of youngsters in the street has led to privacy lawsuits.

The Court of Appeal upheld the appeal by *Harry Potter* author J K Rowling and her husband against a judge's decision to strike out their claim against a photographic agency which photographed them with their son, who was in a pushchair, in a street in Edinburgh. The Court of Appeal said it was arguable that the child had a reasonable expectation of privacy. A child whose parents were not in the public eye could expect that the press would not use his photograph, and the same was true here—the photograph would not have been taken or published had he not been Ms Rowling's son. The law should protect children from intrusive media attention, the Court added (*David Murray (By his litigation friends (1) Neil Murray (2) Joanne Murray) v Big Pictures (UK) Ltd* [2008] EWCA Civ 446, (2008) 3 WLR 1360).

👁 Case study

Rock star Paul Weller and his wife Hannah won £10,000 in damages for their children whose faces were 'plastered' over the MailOnline website in October 2012. Weller, 55, sued the newspaper's publisher, Associated Newspapers, on behalf of his daughter Dylan, who was 16 when the seven unpixelated pictures appeared, and twin sons John Paul and Bowie, who were 10 months old. A paparazzo had followed Weller and the children on a shopping trip through the streets of Santa Monica, California, taking photos without their consent despite being asked to stop. Associated Newspapers said the pictures were entirely innocuous and inoffensive images taken in public places and that the Wellers had previously chosen to open up their private family life to public gaze to a significant degree. Mr Justice Dingemans said:

> In my judgment, the photographs were published in circumstances where Dylan, Bowie and John Paul had a reasonable expectation of privacy. This was because the photographs showed their faces, one of the chief attributes of their personalities, as they were on a family trip out with their father going shopping and to a cafe and they were identified by surname.

The Court of Appeal upheld the decision in November 2015, with Lord Dyson, Master of the Rolls, saying: 'The fact that a child's parent or parents are celebrities or public figures may not, without more, be relied on to argue that the child should have a lower reasonable expectation of privacy.' Mr Justice Dingemans was 'plainly entitled to find that the publication of the photographs did not contribute to a current debate of general interest', he went on, adding that the youngsters 'were only of interest to the MailOnline because they are children of a successful musician' (*Media Lawyer*, 16 April 2014; 20 November 2015).

However, a majority of the Supreme Court held in 2015 that a 14-year-old whose photograph, taken during a riot in Northern Ireland and released by police in an attempt to identify offenders, did not have a 'reasonable expectation of privacy' or a 'legitimate expectation of protection' (*In re JR38* [2015] UKSC 42, [2015] 3 WLR 115 SC(NI)).

▶ Can information be private if it is in the public domain?

A judge may refuse to ban publication of material if it is already widely published—for example, on many sites on the internet—or easily available to anyone. But each case is different.

In 2005 a judge granted an injunction restraining a newspaper from publishing the addresses of buildings acquired for housing vulnerable adolescents, although they would be known to neighbours and others living nearby, and the addresses might also be available from the Land Registry (*Green Corns Ltd v Claverley Group Ltd* [2005] EMLR 31).

What is the position with 'widely published' photographs? The Court of Appeal in the *Douglas* case (referred to elsewhere) said:

> Once intimate personal information about a celebrity's private life has been widely published it may serve no useful purpose to prohibit further publication. The same will not necessarily be true of photographs. Insofar as a photograph

does more than convey information and intrudes on privacy by enabling the viewer to focus on intimate personal detail, there will be a fresh intrusion of privacy when each additional viewer sees the photograph and even when one who has seen a previous publication of the photograph is confronted by a fresh publication of it. 🙶🙶

Any publisher wishing to show that information is in the public domain will have to establish that by evidence—and the court will scrutinise carefully what has been published.

see also ch. 25, p. 327, Information already in the public domain

▎ Information obtained covertly

What if the information is obtained, for example, by bugging or long-lens photography?

One issue is that if a person is unaware of cameras or microphones, he/she may assume the situation is private and act or speak accordingly.

In 2006 the Court of Appeal referred to cases where a duty of confidentiality arose from information having been acquired by 'unlawful or surreptitious means'. The Court regarded the taking of long-distance photographs as being 'an exercise generally considered to raise privacy issues' (*Niema Ash and another v Loreena McKennitt and others* [2006] EWCA Civ 1714, [2007] 3 WLR 194).

In the *Douglas* case the wedding pictures were taken by an uninvited freelance photographer. The photographs of Naomi Campbell leaving a Narcotics Anonymous therapy session were also taken surreptitiously.

In 2007 former Prime Minister Tony Blair and his wife, Cherie, won damages—which they gave to charity—from Associated Newspapers over 'long-lens' pictures taken of them while they were on holiday at Sir Cliff Richards' villa in Barbados. The Blairs said that, while they accepted a certain level of scrutiny, here the photographers had overstepped the mark.

for detail on *Douglas*, see Additional Material for ch. 25 on www. mcnaes. com

▎ The public interest

Even before the Human Rights Act 1998, journalists could plead that the disclosure of confidential information would be in the public interest—for example, to expose crime, other wrongdoing, hypocritical conduct or a threat to public safety. But judges are now much less likely to accept that a claimant's celebrity could generate a public interest in private conduct that would otherwise be protected.

In the *Naomi Campbell* case, publication of some detail was held to be in the public interest and some not. There were five distinct 'elements' of private information:

pp. 329–330, Development of law, outlines *Campbell*

- the fact of Ms Campbell's drug addiction;
- the fact that she was receiving therapy for it;

- the fact that she was having therapy at Narcotics Anonymous (NA);
- details of the NA therapy and her reaction to it; and
- surreptitiously obtained photographs of her emerging from an NA session.

Because the model had publicly denied using drugs previously, the first and second facts could be published in the public interest. But the rest could not, because of the intrusiveness of the disclosure and the likelihood that it would interfere with or disrupt her treatment.

Three of the judges—the majority—held that Article 10 considerations could not justify publication of the information. But two judges said the third, fourth and fifth categories added little of significance to the disclosure of the first and second, and that journalists should be given greater latitude. The difference of opinion between the judges illustrates the difficult decisions journalists might face when considering such stories.

The Data Protection Act 1998

data
protection
law is
explained
in ch. 28

The *Naomi Campbell* case also alerted the media to the implications for the law of privacy of the Data Protection Act 1998.

▌ Electronic 'snooping', intercepting and hacking into communications

Journalists who use electronic equipment to spy on other people could be committing a crime as well as running the risk of being sued for infringing privacy.

> Ch. 35 explains the risks of being charged with hacking into computers, telephone message and email systems, or otherwise 'intercepting' communications—activity intrusive into privacy.

▌ Relevance of ethical codes

see chs. 2
and 3 for
general
detail
on these
codes, and
ch. 27 for
their privacy
provisions

Section 12 of the Human Rights Act 1998 also says a court considering a matter affecting freedom of information must have particular regard to 'any relevant privacy code'. In cases involving the media, judges will consider, depending on the media sector involved, if the journalism has conformed to either the Editors' Code, overseen by Ipso, or any other code operated by any other regulator, or the Broadcasting Code.

If the journalism does conform, judges may be more likely to rule that any breach of confidence or privacy was justified by the public interest. The wording of the parts of each code relating to public interest justifications are, anyway, influenced by case law.

➡ Recap of major points

- The right to privacy is guaranteed by Article 8 of the European Convention on Human Rights.
- The law of privacy developed from the action for breach of confidence, but is now recognised as a separate tort of misuse of private information.
- The test in a privacy claim is whether the claimant has 'a reasonable expectation of privacy'.
- The right to privacy is not necessarily lost because the activity happened in public.
- There is a defence that publication was in the public interest.
- Other protections for privacy are in the Data Protection Act 1998, explained in ch. 28, and the Regulation of Investigatory Powers Act 2000, explained in ch. 35.

((•)) Useful Websites

www.judiciary.gov.uk/wp-content/uploads/JCO/Documents/Guidance/practice-guidance-civil-non-disclosure-orders-july2011.pdf

Master of the Rolls' Practice Guidance on privacy injunctions

27

News-gathering avoiding intrusion

Chapter summary

Journalists should avoid unnecessary intrusion into people's privacy, but know when it can be justified. They should combine knowledge of the legal basics with a good grasp of the codes used by the Independent Press Standards Organisation and the Office of Communications, whose adjudications on complaints about intrusion provide guidance covering a far wider range of situations than is dealt with in privacy case law. Few people can afford to go to court if they feel their privacy is breached, but many complain to regulators about journalists taking photos, filming and audio-recording, and about what is published. Publishing 'user-generated' photographs, or footage supplied by the public, or material from social media sites can create ethical or legal problems. This chapter also explains that the codes seek to minimise intrusion into grief and have particular rules for when children are interviewed, filmed or photographed by journalists.

▶ Civil law on privacy—photography, filming and recording

ch. 1
explains the
Convention

As chs. 25 and 26 show, in cases in privacy law concerning publication of photographs and footage, judges weigh the individual's right to privacy under Article 8 of the European Convention on Human Rights against the media's Article 10 rights to freedom of expression and to impart information, and the public's right to receive it.

This checklist is a rough guide to when civil law may be breached if people are photographed or filmed or audio-recorded without their consent (for convenience, references to 'filming' include videoing).

- Was the person filmed or photographed or recorded in a location where he/she had 'a reasonable expectation of privacy'? An individual could reasonably expect privacy at home, in a secluded garden or on a private beach, but would normally have less or no expectation of it in a public place.
- Have the media persistently harassed the person? If so, the court might decide that his/her privacy was violated even though he/she was pictured or filmed or recorded in a public place—see the *Von Hannover No. 1* (*Princess Caroline*) case in ch. 26, pp. 329–330, Development of the law.
- Was the person in a condition, situation or event giving rise to a reasonable expectation of privacy, even though he/she was in or could be seen from a public place? For example, was the person mentally ill, having medical treatment or therapy or on a private shopping trip with his/her children? See the *Campbell* and *Peck* cases in ch. 26.
- Is the person a child and therefore more likely than an adult to be upset or traumatised by being filmed or photographed, or by what is published?
- Is there a 'public interest' factor in revelations in the journalism which overrides the person's right to privacy, whatever the location or situation?
- Is the photo or footage or recording already so widely published—for example, copied worldwide on hundreds of internet sites—that banning publication is pointless?

Courts also consider the degree of harm which publication might cause, or has caused, the person and might also consider the detail or extent of images captured—was the photograph a long shot or close-up of a face, or was the film a brief clip or lengthy footage? Covert photography, filming or recording with hidden cameras or microphones is likely to be more intrusive as the target is unaware of it, and may assume the situation is private and act accordingly.

✳ Remember

Journalists also need to know the law on trespass, dealt with in ch. 36, p. 446, Trespass and bye-laws.

▌ Law against harassment

There is no criminal or civil law banning photography or filming or recording in the street or other public places.

But paparazzi who hound people could be prosecuted or sued under the Protection from Harassment Act 1997 which created criminal offences and civil remedies.

see also ch. 36 on the right to take photos, film and record

👁 Case study

In 2015 a High Court judge granted an injunction under the 1997 Act against two unknown photographers after a mother complained of harassment. Katherine Kerner's husband Stuart, aged 44, who was vice-principal of a south London school, was convicted by a jury of abuse of trust by having sex with a 16-year-old female pupil. Mrs Kerner told the High Court that—soon after this court case, when she and her 9-year-old son were preparing to leave their home in Kent for his school day—two photographers, whose names she did not know, had leapt from a car and 'aggressively' began taking photographs. She ran back inside but one photographer stayed for more than an hour, taking 'intrusive' photos through a window and of her son (*Kerner v WX and YZ* [2015] EWHC 128 (QB), [2015] EWHC 178 (QB), [2015] EWHC 1247 (QB)).

The 1997 Act—created to deal with obsessive 'stalkers' rather than, specifically, journalists—says harassment can include causing alarm or distress and is 'a course of conduct', which means the conduct must have occurred more than once. It was amended in 2012 to create specific 'stalking' offences. Following, watching or spying on someone could be stalking if they cause alarm or distress.

As this chapter explains, harassment would also normally breach the codes of the media regulators.

 See the Additional Material for this chapter on www.mcnaes.com for recent cases involving 1997 Act. These include the High Court challenge by the *Croydon Advertiser* to a controversial official warning given by police to one of its reporters after he sought comment from a convicted fraudster about a website scam she was running and she complained he was 'harassing' her.

▌ The Editors' Code and Broadcasting Code

The Independent Press Standards Organisation (Ipso) uses the Editors' Code when it adjudicates on complaints against publishers signed up to its system. Some UK newspapers not in the Ipso system also use the Code. The regulator Ofcom requires broadcasters to comply with its Broadcasting Code. Ch. 2 explains press regulation and ch. 3 explains Ofcom. Both codes give guidance on when photography, filming or recording is unethical. These codes have also clauses or sections on covert photography, filming or recording, explained in those chapters.

This chapter's consideration of privacy, intrusion and regulatory boundaries in journalism mainly deals with journalists working openly, including when using cameras or microphones, though it is possible even then that people—for example, in crowds or in the chaos after an accident—might be unaware that their images or voices are being captured.

 See Appendix 2 for the full text of the Editors' Code. See Useful Websites at the end of this chapter for the full text of the Broadcasting Code.

The codes' general protection of privacy

Breaching the codes is not necessarily to breach privacy law, but complying with the codes is ethical and helps reduce the likelihood of a privacy lawsuit.

Clause 2 (Privacy) of the Editors' Code states:

> i)   Everyone is entitled to respect for his or her private and family life, home, health and correspondence, including digital communications.
>
> ii) Editors will be expected to justify intrusions into any individual's private life without consent. Account will be taken of the complainant's own public disclosures of information.
>
> iii) It is unacceptable to photograph individuals, without their consent, in public or private places where there is a reasonable expectation of privacy.

References to photography in the Editors' Code include filming. Neither Ipso nor Ofcom will normally adjudicate against the use of innocuous images of people in public places or in crowds. Ofcom has said that as a general rule there is no obligation to get consent to film or show images of people appearing incidentally as clearly random members of the public. But Ipso and Ofcom, like the courts, will take account of situational factors as well as location.

👁 Case study

clauses 4 and 6 are explained later in this chapter

In 2015 Ipso ruled that the *Derby Telegraph* breached clause 2 (Privacy), clause 4 (Intrusion into shock) and clause 6 (Children) of the Editors' Code because a member of its staff took a photo of two 11-year-old girls—one of them injured—following a traffic accident outside a school. The picture, published online, showed the injured girl lying on the pavement, with her face pixelated, a girl next to her who was identifiable and two passers-by.

The newspaper did not know the girls were sisters and therefore that publishing the image was likely to identify both. Their mother complained that the photo depicted a distressing incident for her daughters, and was taken when everyone involved was in shock and when emergency services had yet to arrive. She said that publication of the photo added to the family's distress and that, as it related to her daughters' welfare, it should not have been published without her consent. She was also concerned that the newspaper had not pixelated the face of her uninjured daughter. The newspaper had not been able to contact the family as the injured girl's name had not been released. After hearing of the complaint, the newspaper immediately removed the image from its website. Ipso said that the injured girl had in the circumstances 'a reasonable expectation of privacy', adding: 'Parental consent should have been sought for publication of the photograph.' The newspaper had suggested that the accident was of public interest, because of previously expressed concerns about the area's road safety. But Ipso said the *Telegraph* had not explained how publishing the photo contributed to that public interest and that no exceptional public interest appeared to exist (*A woman v Derby Telegraph*, adjudication issued 13 February 2015).

see p. 352,
Public
interest
exceptions
in the codes

Publishing an identifying photo of an adult victim at an accident scene is also likely to be deemed a breach of the Code, unless consent is obtained.

Practice 8.16 of the Broadcasting Code says: 'Broadcasters should not take or broadcast footage or audio of people caught up in emergencies, victims of accidents or those suffering a personal tragedy, even in a public place, where that results in an infringement of privacy, unless it is warranted or the people concerned have given consent.'

✳ Remember

Both Ipso and Ofcom will make some exceptions to their normal privacy rules in respect of coverage of major incidents, such as a terrorist bombing, because of the very high public interest in showing what has happened. See the Additional Material for this chapter on www.mcnaes.com for 'Coverage of major incidents' and other case studies about complaints of breach of privacy.

The Broadcasting Code tends to use the phrase 'legitimate expectation of privacy' rather than 'reasonable expectation of privacy'. But most principles in its rules for broadcasters are similar to those in the Editors' Code for newspapers, magazines and websites. Use in the Broadcasting Code of the term 'warranted' refers to public interest exceptions, explained later in this chapter.

Section 8 of the Broadcasting Code says, in rule 8.1: 'Any infringement of privacy in programmes, or in connection with obtaining material included in programmes, must be warranted.' It adds: 'Legitimate expectations of privacy will vary according to the place, and nature of the information, activity or condition in question, the extent to which it is in the public domain (if at all) and whether the individual concerned is already in the public eye. There may be circumstances where people can reasonably expect privacy even in a public place. Some activities and conditions may be of such a private nature that filming or recording, even in a public place, could involve an infringement of privacy.'

👁 Case study

In 2013 Ofcom ruled that the privacy of a woman it referred to as Ms D was unwarrantably infringed by the inclusion of 10 seconds of footage of her with her face visible, including shots of her dancing, in an episode of Channel 4's programme *The Hotel*. It showed a 'ladies night' attended by 300 women and featuring male strippers. Ms D made clear she did not want to appear in the programme. The footage was included because of 'human error'. Ofcom said there were elements of 'personal sensitivity' in attendance at such an event (*Ofcom Broadcast Bulletin*, Issue 236, 27 August 2013).

Ofcom guidance is that property which is privately owned but readily accessible to the public, such as a railway station or shop, can be a public place. Ipso's predecessor the Press Complaints Commission (PCC) ruled that someone had a 'reasonable expectation of privacy' in a café, even though other members of the public were present (*Tunbridge v Dorking Advertiser*, adjudication issued 23 May 2002). The PCC, whose adjudications were based on the Editors' Code, also ruled that a photograph taken from a public highway of someone on their threshold or in their garden did not breach the Code, even if public interest considerations did not apply, if there was no 'reasonable expectation of privacy' and the picture did not show anything private (for example, *A woman v Scottish Sun*, adjudication issued 7 April 2010). Ipso is not bound by PCC adjudications, but can opt to follow them.

The Broadcasting Code adds in practice 8.4: 'Broadcasters should ensure that words, images or actions filmed or recorded in, or broadcast from, a public place, are not so private that prior consent is required before broadcast from the individual or organisation concerned, unless broadcasting without their consent is warranted.'

Ofcom's guidance to section 8 gives, as examples of when people can reasonably expect a *degree* of privacy even in a public place, a child in a state of undress, someone with a disfiguring medical condition or CCTV footage of a suicide attempt.

For legal context, see also ch. 26, p. 334, Reasonable expectation of privacy, on the *Peck* case. See Useful Websites at the end of this chapter for the Ofcom guidance on privacy.

✳ Remember

Practice 8.2 of the Broadcasting Code says that information which discloses the location of a person's home or family should not be revealed without permission, unless this is warranted. Ipso says that the street address of a person's home is not generally considered to be private (*Baird v Motherwell Times & Bellshill Speaker*, adjudication issued 17 March 2015).

❙ Doorstepping

Section 8 of the Broadcasting Code defines 'doorstepping' as 'the filming or recording of an interview or attempted interview with someone, or announcing that a call is being filmed or recorded for broadcast purposes, without any prior warning'.

Doorstepping is an ambush technique which can be used against someone unlikely to agree to an interview—for example, a crook being investigated or a politician in a scandal—when they open the door at their home or workplace.

Practice 8.11 of the Code says: 'Doorstepping for factual programmes should not take place unless a request for an interview has been refused or it has not been possible to request an interview, or there is good reason to believe that an investigation will be frustrated if the subject is approached openly, and it is warranted to doorstep.'

But the practice adds that broadcasters may normally, without prior warning, interview, film or record people in the news when they are in public places.

Also, it makes clear that vox-pops (short surveys sampling the views of random members of the public) are not considered 'doorstepping'.

❙ Privacy in hospital and institutions

Clause 8 of the Editors' Code says journalists must identify themselves and obtain permission from a responsible executive before entering non-public areas of hospitals or similar institutions to pursue inquiries.

Broadcasting Code practice 8.8 says: 'When filming or recording in institutions, organisations or other agencies, permission should be obtained from the relevant authority or management, unless it is warranted to film or record without permission. Individual consent of employees or others whose appearance is incidental or where they are essentially anonymous members of the general public will not normally be required. However, in potentially sensitive places such as ambulances, hospitals, schools, prisons or police stations, separate consent should normally be obtained before filming or recording and for broadcast from those in sensitive situations (unless not obtaining consent is warranted). If the individual will not be identifiable in the programme then separate consent for broadcast will not be required.'

By 'separate consent', the Code means there needs to be a two-stage consent—for example, consent must normally be obtained before filming/recording begins, and then further consent must be obtained from individuals for the broadcasting of footage or audio which identifies them. Broadcasters may need to ask the people filmed or recorded to sign consent forms so that, should there be a complaint, there is proof of consent.

◗ The codes' protection against harassment

Under the Editors' Code and Broadcasting Code, a journalist should normally respect a person's refusal to answer questions or his/her request to stop photographing, filming or recording him/her, although there are 'public interest' exceptions to these rules, as explained later.

 for legal context, see p. 343, Law against harassment

The Broadcasting Code's practice 8.7 says: 'If an individual or organisation's privacy is being infringed, and they ask that the filming, recording or live broadcast be stopped, the broadcaster should do so, unless it is warranted to continue.'

Clause 3 (Harassment) of the Editors' Code says:

i)   Journalists must not engage in intimidation, harassment or persistent pursuit.

ii)   They must not persist in questioning, telephoning, pursuing or photographing individuals once asked to desist; nor remain on property when asked to leave and must not follow them. If requested, they must identify themselves and whom they represent.

iii) Editors must ensure these principles are observed by those working for them and take care not to use non-compliant material from other sources.

◉ Case study

In 2014 the Press Complaints Commission ruled that *The Sun* breached clause 3 (Harassment) of the Editors' Code by making a fourth attempt to contact a woman who was a victim of sexual assault by disgraced publicist Max Clifford. The newspaper—its attempts to contact her spanned 11 months—was told to desist on the third occasion a reporter called at her home (*A woman v The Sun*, adjudication issued 15 August 2014).

◗ Prohibitions on intrusion into grief or shock

Clause 4 (Intrusion into grief or shock) of the Editors' Code says:

In cases involving personal grief or shock, enquiries and approaches must be made with sympathy and discretion and publication handled sensitively. These provisions should not restrict the right to report legal proceedings.

Adjudications on complaints against the media have made clear that articles breaking news of violent or accidental deaths should not contain graphic detail likely to add to the distress of relatives. Broadcast journalists should be aware that images or descriptions of such material could, depending on the context, breach the Broadcasting Code's prohibitions on harm and offence explained in ch. 3.

Journalists should not break news of a death to the deceased's family or close friends, either personally or by detail in what they publish. This would be a breach of clause 4 (PCC adjudication in *Oliver v Manchester Evening News*, Report 43). It should be noted the 'public interest exceptions' in the Editors' Code do not apply to clause 4 and so do not justify intrusion into grief or shock.

It is usually unethical for a media organisation to publish online a photo or footage showing, identifiably, an accident victim at a crash scene or to identify the person in text unless it is sure, or it is not unreasonable to assume, that the authorities have notified his/her family of the accident. Otherwise there is a risk that his/her relatives or friends might not have been told and will thus be shocked by the coverage (a point made in the Ipso ruling in the *Derby Telegraph* case, cited earlier). Also, as this chapter has explained, such an image may breach the person's privacy whenever it is published if his/her face is not obscured or pixelated.

Practice 8.18 of the Broadcasting Code says broadcasters should take care not to reveal the identity of a person who has died, or of victims of accidents or violent crimes, unless and until it is clear that the next of kin have been informed or unless it is warranted.

see also
p. 353,
Material
from social
media sites,
on the need
to avoid
aggravating
grief

Ofcom guidance is that, at funerals, programme-makers should respect requests to withdraw. The PCC censured newspapers for publishing photographs of funerals taken without bereaved families' consent (for example, *Rosemary MacLeod v Scottish Sun*, adjudication issued 23 April 2013). But the Editors' Code does not ban this outright.

The Broadcasting Code warns broadcasters that the bereaved may need special consideration as a 'vulnerable person' who may not be able to give informed consent to be featured in a programme.

ch. 3
explains
informed
consent

Practice 8.19 of the Broadcasting Code says broadcasters should try to reduce the potential distress to victims and relatives when making or broadcasting programmes intended to examine past events that involve trauma to individuals (including crime) unless it is warranted to do otherwise. It adds that, so far as reasonably practicable, surviving victims and the immediate families of those whose experience is to feature should be told of the plans for the programme.

▌ Protecting children's privacy and welfare

The Editors' Code, clause 6 (Children), says:

    i)   All pupils should be free to complete their time at school without unnecessary intrusion.

    ii) They must not be approached or photographed at school without permission of the school authorities.

iii) Children under 16 must not be interviewed or photographed on issues involving their own or another child's welfare unless a custodial parent or similarly responsible adult consents.

iv) Children under 16 must not be paid for material involving their welfare, nor parents or guardians for material about their children or wards, unless it is clearly in the child's interest.

v) Editors must not use the fame, notoriety or position of a parent or guardian as sole justification for publishing details of a child's private life. 🗩🗩

The Code does not seek to place a general inhibition on photographing or filming children. But adjudications have made clear that publishing photographs in which children are identifiable and which could cause embarrassment or show them in distress—for example, in a swimsuit or after an accident, or referring to children's medical conditions—concerns their welfare and therefore should not normally be done without a parent or legal guardian's consent.

see the Derby Telegraph case on p. 345, The codes' general protection of privacy

Obscuring the child's identity could avoid an adverse adjudication, as long as the way in which the picture or information was obtained did not breach the Code.

Parental consent for publishing a child's image can in some instances be implied because of the context—for example, if a parent has allowed the child to be a spectator at a televised sports event—and 'innocuous' pictures of children in crowds or public places will not normally breach the Code (*Quigley v Zoo magazine*, PCC adjudication issued 23 June 2006).

 The Additional Material for this chapter on www.mcnaes.com sets out adjudications on press reports about children, including in 'Images of youngsters committing crime'.

Both the Editors' Code and Ofcom Broadcasting Code accept that exceptional circumstances may justify 'public interest exceptions' to the normal rules about children. But even in exceptional circumstances there must be careful consideration of whether children should be identifiable in what is published.

👁 Case study

In 2007 the PCC criticised a Scottish newspaper for publishing on its website mobile phone footage shot by a child showing disruptive behaviour by some of her classmates. The PCC accepted it was in the public interest to show the behaviour, which the girl said contributed to her poor exam results, but criticised the paper for failing to conceal the children's identities (*Gaddis v Hamilton Advertiser*, adjudication issued 30 July 2007).

ch. 3 explains the Code's general protection for the under-18s

The Broadcasting Code says in practice 8.20: 'Broadcasters should pay particular attention to the privacy of people under 16. They do not lose their rights to privacy because, for example, of the fame or notoriety of their parents or because of events in their schools.'

Practice 8.21 adds:

" Where a programme features an individual under 16 or a vulnerable person in a way that infringes privacy, consent must be obtained from:

- a parent, guardian or other person of eighteen or over in loco parentis; and
- wherever possible, the individual concerned;
- unless the subject matter is trivial or uncontroversial and the participation minor, or it is warranted to proceed without consent. "

The Code says a vulnerable person may include those with learning difficulties, mental health problems, the bereaved, the traumatised and the sick.

The Broadcasting Code, like the Editors' Code, states that normally broadcasters must get a school's permission before filming pupils—see practice 8.8, cited earlier.

▌ Public interest exceptions in the codes

The Editors' Code and the Broadcasting Code allow that some rules may be breached if the journalist is covered by 'public interest' exceptions. The exceptions cover types of valuable journalistic activity, as outlined in chs. 2 and 3, and include exposing crime or negligence imperilling people's safety and exposing deception of the public by an organisation or a hypocritical politician. If the public interest factor is sufficient and any intrusion into privacy proportionate, Ipso and Ofcom will say that a photographer's persistent pursuit of a criminal to take his/her picture or surveillance or undercover filming—even of children— was justified.

chs. 2 and 3 cover use of undercover tactics by journalists

◉ Case study

In 2008 Ofcom rejected complaints by several parents whose children were filmed by the BBC during an undercover investigation into standards at a nursery as part of an inquiry into how nurseries were regulated. Ofcom said the filming was justified by the strong public interest and that the broadcast of the programme *Whistleblower: Childcare*, in which the children's faces were blurred to obscure their identity, had not infringed their privacy. The nursery had broken glass in the garden, power tools were left unattended near children and it had failed to check the false CV of a new member of staff (in fact, the undercover reporter) (*Ofcom Broadcast Bulletin 116*, 1 September 2008).

▌ User-generated content

Pictures and footage supplied by readers and viewers—for example, mobile phone footage—frequently feature in media coverage. This is particularly the case in major events such as the aftermath of the terrorist atrocities. Journalists handling this 'user-generated content' (UGC)—whatever the nature of the coverage—should realise it might breach the privacy of those depicted, or intrude into grief or shock.

Also, some UGC pictures published have turned out to be faked or supplied in breach of someone else's **copyright**. Ch. 29 explains copyright.

→ glossary

▌ Material from social media sites

Journalists routinely search social media sites, including Facebook, Flickr, Tumblr, Instagram and Twitter, for pictures or footage of people in the news, or to find news. Again, publishing this material may breach copyright.

((•))

It might also be an intrusion into privacy if the person was portrayed in a private situation and was unaware that he/she was being pictured or that the material was being posted on the social media site. The Editors' Codebook, produced by the committee which oversees the Editors' Code, suggests these questions can be asked when considering when such material should be used in news coverage: How personal is it? What is the public interest in its publication? Has the person tried to restrict access? Are they responsible for uploading it themselves?

see Useful Websites at the end of this chapter for the Codebook

For case studies about media publication of social media or user-generated content, see the Additional Material for this chapter on www.mcnaes.com.

Even if the person shown is the one who placed his/her own image in the public domain by uploading the material to the social media site, journalists must consider if it is ethical to use the image in the context of a news story projected to a different, and probably much bigger, audience. For example, the grieving family of a teenager who has died might be even more distressed if media reports include a social website picture showing the youngster apparently drunk on a social occasion.

Publishing an innocuous image, obtained from a publicly accessible page on a social media website, of someone who died in shocking event or who is a crime victim is not unethical provided that the manner of publication is sensitive to people's grief or shock—for example, see the Ipso ruling *Cross v Airdrie and Coatbridge Advertiser*, issued 12 February 2015.

Ipso has also ruled that the Editors' Code is not breached when a media organisation quotes comments or messages—for example, tributes to someone who has died—which people make on publicly accessible pages of social media sites (*Hodder v Dorset Echo*, adjudication issued 16 April 2015). Nevertheless, even if the material is publicly available, if it was created by children or teenagers, and publication of it by the media is not warranted and it breaches their privacy by humiliating or embarrassing them, the Code would be breached (PCC ruling in *Mullen, Weir and Cambell v Scottish Sunday Express*, adjudication issued 26 June 2009).

If the social media account has privacy settings—for example, it has been restricted to someone's family or close friends—media publication of material from it will, if a person's privacy is infringed, require a public interest justification under the relevant code—for example, the exposure of a public figure's hypocrisy or of a crime—unless that person consents to its publication.

In 2014 Ipso ruled that, because there was a public interest justification, the *Sunday Mirror* had not breached the Editors' Code in an investigation in which it revealed that married Conservative Minister Brooks Newmark used a private Twitter account to send an explicit image of himself to an undercover reporter posing as a female Conservative Party activist (adjudication issued by Ipso, 26 March 2015).

➡ Recap of major points

- The civil courts use the criterion of 'a reasonable expectation of privacy' when deciding if the media have breached a person's human rights by photographing or filming him/her.
- Intrusion into privacy can be lawful if there is a 'public interest' justification.
- People who object to being filmed or photographed or recorded by the media may complain to Ipso or Ofcom.
- Their codes require journalists to have parental consent for photographing, filming or recording a child if his/her welfare or privacy is involved.
- Journalists must take care when deciding whether to publish pictures or footage supplied by the public or copied from social media sites, as publication may breach privacy or copyright.
- Journalists should not intrude into grief—for example, when filming or photographing funerals or publishing photos from social media sites.

((•)) Useful Websites

http://stakeholders.ofcom.org.uk/broadcasting/broadcast-codes/broadcast-code/
   Ofcom Broadcasting Code

http://stakeholders.ofcom.org.uk/broadcasting/guidance/programme-guidance/bguidance/
   Ofcom's guidance on the Code

www.editorscode.org.uk/
 Editors' Codebook—collates adjudications and provides advice on the
 Editors' Code

www.bbc.co.uk/editorialguidelines/guidelines/privacy
 BBC Editorial Guidelines on filming in public places, sensitive places and private
 property and use of social media material

www.bbc.co.uk/editorialguidelines/guidance/social-media-pictures
 BBC editorial guidance on use of social media pictures

www.bbc.co.uk/editorialguidelines/guidelines/children-young-people
 BBC Editorial Guidelines on children as contributors

28

Data protection

Chapter summary

The privacy of personal information kept on computers and in filing systems is safeguarded by data protection law. This covers data we give about ourselves to government departments, councils, banks, telephone companies, and other commercial and public institutions, and data they generate about us. Journalists who use underhand methods to gain access to people's personal data may be prosecuted, unless they have a 'public interest' or other defence. Institutions—including police forces and schools—sometimes misunderstand data protection law when claiming it stops them releasing information to the media. Also, as journalists obtain and store data about people—in research, news stories, recordings, pictures and footage—media organisations and freelance journalists must be lawful in how they process and publish data, to avoid paying damages for breaching privacy or being fined by the Information Commissioner.

▶ Protection for stored data

In 2000 the Human Rights Act 1998 created a specific right to respect for privacy and family life. But even before then the law recognised privacy rights relating to the vast amount of information held in computer and manual records. Public and commercial bodies—taken as a whole—hold hundreds of databases about each working adult. Privacy rights for personal data, whether held on a computer or in 'structured manual files', are provided by the Data Protection Act 1998.

The Act requires personal data to be kept securely. Many news stories have highlighted cases of huge amounts of data about individuals, including lists of clients or customers, their dates of birth, addresses and bank account details, being lost by companies or government departments, or stolen by online hackers. Such stories remind journalists that they too must take care to protect data—for example, about their sources.

ch. 34 covers the ethics of protecting sources

▌ Data protection principles

The Data Protection Act 1998 defines a 'data controller' as a person or organisation who determines the purposes for which and the manner in which personal data is processed. Data controllers include local authorities, health trusts, government departments, commercial organisations, magistrates' courts and the police—in fact, any organisation or individual keeping personal data about others in a computer or a structured filing system. Media organisations and freelance journalists are data controllers because they decide how they will use the personal data that they hold about individuals. The Information Commissioner keeps a public register of data controllers. The registration requirement mainly affects media managements, but freelances should also register. The Act puts virtually all responsibility for data protection on the data controller.

A 'data subject' is a person about whom the information is held.

The Act says people handling personal data—in reality, any information about someone can be personal data—must comply with data protection principles. Data must, for example, be:

- fairly and lawfully processed;
- processed for limited purposes—for example, for the purpose for which a person (the data subject) provided it to the data controller, such as to open a bank account, claim benefits, get a mobile phone account, etc;
- processed in accordance with the data subject's rights;
- secure.

Section 32 of the Act says that personal data which is processed only for 'special purposes' (journalistic, literary or artistic purposes) is exempt from some of the Act's provisions including those relating to the data protection principles *except* for the legal obligation to keep the data secure. Journalists do not need to rely on the exemption when, for example, they are publishing in a 'fair' way personal data about someone which he/she knowingly supplied for the purpose of that publication. But they may need it in other circumstances—for example, if deception has been used when interviewing the person.

 See the Additional Material for this chapter on www.mcnaes.com for more detail of this exemption for journalism, and see too p. 362, The Information Commissioner's Office guidance, later in this chapter.

▌ Crimes of procuring, gaining or disclosing personal data

Anyone who without a lawful purpose obtains or procures personal data from a data controller, or anyone who unlawfully discloses it—for example, by publishing it—commits an offence under section 55 of the 1998 Act. The section 32 exemption for journalism does not itself shield journalists from how section 55 applies. A conviction is punishable by an unlimited fine.

Section 55 says:

> A person must not knowingly or recklessly, without the consent of the data controller
>
> (a) obtain or disclose personal data or the information contained in personal data, or
>
> (b) procure the disclosure to another person of the information contained in personal data.

see ch. 35 for other offences a journalist might commit in procuring leaks of information

'Blagging' by a journalist—for example, posing as someone else when phoning a bank to get information from that person's account—could be an offence under this section. A journalist who persuades or pays someone to leak personal data from a data controller's records might be committing an offence, as might the source.

Defences are available to those who act in the reasonable belief that they would have obtained permission from the data controller for their actions and to anyone who shows that obtaining, disclosing or procuring the information was 'justified in the public interest'. But the public interest is not defined. Section 55 also contains a defence that obtaining, disclosing or procuring the information was necessary for the purpose of preventing or detecting crime—a defence which might aid investigative journalists.

Although data protection law has been in force for nearly three decades, most journalists know little about it, probably because threats of prosecution against journalists have been rare. But this is changing.

▶ Increasing concern about data breaches

see Useful Websites at the end of this chapter for these reports

In 2006 the Information Commissioner urged Parliament to make the section 55 offence punishable by up to two years' imprisonment. In reports entitled *What Price Privacy?* and *What Price Privacy Now?* he said his office and the police had uncovered evidence of a widespread and organised undercover market in confidential personal information, procured and sold by dishonest private investigators.

Some information was 'blagged' and some obtained corruptly from dishonest individuals—including police officers—whose jobs within institutions and companies gave them access to it. Among the 'buyers' for this information were many journalists wanting details to trace people or inquire about them.

It should be remembered that no journalists were prosecuted in this investigation and that journalists who bought the information may in many instances have had a public interest justification for seeking it out or for accepting it when offered.

But, following publication of the Commissioner's reports, Parliament legislated to introduce jail terms of up to two years for breach of section 55. The measure, in section 77 of the Criminal Justice and Immigration Act 2008, has not yet been implemented at time of writing.

Media lobbying led to the inclusion in the 2008 Act of a new defence for someone charged under section 55—that they obtained, disclosed or procured data 'with a view to the publication by any person of any journalistic, literary or artistic material' and did so with 'the reasonable belief that in the particular circumstances' their actions were 'justified as being in the public interest'. This defence has not yet been brought into force at time of writing.

✳ Remember

The focus on how journalists gain information was intensified by the Leveson Inquiry into 'the culture, practices, and ethics of the press'. The Editors' Code bans accessing digitally held private information without consent.

ch. 2 explains the Inquiry and Code

▶ When journalists' lawful inquiries are thwarted

Organisations asked for information by journalists sometimes cite the Data Protection 1998 Act to justify refusing to give it. But the Act covers personal data, not all data, and even personal data can be lawfully released in some circumstances—for example, if the 'data subject' agrees.

Data is only personal if it can lead to a living individual being identified.

Getting information from police

Police officers who claim the Act prevents them from releasing information may have misunderstood the law. People involved in road accidents and the victims of crime may ask police not to give the media their details. But police are not obliged to agree to requests from victims, witnesses or next of kin not to release information about an incident. It may help police inquiries—or be in the public interest in some other way—if the media publish it. At time of writing, the College of Policing, jointly with the National Police Chiefs' Council, was due in 2016 to issue new guidance to police about relations with the media.

 Check www.mcnaes.com for updates on this new guidance.

The 1998 Act does not apply to dead people, so does not prevent police naming victims who have died once they are positively identified and immediate relatives notified.

Getting information from courts

Journalists sometimes have difficulty obtaining information from courts.

Guidance for court staff from Her Majesty's Courts and Tribunals Service published in August 2014 states, on p. 14: 'The Data Protection Act must not be used as a blanket excuse for withholding information.' It also makes clear, on p. 13, that a defendant's address may be supplied to reporters even if it has not been read out in court.

Getting information from schools

Schools have cited the Act as a reason for refusing to allow photographs of sports and activities or—if photography has been allowed—refusing to name the children in the pictures.

Department of Education guidance is that schools and local authorities are free to decide their own policies about when photos may be taken, and on the release of associated information for publicity, but that it will require the consent of pupils' parents or legal guardians.

The Information Commissioner has issued this guidance about photographs being taken by a local newspaper of a school awards ceremony: 'As long as the school has agreed to this, and the children and/or their guardians are aware that photographs of those attending the ceremony may appear in the newspaper, this will not breach the Act.'

The Commissioner's guidance is also that schools do not breach the Act by releasing exam results to the local media for publication and that in general, because a school has a legitimate interest in publishing results, pupils or parents or guardians do not need to consent to publication.

▌ Privacy law and data law

A privacy case brought against a media organisation or journalist might include an element claiming breach of data protection law.

 Case study

In 2002 supermodel Naomi Campbell was awarded £3,500 damages for breach of privacy and infringement of data protection rights over the *Daily Mirror*'s publication of details about her therapy at Narcotics Anonymous (NA), an award upheld by the House of Lords (*Campbell v Mirror Group Newspapers Ltd* [2004] UKHL 22). But the judgment did not treat the data protection element as a separate issue from the misuse of private information acquired (and therefore processed) by the newspaper—a photo of her leaving the therapy and some detail of it.

---

see also ch. 14, p. 165, What information and help must criminal courts provide?

see Useful Websites at the end of this chapter for the ICO guidance

ch. 26 gives details of the *Campbell* case

The *Campbell* case illustrates that a media organisation which breaches some-one's privacy is also likely, in the processing of information gained, to have breached their data protection rights, but that the courts will examine the total effect on the claimant and not differentiate between the wrong caused by each breach.

▶ Sensitive personal data

The 1998 Act provides particular privacy protection for 'sensitive personal data', which means information about the data subject's:

- racial or ethnic origin;
- political opinions;
- religious beliefs or other beliefs of a similar nature;
- membership of a trade union;
- physical or mental health or condition;
- sexual life;
- criminal offences and any proceedings for offences committed or alleged to have been committed.

The judge in the *Campbell* case ruled that the information about the nature and details of the therapy she was seeking was 'sensitive personal data' in respect of her physical or mental health.

Under the law as originally enacted, sensitive personal data can usually only be processed lawfully if either of two main conditions are met—for example, the person gave 'explicit' consent or deliberately made the information public, or the use to which the information was to be put was necessary for the administration of justice.

After media representations, the government introduced a statutory instru-ment that widened the grounds for any third party's lawful release of information to the media for publication by adding another 'gateway' for the lawful processing of sensitive personal data. This is the Data Protection (Processing of Sensitive Personal Data) Order 2000.

A journalist may need to rely on the section 32 exemption as regards collec-tion of 'sensitive personal data', which means there should be a public interest justification.

 For detail of how the 2000 Order and other exemptions in the 1998 Act protect media activity which is in the public interest, including retaining information, and whether a 'subject access request' could threaten a journalist's protection of the identity of a confidential source, see the Additional Material for this chapter on www.mcnaes.com.

❙ The Information Commissioner's Office guidance

see Useful Websites at the end of this chapter for the guidance

In 2014 the Information Commissioner's Office (ICO) published guidance for the media on data protection law.

This guidance is, on the whole, reassuring for journalists, but underlines that they cannot rely on the 1998 Act's section 32 exemption for journalism to avoid obligations to keep people's personal data secure. So—for example—memory sticks should have passwords.

The guidance covers the Act's requirement for there to be a reasonable belief held by 'the data controller', when relying on the section 32 exemption, that publication of someone's personal data—for example, gathered covertly against their wishes—would be in the public interest. It says: 'If you initially consider that a story will be in the public interest, but in the end change your mind and decide not to publish, the exemption can still cover the information you collected up to that point. On the other hand, it also means that the exemption cannot cover "fishing expeditions" for personal data undertaken with no particular story or journalistic aim in mind.'

ch. 2 explains the term 'fishing expedition'

In considering whether the section 32 exemption applies, the Information Commissioner or a court can consider if there has been compliance with the 'relevant' code, which could be the Editors' Code, the Broadcasting Code or BBC Editorial Guidelines.

chs. 2, 3 and 27 explain these codes

The ICO guidance advocates 'audit trail' procedures. This means that editors and investigative journalists should keep records to show why a public interest justification—for example, for use of deception—was reasonably believed to exist, including records of **prima facie** evidence and decisions. Such procedures are also referred to in ch. 2 as regards undercover journalism and ch. 22 in the context of the 'public interest' defence in defamation law.

→ glossary

The ICO has also issued guidance for members of the public on their data protection rights in relation to the media—see Useful Websites at the end of this chapter.

➡ Recap of major points

- Journalists seeking information should realise that it is a criminal offence to procure the disclosure of personal data unless there is a legal defence.

- Sometimes the Data Protection Act 1998 is mistakenly used as a reason to deny journalists information.

- The 1998 Act has exemptions protecting journalism which is in the public interest.

((•)) Useful Websites

https://ico.org.uk/media/about-the-ico/documents/1042393/what-price-privacy.pdf
   What Price Privacy?

https://ico.org.uk/media/about-the-ico/documents/1042392/what-price-privacy-now.pdf
   What Price Privacy Now?

https://ico.org.uk/media/for-organisations/documents/1136/taking_photos.pdf
   Information Commissioner's guidance for schools about photos

https://ico.org.uk/media/for-organisations/documents/1135/publication-of-exam-results-by-schools-dpa-guidance.pdf
   Information Commissioner's guidance for schools about exam results

https://ico.org.uk/media/for-organisations/documents/1552/data-protection-and-journalism-media-guidance.pdf
   Information Commissioner's guide for the media on data protection law

http://ico.org.uk/for_the_public/topic_specific_guides/media
   Information Commissioner's guidance for the public on their data protection
   rights in relation to the media

29

Copyright

Chapter summary

Copyright is a property right to control who can copy work created by artistic and other intellectual endeavour. Copyright protects journalism articles, website content, books, photographs, films, sound recordings and music, TV and radio broadcasts. This chapter explains how copyright law, by deterring and punishing plagiarism, protects the ability of journalists and media employers to earn profit from their output. Copyright lasts for decades. Copyright also protects work created by others which journalists may wish to copy—for example, by quoting from or showing it.

▌ What material does copyright protect?

→ glossary

The source of most UK law on **copyright** is the Copyright, Designs and Patents Act 1988, as amended by subsequent law.

Section 1 says copyright subsists in:

- 'original literary, dramatic, musical or artistic works'—which includes: all kinds of text whether handwritten, printed or online, such as journalistic and scientific articles, poems, lyrics, books, plays, scripts, shorthand or longhand records of speeches and interviews; musical manuscripts; photographs; design documents, websites, templates; graphic works, maps, plans, sketches, paintings, sculptures; databases and computer programs;
- 'sound recordings, films or broadcasts', including journalism in these media, files and CDs of music, home and cinema movies, and TV and radio output;
- 'the typographical arrangement of published editions'.

Unauthorised copying of all or 'any substantial part' of any work in these catego- →glossary
ries is a criminal offence and a civil tort unless justified by a defence or exception. More than one type of copyright, with different owners, may exist in a single
work—for example, a film will have copyrights in the script, footage and music.

▌ Who owns copyright under the 1988 Act?

- The 'first owner' of copyright in a literary, dramatic, musical or artistic
  work is the author as creator. This definition includes the journalist as an
  article's writer, the photographer as creator of a photo, the artist who makes
  a painting or sculpture, etc. If authorship is joint, each author is a 'first
  owner' and permission is needed from each to copy the work.

The 'first owner' has the copyright unless he/she agrees—for example, for payment—to assign to another party the right to control who makes copies—see later
in this chapter.

- The Act says an employer owns the copyright in a literary, dramatic, musical or artistic work—including a journalistic article or photo—created by
  an employee in the course of his/her employment. This is usually stated in
  the employment contract.
- A staff journalist only has the copyright in an article or photo if the
  employer specifically agrees to this, for example, in the contract of employment (1988 Act, section 11).
- Self-employed journalists, including freelance and commercial photographers, are the 'first owners' of copyright in their works.

The terms, including payment, under which freelances assign copyright or licence
use of their work to media publishers may be specific to each deal, or governed
by custom and practice. 'Assign' means to transfer ownership of the copyright.
'Licence' means to permit a use of the copyright work.

- The 'first owner' of copyright in a sound recording is the producer, defined
  in the Act as the person/organisation who undertook 'the arrangements necessary' for creating the work.
- The 'first owners' of copyright in a film made on or after 1 July 1994, whether
  made for journalism or entertainment, are jointly the producer and principal director. The producer owns the copyright in films made earlier which
  are covered by the Act.
- The 'first owner' of copyright in a broadcast is the person or organisation
  'making the broadcast'—that is, transmitting it, if responsible for content,
  or providing that content and arranging transmission. This is usually a
  broadcast company.

- The 'first owner' of copyright in 'the typographical arrangement of a published edition' is the publisher.
- The 'first owner' of copyright in 'computer-generated work', a category which the Act limits to circumstances of 'no human author', is the person or organisation undertaking 'the arrangements necessary' for the work's creation.

Copying from the internet, including social networking sites

The fact that material, including any photo, can be seen by all on the internet—for example, via Google Images—does not mean that anyone has the right to copy and publish it. Publishing material such as a photo or an extract of 'original' text copied from the internet infringes any copyright in the work, unless the copyright owner consents, or a defence or exception applies. Downloading may be an infringement.

see also
p. 378,
'Open
content'
licences

- Publishing photos copied from a social networking site—such as Facebook, Instagram, Flickr, Twitter, or Tumblr—may infringe the copyright in the site and/or the copyright held by the person who created the picture, who might not even be aware that someone else has uploaded a copy on to the site.

👁 Case study

Commercial photographer Jason Sheldon sued Daybrook House Promotions Ltd, a company running Nottingham dance venue Rock City, after he discovered it used one of his pictures in a poster campaign for its events. The picture was of popstars Ke$ha and LMFAO on their tour bus. Daybrook said the photo had been available on the Tumblr website, which it mistakenly believed meant the photograph was there to be freely used. Daybrook offered to pay Mr Sheldon £150 for its use. But in a preliminary ruling Judge Birss, in the Patents County Court, said that if the case proceeded and he found copyright had been breached, he would award Mr Sheldon £5,682.37 damages, noting that, for this particular photo, he had exclusive access to the pop stars (*Sheldon v Daybrook House Promotions Ltd* [2013] EWPCC 26). It was later reported that Daybrook settled the case—see Useful Websites at the end of this chapter. The Patents County Court is now the Intellectual Property Enterprise Court.

 If the material was posted on a personal webpage, a media organisation may need to consider too whether, apart from copyright law, ethical considerations mean it should not be used in news coverage—see ch. 27, p. 353, Material from social media sites.

Photos of TV images and photos shown on TV

Publishing a photo—for example, a 'screengrab'—of a television or film image without permission can infringe copyright under section 17 of the 1988 Act. Showing a photo on a TV programme without the copyright owner's permission is also an infringement, unless a defence applies.

see p. 373, Defences to alleged infringement of copyright

▌ Commissioner's copyright in older work

Section 4 of the Copyright Act 1956 governs who owns copyright in literary, dramatic and artistic work created before 1 August 1989—that is, before the 1988 Act came into force. Copyright in such a work, including a journalism article, which was created in the course of employment is owned by the employer unless the employer has assigned it to someone else.

see p. 370, Assignment and licensing of copyright

But if a work was created by a freelance paid or commissioned to do it, the 1956 Act says that, in the absence of any other agreement, the copyright is owned by the commissioner—for example, a newspaper or magazine.

This difference between the two Acts decides who, as copyright holder, can successfully object to the use of an archived photo or demand payment for its use.

- Copyright in a commissioned photograph taken before 1 August 1989 is owned by the commissioner, even though the freelance or commercial photographer who took the photo may own the negatives or have digital copies.
- The photographer or his/her employer owns the copyright in a photo taken before 1 August 1989 which was not commissioned.

This summary assumes that copyright in the photograph has not been not assigned to someone else.

A family wedding photo taken by a commercial photographer before 1 August 1989 will almost certainly have been commissioned by someone in the family, who will therefore probably own the copyright.

- Under the 1988 Act, the copyright in a photograph taken on or after 1 August 1989 is owned by the photographer's employer, or by the photographer if he/she is self-employed, *unless* there is an agreement to the contrary.

A celebrity who hires (commissions) a photographer to take pictures of a family occasion may well insist on the copyright being assigned to him/her, to control their use.

▌ Private and domestic photographs and films

Section 85 of the 1988 Act gives a 'moral right', in essence a privacy right, to people who commission photographs or films for 'private and domestic purposes'.

ch. 26 explains general privacy rights

- The right is that no copies of the photograph or film should be published, issued to or exhibited to the public without the commissioner's agreement.
- Commissioners have this right even if they do not own the copyright, and can sue and recover damages from anyone who publishes a commissioned photo or film of a private and domestic occasion without their permission.
- A publisher who uses the photo or film in breach of copyright could also be sued—for example, by a photographer who holds the copyright.

see p. 373, Legal remedies for infringe- ment of copyright

Consider this hypothetical case: a woman is hurt in a train crash. A journalist traces a relative, who emails the journalist a copy of a picture of the woman, taken some years previously at her wedding. If the relative took the picture himself/ herself and agrees for it to be published, there is no infringement of copyright. If the wedding picture was taken by a commercial photographer commissioned by the bridegroom (that is, the injured woman's husband), the photographer will probably own the copyright and may be glad to accept a fee for media publication of the picture. But the husband may not want it published. He may sue for breach of his moral right and win, even if he is not in the photo.

This 'moral right' can be waived. But otherwise it lasts as long as the copyright— see later in this chapter.

see also, p. 379, Moral rights for creators

> A judge ruled in 2012 that photos created by a photographer as a present for his friend Carina Trimingham, who appeared in them, were not 'commissioned' because he was not obliged by any financial deal to create them and so she had no moral right under section 85 to control their use. See Additional Material for ch. 29 on www.mcnaes.com for this case.

When a big story breaks, the media tend to rush to get 'pick-up' pictures or family-held footage of those involved and adopt a 'publish first, worry later' approach. Most families know little about copyright or moral rights, so financial conse- quences for media organisations are rare—but they could occur.

▌ The scope of copyright protection

Copyright is automatically in force as soon as a work is created in any permanent form. In the UK, copyright does not have to be registered.

What is 'original'?

Copyright protects an 'original literary, dramatic, musical or artistic work'. 'Literary' in this context includes any work, written or spoken, which exists in some permanent form—it has no reference to a work's literary or artistic merits. The legal definition of 'original' has for some decades in UK law simply required that the work was originated by the creator(s) using some element of 'skill, labour and judgment' (see, for example, *Express Newspapers plc v News (UK) Ltd* [1990] 3 All ER 376).

The elements of skill, labour, judgment, time or expense have not needed to be great. Judges cite the rough guideline that 'anything worth copying is usually worth protecting'.

- Skill, labour and judgement spent in creating a bus or rail timetable, or tide table or a database, mean that that such works have been protected by copyright, vested in the 'first owner' as creator or, if employed, his/her employer.
- Copyright could also subsist in even a fairly basic form of map, diagram, drawing or sketch, so journalists should also beware of reproducing these without permission.

But a commonplace expression such as 'love is blind', if used in a book title, will not be protected by copyright because of lack of originality.

 See the Additional Material for ch. 29 on www.mcnaes.com for detail on copyright which exists in TV and radio programme listings, and for the 2012 ruling by the European Court of Justice that copyright did not exist in lists of Premier League football fixtures.

No copyright in news or in unrecorded ideas

Copyright does not protect ideas—it controls the right to copy the form or manner in which ideas are expressed or executed. The law of breach of confidence, explained in ch. 25, would apply in some circumstances if a considered 'idea' with commercial value were exploited in breach of 'confidential' discussions about it.

- There is also no copyright in facts, news or information. Copyright exists in the form—for example, sentences, a photo, footage—in which these things are expressed, and in the selection and arrangement of the material for publication.

'Lifting' stories

News organisations often include in their stories facts—such as political initiatives or a famous person's death—which are 'broken' by rivals. This is known as 'lifting' a story. There is no copyright infringement in reporting in a *re-written* version the facts uncovered or published by others (*Springfield v Thame* (1903) 89 LT 242). But there may be infringements in 'lifting' verbatim phrases and quotes from the original report, depending on the extent—see p. 373, What is 'substantial'?, and p. 371, Copyright in speeches and interviews.

ch. 19 explains the defamation danger in lifting stories

see p. 378,
Acquiescence

👁 **Case study**

High Court judge Sir Nicolas Browne-Wilkinson said in 1990: 'For myself, I would hesitate a long time before deciding that there is copyright in a news story which would be infringed by another newspaper picking up that story and reproducing the same story in different words … That would not be in the public interest …' He also observed that, as the practice among UK national newspapers of copying quotes from each other was so widespread and rarely led to copyright disputes, it could be argued that the newspapers gave each other implied licence for the practice by 'acquiescence' (*Express Newspapers plc v News (UK) Ltd* [1990] 3 All ER 376).

Changing the odd word or two when writing a news report by 'lifting' facts from a rival report will not be enough to avoid copyright infringement. But the 1988 Act's defence of 'fair dealing' for reporting current events can allow a media organisation to copy some quotes and other sentences from a rival's report, and to broadcast short extracts of film or sound footage already broadcast by a rival— see later in this chapter.

▌ Assignment and licensing of copyright

Copyright holders can 'assign' copyright, wholly or in part, to another person or organisation, either temporarily or for the copyright's duration. This transfers control to exploit the work. Or the owner can, while retaining the copyright, 'licence' another party to exploit the work in a particular deal or territory. Section 90 of the 1988 Act says an assignment of copyright is not effective unless it is in writing and is signed by or on behalf of the person assigning it—for example, the 'first owner'.

A licence need not be in writing. In journalism, licences are often agreed verbally, or implied by what has become custom and practice. For example, freelance journalists who regularly send articles or photos to newspapers know their fee rates, and whether they also want the right to use the work in magazine supplements and on websites, or possibly in overseas editions and for syndication. Any doubts on either side about licence terms should be discussed then agreed in writing before the work is published.

Material from non-journalist contributors

- A reader sending a letter for publication has by implication licensed the media organisation to publish it once, but retains the copyright.

If the organisation subsequently wants to publish a compilation of readers' letters as a book, it will need to contact each letter-writer to seek a licence to re-publish the letters.

▶ Copyright in speeches and interviews, and in notes or recordings of them

Copyright exists in spoken words such as public speech as soon as the speaker's words are recorded in some form, with or without permission. The copyright arises even if the speech is not delivered from a script, but is, for example, uttered in an improvised comedy show or in an interview with a journalist. The speaker, as the author of a 'literary work'—that is, his/her words as recorded—owns the copyright in that work, unless he/she is speaking in the course of his/her employment, in which case the employer owns the copyright, or is reciting words in which someone else holds copyright (for example, from a play script).

As copyright protects the 'original' product of 'skill, labour and judgment', there is no copyright in casual conversational or trite remarks, in short jokes already in circulation, or in commonplace or ill-judged sayings.

Section 58 of the 1988 Act—a specific defence for journalism—says it is not infringement of copyright to use a record of all or part of a speaker's words for reporting current events, as long as:

(1) the record of the words—that is, as recorded on tape or digitally, or in shorthand or longhand—is a direct record of their utterance and is not taken from a previous record or broadcast (as taking the record from such sources could infringe the copyright in those sources);

(2) the speaker did not forbid any note or recording being made of his/her words and making the record of them did not infringe any pre-existing copyright (it might, if the speaker were quoting someone else's words);

(3) the use made of the record of the words, or extracts from it, is not of a kind prohibited by the speaker (or anyone else who owns copyright in words used by the speaker) before the record was made;

(4) the record is used with the authority of the person who is lawfully in possession of it—who would usually be the journalist who took notes or made a recording of the speaker's words, or his/her employer.

A journalist should not be overly concerned about infringing a speaker's copyright when reporting verbatim a speech from a note or recording made of a speech or an interview, as usually a speaker who knows he/she is a journalist has consented to publication, expressly or by implication. Even if a speaker withholds consent, one or both of the fair dealing defences can apply—see later in this chapter.

The first and fourth conditions listed earlier reflect the fact that, apart from the speaker's copyright in the recorded words, a separate copyright exists in the actual record—the audio-recording, shorthand or longhand note—because of the skill, labour and judgement involved in making it (*Walter v Lane* [1900] AC 539). The journalist who made the record will, if a freelance, be 'first owner' of that copyright. If the record was made in the course of his/her employment, the employer owns it.

▶ Parliament and the courts

Section 45 of the 1988 Act says copyright is not infringed by anything done for the purposes of reporting parliamentary and judicial proceedings. This means there is no copyright infringement in reporting what is said in proceedings of the UK and Scottish Parliaments, the Northern Ireland and Welsh Assemblies, or in the proceedings of statutory public inquiries and court cases.

! Remember your rights

Section 45 means that the media does not infringe copyright if, when it covers court cases, it publishes copies of documents, photographs or footage supplied by the prosecution under the 2005 protocol—see ch. 14, p. 171, The 'Publicity and Criminal Justice System' protocol—or with the court's permission for publication—see ch. 14, p. 169, Practice Direction Part 5B. See the Additional Material for ch. 29 on www.mcnaes.com for a section 45 case study.

▶ How long does copyright last?

Durations of copyright, set out in sections 12–15 of the 1988 Act, can be summarised as follows.

- Copyright in a literary, dramatic, musical or artistic work—including a journalism article or a photo—lasts for the author's (that is, creator's) lifetime and then a further 70 years from the end of the calendar year in which he/she dies. The copyright can be bequeathed to the creator's heirs. The duration is the same even if the copyright is owned by an employer or has been assigned to a company.
- Copyright in a work of computer-generated music or graphics lasts for 50 years from the end of the year in which it was made.
- Copyright in a sound recording published or communicated to the public lasts 70 years from the end of the year in which that first happened.
- Copyright in a broadcast lasts 50 years from the end of the year in which it was made.

There are different (but still lengthy) periods of copyright for various other works, such as films, works of unknown authorship and for some particular circumstances.

 See Additional Material for ch. 29 on www.mcnaes.com about copyright in 'orphan works'—that is, copied when the owner of the copyright could not be traced to gain permission.

Crown copyright

Work produced by civil servants in the course of their employment is protected by Crown copyright, which can last up to 125 years.

▌ Legal remedies for infringement of copyright

Civil law

- A copyright holder who discovers that someone plans to infringe that right can get a High Court or county court injunction to stop it.
- If the infringement has happened, an injunction can ban any repetition. The copyright owner can also sue the infringer for damages or for 'an account of profits', to claim any profit made.
- The court can also order all infringing copies of the work to be handed to the copyright owner or destroyed.

→ glossary

The damages awarded by a court may reflect its view that there has been a flagrant breach of copyright.

Criminal law

Infringing copyright is a criminal offence. Prosecutions tend to be confined to cases of large-scale piracy. In 2014 a Walsall man who helped make more than 700,000 pirate copies of the Hollywood film *The Fast and the Furious* was jailed for 33 months (Press Association, 3 September 2014).

▌ Defences to alleged infringement of copyright

A question regularly asked by journalists is: 'How much can we copy or quote without infringing copyright?' One consideration is whether the copyright owner, in the case of copied text or quotes, will think it worth the effort to sue—but copyright can reside in a single sentence.

What is 'substantial'?

Section 16 of the 1988 Act says it is an infringement of copyright to copy the whole or 'any substantial part' of a work. 'Substantial' refers to 'the quality of the originality', including the importance of the copied material in relation to the rest of the original work, rather than merely to how much was copied (*Newspaper Licensing Agency Ltd v Meltwater Holding BV* [2010] EWHC 3009 (Ch)).

For example, a face may be a small part of a photograph but is probably more important, as regards its commercial value, than the rest of the picture. A court dealing with a 'literary work' would consider to what degree unauthorised verbatim publication of part of it might devalue the work's copyright.

In the *Meltwater* case High Court judge Mrs Justice Proudman drew on the 2009 judgment in which the European Court of Justice ruled that a single extract of 11 consecutive words from a newspaper article could be protected by copyright if the work had sufficient originality (Case C-5/08 *Infopaq International A/S v Danske Dagblades Forening* [2010] FSR 495).

see p. 368, What is 'original'?

Mrs Justice Proudman said: 'The ECJ makes it clear that originality rather than substantiality is the test to be applied to the part extracted. As a matter of principle this is the only real test.'

The issue of what is a 'substantial part' is not always relevant for the news media, as documents can be paraphrased or summarised to avoid quoting verbatim. Also, editors can aim to rely on a fair dealing defence, because then the issue of how much can be copied/quoted must be assessed in terms of 'fairness' rather than substantiality.

 See Additional Material for ch. 29 on www.mcnaes.com for the *Meltwater* judgment. It upheld copyright protection for headlines and short text extracts electronically 'scraped' from newspapers' websites by a company monitoring various news subjects for its subscribers.

Fair dealing defences

The four 'fair dealing' defences in section 30 of the 1988 Act recognise the public interest in news coverage and some other types of publication being free of some copyright restraints.

Defence of fair dealing for the purpose of reporting current events

- Section 30 of the Act allows publication of work protected by copyright 'for the purpose of reporting current events', even if there is no consent from the copyright owner.
- But there must be 'fair dealing' by those publishing it for this purpose and an accompanying 'sufficient acknowledgement' of the work copied.
- 'Fair dealing' means fair practice—for example, the publisher should not take unfair commercial advantage of the copyright owner by excessive publication of the copied work.
- 'Sufficient acknowledgement' means that a report, in a newspaper, magazine, website or other textual medium, must:
  - cite the work's title, or include some identifying description of it; and
  - name its author/creator, unless it was published anonymously (section 178).

- Photographs are specifically excluded from the fair dealing defence of 'reporting current events', because otherwise no news photographers could earn their living by selling their pictures.

Case law suggests that a court will be less likely to uphold the fair dealing defence if the work copied has been 'leaked' to the media organisation. But the defence will probably not be undermined if the leak—for example, of an internal company memo—reveals wrongdoing or a threat to public safety. In such a case, the defence may protect verbatim publication of an entire document. But if the copyright in a text or document has a legitimate commercial value, judges will expect the media to make only limited use of verbatim extracts, so that the copyright owner's ability to exploit that value is not compromised unfairly. See, for example, the *Ashdown* case discussed in the Additional Material for ch. 29 on www.mcnaes.com in which the Court of Appeal ruled that *Sunday Telegraph*, by quoting verbatim or nearly verbatim some 20 per cent of a nine-page document, was unfair in that case's circumstances and that 'one or two short extracts from it would have sufficed' to satisfy readers than the reporting was authoritative.

In *Ashdown* the judgment suggested that the term 'current events' could cover events which occurred two years before the disputed copying—or possibly, in some circumstances, events from 30 years ago—if the copied work helped them be re-examined in new revelations in media coverage.

Although the fair dealing defence does not cover still photographs, it does cover media use—that is, if 'fair'—of copied film footage and sound recordings, including in digital forms.

👁 Case study

In 1991 the High Court dismissed a copyright action by the BBC against British Satellite Broadcasting (BSB) over the use by the satellite company's sports programme of highlights from BBC coverage of the World Cup football finals, to which the Corporation had bought exclusive rights. The court said BSB's use of short clips showing goals scored, 14–37 seconds in length and up to four times in 24 hours, with a BBC credit line included as acknowledgement, was protected by the defence of fair dealing for reporting current events (*BBC v British Satellite Broadcasting* [1991] 3 All ER 833 (Ch D)).

Rival broadcast organisations sometimes agree protocols for limited copying of each other's output.

The Act says sound recording, film or broadcast reports of current events do not need to acknowledge the copied work's title, or other description of it, or the identity of its author/creator 'where this would be impossible for reasons of practicality or otherwise'. This reflects the difficulty of including all such detail in a broadcast of a short piece of copied footage. But acknowledgements help prove fairness.

Defence of fair dealing for the purpose of criticism or review

Section 30 of the Act allows publication of copies of a work, even without the copyright owner's consent, 'for the purpose of criticism or review'.

- But the work must already have been 'made available to the public' *with* the copyright owner's consent—for example, published or exhibited. The defence does not protect use of leaked or stolen material.
- There must also be 'fair dealing' by those publishing it for criticism or review and an accompanying 'sufficient acknowledgement' of the work.

The 'fair dealing' and 'sufficient acknowledgement' requirements are in essence the same as those required for the defence of fair dealing in reporting current events.

Authors or creators who have released works to the public may well be happy for extracts from them to appear in criticisms or reviews, as they will receive wider publicity. But the defence applies irrespective of whether they object. The defence would, for example, cover publication of a whole photo from an exhibition or book of artistic photos. Case law says the defence can protect copying for the purpose of a critique or review of the 'ideas or philosophy' manifest in the copied work, not just assessment of the work's quality as literature or art.

The requirement of fairness means that in a dispute about the extent of the use of copied material a court would consider if the media organisation genuinely sought to critique the copied work(s) or had the baser motive of taking commercial advantage.

> See the Additional Material for ch. 29 on www.mcnaes.com for case studies of media organisations relying on these fair dealing defences.

Defence of fair dealing for use of quotation

In 2014 section 30 of the 1988 Act was amended to create a general defence for use of quotation. The requirements, all of which must be met, are that the work being quoted has been made available for the public (it is not—for example—a leaked or stolen document/recording), that the use is 'fair dealing' (see earlier), that the extent of the quotation is no more than is required 'by the specific purpose for which it is used' and that the quotation is accompanied by 'sufficient acknowledgement' (see earlier), 'unless this would be impossible for reasons of practicality or otherwise'. The 'quotation' could be by use of part of a recording otherwise protected by copyright (see Schedule 2 to the Act).

see Useful Websites at the end of this chapter for IPO guidance

This new defence can protect quotation in journalism of short extracts when this is not covered by the other fair dealing defences—because it is not to report 'current events' or to review. It also protects, for example, theatres and record companies when they use in promotional material quotes from newspaper reviews.

The Intellectual Property Office (IPO) guidance is that the quotation defence can cover copying of a photograph but only in 'exceptional' circumstances.

Defence of fair dealing for the purpose of caricature, parody or pastiche

The amendment in 2014 to section 30 also created a defence of copying for the purposes of caricature, parody and pastiche. Again, the copying must be limited so that it does not take 'unfair' commercial advantage of the copyright owner by excessive publication of the copied work.

Public interest defence

The public interest defence in copyright case law is narrow, reflecting the fact →glossary that the 'fair dealing' defences have a public interest element. But whereas the defence of fair dealing for the purpose of reporting current events cannot protect the unauthorised copying (publication) of a still photo, the 'public interest' defence can protect publication of any copyrighted work, including a still photo, if the purpose is to expose it as an immoral work, or one damaging to public life, health, safety or the administration of justice, or as a work which incites immoral behaviour, and in some other circumstances—for example, if police ask the media to publish a photo (for which the police do not own the copyright) of a person whom they wish to trace.

👁 Case study

In 2010 the *Reading Post* succeeded with the public interest defence in the small claims court after being sued by the owner of copyright in several photos which it had copied from a website. Police had directed the *Post* to the site, which showed the apparent exploits of 'urban explorers' inside abandoned buildings. The *Post* said it published the pictures to highlight police concerns that these activities involved criminal damage, including graffiti, and to help identify those involved. The judge said he felt the pictures were posted on the website to encourage the activities, which could cause an accident, and the public to suffer, and were a serious social problem (*Newspaper Society website*, 28 January 2010).

 See the Additional Material for ch. 29 on www.mcnaes.com for other examples of journalistic use of the 'public interest' defence.

Incidental infringement and publicly displayed artworks

Section 31 of the Act says copyright in a work is not infringed by its incidental inclusion in a photo, sound recording, film or a broadcast. So there is no infringement if a TV news report incidentally shows, in the background, a work of art, or its sound track of coverage of a wider event incidentally includes a band playing, although deliberately including music would need to be covered by another defence or exception—for example, fair dealing.

Innocent infringement

If an infringer did not know and had no reason to believe the copied work was subject to copyright—for example, he/she genuinely believed the copyright had run out—the copyright owner would be entitled to an account of profits but not to damages.

> 📖 P. 373, Legal remedies for infringement of copyright, explains what 'account of profits' means.

Acquiescence

A copyright holder who encourages or allows another to make use of a work without complaining may destroy any claim for infringement.

▌ Mere use of hyperlinks does not breach copyright

The European Court of Justice ruled in 2014 that a news-monitoring website's use of hyperlinks merely to direct its client readers to items on the *Göteborgs-Posten* newspaper's website (among others) had not infringed copyright in that material because it was freely available online—that is, the newspaper site was not behind any paywall or other barrier (Case C-466/12 *Svennson and others v Retriver Sverige AB*, 13 February 2014).

▌ 'Open content' licences

see Useful Websites at the end of this chapter for Creative Commons site

Some creators—including some who post photographs on social media sites such as Flickr—give a general, 'open content' licence for people to copy and distribute their work free of charge, provided that attribution to the creator is included and specified conditions are honoured. The licence may be in the Creative Commons format. One condition may be that the use of the work is not commercial, which would exclude use in journalism for which consumers pay. A different licence would have to be agreed with the copyright owner to permit such journalistic use, unless a defence applied.

◗ Moral rights for creators

The 1988 Act, to comply with an international convention, gives 'moral rights' to authors (creators) of some categories of copyright work, including literary and artistic work—for example, a photo—and to the director of a film. He/she can assert the right to be identified when his/her work is published and has the right not to have it subjected to 'derogatory'—for example, distortive—treatment. A person has a moral right not to have a work falsely attributed to him/her. This law is in sections 77–84 of the Act. The rights to be identified and not to have the work subject to derogatory treatment do not apply to work created in the course of employment, or for reporting current events, or to other types of content in a newspaper, magazine or periodical. But a freelance with sufficient clout can insist, as a term of the copyright licence, on being identified by a media publisher as the work's author.

◗ 'Passing off' and trade marks

Other civil law provides remedies against someone who, to gain profit, falsely 'passes off' their products or services as being retailed by a more prestigious organisation. A celebrity could use this to stop his/her name or image being falsely used to endorse a product. The system of registration of trademarks gives similar protection in the retail of goods and services.

➡ Recap of major points

- Copyright law controls who can commercially exploit literary, musical, dramatic and artistic works, including journalism articles and photos, as well as the exploitation of sound recordings, film, broadcast and typographical arrangements.
- There is no copyright in news in itself, only in the form in which it is expressed.
- Defences of fair dealing are available for publication of copyrighted work if the copying is not excessive and if the publisher honours requirement for attribution to the creator(s).
- But photographs are excluded from the fair dealing defence which covers reporting news and current events.
- A copyright owner whose rights are infringed can seek an injunction and/or damages.

((•)) Useful Websites

www.ipo.gov.uk/types/copy.htm
Intellectual Property Office, a Government agency—see its guides to copyright and trade marks

www.gov.uk/government/uploads/system/uploads/attachment_data/file/448269/Exceptions_to_copyright_-_An_Overview.pdf
Intellectual Property Office guide, *Exceptions to Copyright*

www.londonfreelance.org/advice.html
London freelance branch of the National Union of Journalists—advice on copyright

www.justice.gov.uk/courts/rcj-rolls-building/intellectual-property-enterprise-court
Intellectual Property Enterprise Court

www.epuk.org/
Editorial Photographers group, whose site features copyright issues

www.epuk.org/News/1039/infringer-who-originally-offered-150-forced-to-pay-20000-in-settlement
Editorial Photographers article on the *Sheldon* case

http://creativecommons.org/licenses/
Guide to Creative Commons copyright licences

Part 5

Information and expression

The Freedom of Information Act 2000

Chapter summary

The Freedom of Information (FoI) Act 2000, which came into effect in 2005, created the UK's first general right of access to information held by government departments and public authorities. Use of the Act has produced many exclusive stories, some about the highest reaches of government. But FoI is bedevilled by bureaucratic delay and wide-ranging exemptions, and a requestor must be prepared to argue that the 'public interest' justifies disclosure of information. This chapter deals with FoI law as it applies in England, Wales and Northern Ireland, and information access rights in the Environmental Information Regulations 2004.

▶ Introduction to the Act

The Freedom of Information Act 2000 gives people the right to require 'public authorities' to disclose information they would not otherwise publish. Authorities must supply information without charging for finding and collating it, subject to cost limits.

The parliamentary expenses scandal in spring 2009 highlighted the Act's shortcomings. FoI requests by campaigner and journalist Heather Brooke forced House of Commons officials to disclose some details of what some MPs were claiming in expenses for their second homes.

But these official disclosures were anodyne in comparison with the truth, which emerged when full details of MPs' expenses was leaked to the Telegraph Media Group—and showed that MPs 'flipped' their main and second homes to maximise expenses, claimed for items such as moat-clearing and duck houses, could make claims without producing receipts and had reclaimed the cost of things ranging from dog biscuits to bath plugs, none of which emerged in the official disclosures.

see p. 386, Cost limits

As the main text of this book was being completed in late 2015, the government was due to begin considering proposals which, if implemented, would weaken the effect of FoI law—for example, if authorities were permitted to require requestors to pay a fee for information. The National Union of Journalists and Society of Editors were among those campaigning against the proposals. For updates, check www.mcnaes.com.

Difficulties with FoI obligations

The Act has brought many newsworthy disclosures by national, regional and local journalists.

Although many public bodies are helpful when responding to FoI requests, many others delay answering requests and are extremely slow when considering the 'public interest test' (discussed later in the chapter). The Information Commissioner has monitored a number of public bodies for three-month periods because of their tardiness in answering FoI requests. These include the Cabinet Office—monitored twice—which is now responsible for FoI policy, but which the Information Commissioner described in April 2011 as being among the worst offenders for delays in responding to FoI requests.

Government departments and other public bodies often seek to use the Act's exemptions to thwart requests for information, and numerous requestors win appeals to the Information Commissioner and the First-tier Tribunal (Information Rights). Journalists using the Act need to be systematic and persistent. Despite the drawbacks it is a worthwhile tool for investigative journalism.

▌ What is a 'public authority' under the Act?

The Act covers about 100,000 major and minor bodies in the public sector, including:

- national government departments and ministries such as the Home Office, Foreign Office and Prime Minister's Office;
- the House of Commons, the House of Lords, and the National Assemblies of Northern Ireland and Wales;
- the armed forces;
- local government—metropolitan, city, county, district and parish councils, transport executives, waste disposal agencies, police forces, fire services;
- national park authorities;
- universities, colleges and schools in the state sector;
- the National Health Service, including primary care trusts, hospital trusts, health authorities, and doctors' and dentists' practices;
- various advisory councils and regulatory bodies with statutory powers, such as Ofcom and the General Medical Council.

It does not define 'public authority', but lists, in Schedule 1, the bodies and organisations it covers. More have been added by statutory instruments.

▶ Institutions and agencies not covered by the Act

The security and intelligence agencies—MI5, MI6 and GCHQ—are exempt, and so not required to respond to FoI requests. Courts and tribunals are not covered, though some information gathered or created in their functions will be available if a request is made to the government department holding it, such as the Ministry of Justice.

The following are not public authorities under the Act: housing associations; charities; private prisons; harbour authorities; and MPs and Peers, as individuals.

The Royal Family never came under the Act. But an amendment introduced in section 46(1) of and Schedule 7 to the Constitutional Reform and Governance Act 2010, which came into force in January 2011, gives the Queen, the Prince of Wales and Prince William absolute exemption from any application for information. Other members of the Royal Family, such as the Duke of Edinburgh and Prince Harry, remain subject to a qualified exemption—public bodies holding information relating to them should release it if there is a public interest in disclosure.

The Coalition government which was in power from 2010 to 2015 made many more bodies, including the Universities and Colleges Admissions Service (UCAS), the National Police Chiefs' Council, the Financial Ombudsman Service (FOS) and companies entirely owned by local authorities subject to the Act.

 Check www.mcnaes.com for updates on the FoI Act covering more bodies.

▶ How the Act works

A public authority should respond to a request for information within 20 working days, either supplying the information or explaining that it cannot do so because:

- it does not hold it—in most circumstances this must be made clear;
- providing it would exceed the cost limits for free provision—see later in the chapter;
- it is exempt from disclosure.

see p. 387, Exemptions

In the case of some exempt categories—for example, information held in confidence or concerning national security—an authority does not have to say what it holds if denying or confirming the information's existence would undermine the purpose of the exemption.

Journalists should check an authority's website for information before making an FoI request, as it might already publish the material there. The Act says each authority must have a 'publication scheme'. If the information sought is not listed there, the journalists should ask the official who coordinates the authority's FoI matters about the types of information it holds. Section 16 of the Act says authorities must offer 'advice and assistance', including on how to frame requests to stay within the cost limits for free information—although sometimes this is not done.

A requestor's reason for wanting information plays no part in an authority's decision on providing it (unless a request is 'vexatious'—for example, from someone who repeatedly seeks the same or similar information).

An authority which has to apply the 'public interest test' (see later) to consider if an exemption applies may take more than 20 working days to give its final response. It must consider, even if some information specified in a request is deemed exempt from disclosure, if the request can be met in part by releasing non-exempt information.

What is information?

Section 84 of the Act defines information as 'information recorded in any form'. An authority is not required to gather information it does not already have. The right under the Act is for *information* to be communicated to the requestor, not necessarily in the form of particular documents, though requests often refer to particular documents, which are supplied. 'Document' includes electronic documents (*Dominic Kennedy v Information Commissioner and Charity Commission* [2010] EWHC 475 (Admin), [2010] 1 WLR 1489).

The Protection of Freedoms Act 2012, by amending the 2000 Act, gave requestors greater rights to have datasets held by public authorities sent to them in electronic, re-usable form.

((•))

for dataset guidance, see Useful Websites at the end of this chapter

Cost limits

A government department required to disclose requested information must do so free if it costs no more than £600. All other public authorities covered by the Act must provide such information free if doing so costs no more than £450. Cost is estimated by assessing—at £25 an hour—the staff time reasonably needed to determine whether a body holds the information, to find and retrieve it, and if necessary to extract it from a document. If after a bona fide estimating process the cost limit exceeded, the authority is not obliged to supply any information requested, but may *choose* to supply it without charge, or at a price which reflects the cost of providing it if the requestor is willing to pay. An authority which can comply with part, but not all, of a request within the cost limits has a duty under section 16 to offer a requestor advice to see if he/she wishes to re-define or limit the request. If the information is to be provided on paper, the requestor can be charged a reasonable price for photocopying. Information can often be sent by email.

Journalists should make requests as specific as possible. A requestor may get round a cost limit by breaking a 'large' request into several smaller ones, sent serially. But authorities may 'aggregate' the cost of two or more requests made within 60 days by the same person for the same or similar types of information—that is, treat them as being part of a single request—and refuse them if in total they breach the cost limit for one request. Authorities should not use aggregation powers to frustrate a sequence of requests each of which, on the basis of information sent previously, digs further into a topic by asking for further different information.

Advice and assistance

Section 16 requires a public body to give prospective or actual requestors 'advice and assistance, so far as it would be reasonable to expect the authority to do so'.

- It should, if asked, tell a requestor *before* he/she makes a request what information of the type sought might be available and help him/her to frame a request.
- It should give guidance to avoid a request breaching the cost limit for providing information free.

The First-tier Tribunal has made clear that it expects the Information Commissioner, when adjudicating an appeal against a refusal to supply information, to consider the extent to which a body met its obligations under section 16, so a requestor should if necessary remind the body, in writing, of these obligations. The Act says an authority which, in relation to the duty to advise and assist, conforms to the Code of Practice issued by the Ministry of Justice is to be taken as complying with that duty.

((•))
see Useful Websites at the end of this chapter for the Code of Practice

Paragraph 8 of the Code says 'authorities should, so far as is reasonably practicable, provide assistance to the applicant to enable him/her to describe more clearly the information requested'. The Information Tribunal has said of the duty to help: 'An applicant does not have to ask for it ... nothing [in the Act] restricts the duty to advise and assist only to those cases when some form of request has [already] been made ... the duty must include at least one to advise and assist an applicant with regard to the formulation of an appropriate request' (Appeal number EA/2006/0046).

Section 1(3) allows a body which 'reasonably requires' further detail to identify and locate information to clarify this with the requestor, and, if such further detail is not provided, not to comply with the request. The Information Commissioner has made clear that a public authority which tells a requestor that the information is already in the public domain should also indicate where it can be found.

((•))
see Useful Websites at the end of this chapter for ICO guidance

▌ Exemptions

Bodies may refuse to supply information on various grounds—exemptions. The Information Commissioner's Office website has guidance on these.

Absolute exemptions

Some exemptions are 'absolute'—the authority does not have to give a reason for refusing disclosure beyond stating that the exemption applies because of the nature of the information. Absolute exemptions include the following.

Section 21—information reasonably accessible by other means

Section 23—information supplied to the public authority by or relating to bodies dealing with security matters This may be supplied by eg MI5, MI6 and GCHQ.

Section 32—court records This exemption covers documents held by a public authority because it is a litigant or an interested party in a court case—for example, copies of material filed with a court for the purposes of proceedings.

ch. 28 explains data protection law

Section 40—personal information The Act does not override data protection law. A public body may decide that an FoI request encompasses exempt 'personal data'. But it should consider whether deleting references which could identify an individual could allow disclosure of non-exempt information.

The Commissioner has made clear that, when considering personal data issues, authorities should distinguish between 'professional personal information', such as staff job descriptions and details of their responsibilities, and 'private personal information', such as sickness records.

Section 41—information provided to the authority in confidence by another party This does not cover information which the public body has generated itself, so does not cover any contract the authority has entered into.

But the Information Tribunal, as it was, has said that the section 40 or 41 exemptions are not as absolute as they first appear, because a body should apply a public interest test under data protection law and/or the law of confidence when deciding on disclosure.

Section 44—information the disclosure of which is forbidden by other law For example, the Information Tribunal upheld a ruling that the Independent Police Complaints Commission could not, because of a provision in the Police Act 1996, disclose under the FoI Act copies of files relating to complaints against the police.

Qualified exemptions

The other exemptions are 'qualified'—the Act says information may be withheld only if the public interest in withholding it is greater than the public interest in disclosure. A public body which declines to supply information in these categories must give reasons showing how it has applied the public interest test.

see Useful Websites at the end of this chapter for this ICO guidance

The Act does not define 'public interest'. But in guidance in 2013 the Information Commissioner said that public interest factors which should encourage public authorities to disclose information included:

- general arguments in favour of promoting transparency, accountability and participation;

- that disclosure might enhance the quality of discussions and decision making generally;
- that the balance might be tipped in favour of disclosure by financial issues—such as if the information requested involves a large amount of public money;
- the specific circumstances of the case and the content of the information requested in relation to those circumstances;
- the age of the information;
- the timing of a request which, in respect of information relating to an investigation, may be relevant;
- the impact of disclosure upon individuals and/or the wider public.

The Campaign for Freedom of Information has stressed the importance of applicants pursuing requests all the way to the First-tier Tribunal (Information Rights) if necessary and not accepting a public authority's initial refusal. Requestors should not assume that the Information Commissioner will automatically recognise the public interest case for disclosing information and should raise it in appeal correspondence. But appeals take time, even when authorities have clearly misapplied absolute or qualified exemptions, as the Information Commissioner's office is overworked and under-resourced.

Qualified exemptions include the following.

Section 24—information which if disclosed is likely to prejudice national security This concerns information other than that already absolutely exempt under section 23.

Section 27—information which if disclosed is likely to prejudice international relations

Section 31—information held by an authority for law enforcement functions This is exempt if its disclosure would, or would be likely to, prejudice the prevention or detection of crime, the apprehension and prosecution of offenders, or the administration of justice. So details of when a speed camera at a particular site is active do not have to be disclosed as this would compromise the camera's effect. But more general information, such as how many drivers a particular camera caught speeding on a particular day, could be published.

Section 35—information relating to formulation or development of government policy The First-tier Tribunal (Information Rights) has been robust in disapproving of some attempts to use this exemption, noting that there is a public interest in involuntary disclosure of information under the Act as it acts as a check on information disclosed voluntarily. The older the information, the less sensitive it is as an indication of an authority's policy options.

Section 36—information the disclosure of which is likely to prejudice effective conduct of public affairs This exemption is controversial as it is so vague. Parliament intended it to cover material which did not fall into other categories but which, if disclosed, would damage a public body's ability to carry out its duties. Heather Brooke says a public authority relying on it 'is desperate and grasping at straws'.

Section 43—commercial interests This covers trade secrets and information which if disclosed 'would, or would be likely to, prejudice the commercial interest of any person (including the public authority holding it)'.

👁 Case study

In *John Connor Press Associates v Information Commissioner* (EA/2005/ 0005), the Information Tribunal held that the National Maritime Museum should have disclosed financial information concerning its purchase of a set of artworks. The Museum had argued that when it received the free-lance news agency's FoI request it was negotiating with another artist about another project and its ability to ensure value for public money would have been prejudiced had financial details about the previous deal been released. The Tribunal held that no real and significant risk of such prejudice existed, partly because the deal under negotiation—which included payment for 'performance art'—differed in scope from the Museum's previous deal for artworks.

Delays in the public interest test

The Act does not set a deadline for completing the 'public interest test' over an FoI request—considering it may mean the 20-day period for responding to requests instead becomes months. But a public body must tell a requestor within the 20-day limit that a qualified exemption might apply.

▌ If the information is not supplied

If an authority takes no decision on supplying the information within the 20-day limit, or refuses to supply it because of the cost limit or an exemption, a requestor can request an 'internal review' of the decision, which should be conducted by an official other than the one involved in the refusal. There is no timescale for completing this review. The Information Commissioner's Office has said that 20 working days (from the time a request for a review is received) is a reasonable time for a review and that in no case should the time exceed 40 working days. A requestor dissatisfied with the result of a review can appeal to the Information Commissioner.

The Information Commissioner and the First-tier Tribunal (Information Rights)

The Freedom of Information Act 2000 is enforced by the Information Commissioner, who also oversees the Data Protection Act 1998. The current Commissioner is Christopher Graham.

The Commissioner can: order a body to release information if he/she disagrees with a refusal to disclose it; question an authority's claim not to hold requested information; and question its estimate that disclosure would exceed the cost limit.

If a requestor claims an authority has not responded within the 20-day limit, the Commissioner can, under section 52, serve it with an enforcement notice requiring compliance with the Act. As an ultimate sanction, he/she can ask the High Court to punish an authority's failure to comply with the notice as contempt of court. Section 48 gives him/her the power to issue a 'good practice recommendation' specifying the steps an authority should take to improve compliance. FoI campaigners have criticised the Commissioner for not using his/her powers enough.

Requestors and public authorities dissatisfied with the Information Commissioner's decision can appeal to the First-tier Tribunal (Information Rights). Appeals should be made within 28 days of receipt of the Commissioner's decision. The Tribunal, part of the First-tier Tribunal in the administrative justice system—see ch. 17—publishes its decisions online.

((•))

see Useful Websites at the end of this chapter for the Tribunal's site

Ministers' power of veto

Cabinet Ministers can veto notices issued by the Commissioner requiring government departments to disclose requested information. A veto can be challenged in law.

👁 Case study

In March 2015 the Supreme Court upheld a Court of Appeal decision which paved the way for publication of letters to government Ministers from the Prince of Wales. The Court of Appeal had unanimously ruled the previous year that Attorney General Dominic Grieve had 'no good reason' for using his ministerial veto to override the decision of an independent tribunal, chaired by a High Court judge, in favour of disclosure of this royal correspondence. The content of the letters had been the subject of an FoI request by *Guardian* journalist Rob Evans. Mr Grieve had said his use of the veto was based on his view that the correspondence was undertaken as part of the Prince's 'preparation for becoming king', and that making it public could potentially damage the principle of the heir to the throne being politically neutral and so undermine his ability to fulfil his duties when king. But the Supreme Court said there was a 'fundamental composite principle' behind the Court's dismissal of the appeal— that a decision of a judicial body should be final and binding, and should not be capable of being overturned by a member of the executive (*R (on the application of Evans and another) v Attorney General* [2015] UKSC 21).

The government has since indicated that it wishes to amend the FoI Act to strengthen the veto.

The FoI Act's coverage of media organisations

The BBC, Channel 4 and S4C—public service broadcasters—were made subject to the Act, but in a limited way as disclosure provisions only apply to information they hold 'for purposes other than those of journalism, art or literature'. It does not require these broadcasters to comply with:

(1) requests attempting to reveal journalists' confidential sources;

(2) requests by rival news organisations, or by the subjects of journalistic investigations (that is, 'data subjects'), aimed at securing, before or after broadcast, material gathered in a journalistic investigation, including any footage/audio not broadcast.

The Supreme Court has ruled that that if information was held for journalistic purposes, it was exempt from disclosure even if it was also held for other purposes (*Sugar (Deceased) (Represented by Fiona Paveley) v BBC and another* [2012] UKSC 4, [2012] 1 WLR 439, [2012] 2 All ER 509). This decision marked the end of the BBC's battle over the Balen Report, an internal document which reviewed and made recommendations about its coverage of the Middle East, including best practice on matters such as impartiality.

chs. 2 and 3 explain the roles of Ipso and Ofcom

Ofcom is subject to the Act, but Ipso, which is not a public authority, is not.

Environmental information

ch. 1 explains EU directives

The Environmental Information Regulations 2004 (EIR), which came into force in 2005, require public authorities to provide information about environmental matters. They implement a European Union directive and give, in the environmental field, the public—and journalists—more powerful rights of access to information than those in the FoI Act. A public authority receiving a request for information within the scope of the EIR should automatically deal with it under the EIR rather than under the Act (ideally the request should refer to the EIR). For guidance on using the EIR, see Useful Websites at the end of this chapter.

Environmental information covers air, water, land, natural sites and living organisms—including genetically modified (GM) crops—and discharges, as well as noise and radiation. The EIR cover more bodies than the FoI Act, with fewer exemptions—for example, information about emissions cannot be withheld because of commercial confidentiality.

All bodies subject to the FoI Act are also subject to the EIR and the same 20-day deadline applies to requests for information. Privatised water and sewerage companies in England and Wales are not subject to either the Act or the EIR, although they are in Scotland.

The EIR require that public authorities must assist those requesting information.

EIR requests can be turned down on grounds of national security. But all refusals are subject to a public interest test and requests can be refused only if the public interest in non-disclosure far outweighs the public interest in disclosure. A 'reasonable' fee can be charged for EIR requests.

The EIR, which are enforced by the Information Commissioner, can be used, for example, to obtain reports of hygiene inspections at factories and restaurants as they cover information on 'the state of human health and safety, including the contamination of the food chain'.

👁 Case study

The Times used the Scottish EIR to bypass the exemption in the FoI Act to force local authorities north of the border to disclose details of lobbying by the Prince of Wales. The Scottish Information Commissioner held (Decision 039/2011, *Mr Dominic Kennedy of The Times and the Scottish Ministers*) that the newspaper had more right to the information than the Prince had to keep it quiet. The newspaper pointed out that the EIR, which were imposed by Brussels, had no opt-outs or exemptions for royalty.

▶ Legal issues in using FoI disclosures in stories

Publication of material disclosed under the FoI Act or the EIR brings no special protection against an action for defamation. The FoI Act and EIR do not confer statutory qualified privilege on such reports.

Material disclosed under either the Act or the EIR will be protected by copyright, which must be respected. If you have any doubts about copyright, consult the public authority about the status of information. In some cases copyright

chs. 21 and 22 explain defamation defences

→ glossary

ch. 29
explains
copyright
law

→ glossary

may be waived or information licensed for re-use. Copyright protects photographs, maps and diagrams, but does not protect facts as such, only the way in which they are recorded. Thus, a journalist using information from material supplied under FoI and putting it into a news story does not have to fear that factual revelations will raise copyright issues. Also, a **fair dealing** defence applies to citing some text verbatim for the purposes of reporting current events.

➡ Recap of major points

- The Freedom of Information Act 2000 gives a general right of access to information held by public authorities including government departments and local authorities.
- But there are wide-ranging exemptions and plenty of potential for delays in responding.
- The Act obliges public authorities to offer requestors advice to enable them to word their requests in such a way that they are more likely to succeed.
- The Information Commissioner hears appeals against a body's refusal to supply information. The First-tier Tribunal (Information Rights) can hear appeals against the Commissioner's decisions.
- The Environmental Information Regulations 2004 provide powerful rights of access to information in fields they cover.

((•)) Useful Websites

https://ico.org.uk
Information Commissioner's Office (ICO)

http://ico.org.uk/for_the_public/official_information
ICO guidance on advice and assistance for requestors

www.ico.org.uk/~/media/documents/library/Freedom_of_Information/Detailed_specialist_guides/the_public_interest_test.ashx
ICO guidance on the public interest test

http://foia.blogspot.com/
Campaign for Freedom of Information's UK FoI Blog

http://heatherbrooke.org/category/freedom-of-information/
Heather Brooke's articles on FoI

www.holdthefrontpage.co.uk/day/FoI/FoIindex.shtml
Holdthefrontpage stories on journalists using the FoI Act

www.gov.uk/government/uploads/system/uploads/attachment_data/file/235286/0033.pdf
Code of Practice for public authorities on FoI requests

www.justice.gov.uk/downloads/information-access-rights/foi/code-of-practice-datasets.pdf
  Code of Practice on release of datasets

www.opsi.gov.uk/Acts/acts2000/ukpga_20000036_en_1/
  Freedom of Information Act

https://ico.org.uk/media/for-organisations/documents/1151/datasets-foi-guidance.pdf
  ICO guidance on datasets

https://ico.org.uk/for-organisations/guide-to-the-environmental-information-regulations/what-are-the-eir/
  ICO guidance to public authorities on EIR

http://Folman.com
  Blog written by an FoI practitioner, including a useful guide on making FoI requests

31

Other information rights and access to meetings

Chapter summary

The public and journalists have rights to information under various laws, most notably as regards the workings of local government. These rights can be used to get policy documents from public bodies and to ensure journalists can report important meetings. For some types of material the laws are better than the Freedom of Information Act 2000 (see previous chapter), as they offer quicker rights to obtain copies of or inspect documents. Because there is much detail in these laws, a longer version of this chapter is provided on www.mcnaes.com.

Local government

Local government is a major source of stories and should be subjected to rigorous scrutiny by journalists. But devolution means that at present journalists' and citizens' rights to access to information from principal authorities differs in England and Wales.

Authorities fall into two categories. Principal authorities include county councils, district councils, London boroughs, the London Assembly and fire authorities.

The others—parish councils and community councils—are not principal authorities.

Principal authorities

The Local Government Act 2000, which has since been amended by the Localism Act 2011, reformed the way authorities are run, introducing new models of 'cabinet style' local government, of which two survive—a leader (elected by council members) and cabinet, and a directly elected mayor and cabinet. Access to information from principal authorities which have not adopted these models remains governed by the Local Government Act 1972, as amended by the Local Government (Access to Information) Act 1985. Law in these Acts is explained later in this chapter.

Some details of the rights of journalists and the public to attend and report on meetings of local authorities and some other public bodies are available in the guidance *Open and Accountable Local Government* published by the Department for Communities and Local Government—see Useful Websites at the end of this chapter.

See too the longer version of this chapter on www.mcnaes.com for fuller details of these rights, and about the laws which require parish councils and community councils to hold public meetings and provide information. Such laws as regards Police and Crime Commissioners, health authorities and NHS trusts are discussed later in the chapter.

▶ The Local Government Act 2000

Regulations covering access to information under the 2000 Act are contained in statutory instruments and apply to unitary authorities, London borough councils, county councils and district councils in England operating executive arrangements under the Act.

The main regulations are now provided for in the Local Authorities (Executive Arrangements) (Meetings and Access to Information) (England) Regulations 2012 and the Openness of Local Government Bodies Regulations 2014, which now allow journalists and anyone else reporting on authorities in England do so by filming or recording meetings, and by live blogging and tweeting from them. In Wales, journalists need the permission of the local authority, although the Welsh government is actively encouraging policies of openness. References in this chapter are to the 2012 Regulations, unless otherwise stated.

When bodies must meet in public

Meetings of decision-making bodies—local authority executives and their committees—must be open to the public (regulation 3).

But the public may be excluded if it is likely that:

- confidential information would be disclosed in breach of the obligation of confidence;
- the decision-making body concerned passes a resolution to exclude the public during an item in which disclosure of exempt information is likely—the resolution must describe the exempt information concerned; or
- it is necessary to maintain orderly conduct or prevent misbehaviour at a meeting.

The public may only be excluded under the first two for the part or parts of the meeting during which confidential or exempt information is likely to be disclosed.

Confidential information

'Confidential information' is information provided to the local authority by a government department upon terms (however expressed) forbidding its disclosure to the public, or information the disclosure of which to the public is prohibited by or under any enactment or a court order.

Exempt information

Exempt information in England is information relating to a variety of subjects, including, for example: an employee or office holder of the authority, or of the magistrates' courts or probationary committee; a particular council tenant or applicant for council services or grants; care of children; an individual's financial or business affairs; and labour relations matters between the council and its employees.

Any part of an agenda, report or other document which contains exempt information does not have to be made available for inspection.

Exempt information in Wales is similar, but less wide-ranging.

The fact that exempt information is to be discussed at a meeting does not impose an obligation on the authority to discuss it in private.

ch. 30 explains the FoI Act

The categories of exempt information are wider than the categories of information which an authority is not obliged to disclose under the Freedom of Information Act 2000—so exempt material might be obtained through an FoI request.

Notice of public meetings

A decision-making body must display a notice giving the time and place of a public meeting at its offices, and on its website, at least five clear days before the meeting or, if it is convened at shorter notice, when it is convened (regulation 6).

Access to agendas and reports

A copy of the agenda and every report for a meeting must be available for public inspection at the authority's office and on its website (regulation 7). Copies of reports do not have to include material relating only to matters to be dealt with in private.

Any document which has to be available for inspection by the public must be available for at least five clear days before the meeting or, if the meeting is convened at shorter notice, when it is convened.

If all or part of a report for a public meeting is not available for public inspection, it must be marked 'not for publication' and say that it contains confidential information, or exempt information, which must be described.

Journalists and members of the public who ask must, on paying for postage, copying or other necessary charge for transmission, be supplied with:

- a copy of the agenda and each report for a public meeting;
- the further statements or details necessary to indicate the nature of the items in the agenda; and
- if the proper officer thinks fit, in the case of an item, a copy of any other document supplied to the executive's members in connection with it.

Regulation 20 says this does not authorise the disclosure of confidential information in breach of the obligation of confidence, or of anything likely to contain exempt information or the advice of a political adviser or assistant.

Notification of private meetings

A decision-making body planning to meet in private must give at least 28 days' notice of its intention by publishing a notification explaining the reasons at its offices and on its website (regulation 5).

It must publish a further notice at least five days before the meeting takes place, with a statement of the reasons for holding it in private, details of any representations made about why it should be in public and a statement of its response.

A decision-making body which wishes to hold a meeting so quickly that it cannot comply with these requirements must obtain consent to do so from the chair or deputy chair of a relevant scrutiny committee or, in their absence, the authority's chair or deputy chair.

Key decisions

Special rules apply when a 'key decision' is to be made—this is covered by regulations 9 and 10. A key decision is one which is likely:

- to result in the authority incurring spending or making savings which are significant having regard to its budget for the relevant service or function; or
- to be significant in terms of its effects on communities living or working in an area comprising two or more wards or electoral divisions.

Publicity in connection with key decisions

At least 28 days before a key decision is made, a local authority must publish a document giving details about it. Regulation 10 says this must specify, among other things, the issue to be decided and a list of the documents submitted to the decision maker for consideration in relation to it.

If the public might be excluded from the meeting at which the issue is to be discussed, or documents relating to the decision do not have to be disclosed to the public, the notification must contain particulars of the matter, but cannot contain any confidential exempt information or details of advice from a political adviser or assistant.

If the required notification period for a meeting to make a key decision is impractical, the decision may only be made five clear days after various authority members have been notified of the fact in writing, and a copy of that notification has been made available for public inspection and published on the authority's website.

For more detail of regulations 9 and 10, see the longer version of this chapter on www.mcnaes.com.

Documents that must be made available after a meeting

Regulation 12 requires a written statement to be produced 'as soon as reasonably practicable' after a public or private meeting at which an executive decision is made. It must include a record of the decision and the reasons for it.

An executive decision made by an individual or a key decision made by an officer must be recorded similarly.

A media organisation which requests copies of any of the documents available for public inspection must be supplied with them on payment of postage, copying 'or other necessary charge for transmission' (regulation 14).

▌ Register of interests

The Localism Act 2011 places a duty on councillors to enter certain personal interests on a publicly available register. Failure to disclose interests is a criminal offence punishable by an unlimited fine and possible disqualification from membership of the authority for up to five years.

! Remember your rights

If you encounter someone who has custody of a document which must be available for public inspection but who intentionally obstructs you exercising a right to inspect or make a copy of it, or refuses to supply a copy of it, you can warn them that they are committing an offence punishable by a fine of up to £200 under section 100H(4) of the Local Government Act 1972 and under regulation 22 of the Local Authorities (Executive Arrangements) (Meetings and Access to Information) (England) Regulations 2012.

▌ Copyright and defamation

ch. 29 explains copyright law

Regulation 21(3) and (4) of the 2012 Regulations say any member of the public may reproduce any document supplied to him/her or made available for public inspection under the Regulations, or provide commentary on it, in any publicly

available medium. This will not infringe **copyright** in the document as long as →glossary
the local authority is the copyright holder. But this regulation does not authorise
infringement of anyone else's copyright.

On defamation, it extends the protection of qualified privilege to the publication
of any defamatory matter contained in any document required by the Regulations
to be open to inspection by the public and supplied to, or available for inspection
by, members of the public or supplied for a newspaper's benefit.

✳ Remember

If a local authority holds a meeting in private under any of the legislation referred
to, a defamatory media report of the discussion in such meetings and of documents
considered in them, if leaked unofficially to the media, would not be protected by
qualified privilege under Schedule 1 to the Defamation Act 1996.

Media coverage of an official statement issued to journalists about a meeting
held in private will be privileged under the 1996 Act if the defence's requirements
are met.

Media coverage of the public proceedings of local authorities, whether in full
council, committees or sub-committees, and of minutes, agendas, reports or
other documents officially made available to journalists or the public, will also
be privileged.

 Ch. 21, pp. 286–291, Qualified privilege, explains the requirements of this defence.

▌ The Local Government (Access to Information) Act 1985

The Local Government (Access to Information) Act 1985 predates the introduction of cabinet-style councils. Although the 1985 Act, as a major reform, tends to
be referred to in its own right, the reform was achieved by it inserting new parts—
Part VA and Schedule 12A—into the Local Government Act 1972, containing the
requirements set out in the following passages (which include later amendments).

When meetings must be in public

All meetings of principal authorities, their committees and their sub-committees
must be open to the public unless dealing with confidential or exempt information
(but the position about working parties and advisory or study groups, which may
in effect act as sub-committees without the name, is unclear in this law).

Principal authorities, their committees and their sub-committees must exclude
the public when confidential information is likely to be disclosed.

A local authority may exclude the public when disclosure of exempt information is likely by passing a resolution, which must state the part of the meeting to which the exclusion applies and describe the category of exempt information (the categories are in Schedule 12A to the 1972 Act).

While the meeting is open to the public, 'duly accredited representatives' of newspapers or news agencies must, under section 100(6)(c) of the 1972 Act, be afforded reasonable facilities for taking their report.

Documents that must be made available

A newspaper or news agency must on request (and on payment of postage or other transmission charge) be supplied with (a) agendas, (b) further particulars necessary to indicate the nature of the items on the agenda and (c) if the 'proper officer' thinks fit, copies of any other documents supplied to council members, although he/she may exclude from what he/she sends out any report, or part of a report, relating to items not likely to be discussed in public.

Late items, reports and supplementary information can be admitted at the meeting only if the chair regards the matter as urgent and specifies the reason for the urgency.

Copies of agendas and of any report for a meeting of a council must be open to public inspection at least five working days before the meeting (except for items not likely to be discussed in public). Where a meeting is called at shorter notice they must be open to inspection when the meeting is convened.

Fire authorities and joint bodies

The 1972 Act also applies to fire authorities, meetings of joint consultative committees of health and local authorities, and to some joint boards.

! Remember your rights

There are other rights to inspect council records—for example, planning applications. For details, see the longer version of this chapter on www.mcnaes.com.

▌ Parish and town councils, and Water Act bodies

The Public Bodies (Admission to Meetings) Act 1960 sets out information and access rights relating to parish, town and community councils, parish meetings and meetings of bodies set up under the Water Act 1989—regional and local flood defence committees, regional rivers advisory committees, salmon and freshwater fisheries advisory committees, and customer service committees. The longer version of this chapter on www.mcnaes.com explains these rights.

▌ Access to financial accounts

Journalists often miss golden opportunities to find local authority stories by using the rights now granted under section 26 of the Local Audit and Accountability Act 2014 and the Accounts and Audit (England) Regulations 2011. 'Local authorities' includes fire and civil defence authorities.

Section 26 of the Act says 'any persons interested' may—in a period of 20 full working days before a date appointed by the local authority's auditor—inspect its accounts and 'all books, deeds, contracts, bills, vouchers and receipts and other documents relating to those records', and make copies.

! Remember your rights

The 2014 Act makes it a criminal offence for any officer or councillor to obstruct local taxpayers or electors exercising their rights to view and copy the (non-exempt) material. Authority press officers who try to involve themselves in the actual inspection should be warned off. For detail of these and other inspection rights to probe an authority's financial matters, including expenses paid to councillors, see the longer version of this chapter on www.mcnaes.com.

▌ Health authorities and NHS trusts

Admission to meetings of local health authorities and NHS trusts, and rights to their agendas, are subject to the Public Bodies (Admission to Meetings) Act 1960.

Department of Health guidance to these bodies in 1998 (Health Service Circular no. 1998/207) said the government was 'committed to ending what it sees as excessive secrecy in decision making in public bodies', and that although authorities and trusts could exclude press and public in the public interest under the terms of the 1960 Act, they were expected to conduct their business in public in as open a manner as possible.

The 1960 Act gives the same rights of admission to any committee of a health authority consisting of all members of the authority.

The Health and Social Care Act 2001 gave new powers to overview and scrutinise committees of those local authorities with social services responsibilities (county councils, London borough councils, unitary authorities), and these are subject to similar access to information provisions as other committees covered by Local Government (Access to Information) Act 1985, explained earlier.

But extended exemptions apply, which go further than the exemptions in the 1985 Act by exempting also information on (1) a person providing or applying to provide NHS services, (2) an employee of such a person or (3) information relating to a person's health. Minutes, agendas and reports are open to public inspection for only three years, and background papers for only two years.

❚ Police and Crime Commissioners

Police and Crime Commissioners must, under provision in sections 5 and 12 of the Police Reform and Social Responsibility Act 2011, publish a Police and Crime Plan and annual reports. Financial and other information, including a register of interests, must be published, as specified in the Elected Local Policing Bodies (Specified Information) Order 2011.

((•))
see Useful
Websites at
the end of
this chapter
for the
Order and
Regulations

Police and crime panels

Much of the law on access to information referred to in this chapter also applies to the police and crime panels in each police area—see the Police and Crime Panels (Application of Local Authority Enactments) Regulations 2012.

❚ Quangos

Many day-to-day services to the public which were administered by bodies on which representatives of the public served have become semi-independent agencies with managing bodies staffed by appointees rather than representatives.

The term 'quango' (quasi-autonomous non-governmental organisation) describes taxpayer-funded non-elected public bodies operating outside the Civil Service. Generally, there is no right of access to meetings of quangos, although there is a right to information to most of them under the FoI Act, explained in ch. 30.

✳ Remember

The public must be admitted to meetings of local magistrates advisory committees at least once a year. For detail, see the longer version this chapter on www.mcnaes.com.

➡ Recap of major points

- People have rights to other information from local authorities, such as annual budget figures and agendas, as well as rights to attend meetings.
- In certain circumstances authorities have the right to withhold documents or to deny public access to meetings.
- Laws giving rights to examine accounts can be very good sources of stories, provided the journalist knows where to look.
- There are rights to attend the meetings of health authorities and these bodies are required to publish each year their performance in key areas of health provision.

((•)) Useful Websites

www.gov.uk/government/uploads/system/uploads/attachment_data/file/343182/140812_Openness_Guide.pdf

> Department for Communities and Local Government guidance, *Open and Accountable Local Government*

www.legislation.gov.uk/uksi/2012/2089/contents/made

> Local Authorities (Executive Arrangements) (Meetings and Access to Information) (England) Regulations 2012

www.legislation.gov.uk/uksi/2012/2479/article/1/made

> Elected Local Policing Bodies (Specified Information) Order 2011 and amendments

www.gov.uk/government/uploads/system/uploads/attachment_data/file/143836/publishing-information.pdf

> Government guidance to Police and Crime Commissioners on publishing information

www.legislation.gov.uk/uksi/2012/2734/made

> Police and Crime Panels (Application of Local Authority Enactments) Regulations 2012 and their Explanatory Notes

32

Reporting elections

Chapter summary

The Representation of the People Act 1983 makes it a criminal offence to make or publish false statements about election candidates. There are restrictions on publishing 'exit polls'. Broadcast journalists must maintain impartiality in coverage of elections and referendums.

▶ False statements about election candidates

Section 106 of the Representation of the People Act 1983 makes it a criminal offence to:

- make or publish a false statement of fact about the personal character or conduct of an election candidate, if the purpose is to affect how many votes he/she will get.

To constitute such an offence, the falsity must be expressed as if it were a fact, as distinct from a statement which is clearly merely a comment or opinion about the candidate. It is a defence for someone accused of publishing such a false statement to show that he/she had reasonable grounds for believing when the statement was published that it was true and did at that time believe it was true (even if it turns out to be untrue).

Section 106 (5) makes it an offence:

- to publish a false claim that a candidate has withdrawn from the election, if the publisher knows it to be false and published it to promote or procure the election of another candidate.

Breach of section 106 is punishable by a fine for which there is no specified limit. If the publisher is a company, its directors can be convicted. The law is to deter 'dirty tricks' by those campaigning in elections, or by their supporters, and is not aimed specifically at the media.

👁 Case study

In 2010 Labour MP Phil Woolas lost his seat when his election was declared void after he was convicted of illegal practices under section 106 by publishing election addresses containing statements of fact about the character and conduct of a Liberal Democrat candidate Robert Elwyn Watkins—involving where he lived, his attitude to Muslim extremists and his election expenses—which he had no reasonable grounds for believing were true and did not believe were true (*Robert Elwyn James Watkins v Philip James Woolas* [2010] EWHC 2702 (QB)).

The ban in criminal law on such false statements applies from the time formal notice is given that an election is to take place until the election ends. For local government elections, this period is about five weeks. For national parliamentary elections, it begins with the date of the dissolution of Parliament or any earlier time at which Her Majesty's intention to dissolve Parliament is announced.

If the false statement is defamatory, the publisher may—of course—also face a libel action. But the criminal sanction in the 1983 Act enables quicker remedial action, in that a candidate who can prove a **prima facie** case that he/she has been traduced by such a false statement can obtain a court **injunction** preventing its repetition, whereas the legal rule against **prior restraint** means it is harder to get an injunction in a libel action, which could take months to be settled or resolved at trial. The 1983 Act also prohibits such false statements even if they are not defamatory. A journalist who in 1997 published false allegations on the internet that an election candidate was a homosexual was fined £250 under the Act. An inaccurate statement that someone is homosexual is not, in itself, defamatory. But in the context of an election, it could cost a candidate votes if, for example, voters with anti-gay religious beliefs decide, because of the false statement, not to support that candidate.

→ glossary

→ glossary

→ glossary

see ch.
19, p. 259,
Changing
standards,
on whether
it is
defamatory
to call
someone
'gay'

▌ Defamation dangers during elections

Election candidates and their supporters may make defamatory allegations about rivals, using, for example, terms such 'racist', 'fascist' and 'liar'.

A media organisation which publishes them may be successfully sued for defamation if it has no defence. The media has no specific statutory privilege for publishing election material produced by candidates or what they say. But qualified privilege protects fair and accurate reports of public meetings and press conferences, if all requirements of that defence are met.

 Ch. 19 has definitions of defamatory statements and ch. 21 explains qualified privilege.

✳ Remember

Journalists reporting speeches by extremist candidates should remember that such speakers, and reports of their speeches, are subject to the laws against stirring up hatred, including on racial and religious grounds. See the www.mcnaes.com chapter on hate crimes.

▶ Election advertisements

In election law, only an election candidate or his/her agent may incur any expenses relating to his/her campaign, including for publishing an advertisement. It is an offence for anyone else to pay for such an advertisement unless the election agent authorises him/her to do so, in writing. This stops well-wishers from putting advertisements in newspapers on behalf of candidates without their express authority.

▶ Broadcasters' duty to be impartial

Section 6 of the Broadcasting Code has detailed rules on how broadcast output must be impartial in election and referendum periods. Ofcom has fined several radio stations after presenters or others made partial declarations of support for political candidates or parties. The BBC is not subject to this section but has similar provision in its Editorial Guidelines.

 See also ch. 3 on impartiality and Useful Websites at the end of this chapter.

In May 2014 Ofcom warned broadcasters of the need to ensure impartiality in reporting on the Scottish independence referendum period, which started at the end of that month. An academic study published earlier had claimed that the mainstream TV coverage of the first year of the independence referendum campaigns had not been fair or balanced and seemed to have damaged the 'Yes' campaign.

see also the
Bangla TV
impartiality
case study
in ch. 3, p. 30

👁 Case study

In 2008 Ofcom fined *Talksport* radio £20,000 for breaching the impartiality requirement after presenter James Whale directly encouraged listeners to vote for Conservative candidate Boris Johnson in the London mayoral elections and criticised Labour candidate Ken Livingstone (*Ofcom Broadcast Bulletin*, No. 123, 8 December 2008).

Among the rules in section 6 of the Broadcasting Code are that:

- due weight must be given to the coverage of major parties during the election period, and broadcasters must also consider giving appropriate coverage to other parties and independent candidates with significant views and perspectives (rule 6.2);
- if a candidate takes part in an item about his/her particular constituency, or electoral area, then candidates of each of the major parties must be offered the opportunity to take part (rule 6.9);
- broadcasters must offer the opportunity to take part in constituency or electoral area reports and discussions to all candidates within the constituency or electoral area representing parties with previous significant electoral support or where there is evidence of significant current support, including any such independent candidate (rule 6.10); and
- any constituency or electoral area report or discussion after the close of nominations must include a list of all candidates standing, giving first names, surnames and the name of the parties they represent or, if a candidate is standing independently, the fact that he/she is an independent. This must be conveyed in sound and/or vision. Where a constituency report on a radio service is repeated on several occasions in the same day, the full list need only be broadcast on one occasion, but the audience should be directed to where the list can be seen—for example, a website (rule 6.11).

▌Exit polls

The term 'exit poll' describes any kind of survey in which people who have voted are asked which candidate and/or political party they voted for. When conducted scientifically, such surveys of people leaving polling stations can often produce data accurately predicting an election result, hours before it is officially declared. A number of democratic nations, including the UK, restrict when such data/ predictions can be published. The rationale, disputed by some, is that publishing the information, or predictions based on it, before polls close could skew the election result. The concern is that telling people who have yet to vote which candidate/party seems likely to win, with that information being apparently soundly based on votes already cast, could cause people to change their original voting intentions—for example, by switching to support another candidate who appears, from the exit poll data, to have a better chance of victory, or deciding not to vote at all because the exit poll data shows that their favoured candidate cannot win or will win so easily that no further votes are needed. These possible effects are seen as potential contamination of the democratic process, in that: (a) the later group of voters will have made choices on data not available to those who voted earlier; and (b) the data, and any prediction apparently based on them, might be inaccurate or, in the worst cases, might have been falsified to influence voting.

Section 66A of the Representation of the People Act 1983, as inserted by the 2000 Act of the same title, makes it a criminal offence to:

- publish, before a poll is closed, any statement about the way in which voters have voted in that election which is, or might reasonably be taken to be, based on information given by voters after they have voted; and

- publish, before a poll is closed, any forecast—including any estimate—of that election result, if the forecast is based on exit poll information from voters or might reasonably be taken to be based on it.

So, for example, it would be illegal to broadcast, or put on a website, before polling stations closed, the statement 'Fifty-five per cent of the people we have questioned say they have voted Conservative today'.

This law applies to parliamentary, council and Welsh Assembly elections, and to by-elections. It applies in respect of exit polls conducted to focus on an individual constituency or ward, or on voting nationally, and either does or can be made to apply to various types of referendum. Publication of material in breach of section 66A leaves the publisher liable to a fine for which there is no specified limit or a jail term of up to six months. Publication of exit polls during polling for European parliamentary elections is also prohibited under the 2004 Regulations.

It is perfectly legal to publish, at any time, opinion poll data on voting intentions which was gathered before voting begins, because the information was not based on how people say they actually voted. Also, it is legal to report the results of exit polls, and any forecast based on them, as soon as polling has finally closed, as TV programmes frequently do. But it is not always accurate now to talk of 'an election day'. For example, experiments to encourage more people to vote may mean that in some places voting takes place over several days. It will be an offence to publish an exit poll, or forecast apparently based on it, during any of the polling days, until the polls close on the final day.

◉ Case study

During elections for the European Parliament in June 2004, *The Times* published an opinion poll which had asked people how they had voted in areas using all-postal ballots. The Electoral Commission, the independent elections watchdog, said this amounted to an exit poll and referred the matter to the Crown Prosecution Service, but later reported that the CPS had concluded that it would not be appropriate to take any further action (Electoral Commission report on European Parliamentary elections, 21 December 2004).

Regulatory codes for broadcast journalists have, for some time, placed similar controls on the publication of exit polls, and indeed go further. Rule 6.5 of the Broadcasting Code states: 'Broadcasters may not publish the results of any opinion poll on polling day itself until the election or referendum poll closes. (For European Parliamentary elections, this applies until all polls throughout the European Union have closed.)' Rule 6.4 bans discussion and analysis of election and referendum issues during polling, a period which begins when polling stations open. This rule does not apply to any poll conducted entirely by post.

BBC Editorial Guidelines take the same approach.

Election counts

Journalists, including photographers and TV crews, attend election counts so declarations of the result can be quickly aired. There is no statutory right to attend a count—admission is at the discretion of the returning officer, who has legal responsibility for security and procedures at the count. The Electoral Commission's media handbook for the 2015 General Election said members of the media wishing to attend a count had to contact the relevant local authority communications department to request permission to attend the count and declaration of the results.

👁 Case study

In the 2010 General Election, the media were initially banned from the count at Staffordshire Moorlands and told by council officials running it that they had to stay in a separate room, apparently because of fears that their presence in the counting hall would be disruptive. The ban was lifted after lawyers for the *Staffordshire Sentinel, Leek Post and Times* and the BBC wrote to the acting returning officer protesting that it was undemocratic and a breach of the right to freedom of expression under Article 10 of the European Convention on Human Rights. The *Sentinel* also planned to get round the ban by having three staff members accredited as 'observers' at the count (*Media Lawyer*, 6 May 2010).

Registering as an observer takes 10 days, and it seems observers cannot be barred from a count—see Useful Websites at the end of this chapter.

The returning officer at the high-profile by-election at Oldham East and Saddleworth in January 2011, which followed Phil Woolas's removal as MP—see the earlier case study—refused to allow journalists into the count, despite protests from the BBC and Press Association, saying there would be too many of them to accommodate comfortably. Journalists had to stay on a balcony overlooking the hall, with any communication with candidates, agents and others being 'facilitated' by Oldham Council press officers.

➡ Recap of major points

- Once an election has been called it is a criminal offence to publish a false statement about the personal character or conduct of a candidate for the purpose of affecting the number of votes he/she gets.

- It is an offence to publish before the end of polling any data obtained in exit polls on how people have voted or any prediction of the election result based on such data.

- The Broadcasting Code and the BBC Editorial Guidelines require broadcasters to follow certain practices to ensure impartiality in coverage of elections and referendums, and restrict use of opinion (including exit) polls.

((•)) Useful Websites

http://stakeholders.ofcom.org.uk/binaries/broadcast/code-july-15/Ofcom_Broadcast_Code_July_2015.pdf
   Broadcasting Code—see section 6, on elections and referendums

www.bbc.co.uk/guidelines/editorialguidelines/edguide/politics/broadcastingdur.shtml
   BBC Editorial Guidelines on elections, opinion polls, surveys, questionnaires, votes and straw polls

www.electoralcommission.org.uk/
   Electoral Commission

www.electoralcommission.org.uk/elections/electoral_observers
   Electoral Commission guidance on observers

33

Official secrets

Chapter summary

Official secrets legislation protects national security. It has not been used in recent years to prosecute journalists, but has been used to jail civil servants and others who have given journalists sensitive information. Police could search the home and newsroom of a journalist who is thought to have breached this law, seize their records and try to identify the source. There is no public interest defence for anyone facing prosecution.

▌ Introduction

The Official Secrets Acts of 1911 and 1989 protect national security, and can be used to enforce the duty of confidentiality owed to the UK state by Crown servants or employees of companies doing military and other sensitive work. Crown servants include civil servants, members of the armed services, the police and civilians working for them. The Acts impose a similar duty on members of the security and intelligence services.

Part of the legislation was designed to punish those who spy or plan to spy on the UK for foreign powers. Royal Navy Petty Officer Edward Devenney, aged 30, was jailed for eight years in 2012 when he admitted breaching the Official Secrets Act 1911. Aggrieved by failure to gain promotion, he planned to pass code material for NATO communications to the Russian embassy and rang it, but was arrested by MI5 (Metropolitan Police press release, 12 December 2012).

Official secrets legislation can also punish the leaking of sensitive information to a journalist or a member of the public. Publishing such material makes it available to hostile powers, terrorists and criminals, and can embarrass the UK's allies—for example, by disclosing diplomatic correspondence.

ch. 1, p. 9,
High offices
in law,
explains the
Attorney
General's
role

Using the law to punish leaks is controversial. Attorney Generals have approved prosecutions of Crown servants and others who, on grounds of conscience, leaked information to the media to throw light on controversial government policies. In such cases the media and others have questioned whether the prosecution was intended to protect vital state secrets or to stifle debate about matters embarrassing to the government. A journalist seen as being an accomplice to a leak could be prosecuted. Journalists and their editors could also be prosecuted for circulating or publishing such information. As the law is complex, there is a longer version of this chapter on www.mcnaes.com.

◗ The law's consequences for journalists

As this book went to press no journalist had been successfully prosecuted, let alone jailed, under official secrets legislation for many years.

👁 Case study

In 2013 Edward Snowden leaked to journalists material he copied when he was a contractor with the US National Security Agency. After travelling to Hong Kong, Snowden publicly revealed he was the leaker, saying he wanted to expose the extent of the USA's and UK's secret surveillance of the world's communications systems. *The Guardian*, drawing on this material, revealed some detail of the UK's secret cooperation with the USA in this surveillance, including emails. *The Times* quoted a former head of the UK's surveillance base GCHQ as saying that it had to be assumed that Snowden's travels meant UK intelligence files had been hacked from his computer by China and Russia, which was 'the most catastrophic loss to British intelligence ever'. But by late 2013 *The Guardian* had not been charged with breaching official secrets law for receiving or publishing some of Snowden's material, although a threat of legal action meant that the newspaper complied with a demand by government officials that they should destroy computer hard drives containing copies of files he leaked (*The Guardian*, 10 June, 19 and 20 August 2013; *The Times*, 11 October 2013).

See the chapter on Terrorism and the effect of counter-terrorism law on www.mcnaes.com for David Miranda's detention in the Snowden saga.

But although officialdom is reluctant to use official secrets law to prosecute journalists, for reasons discussed later, journalists must know about the law to be ready to protect confidential sources of information. The journalist might not be jailed for his/her story—but the source might. Police seeking to identify the source of leaked information could raid a journalist's newsroom, office or home. The journalist might be arrested and threatened with prosecution.

Sources are generally dealt with more severely than journalists. In 2007 a former civil servant, David Keogh, and Leo O'Connor, who had worked as an MP's researcher, were jailed for six months and three months respectively for leaking a memo to the *Daily Mirror* about a conversation US President George Bush and UK Prime Minister Tony Blair had about the Iraq war.

 The longer version of this chapter on www.mcnaes.com provides detail of the above case, others in which sources were jailed and how a journalist's home was raided by police. Ch. 34 in this book explains police powers to search.

👁 Case study

The Official Secrets Acts continue to be cited when officialdom wants to stop police 'whistleblowers' speaking to the media. In 2015 the *Grimsby Telegraph* reported from an unnamed police source that, after a 'restructure' in staffing, on some 3am–7am shifts, there were only four officers working in the whole of North East Lincolnshire. Humberside Police and Crime Commissioner Matthew Grove denied the claim, telling the paper: 'If any police officers are telling you the number of officers on duty, they are breaking the Official Secrets Act and becoming criminals.' *The Times* described his comment as 'ridiculous'. Mr Grove later said: 'I signed the Official Secrets Act on taking office as Commissioner, and felt that to provide sensitive information such as that disclosed would breach the principles of the Act.' He added: 'I would never try to "gag" police officers from giving their views as has been implied, but ask them to consider the wider impact on the public and their colleagues before they do' (*Grimsby Telegraph*, 15 May and 5 June 2015; *Press Gazette*, 4 June 2015).

Reluctance to prosecute journalists

The reluctance of officialdom to use official secrets law against UK journalists is partly an effect of the legislation. The 1989 Act contains defences which journalists can use, but sources cannot—for example, a journalist has a defence that disclosure of the information was not 'damaging' to state interests.

John Wadham, former director of the civil rights organisation Liberty, has said of the lack of prosecutions of journalists:

❝ It is partly because governments don't like to be seen to be trying to put journalists in prison and partly because juries are less sympathetic to civil servants—who are employed to keep their mouths shut, who are aware of the rules but break them, and who breach the trust with employers and colleagues—compared with journalists, who are paid to find things out and publish them. 🗩🗩

 See the longer version of this chapter on www.mcnaes.com about how UK governments have used injunctions to stop publication of leaked 'official secrets'. See too ch. 25, p. 322, Breach of confidence and official secrets, about the *Spycatcher* case.

▌ The 1911 Act

Section 1 of the 1911 Act is concerned with spying, but journalists need to know about it. Section 1 makes it an arrestable offence, carrying a penalty of up to 14 years' imprisonment, to do any of the following 'for any purpose prejudicial to the safety or interests of the state':

(a) approach, inspect, pass over, be in the neighbourhood of or enter any prohibited place (see below);

(b) make any sketch, plan, model or note that might be or is intended to be useful to an enemy;

(c) obtain, collect, record or communicate to any person any information that might be or is intended to be useful to an enemy.

Offences under (c) are most relevant for journalists. Section 3 of the 1911 Act gives a lengthy and wide-ranging definition of a 'prohibited place' as including 'any work or defence, arsenal, naval or air force establishment or station, factory, dockyard, mine, minefield, camp, ship, or aircraft', as well as 'any telegraph, telephone, wireless or signal station, or office' when any such property is used by the state. Statutory instruments added British Nuclear Fuels plc and Atomic Energy Authority sites to the list of prohibited places.

The media must remember that taking photos or gathering information outside or near prohibited places, even for routine news coverage of events such as peace protests, could be held to be a breach of the Act if, for example, material gathered and published jeopardises security at a defence base.

▌ The 1989 Act—the journalist's position

The 1989 Act defines offences of disclosure by reference to various classes of information. These include information about: security and intelligence; defence; international relations; official investigations into crime—for example, by police or other agencies; official phone-tapping and interception of letters or other communications; prison and custody facilities; and matters entrusted in confidence to other states or international organisations.

Section 5 of the 1989 Act says a person—for our purposes, a journalist—commits an offence by disclosing without lawful authority information protected by the Act, knowing or having reasonable cause to believe that it is protected against disclosure, if he/she receives it from a Crown servant or government contractor either without lawful authority or in confidence, or receives it from someone else who received it in confidence from such a person.

 See the version of this chapter on www.mcnaes.com for more detail of what must be proved.

Damage test but no public interest defence

Though the 1989 Act can catch journalists and members of the public, it is directed particularly at security service members, other Crown servants and government contractors. The degree of damage (by disclosure) to state interests necessary for conviction under the Act varies according to the class of information and the category of person accused. The damage alleged to have occurred could be, for example, to the capacity of the armed forces to carry out certain duties or to British relations with another state.

There is no public interest defence in official secrets cases—and information can be classed as secret even if it has been published previously.

Breaching the 1989 Act is punishable by a jail term of up to two years and/or a fine.

▌ The public and media may be excluded from secrets trials

Section 8 of the Official Secrets Act 1920 allows the public and media to be excluded from secrets trials when publishing evidence would be 'prejudicial to the national safety'.

▌ Defence and Security Media Advisory Notice system

In 2015 what was the Defence Press and Broadcasting Advisory Committee was reformed to become the Defence and Security Media Advisory (DSMA) Committee. The Committee is, as its predecessor was, the head of a joint government/media system through which the media can get specific guidance on how to avoid inadvertent disclosure of information damaging to the UK's national security and defence. It also has five standing 'notices' giving general guidance. These are widely known as 'D-Notices' (defence notices) but are now officially known as 'DSMA-Notices'.

((•))
see Useful Websites at the end of this chapter to read the DSMA-Notices

These five standing DSMA-Notices cover:

(1) military operations, plans and capabilities;

(2) nuclear and non-nuclear weapons, defence equipment and counter-terrorism equipment;

(3) ciphers and secure communications;

(4) identification of sensitive installations and home addresses;

(5) UK security and intelligence services, and special forces.

The system is based on voluntary self-censorship by the media. Editors who consult the DSMA-Notice secretary sometimes decide to limit what is published and sometimes publish information that they might otherwise have left out. The DSMA Committee has no statutory enforcement powers.

 See the longer version of this chapter on www.mcnaes.com for further details about the DSMA-Notice system, including its evolution as a reform after *The Guardian* decided not to contact the former committee before publishing the first tranche of material leaked by Edward Snowden.

➡ Recap of major points

- Official secrets law is complex and frequently controversial. There is a longer version of this chapter on www.mcnaes.com.

- This law protects national security and the safety of citizens, and can be used against foreign spies, terrorists or other criminals.

- But journalists say it is sometimes used to punish those who leak information which is politically embarrassing for the government and to deter the media from revealing such information.

((•)) Useful Websites

www.dsma.uk/
Defence and Security Media Advisory Notice system

www.parliament.uk/briefing-papers/SN02023
House of Commons Library, *Note on Official Secrecy*

The journalist's sources and neutrality

Chapter summary

It is an ethical principle that journalists do not disclose sources of confidential information. Journalists often have to rely on information from people whose safety or careers would be at risk if they were known as the sources. If disclosing such sources were to become commonplace, journalists' jobs would be much harder—fewer people would be willing to speak to them, and many important stories would not be revealed. Various bodies have legal powers to demand that journalists reveal where they got a story, or get journalists' phone, internet and email records. This chapter explains those powers and how journalists can protect confidential sources, and warns that investigative journalists suspected of receiving leaks of sensitive official information may be placed under secret surveillance. On some occasions when journalists refuse to hand over material or give evidence, their object is not to protect an individual source but to maintain a reputation for neutrality.

▶ Protecting your source— the ethical imperative

Clause 14 of the Editors' Code says simply: 'Journalists have a moral obligation to protect confidential sources of information.' This clause is not subject to the Code's 'public interest' exceptions and does not give any circumstance which justifies breaching it. The Editors' Code is explained in ch. 2.

((•)) See Useful Websites at the end of this chapter for the NUJ Code.

The National Union of Journalists' Code of Conduct has a similar clause. It too has no exception to the principle.

Journalists' codes in nations all round the world state the same principle. If confidential sources were not sure that journalists would protect their identities, many stories of great public interest would never be published.

The Broadcasting Code, explained in ch. 3, says in practice 7.7: 'Guarantees given to contributors, for example relating to the content of a programme, confidentiality or anonymity, should normally be honoured.'

Remember that, whether the story is local or national, if a confidential source's employer or anyone hostile to him/her discovers the source's identity, this could have life-changing consequences for him/her.

👁 Case study

In 2007 the Press Complaints Commission ruled that a newspaper breached clause 14 in an article about the possible closure of Burnley mortuary. A man who spoke to the paper on condition he was not identified was referred to in the article as 'a worker at Burnley's mortuary'. As he was one of only two people who worked there—the other was his boss—his employers identified him as the paper's source, and he was sacked for gross misconduct. The paper said the reporter had not known, and had no reason to know, that the man was one of only two employees. But the PCC said it should have established with the man how he should be described (*A man v Lancashire Telegraph*, adjudication issued 31 October 2007).

All journalists and their employers should do everything they can to protect the identity of a source who needs confidentiality. This includes ensuring that if a source is paid, the payment is untraceable, and that a source's details are not kept anywhere where they might be found or accessed, including on computers or devices such as memory sticks, or in a manner which might link them to stories done as a result of information or material they provided.

Journalists have needed to protect the identities of sources from companies or public agencies which resorted to court action when attempting to discover who leaked information.

If a court orders a journalist to identify a source, the journalist and his/her editor may take an ethical decision to defy the order. But they may then face the legal consequences—a substantial fine, or possibly a jail sentence for contempt of court, although in the past four decades no UK journalist has been jailed for such a contempt.

When deciding what to do to protect a source's identity, a journalist should anticipate what measures may be used by officialdom to discover it.

▌ Expect your phone records and emails to be accessed

Later sections of this chapter explain the powers judges have to order journalists to 'produce'—to police investigating crime—information received from or about a source, or to disclose in court proceedings the identity of a source alleged by an employer to have breached a duty of confidence by leaking information to the media.

In 2014 the UK media realised, because of events arising from the *Plebgate* case (see below), that police wanting to discover journalists' sources had for some time been using the Regulation of Investigatory Powers Act 2000 (RIPA) to get journalists' 'communications data' from phone companies and did not need—at that time—to get a judge's approval to do so.

The ease with which police had gained such data, which can show who the journalists have been communicating with—for example, numbers called, email addresses, with dates and times—made a mockery of journalists' rights to have confidential sources and to be able to argue in court that the identity of such a source should remain secret. Those rights have been established in case law— outlined in this chapter—based on Article 10 of the European Convention on Human Rights.

👁 Case study

Three police officers were sacked after details of the so-called Plebgate scandal were leaked to *The Sun* in September 2012. The newspaper was probing an incident in which MP Andrew Mitchell, then Conservative Chief Whip, had called a police officer a '****ing pleb' during an altercation at the gates of Downing Street. Metropolitan Police detectives investigating the leak obtained from phone company records a week's worth of three *Sun* journalists' phone data, including GPRS location data, and details of 90 minutes of calls to and from two of *The Sun's* newsdesk landlines. Part of the data showed a series of contacts by text and voice calls between *The Sun's* political editor Tom Newton Dunn and one of the officers later sacked. The detectives got this data using RIPA (Operation Alice Closing Report, September 2014; *The Guardian*, 21 July 2015).

The Sun took a complaint about this use of RIPA to the Investigatory Powers Tribunal, which ruled in late 2015 that the use had breached the Article 10 rights of the newspaper and three of its journalists—see the Late News section for detail.

 See ch. 17, p. 215, Tribunals in the administrative justice system, for this tribunal's role.

New 'safeguards' made law

Controversy over police use of RIPA powers led to the *Press Gazette's* campaign 'Save Our Sources' and other protests. The government responded by introducing a legal requirement for police to apply to a Crown court judge for a 'production order' if they want to obtain journalists' communications data. This requirement is in the Acquisition and Disclosure of Communications Data Code of Practice, which came into force in March 2015, governing use of RIPA. The applications must be made under a procedure detailed in the Police and Criminal Evidence Act 1985 (PACE), explained later in this chapter. This means that journalists or media organisations whose data is being sought must be given the opportunity to oppose the application in court.

But it soon emerged that Police Scotland had failed to obey the requirement five times within a couple of months when seeking journalists' sources (*Media Lawyer*, 25 November 2015).

 Check www.mcnaes.com for updates on RIPA and on the Investigatory Powers Bill 2015–16, and for RIPA background see the Additional Material for this chapter on www.mcnaes.com.

✳ Remember

A journalist who needs to protect a source's identity should, if possible, avoid contact which uses emails and other forms of electronic communication, use only untraceable pay-as-you-go mobile phones and avoid keeping any other material which might help identify the source.

◗ You may be put under surveillance

Journalists in touch with secret sources yielding information on crime or what the state considers should be secret should realise that various statutes, including RIPA, give police and other agencies the right to keep journalists personally under surveillance. They have the right to take their suspicions to the Investigatory Powers Tribunal.

👁 Case study

In 2008 *Milton Keynes Citizen* reporter Sally Murrer and Mark Kearney, a former detective accused of leaking information to her, walked free after a court ruled that prosecution evidence gathered by police bugging Mr Kearney's car was inadmissible. Mr Kearney faced charges of misconduct in public office, and Ms Murrer was charged with aiding and abetting misconduct in public office. At Kingston Crown court Judge Richard Southwell said gathering evidence by using the listening device was an unjustifiable violation of the freedom of expression rights of both, as well as a breach of Ms Murrer's right to protect her sources. The information allegedly leaked was not sensitive, let alone 'highly sensitive', and the police action could not be justified.

Ms Murrer's counsel, Gavin Millar, QC, told the court: 'One of the protections of the Strasbourg [European Court of Human Rights] law is a practical one … It is the right to be brought before a court and have a court decide whether you are required to disclose your source. What they did here was a no-no in Strasbourg terms—and a pretty big no-no' (*R v Kearney and Murrer*; *Media Lawyer*, 28 November 2008).

The Police Act 1997

Journalists in touch with secret sources yielding information on crime should know that the Police Act 1997 enables police to put them under electronic surveillance. The Act allows police to authorise themselves to break into premises and place bugs if they believe doing so will help them investigate serious crime. Sections 92–98 make entering or interfering with property or 'wireless telegraphy' lawful when a chief constable or, in urgent cases, an assistant chief constable, 'thinks it necessary … on the ground that it is likely to be of substantial value in the prevention or detection of serious crime'.

Under the Act, the government appoints a small number of Commissioners, current or former High Court judges. Police must obtain a Commissioner's prior approval for bugging homes, offices and hotel bedrooms, and in respect of doctors, lawyers and 'confidential journalistic material'. Prior approval is not necessary in urgent cases.

� Article 10 in breach of confidence cases

In common law judges have the power to order disclosure of the identities of wrongdoers (*Norwich Pharmacal Co v Customs and Excise Comrs* [1974] AC 133). In law the term 'wrongdoer' may include a person who breaches a duty of confidence—for example, owed by an employee to a government department or company—by leaking sensitive information gained in that employment to the media.

Until fairly recently, UK judges—for example, in the *Goodwin* case, explained later—tended not to give much weight to the idea that there is a general public interest in journalists protecting confidential sources. But judgments in the European Court of Human Rights (ECtHR) and the UK's adoption of the European Convention on Human Rights have improved the legal climate. As this chapter has outlined earlier, journalists can point to their, and the public's, rights under the Convention's Article 10, guaranteeing freedom of expression and the right to impart and receive information.

→ glossary

ch. 25
explains
breach of
confidence

ch. 1
explains
Convention
rights

Case study

In 1989 a High Court judge ordered Bill Goodwin, a trainee reporter on *The Engineer* magazine, to disclose his source of information for a story about an engineering company's financial difficulties. He refused and was fined £5,000 for contempt of court (*X Ltd v Morgan-Grampian (Publishers) Ltd* [1991] 1 AC 1).

The Court of Appeal and House of Lords upheld the decision, saying disclosure was 'necessary in the interests of justice' because the company had a right to know who was leaking information about it. Mr Goodwin went to the ECtHR which in 1996 agreed that the UK courts had breached his Article 10 rights (*Goodwin v United Kingdom*, Application no. 17488/90 (1996) EHRR 123). It said protection of journalistic sources was a basic condition for press freedom, and a court order to disclose a source could not be compatible with Article 10 unless it was justified by an overriding requirement in the public interest.

 see ch. 25, p. 326, Order to reveal source, for more detail on the *Goodwin* case

Article 8 privacy rights may be engaged

A decision by a Chamber of the Fifth Section of the ECtHR in 2013 illustrates that its judges continue to recognise that it is necessary to protect journalists' sources to uphold human rights and freedoms.

It ruled that a warrant for a search of a newspaper's office issued by a Luxembourg court breached both Article 8, covering the right to respect for privacy and family life, and Article 10, guaranteeing the right to freedom of expression. In its judgment the ECtHR rejected the notion that Article 8 only protected individuals' homes, saying the term 'home' should be interpreted 'as also including the official office of a company run by an individual, and the official office of a legal person, including subsidiaries and other business premises' (Application no. 26419/10 *Case of Saint-Paul Luxembourg SA v Luxembourg* [2013] ECHR 340).

> For more detail of this case, see the Additional Material for this chapter on www.mcnaes.com.

Article 2 'right to life' may be engaged

Journalists, like other citizens, have no general obligation to give police information.

If police want journalistic material to assist investigations, they normally have to apply to a judge. They also generally need a judge's consent before searching a journalist's premises for it. See this chapter's explanation of the Police and Criminal Evidence Act 1984 and other statutes.

In some circumstances a journalist, while citing Article 10 of the Convention, may need to rely on Article 2, the right to life.

👁 Case study

In 2009 a judge accepted that the Article 2 rights of Suzanne Breen, the then northern editor of Ireland's *Sunday Tribune* newspaper, meant that she should not be compelled to produce to the police notes and records of a phone call she received from a spokesperson for the Real IRA terrorist group claiming responsibility for two murders. A judge ruled that her life would be at 'real and immediate' risk from the Real IRA were she to be forced to produce the information. She has condemned terrorist violence (*In the matter of an application by D/Inspector Justyn Galloway, PSNI, under paragraph 5 Schedule 5 of the Terrorism Act 2000 and Suzanne Breen* [2009] NICty 4).

▶ Tribunals of inquiry

A journalist who, by refusing to name a source, refuses to cooperate with an inquiry held under the 2005 Act could be punished by the High Court for contempt. For more detail, see the Additional Material for ch. 17 on www.mcnaes.com.

▶ Be ready for a long battle

A journalist protecting a source's identity must be ready for a long and tortuous legal battle. In 2000 Ashworth High Security Hospital obtained an order that the *Daily Mirror* should disclose the source of a story on Moors murderer Ian Brady, concerning his treatment at the hospital, starting a legal case which lasted six years and involved a freelance journalist, the Court of Appeal and the House of Lords. In 2006 in the High Court Mr Justice Tugendhat rejected the hospital's argument that the need to protect the confidentiality of medical records overrode, in that case's circumstances, the public interest in protecting the journalist's sources (*Mersey Care NHS Trust v Robin Ackroyd* [2006] EWHC 107 (QB)).

▶ The 'shield law' has not always shielded

In section 10 of the Contempt of Court Act 1981 Parliament created what is sometimes referred to as a 'shield law' to protect journalistic activity.

Section 10 says: 'No court may require a person to disclose, nor is any person guilty of contempt of court for refusing to disclose, the source of information contained in a publication for which he is responsible, unless it is established to the satisfaction of the court that disclosure is necessary in the interests of justice or national security, or for the prevention of disorder or crime.'

Journalists hoped the section would lead judges to create a high threshold of 'necessity' in cases involving corporate or official attempts to flush out the identities of a journalist's source.

But judges may well accept the arguments of the police and other official agencies, rather than the counter-arguments of the media, about what is necessary to be disclosed by a journalist 'for the prevention of disorder or crime'. History also shows that judges tend to accept the government's interpretation what is needed to protect 'national security'.

👁 Case study

In 1983 *The Guardian* was ordered to return to the government a leaked photocopy of a Ministry of Defence document revealing the strategy for handling the controversial arrival of US Cruise nuclear missiles, due to be based in the UK. *The Guardian* did not know the informant's identity, but, realising that it might be revealed by examination of the document, argued that section 10 meant it did not have to hand it over. The House of Lords said the interests of national security required disclosure of the informant's identity—publishing this document posed no threat to national security, but the person who leaked it might leak another.

The Guardian handed over the document, and consequently the informant, Foreign Office clerk Sarah Tisdall, was convicted under the Official Secrets Act and jailed for six months (*Secretary of State for Defence v Guardian Newspapers Ltd* [1985] AC 339).

ch. 33 deals with official secrets law

✳ Remember

Had *The Guardian* destroyed the document after using it to prepare the article but before being ordered to hand it over, Ms Tisdall's identity would probably have remained secret.

▌ Statutory powers of investigators

Various statutes have provision for the police and other official investigators, when investigating crime, to get a court order requiring a person to surrender material or in some circumstances to search premises without warning to seize it. In the case of a journalist, this could be notes of interviews, computers or phones, etc, which could reveal the identity of a source of published stories about the crime being investigated.

The Police and Criminal Evidence Act 1984 (PACE)

Police, if they wish someone to be compelled to surrender documents or other material, need a court order in most circumstances. PACE is the legislation they use most when applying for these orders.

Special procedure material

PACE gives special protection to 'journalistic material', defined as 'material acquired or created for the purposes of journalism'. When seeking to compel journalists or media organisations to surrender such material, police investigating a crime must use PACE's 'special procedure', which means they must apply to a High Court judge, a recorder or a circuit judge. If the application succeeds →glossary the judge makes a 'production order'—that is, an order requiring the person or organisation holding the material to produce it to the police.

The application is normally 'on notice', so the holder of the material has the chance to attend the hearing to argue against the order being granted.

Before making the order a judge must be satisfied that there are reasonable grounds for believing that a serious offence has been committed, that the material the police want would be admissible evidence at a trial for that offence and of substantial value to the investigation, that other methods of obtaining it have been tried without success, or have not been tried because it appears they would be bound to fail, and that production of the material to the police would be in the public interest, having regard to:

(1) the benefit likely to accrue to the investigation if the material is obtained; and

(2) the circumstances under which the person in possession of the material holds it.

The Act's 'special procedure' appears to give journalistic material useful protection. But judges have interpreted it in a way which makes the protection less valuable than was hoped.

! Remember your rights

Courts must allow media organisations access to all the evidence when dealing with police requests for orders under PACE, the Supreme Court ruled in March 2014 (*R (on the application of British Sky Broadcasting Ltd) v The Commissioner of Police of the Metropolis* [2014] UKSC 17).

Photos and footage of disorder

see also
p. 431,
Maintaining
a reputation
for
neutrality,
on this
principle

In several cases, applications by the police for production orders have concerned photographs or film taken during rioting and other public disturbances. Although such material does not reveal the identity of any sources promised anonymity, there is another principle involved for the media—that of maintaining neutrality.

Most editors and journalists take the view that they should hand over such material only after careful consideration, and generally only after a court order, arguing that if it becomes routine for police to obtain unpublished photographs or film, journalists, photographers and camera operators will be seen as an arm of the state. This could increase the danger that they will be attacked when covering such events. For example, untransmitted footage of the riots in London in August 2011 was handed to the police by BBC, ITN and Sky News only after police obtained production orders.

A judge might reject the application for a production order if, among other things, he/she does not consider it in the public interest to grant it. Media lawyers have argued that it is not in the public interest to prevent the media doing their job. In nearly every case judges have found that the police's need for evidence outweighed that argument, though the case described below was a welcome exception.

👁 Case study

In 2012 the High Court overturned an order made by a judge at Chelmsford Crown court for broadcasters to hand over more than 100 hours of footage of evictions from the Dale Farm travellers' site. The High Court said there were no reasonable grounds to believe that the footage included material likely to be of substantial value to the police investigation. Applicants for such an order had to produce 'clear and compelling' evidence that it was necessary. Lord Justice Moses said a judge facing such an application also had to exercise his discretion in a manner compatible with Article 10, even if the conditions for having the material were satisfied, and added: 'First, the objective must be sufficiently important to justify the inhibition such orders inflict on the exercise of the fundamental right to disseminate information. Second, the means chosen to limit the right must be rational, fair and not arbitrary, and third, the means used must impair the right as little as is reasonably possible' (*R (on the application of BSkyB, the BBC, ITN, Hardcash Productions Ltd and Jason Parkinson) v Chelmsford Crown Court* [2012] EWHC 1295 (Admin), [2012] 2 Cr App R 33, [2012] EMLR 30).

Excluded material

→ glossary

Under PACE, excluded material is exempt from compulsory surrender. It includes journalistic material which a person holds in confidence—for example, from a source promised confidentiality by a journalist.

But material which was already liable to search and seizure under the previous law is not protected—for example, a stolen document acquired by a journalist, even from a confidential source, would not be 'excluded material' because it would already be liable to seizure under a warrant issued under the Theft Act 1968.

▶ Expect your premises to be searched

Freedom from an oppressive search is an important civil liberty, safeguarded as early as 1765 in a case concerning a clerk called Entick whose house was entered and papers seized by 'the King's messengers' on the authority of a warrant from the Secretary of State (*Entick v Carrington* (1765) 19 State Tr 1029). In that case, a court condemned the action as unlawful.

That ruling was referred to and endorsed by the High Court in 2000 when it rejected a police application for an order that *The Guardian* and *Observer* should hand over all files, documents and records they had relating to a letter in *The Guardian* from former M15 officer David Shayler and an article in the *Observer* by reporter Martin Bright repeating allegations that M16 officers were involved in a failed attempt to assassinate Libyan leader Colonel Gaddafi (*R v Central Criminal Court, ex p Martin Bright* [2001] 2 All ER 244).

 See ch. 33 on www.mcnaes.com about official secrets law for more detail about Shayler.

But a journalist protecting the identity of a source should be alert to the possibility of his/her home or office being searched by police arriving with a search warrant.

Search warrants under PACE

Instead of asking for an order for a journalist or media organisation to produce (surrender) material, police can apply to a circuit judge for a search warrant under PACE to obtain either non-confidential or confidential material. The person or media organisation does not have to be told of the application and has no right to be heard by the judge.

Before granting a warrant, a judge must be satisfied that the criteria for ordering the production of the material are satisfied and that one of the following circumstances applies:

- it is not practicable to communicate with anyone entitled to grant entry to the premises;
- it is not practicable to communicate with anyone entitled to grant access to the material;
- the material contains information which is subject to an obligation of secrecy or a restriction on disclosure imposed by statute—for example,

material subject to the Official Secrets Acts—and is likely to be disclosed in breach of that obligation if a warrant is not issued; or

- giving notice of an application for an order may seriously prejudice the investigation.

The Serious Organised Crime and Police Act 2005

The Serious Organised Crime and Police Act 2005 allows police, subject to the PACE procedure for search warrants for journalistic material (described earlier), to obtain a warrant to search all property occupied or controlled by the person named in the warrant and not merely specific premises.

But before issuing an all-premises warrant a judge must be satisfied that:

(1) there are reasonable grounds for believing that it is necessary to search premises occupied or controlled by the person in question which are not specified in the application, as well as those which are, in order to find the material in question; and

(2) it is not reasonably practicable to specify all the premises which he/she occupies or controls which might need to be searched.

 See the Additional Material for this chapter on www.mcnaes.com for further detail of the 2005 Act.

The Official Secrets Acts

Section 9 of the Official Secrets Act 1911 gives police powers to make searches, subject to PACE as regards journalistic material.

The Official Secrets Act 1920 gives a chief officer of police, with the Home Secretary's permission, power to authorise a senior police officer to require anyone to furnish information about a suspected case of espionage. Failing to comply is an offence. For more detail, see ch. 33, Official secrets, on www.mcnaes.com.

▌ Counter-terrorism legislation

Counter-terrorism legislation includes a number of offences which could relate to journalist's sources and gives police powers to seize a journalist's research material.

The Terrorism Act 2000 enables a court to issue a warrant for police investigating a terrorist offence to search premises. But the requirements for police seeking an order are much easier to meet than those under PACE. Journalists and news organisations facing the possibility of an application for a production order should make clear that they intend to take a stand on the issue of public interest journalism—by arguing that handing over the material would have a seriously chilling effect on investigative journalism—as well as on the issue of the right to protect sources under Article 10 of the European Convention on Human Rights.

 See www.mcnaes.com for the online chapter, Terrorism and the effect of counter-terrorism law, including the *Malik* case and how various laws might affect journalists who interview sources who joined the so-called Islamic State in Syria or Iraq.

▌ Other statutes

Various other statutes could affect journalists by placing them under a legal obligation to disclose information, for example to an official investigation into fraud or share-dealings—see the Additional Material for ch. 34 on www.mcnaes.com for further detail.

! Remember your rights

The Data Protection Act 1998 does not require journalists to disclose material which could help reveal a source's identity. For detail and a case study, see the Additional Material for ch. 28 on www.mcnaes.com.

▌ Maintaining a reputation for neutrality

Reporters who cover events which lead to prosecutions of those involved or civil lawsuits may be asked—by the prosecution or defence—to give evidence of what they themselves have seen. Most journalists in this situation will wish to retain their reputation for neutrality and will agree to be a witness only after receiving a **subpoena** (in civil cases) or witness summons (in criminal cases).   → glossary

➡ Recap of major points

- It is a matter of professional principle that a reporter does not reveal his/her source of confidential information.
- The European Court of Human Rights has said that an order to disclose the source of information cannot be compatible with Article 10 of the Convention (freedom of expression) unless it is justified by an overriding requirement in the public interest.
- Section 10 of the Contempt of Court Act 1981 says that a disclosure order must not be made 'unless it is established to the satisfaction of the court that disclosure

is necessary in the interests of justice or national security, or for the prevention of disorder or crime'.

- Various laws allow the authorities to put journalists and others under surveillance.

((•)) Useful Websites

www.nuj.org.uk/about/nuj-code/
National Union of Journalists Code of Conduct

The risks of being charged with bribery, misconduct, hacking or intercepting

Chapter summary

The way journalists gain information may leave them and their sources at risk of prosecution. Journalists offering or paying money to sources may be accused of conspiring with the source to commit 'misconduct in public office', or of bribery. Hacking into a computer, a phone voicemail or email system, or intercepting communications may also be prosecuted as an offence. Few of the relevant statutes contain a public interest defence. But the Director of Public Prosecutions has said in guidance to prosecutors that the public interest should always be considered when decisions are taken on whether to prosecute journalists in cases arising from their work. Journalists who realise they may be suspected of such offences should consider whether there is a sufficient public interest to justify what they plan to do—and remember that some offences may also leave them open to being sued in the civil courts for damages. This chapter details the main risks.

▌ More than 60 journalists arrested or charged

In 2011 the Metropolitan police re-opened inquiries into the hacking scandal at the *News of the World* after media revelations suggested that the police's original investigation, which led to a reporter and a private detective being jailed in 2007, had failed to result in all those responsible being prosecuted.

see p. 440, Regulation of Investigatory Powers Act (RIPA) 2000, for this 2007 case

Police also investigated other alleged offences. In December 2015, *Press Gazette* reported that at least 67 journalists who had worked or were working for London-based national newspapers had been arrested or charged in connection with alleged offences including hacking into mobile phone messages, hacking into emails, and making corrupt payments to police officers and other public servants.

The scale of these police inquiries into alleged criminality in or associated with journalism is unprecedented in the UK, and possibly in any democracy. Yet it should be noted that the journalists who were arrested and/or charged were almost all from only two national newspaper groups—News International and the Mirror Group Newspapers, and mainly from the former.

The police investigation into corrupt payments was called Operation Elveden, and it led to 34 journalists being arrested or charged, according to *Press Gazette*. Although only two journalists have been convicted because of Elveden—the convictions of two others were overturned on appeal—police investigations continue. Many public servants—police officers, prison officers and civil servants—who sold information to newspapers were also jailed, some after information about payments to them was passed to police by News International, owner of *The Sun* and the *News of the World*. In late 2015 *Press Gazette* reports indicated that Elveden had led to more than 30 public officials being convicted of selling information to journalists.

The Crown Prosecution Service has issued a list of offences 'most likely to be committed' in cases involving journalists. The consent of the Director of Public Prosecutions or Attorney General is needed before proceedings can be launched for some of these offences. Some are outlined below.

▶ Guidance for prosecutors on whether a journalist should be prosecuted

see Useful
Websites at
the end of
this chapter
for this
guidance,
which
includes
the list of
possible
offences

ch. 1
explains
the Article
10 rights

The Director of Public Prosecutions published guidance for prosecutors on the factors to be considered when they are deciding whether journalists—or their sources—should be charged with criminal offences that may have been committed in the course of the journalists' work. The guidance acknowledges that prosecuting journalists might have an impact on the Article 10 rights of the media and public to freedom of expression and to receive and impart information, both at common law and under the European Convention on Human Rights.

The guidance points out that it is important at the outset to distinguish between the public interest served by these rights and the separate question of whether a prosecution is in the public interest—for example, the public interest in punishing criminality. In general terms, it says that, once prosecutors have decided that there is sufficient evidence to continue with a case, they must consider whether it is in the public interest to go ahead with a prosecution.

The guidance indicates that this decision involves considering a variety of factors. The nature of the information gained or sought by the journalist would be one factor—for example, is the information that a crime has been, is being or is likely to be committed by someone? Or does it show that someone has failed or is likely to fail to comply with any legal obligation? Or that conduct capable of disclosing a miscarriage of justice has occurred, is occurring or is likely to occur? Or is the conduct capable of raising or contributing to an important matter of public debate?

The guidance indicates that if the journalist gained or sought information in these categories, the public interest in such information coming to light weighs against the public interest in prosecuting the journalist for alleged criminality in his/her news-gathering methods.

On the other side, prosecutors also have to consider the overall criminality of that activity—including its effects, the vulnerability of any of its victims and whether the journalist's or source's behaviour was repeated or involved corruption.

Misconduct in public office

This is a common law offence dating from the thirteenth century with which public officials will be charged when accused of disclosing to the media (or others) information which is not specifically protected by legislation such as the Data Protection Act 1998 or Official Secrets Acts.

The 'misconduct' may be by an act, or an omission, but must be wilful, and the offender must be a public officer acting as such. Public officials include police and prison officers, civil servants, magistrates, judges, registrars, and council and court officials. The offence can be committed even if no money changes hands. Lord Justice Pill, in the Court of Appeal in *Attorney General's Reference No. 3 of 2003* [2004] EWCA Crim 868, [2005] QB 73, [2004] 3 WLR 451, [2005] 4 All ER 303 said that there must be 'a serious departure from proper standards before the criminal offence is committed; and a departure not merely negligent but amounting to an affront to the standing of the public office held. The threshold is a high one requiring conduct so far below acceptable standards as to amount to an abuse of the public's trust in the office holder. A mistake, even a serious one, will not suffice.'

ch. 28 deals with data protection law affecting journalism and ch. 33 with official secrets law

---

👁 Case studies

In June 2015, Robert Norman, aged 54, a prison officer at top-security Belmarsh jail, was jailed for 20 months for misconduct in public office after being convicted of having been the paid mole of the *Daily Mirror* and *News of the World* for five years. The jury heard he was paid more than £10,000 for 40 tips to a reporter between 30 April 2006 and 1 May 2011 (*Media Lawyer*, 2 June 2015).

In January 2015, a senior Ministry of Defence official who pocketed £100,000 from the sale of scoops to *The Sun* was jailed for 12 months. Bettina Jordan-Barber, aged 42, was cultivated by a reporter as his 'number one military contact', providing him with exclusive details of army disciplinary investigations, sex scandals and casualties in Afghanistan. The mother-of-two, who is married to an army officer, admitted conspiring to commit misconduct in public office between January 2004 and January 2012. The Old Bailey heard she came across confidential information in her senior Andover-based job compiling briefing notes to pass on to Ministers and the Ministry of Defence press office (*Media Lawyer*, 20 March 2015).

In March, 2013, prison officer Richard Trunkfield was jailed at the Old Bailey for 16 months after admitting misconduct in public office by selling *The Sun* information about Jon Venables, one of the killers of James Bulger, who was being held at Woodhill Prison where he worked. On the same day former Surrey policeman Alan Tierney was jailed for 10 months for selling *The Sun* details of the separate arrests of footballer John Terry's mother and Rolling Stone Ronnie Wood. Another officer who sold information was jailed for two years (*Media Lawyer*, 27 March 2013).

Conspiracy to commit the misconduct

see the *Murrer* case, ch. 34, p. 422, You may be put under surveillance

The associated charge for a journalist would be conspiring to commit the misconduct—for example, an alleged plot involving the public official and/or another person for information to be supplied in breach of this law—or aiding and abetting the offence. The recent use of the offence against journalists has prompted calls for legislation to introduce a proper public interest defence for media organisations and those working for them. The offence was the basis for the controversial and discredited prosecution of journalist Sally Murrer in 2008.

see Late News on related law

The convictions of former *News of the World* crime editor Lucy Panton and former *News of the World* and *The Sun* journalist Ryan Sabey on charges of conspiring to commit misconduct in public office were overturned by the Court of Appeal in 2015, on the grounds that the judges at their trials should have told the juries that, in order to convict, they had to be satisfied that the alleged misconduct had positively harmed the public interest.

see also Late News section about 'misconduct' and bribery law

A third journalist, *The Sun* crime reporter Anthony France, was convicted in May 2015 of conspiring to commit misconduct in public office by paying a police officer for stories. Mr France, who was given a suspended sentence by a judge who described him as being of 'hitherto unblemished character' and 'essentially a decent man of solid integrity', was given the source, a police officer, by *The Sun*'s newsdesk. At time of writing, Mr France has appealed the conviction.

▌ The Bribery Act 2010

A journalist who pays a source for information could in some circumstances be charged under the Bribery Act 2010. A source could also be charged under the Act if he/she could be accused by another party—for example, his/her employer—of acting improperly by giving the journalist information. Offences under the Act can be committed by anyone, not just public officials.

When the Act first came into force it was described as the toughest bribery legislation in the world, and there were fears that it could mean that journalists, particularly those working on investigations, would be breaking the law by paying confidential sources.

By late 2015 no journalist had been charged under the Act. But this legislation, and the 'misconduct' cases, have caused media organisations to review procedures about paying or otherwise rewarding sources of information, to avoid breaching these laws.

The bribery offences

The 2010 Act creates four main offences—bribing someone, accepting bribes, bribing foreign officials and failing, as a commercial organisation, to prevent bribery. All four can only be prosecuted with the consent of the Director of Public Prosecutions. The Act does not include the public interest defence.

It is an offence to offer, promise or give a financial or other advantage to get someone 'improperly to perform a relevant function or activity', or to reward someone for such improper performance, or to do so knowing or believing that accepting the inducement would itself be improper performance.

It is irrelevant whether the person to whom the advantage is offered, promised or given is the same person who performs the function or activity concerned, and it does not matter whether the offer is made directly or through a third party.

The offence of being bribed is covered by four sets of circumstances:

- where someone requests, agrees to receive or accepts a financial or other advantage—a bribe—intending that as a result he/she or someone else will improperly perform a relevant function or activity;
- where someone seeks or accepts a bribe when doing so constitutes improper performance of a relevant function or activity;
- where someone seeks or accepts a bribe as a reward for his/her own or someone else's improper performance of an activity;
- where someone improperly performs an activity in anticipation of or as a consequence of him/herself or someone else having sought or accepted a bribe.

The Act states that in all four of these cases it does not matter whether the bribe is accepted directly or through a third party, or whether it is, or is to be, for the benefit of that person or another person.

In the second, third and fourth cases it is irrelevant whether the person receiving the bribe knows or believes that the performance of the function or activity is improper. In the final case, if the function or activity is being performed by someone other than the person receiving the bribe, it does not matter whether that other person knows or believes that the performance is improper.

Section 3 says the Act covers

- any function of a public nature,
- activities connected with a business, trade or profession,
- things done in the course of employment,
- activities performed by or on behalf of a body, whether corporate or unincorporated,

as long as a person performing it is expected to do so in good faith, or impartially, or is in a position of trust by virtue of what he/she is doing. He/she is covered by the Act even if he/she has no connection with the UK and acts are performed outside the UK.

Penalties

The penalties on summary conviction are up to six months in prison and/or an unlimited fine, and on conviction on indictment, up to 10 years in jail and/or an unlimited fine.

Section 6 creates the offence of bribing a foreign public official if the person paying intends to influence the official in his/her capacity as a public official and also intends to obtain or retain business or an advantage in the conduct of business.

Companies

A company is guilty of the section 7 offence of failing to prevent bribery if someone associated with it bribes someone with the intention of obtaining or keeping business for the company, or getting or keeping an advantage in the conduct of the company's business.

This is a strict liability offence—meaning the prosecution does not have to prove any intention to commit it—but it is a defence for a company to prove that it had adequate procedures in place intended to stop people associated with it from bribing others. The offence is punishable by an unlimited fine.

▶ Cases in which the public interest was clear

There are clear examples of when a possible breach by journalists of the law of 'misconduct in public office' or of the Bribery Act 2010 might be considered to be justified as being in the public interest.

see also ch. 30, p. 383, Introduction to the Act, on the expenses story

One was the exposure by the *Daily Telegraph* of the scandal of MPs' unjustifiable and inflated expenses claims, in that the newspaper had paid a considerable amount of money for the information on which its exposés were based.

This was before the Bribery Act came into force, but it was later made clear that prosecutors would not have brought a case.

The first criminal conviction under the Bribery Act came after *The Sun*, in the public interest, risked being prosecuted itself under the Act by paying Redbridge magistrates' court office worker Munir Yakub Patel a £500 bribe—which it secretly filmed him accepting—to stand up a story that he was taking bribes to keep details of a traffic offence summons off a court database. This led to him being jailed. So far no journalists have been charged with or convicted of bribery.

See the Additonal Material for ch. 35 on www.mcnaes.com for hypothetical case studies on whether a journalist paying for information could be deemed to breach the Bribery Act 2010.

▌ The Computer Misuse Act 1990

The Computer Misuse Act 1990 creates computer hacking offences of unauthorised access to a computer with the intention of:

- getting to any program or information it holds; or
- committing or facilitating the commission of an offence; or
- impairing a computer so as to stop or hinder access to any program or data held in any computer; or
- impairing or intending to impair the operation of any such program or the reliability of any such data.

It is also an offence to make, adapt, supply or offer to supply any article intending or believing that it will be used to commit or help the commission of one of these offences.

Penalties range from six months in prison and/or an unlimited fine on summary conviction, and up to 10 years in prison and/or an unlimited fine if convicted on indictment.

These offences clearly cover computer hacking activities, such as hacking into someone's emails. The unauthorised access offences require that the defendant must have known that the intended access was unauthorised—which will generally not be an issue if a journalist has accessed someone else's computer.

The Act itself does not contain a public interest defence, but acting in the public interest will help protect journalists.

◉ Case study

The Crown Prosecution Service announced in March 2013 that Sky News reporter Gerald Tubb would not be prosecuted for hacking into the emails of back-from-the-dead canoeist John Darwin and his wife Anne, who were jailed in 2008 after staging his 'death' to make a fraudulent life insurance claim.

Malcolm McHaffie, CPS deputy head of special crime, said a prosecution would not be in the public interest. In July 2013 Ofcom cleared Sky News of having breached the Broadcasting Code, saying that it had concluded that the 'exceptional circumstances of this case outweighed Mr and Mrs Darwin's expectation of privacy', and that Sky's conduct was 'warranted in the particular circumstances of this case' (*Media Lawyer*, 29 March and 1 July 2013).

ch. 3 explains Ofcom's role, and ch. 27 explains the Code's privacy section

---

The Regulation of Investigatory Powers Act 2000 (RIPA)

This Act creates a series of offences which could affect journalists, all of which can be prosecuted only with the consent of the Director of Public Prosecutions. There is no public interest defence in the Act itself.

Section 1 creates the offences of unlawfully intercepting any communication being transmitted through a public postal service, or through a public or private telecommunication system.

Private investigator Glenn Mulcaire, who hacked phone messages for *News of the World* royal correspondent Clive Goodman, admitted five offences under this Act when the two men were jailed in January 2007. Mulcaire was given a six-month sentence and Goodman received four months.

The two men had also admitted the Criminal Law Act 1977 offence of conspiring to intercept communications without lawful authority.

In July 2014 former *News of the World* editor Andy Coulson was given an 18-month jail term after being convicted of conspiring to intercept voicemail messages. Six other former *News of the World* journalists have also been convicted of phone-hacking. Penalties for the RIPA offences are an unlimited fine on summary conviction or two years' imprisonment and/or an unlimited fine on conviction on indictment.

The Mulcaire and Goodman case came to light when Prince William began to fear aides' mobile phone voicemail messages were being intercepted after a story about his knee injury appeared in *News of the World* in November 2005.

Section 2(7) of RIPA classifies messages stored for later retrieval as still being 'in the course of transmission', thus putting voicemail within the scope of 'interception'.

The scandal erupted again in 2011 when *The Guardian* revealed the huge scale of phone-hacking at the *News of the World* and that it had hacked into the voicemails on a murdered schoolgirl's phone. This led to the *News of the World's* closure in June 2011.

 Ch. 26 refers to privacy lawsuits arising from hacking by Mirror Group journalists—see ch. 26, p. 331, Damages.

✱ Remember

As ch. 2 explains, the Editors' Code specifically protects the privacy of 'digital communications' and bans the interception of private or mobile telephone calls, messages or emails.

Recording phone calls

Journalists frequently record the calls they themselves make or receive. Under RIPA, interception occurs in the course of transmission, so recording telephone conversations by a device at either end of the communication is not interception and is lawful. For ethical considerations on recording phone calls, see the Editors' Code at ch. 2, pp. 19–20, and Broadcasting Code at ch. 3, p. 35.

◗ The Wireless Telegraphy Act 2006

The Wireless Telegraphy Act 2006 prohibits the use without authority of wireless apparatus with intent to obtain information about the contents, sender or addressee of any message, and prohibits the disclosure of any such information.

◗ Perverting the course of justice

Perverting the course of justice is a common law offence. It includes falsifying, concealing or destroying evidence or potential evidence, such as emails, records or files, and so on. Criminal proceedings do not have to be in progress when the act is done for an offence to be committed. Police who reopened inquiries into allegations of widespread phone-hacking by the *News of the World* arrested a number of people in connection with allegations of perverting the course of justice in relation to the inquiry.

◗ The Serious Crime Act 2007

Sections 44–46 of the Serious Crime Act 2007 make it an offence intentionally to encourage or assist an offence, or to do so believing the offence will be committed, or to do so believing that that offence or another will be committed.

The penalty for each offence is any penalty the offender would be liable to face if he/she were convicted of the anticipated offence.

These offences would cover, for example, the position of a journalist or editor who commissions a private investigator or someone else to hack into someone's emails.

 Ch. 27 deals with the risk of journalists being charged with harassment. The risk of journalists being charged under counter-terrorism law is discussed in the www.mcnaes.com chapter on Terrorism and the affect of counter-terrorism law.

➡ Recap of major points

- News-gathering activities may leave journalists at risk of being charged with criminal offences such as conspiracy to commit misconduct in public office or with bribery.

- Public officials—police, prison officers and others—who sell information to the media may also face criminal prosecution for misconduct in public office.

- Hacking into computers, emails and voicemail messages is a criminal offence.

- The Director of Public Prosecutions has issued guidance saying that the issue of public interest must be considered before journalists are prosecuted in connection with news-gathering activities.

((•)) Useful Websites

www.cps.gov.uk/legal/d_to_g/guidance_for_prosecutors_on_assessing_the_public_interest_in_cases_affecting_the_media_/
  Crown Prosecution Service guidelines for prosecutors assessing whether journalists should be charged—the list of offences most likely to be concerned in such cases appears in Annex A to the document

www.sfo.gov.uk/publications/guidance-policy-and-protocols/bribery-act-guidance/
  Serious Fraud Office and Director of Public Prosecutions guidance on the Bribery Act 2010 is available via this website

36

The right to take photographs, film and record

Chapter summary

Journalists should know their rights when gathering visual images or making recordings in the streets or countryside. There is no criminal law restricting photography or filming or recording in public places. As this chapter explains, concern has grown in the media that over-zealous police officers, security guards and members of the public raise invalid objections to journalists using cameras. Photographers have been wrongly arrested. This chapter covers laws which are sometimes officiously cited or used against journalists and the civil law of trespass.

▌ Introduction

Many police officers and members of the public offer help to the media. But some do not and become officious or hostile to journalists going about their lawful business. In tense situations, journalists may find laws being invalidly used or cited against them. Official guidance issued to police reflects the law—that officers have no power to prohibit the taking of photographs, film or digital images in a public place.

Some 'public places' such as shopping malls are private property, and security staff may intervene unless journalists get permission to take pictures, film, or record there.

▌ Trouble with the police in public places

A photographer, radio reporter, video-journalist or film crew must get in close for their pictures and/or sound. They may be attacked by disorderly people and—even during a small-scale event—be improperly arrested by police as tension rises.

👁 Case study

In 2010 the Metropolitan Police paid photo-journalists Marc Vallée and Jason Parkinson £3,500 each in damages after armed officers stopped them from taking video footage and photos at a protest outside the Greek Embassy. Diplomatic Protection Group officers, claiming the pair were not allowed to film them, pulled Vallée's camera away from his face and covered the lens of Parkinson's camera (*Media Lawyer*, 28 June 2010).

((•))

for this guidance see Useful Websites at the end of this chapter

Police guidelines on media photography and filming

Journalists having problems at an incident or crime scenes may need to refer police to 'authorised professional practice' guidance issued by the College of Policing, in which the section on 'Public order—communication' says:

- journalists have a right to report from incident scenes, and their movement should not be restricted if they do not interfere with the police operation, or jeopardise their own or anyone else's safety;
- the early identification of good media vantage points, in liaison with the media, may help minimise risk to the police operation, but providing an area for journalists does not exclude them from using other areas to which the public have access unless there is a legal basis for restricting access— for example, breach of the peace;
- police cannot give or deny permission to the media to enter private premises whether the premises are directly involved in the police operation or not—the person who owns or controls the property makes that decision;
- police have no legal power or moral responsibility to restrict what is recorded or photographed, nor can they delete images, though in limited circumstances— for example, terrorism cases—they may have a power to seize images;
- if someone who is distressed or bereaved asks for the police to intervene to prevent members of the media filming or photographing them, the police may pass on their request, but there is no power to prevent or restrict media activity.

The College also refers to guidance issued by the (now defunct) Association of Chief Police Officers (ACPO) which says: 'Once an image has been recorded, police can only seize the film or camera at the scene on the strictly limited grounds that it is suspected to contain evidence of a crime. Once the photographer has left the scene, police can only seize images with a court order.'

❗ Remember your rights

If police want to view or seize journalistic material, they must first get a court order under the Police and Criminal Evidence Act 1984, explained in ch. 34.

False imprisonment

A journalist who is subject to unlawful physical restraint—such as being locked in the cells or physically restrained by a police officer—might be able to sue for false imprisonment. Movement must be completely restricted; barring a photographer from going in one particular direction—for example, towards the scene of a crash—is not false imprisonment.

👁 Case study

Wiltshire police paid compensation to photo-journalist Robert Naylor after an incident in 2009 when he went to a canal to report on a death in a boat fire. A police sergeant told him he could not take photos because of 'respect for deceased'. Soon afterwards, as he started back to this car, he was dragged to the ground, arrested and handcuffed for allegedly 'breaching the peace'. Wiltshire police later accepted he was unlawfully detained and apologised (*Media Lawyer*, 30 March 2011).

Public order offences

Police officers sometimes warn media photographers or video-journalists that they may be arrested. The arrest would probably be under common law for breach of the peace or under section 5 of the Public Order Act 1986.

Arrest for breach of the peace is only justified if harm has been done or is likely to be done to a person or his/her property in his/her presence, or when a person is in fear being harmed.

Section 5 allows arrest if anyone uses threatening or abusive words or behaviour, or disorderly behaviour, likely to cause 'harassment, alarm or distress' to another person. Though the journalists is not intending to cause distress, etc, in some situations the mere fact that he/she is taking pictures or shooting footage, perhaps of someone or a group who object to this, may prompt an arrest.

((•))

see Useful Websites at the end of this chapter for further guidance on public order offences

Obstructing the highway

Section 137 of the Highways Act 1980 make it an offence for someone 'without lawful authority or excuse' to obstruct free passage along a highway in any way. This power allows police to arrest journalists in a public place who fail to move on when asked to do so.

Obstructing the police

Section 89 of the Police Act 1996 says that a person commits an offence if he/she 'resists or wilfully obstructs a constable in the execution of his duty, or a person assisting a constable in the execution of his duty'. The obstruction does not have to be a physical act—it may occur, for example, if someone makes it more difficult for the constable to perform his/her duty. A journalist who persists in taking photographs or shooting footage, and engages in argument with a police officer, therefore runs the risk of arrest.

for an outline of the police's general powers of arrest, see ch. 4, pp. 41–42, Arrests

---

👁 Case study

A freelance photographer was arrested in 2007 as he tried to take pictures of a man threatening to jump from the Tyne Bridge in Newcastle. He was later charged with obstructing the police. A district judge at the city's magistrates' courts acquitted the photographer, saying he had acted 'professionally' (*Media Lawyer*, 15 October 2007).

'Stop and search' under the Terrorism Act 2000

Complaints by photographers of excessive use by police of 'stop and search' powers under the Terrorism Act 2000—for example, if a photographer were taking pictures of buildings—have decreased since the government amended the law to produce a more tightly defined 'stop and search' power in the Act's section 47A. This change is primarily concerned with the criteria police can use to designate areas as being at risk of terrorist attack. Police in such areas are still permitted to stop and search an individual without 'reasonable suspicion'. A revised code of practice issued to police makes clear that they have no power under the 2000 Act to stop filming or photography of incidents or of police officers and that it is not an offence to film/photograph a public building or in public places. Police retain power under section 43 of the Act to stop and search, and to seize equipment, if they reasonably suspect someone is a terrorist.

((•)) See Useful Websites at the end of this chapter for the code of practice in full. See the www. mcnaes.com chapter, Terrorism and the effect of counter-terrorism law, for other counter-terrorism laws which could affect journalists.

▌ Trespass and bye-laws

Property and land owners who object to photography or filming or recording on their sites may decide to enforce objections by using the civil law of trespass, which forbids unlawful entry to land or buildings. Because trespass is a **tort**, the remedy is an action in the civil courts which could result in an injunction to prevent further trespass and/or damages. Also, the occupier of property or land may use reasonable force to eject the trespasser. Police may lawfully assist, though they have no duty to do so.

→ glossary

There is no trespass if a journalist photographs, films or records an event on adjoining private land from a site where he/she has permission or a right to be—for example, on a public highway. But such media activity might lead to a subject suing for intrusion into privacy, or complaining to Ipso or Ofcom.

see ch. 27 on news-gathering avoiding intrusion

Trespass can also include 'trespass to the person'—for example, compelling a person to be filmed by stopping him/her from entering home or a workplace. Trespass to goods means, for instance, picking up a document without permission and photographing it.

Trespass is not usually a criminal offence, and so a police officer threatening an arrest for civil trespass is wrong in law. However, there are trespass offences for certain sites—for example, Ministry of Defence (MoD) land and railway property—and there is a specific offence of aggravated trespass. Also, bye-laws ban photography in and of MoD establishments.

 Ch. 33 explains official secrets law on 'prohibited places'.

Aggravated trespass

Section 68 of the Criminal Justice and Public Order Act 1994 created the offence of aggravated trespass. It has been used against protesters—for example, those who, demonstrating over alleged tax evasion by the rich, occupied the Fortnum and Mason store in London in 2011. A journalist covering such an event could be accused of the offence. A person commits aggravated trespass if he/she trespasses and, in relation to any lawful activity which other persons are engaged in on that or adjoining property, does anything intended to have the effect of:

see Useful Websites at the end of this chapter for CPS guidance on this offence

- intimidating any of them so as to deter them from engaging in that activity; or
- obstructing that activity; or
- disrupting that activity.

The penalty for aggravated trespass is up to three months' imprisonment or a fine.

Section 69 of the Act says a senior police officer present at the scene has power to order any person believed to be involved in aggravated trespass to leave the property. Failure to leave, or returning within three months, is an offence. A journalist who fails to leave may have a defence under the Act that he/she had 'a reasonable excuse' to stay.

 Ch. 27 covers privacy issues in photography, filming and recording, including when a child is the subject. That chapter also covers intrusion into grief and explains that paparazzi who stalk people could be sued or prosecuted for harassment.

➡ Recap of major points

- There is no law against photography, filming or recording in public places.

- But journalists need to be familiar with the law on trespass and the general powers police have to arrest those 'obstructing' them or the highway.

- Police have been issued with guidelines that they should help the media take photos and gain footage, but individual officers may need reminding of these

((•)) Useful Websites

www.app.college.police.uk/app-content/public-order/planning-and-deployment/communication/?s=public+order+communication
　　College of Policing guidance

http://content.met.police.uk/Site/photographyadvice
　　Metropolitan Police 'Photography advice'

www.gov.uk/government/uploads/system/uploads/attachment_data/file/97944/stop-search-code-of-practice.pdf
　　Code of Practice for police 'stop and search' powers under the Terrorism Act 2000

www.cps.gov.uk/legal/s_to_u/trespass_and_nuisance_on_land/
　　Crown Prosecution Service guidance on trespass offences

http://media.gn.apc.org/photo/index.html
　　National Union of Journalists London Freelance branch advice for photographers

www.digitalcameraworld.com/2012/04/14/photographers-rights-the-ultimate-guide/
　　Digital Camera World guide to the law

37

Northern Ireland

Chapter summary

Media law in Northern Ireland is—with some exceptions, particularly in defamation law—the same as that in England and Wales. In the few important cases involving the media which have gone to the High Court, cases in England have been freely cited. The Supreme Court in London is the final court of appeal for criminal and civil cases on major points of law. Restrictions on reports of preliminary hearings before magistrates, prior to committal to Crown court, follow Northern Ireland law but restrictions on reports of criminal proceedings involving juveniles are along the lines of those on the mainland. Victims/alleged victims of sexual offences must remain anonymous. It is an offence to disclose the identity of a juror who is serving or has served on a trial in Northern Ireland, or of a person who is on the jury list there.

▶ The law is broadly the same as in England and Wales

The law in Northern Ireland, including the courts structure, is broadly the same as that in England and Wales. Scotland has its own system.

 See the www.mcnaes.com chapter on Scotland.

Many of the laws applicable in England and Wales extend to Northern Ireland by means of Orders made by the Secretary of State.

The Lord Chief Justice of Northern Ireland is assisted by High Court judges and circuit judges who try cases in the Crown court, which also hears appeals from magistrates' courts. Civil cases are heard by High Court judges sitting in the Northern Ireland High Court or circuit judges sitting in the county court. Three Lords Justices of Appeal, sometimes sitting with other High Court judges, hear appeals from the Crown court, county court or High Court in the Court of Appeal in Belfast.

→ glossary

Most cases in magistrates' courts are heard by a **district judge**. Two lay magistrates and a district judge sit for youth and family law cases. The media has restricted reporting rights on these.

The UK Supreme Court is the final court of appeal for criminal and civil cases on major points of law.

▶ Defamation

Defamation law in Northern Ireland and England diverged when the Westminster Parliament passed the Defamation Act 2013 to reform the law, and Northern Ireland's government, the Executive, decided against adopting the legislation automatically. A consultation process took place and was completed in early 2015 but it is expected to be some time before the law is changed.

> Check www.mcnaes.com for updates.

The result is that reforms in the 2013 Act have no effect, and Northern Ireland continues to operate under the Defamation Act (Northern Ireland) 1955 and the relevant parts of the Defamation Act 1996. Thus, there will be no requirement in Northern Ireland for claimants to show that they have suffered serious harm when suing for defamation, while website operators will have fewer defences in relation to user-generated content. Even if such a website publisher has procedures to enable complaints to be remedied, it can be sued in Northern Ireland much more easily than in England or Wales. Also the new statutory defences in England and Wales of responsible publication on matters of public interest, truth and honest opinion do not apply. Instead defendants in Northern Ireland have to rely on the often difficult to prove common law defences of justification and honest comment.

> The 'justification' and 'honest comment' defences are explained on www.mcnaes.com in the Additional Material for this chapter. For general principles of defamation law, see chs. 19–24 where some explanation is in the context of the law in England and Wales.

ch. 18
explains
contempt
law

▶ Contempt of court

The Contempt of Court Act 1981 is effective in Northern Ireland and the many contempt decisions by the High Court in London are equally applicable there.

The only significant difference is the reporting of courts unique to Northern Ireland known as 'Diplock courts'. These were introduced during the Troubles to allow terrorists charged with scheduled offences to be tried by a judge sitting without a jury. The reduction in terrorist activity with the peace process now means these sit extremely rarely. It has been argued that the absence of a jury means that reporting on Diplock cases involves a much reduced risk of contempt through creating a substantial risk of serious prejudice to the proceedings. But the danger remains that the evidence of witnesses might be coloured by accounts given by others.

◗ Reporting restrictions

Guidelines on reporting restrictions issued in 2008 by the Judicial Studies Board for Northern Ireland say courts are encouraged to exercise their discretion to hear media representations when considering discretionary reporting restrictions.

((•))
see Useful Websites at the end of this chapter for this guidance

Preliminary hearings

Committal proceedings must be in open court except where it appears to the court that the ends of justice would not be served by reports of the whole or part of the hearing. The Magistrates' Courts (Northern Ireland) Order 1981 prohibits publication of a report of any opening statement made by the prosecution. There is no automatic ban on reporting evidence, but the Act allows a court to prohibit publication of any evidence if it is satisfied that publication would prejudice the defendant's trial. The court may impose additional restrictions where objection is taken to the admissibility of evidence. The court may, if satisfied that the objection is made in good faith, order that such evidence and any discussion on it shall not be published.

Crown courts

Restrictions under the Criminal Justice Act 2003 on reporting prosecution appeals against the termination of a trial by a judge, or against an acquittal, were extended to Northern Ireland under the Criminal Justice (Northern Ireland) Order 2004.

The Court of Appeal in Belfast ruled in 1995 that hearing plea bargaining submissions in open court could inhibit rather than secure the achievement of justice.

ch. 8, p. 83, Appeals against rulings by judge— reporting restrictions, explains this law

Juveniles in court

A child aged under 10 cannot be charged with a criminal offence in Northern Ireland. Youth courts deal with offences committed by those below the age of 18. The Criminal Justice (Children) (Northern Ireland) Order 1998, as amended, makes it an offence in reporting the proceedings to publish the name, address or school, or any particulars likely to lead to the identification of anyone under 18 involved in youth court proceedings, or in an appeal from a youth court, as defendant, witness or alleged victim/victim. It is also an offence to publish a picture of or including anyone under 18 so involved. A youth court may lift the restrictions on a convicted young offender in the public interest but must first afford parties to the proceedings an opportunity to make representations.

Under article 22 of the 1998 Order, an adult court may order that nothing should be published which would identify anyone under 18 involved in the proceedings as a defendant, witness or party. An order is not effective if the person has reached 18.

> See ch. 9 on juveniles, which explains law applying to media reports of youth court cases in England and Wales, which is similar to that in Northern Ireland, and explains too the 'section 45' orders used in England and Wales which are comparable to article 22 orders.

ch. 14, pp. 161–162, Statute law on open and private hearings, explains section 37

The 1998 Order empowers a court in any criminal proceedings to exclude everyone not concerned in the case where it considers the evidence of a child is likely to involve matter of an indecent or immoral nature. There is no specific provision for the press to remain, unlike the position in England and Wales under section 37 of the Children and Young Persons Act 1933.

Domestic and family proceedings

see also ch. 13 on family cases

Representatives of newspapers and news agencies may attend domestic proceedings but reports must be confined to four points and there is automatic anonymity for children involved in family cases, as in England and Wales. For detail, see the Additional Material for this chapter on www.mcnaes.com. The court may, under the Children (Northern Ireland) Order 1995, direct that any report of non-criminal proceedings must not lead to the identification of any person under 18 as being involved where any power is being exercised under that order, except to the extent which the court may allow. The court has power to sit in private when exercising any power under the 1995 Order.

→ glossary

Sexual, human trafficking and female genital mutilation offences

The Sexual Offences (Amendment) Act 1992 and the Criminal Justice (Northern Ireland) Order 1994 apply in relation to media reports of sexual offences in Northern Ireland. This law, which provides anonymity for victims/alleged victims of sexual offences, is essentially the same as in England and Wales, as is the law providing anonymity for victims/alleged victims of female genital mutilation. These laws are explained in ch. 10. Although the law against 'human trafficking' in section 2 of the Modern Slavery Act 2015, referred to in ch. 10, does not apply to Northern Ireland, a victim/alleged victim of an offence of trafficking for the purposes of sexual exploitation—for example, prostitution—which arises there has anonymity under the 1992 Act.

Identifying defendants in sexual offence cases

There is nothing in the 1994 Order giving a court discretionary powers, in addition to the automatic restrictions protecting victims/alleged victims, to impose further restrictions such as prohibiting identification of the defendant.

Yet it continues to be the case that courts have made or attempted to make orders banning the naming of a defendant, citing the 1994 Order, on the grounds that publishing his/her name would either lead to the identification of the complainant or be detrimental to the complainant's well-being.

Such purported orders are *ultra vires*. The Order's article 19 prohibits publication of particulars which would lead to the identification of the complainant, but there is no provision in the article for a court to determine which particulars they might be.

See also ch. 15, p. 201, Sexual offence law does *not* give anonymity for defendants, and *R v Newtownabbey Magistrates' Court, ex p Belfast Telegraph Newspapers Ltd* [1997] NI 309, cited in ch. 15, p. 184, Has the name or the matter been withheld from the public?

 See too Additional Material for ch. 37 on www.mcnaes.com, 'Bans on identifying defendants', for recent instances in which defendants in various types of criminal case in Northern Ireland have been given anonymity, leading journalists and others to protest that the open justice principle has been eroded.

Identifying jurors

It is an offence to identify someone as being or having been a juror in Northern Ireland, or as being listed as a juror or selected for inclusion on the jury list. The offence is contained in the Juries (Northern Ireland) Order 1996, as amended, which provides a defence that there was reasonable belief that disclosure of the juror's identity was lawful.

 See also ch. 11, pp. 127–128, Contempt risk in identifying or approaching jurors. Note that in Northern Ireland the law protecting the confidentiality of jury deliberations remains in section 8 of the Contempt of Court Act 1981—see ch. 11, pp. 126–127, Confidentiality of jury deliberations.

Photography, filming and recording at court

The Criminal Justice (Northern Ireland) Act 1945, operating in a similar way to the mainland Criminal Justice Act 1925, prohibits photography, filming or sketching in a court or its precincts. Guidelines from the Judicial Studies Board say the court can issue guidance, by way of a map, on the extent of the precincts.

 ch. 11 explains the 1925 Act and also covers the ban on audio-recording in courts

✳ Remember

 www.mcnaes.com has a chapter outlining Scottish media law.

➡ Recap of major points

- The law in Northern Ireland, including the courts structure, is broadly the same as in England and Wales, with minor variations.
- It is easier to sue for defamation in Northern Ireland than in England and Wales, as a claimant does not have to prove any damage and the defences are weaker.
- Reporting restrictions in Northern Ireland broadly follow those in England and Wales but many of them are contained in Orders made by the Secretary of State rather than in Acts of Parliament.

((•)) Useful Websites

www.jsbni.com/Publications/reporting-restrictions/Pages/default.aspx
   Judicial Studies Board for Northern Ireland guide to reporting restrictions

www.courtsni.gov.uk
   Northern Ireland Courts and Tribunals Service

Part 6

Online chapters

38

The incitement of hate

Chapter summary

Freedom of expression has boundaries. One boundary is that making or publishing some kinds of threatening statement is a crime. As this chapter explains, it is an offence to stir up hatred against people because of their race, religious beliefs or their sexual orientation.

Full chapter available at www.mcnaes.com.

39

Scotland

Chapter summary

The law of Scotland affects journalism in different ways from that in England and Wales. This chapter briefly outlines the Scottish legal system and its judiciary, and shows how reporting restrictions affect coverage of criminal proceedings, especially cases involving children. Media organisations based in other parts of the UK may need to pay special consideration to what they publish in Scotland, because contempt laws are interpreted differently.

Full chapter available at www.mcnaes.com.

Terrorism and the effect of counter-terrorism law

Chapter summary

The heightened threat of terrorism in recent years has led to more counter-terrorism laws in the UK, some controversial because of their actual or potential interference with journalists' work. These laws ban the gathering of certain information and restrict what can be published. As this chapter shows, the wide scope of counter-terrorism law has the potential to deter journalistic investigation of the causes and control of terrorism. Journalists who interview people who have joined terrorist groups—for example, the so-called Islamic State—should be aware that a court may order that the interview records and these sources' identities must be disclosed to the police.

Full chapter available at www.mcnaes.com.

Appendix 1
Extracts from the European Convention for the Protection of Human Rights and Fundamental Freedoms (known as the European Convention on Human Rights)

Article 2—Right to life

1. Everyone's right to life shall be protected by law. No one shall be deprived of his life intentionally save in the execution of a sentence of a court following his conviction of a crime for which this penalty is provided by law. [See also * at the end of this Appendix]
2. Deprivation of life shall not be regarded as inflicted in contravention of this Article when it results from the use of force which is no more than absolutely necessary:
   (a) in defence of any person from unlawful violence;
   (b) in order to effect a lawful arrest or to prevent the escape of a person lawfully detained;
   (c) in action lawfully taken for the purpose of quelling a riot or insurrection.

Article 3—Prohibition of torture

No one shall be subjected to torture or to inhuman or degrading treatment or punishment.

Article 6—Right to a fair trial [article quoted in part]

1. In the determination of his civil rights and obligations or of any criminal charge against him, everyone is entitled to a fair and public hearing within a reasonable time by an independent and impartial tribunal established by law. Judgment shall be pronounced publicly but the press and public may be excluded from all or part of the trial in the interest of morals, public order or national security in a democratic society, where the interests of juveniles or the protection of the private life of the parties so require, or to the extent strictly necessary in the opinion of the court in special circumstances where publicity would prejudice the interests of justice.

2. Everyone charged with a criminal offence shall be presumed innocent until proved guilty according to law.

[...]

Article 8—Right to respect for private and family life

1. Everyone has the right to respect for his private and family life, his home and his correspondence.
2. There shall be no interference by a public authority with the exercise of this right except such as is in accordance with the law and is necessary in a democratic society in the interests of national security, public safety or the economic wellbeing of the country, for the prevention of disorder or crime, for the protection of health or morals, or for the protection of the rights and freedoms of others.

Article 10—Freedom of expression

1. Everyone has the right to freedom of expression. This right shall include freedom to hold opinions and to receive and impart information and ideas without interference by public authority and regardless of frontiers. This Article shall not prevent States from requiring the licensing of broadcasting, television or cinema enterprises.
2. The exercise of these freedoms, since it carries with it duties and responsibilities, may be subject to such formalities, conditions, restrictions or penalties as are prescribed by law and are necessary in a democratic society, in the interests of national security, territorial integrity or public safety, for the prevention of disorder or crime, for the protection of health or morals, for the protection of the reputation or rights of others, for preventing the disclosure of information received in confidence, or for maintaining the authority and impartiality of the judiciary.

* Article 1 of the Thirteenth Protocol to the Convention, which was adopted into UK law in 2004, stated: 'The death penalty shall be abolished.' The UK had, in reality, already abolished it.

For the Convention's full text, see www.echr.coe.int/Documents/Convention_ENG.pdf

Appendix 2
The Editors' Code of Practice

The Independent Press Standards Organisation (IPSO), as regulator, is charged with enforcing the following Code of Practice, which was framed by the Editors' Code of Practice Committee and is enshrined in the contractual agreement between IPSO and newspaper, magazine and electronic news publishers.

Preamble

The Code – including this preamble and the public interest exceptions below – sets the framework for the highest professional standards that members of the press subscribing to the Independent Press Standards Organisation have undertaken to maintain. It is the cornerstone of the system of voluntary self-regulation to which they have made a binding contractual commitment. It balances both the rights of the individual and the public's right to know.

To achieve that balance, it is essential that an agreed Code be honoured not only to the letter, but in the full spirit. It should be interpreted neither so narrowly as to compromise its commitment to respect the rights of the individual, nor so broadly that it infringes the fundamental right to freedom of expression – such as to inform, to be partisan, to challenge, shock, be satirical and to entertain – or prevents publication in the public interest.

It is the responsibility of editors and publishers to apply the Code to editorial material in both printed and online versions of their publications. They should take care to ensure it is observed rigorously by all editorial staff and external contributors, including non-journalists.

Editors must maintain in-house procedures to resolve complaints swiftly and, where required to do so, cooperate with IPSO. A publication subject to an adverse adjudication must publish it in full and with due prominence, as required by IPSO.

1. Accuracy

i) The Press must take care not to publish inaccurate, misleading or distorted information or images, including headlines not supported by the text.

ii) A significant inaccuracy, misleading statement or distortion must be corrected, promptly and with due prominence, and – where appropriate – an apology published. In cases involving IPSO, due prominence should be as required by the regulator.

iii) A fair opportunity to reply to significant inaccuracies should be given, when reasonably called for.

iv) The Press, while free to editorialise and campaign, must distinguish clearly between comment, conjecture and fact.

v) A publication must report fairly and accurately the outcome of an action for defamation to which it has been a party, unless an agreed settlement states otherwise, or an agreed statement is published.

2. *Privacy

i) Everyone is entitled to respect for his or her private and family life, home, health and correspondence, including digital communications.

ii) Editors will be expected to justify intrusions into any individual's private life without consent. Account will be taken of the complainant's own public disclosures of information.

iii) It is unacceptable to photograph individuals, without their consent, in public or private places where there is a reasonable expectation of privacy.

3. *Harassment

i) Journalists must not engage in intimidation, harassment or persistent pursuit.

ii) They must not persist in questioning, telephoning, pursuing or photographing individuals once asked to desist; nor remain on property when asked to leave and must not follow them. If requested, they must identify themselves and whom they represent.

iii) Editors must ensure these principles are observed by those working for them and take care not to use non-compliant material from other sources.

4. Intrusion into grief or shock

In cases involving personal grief or shock, enquiries and approaches must be made with sympathy and discretion and publication handled sensitively. These provisions should not restrict the right to report legal proceedings.

5. *Reporting suicide

When reporting suicide, to prevent simulative acts care should be taken to avoid excessive detail of the method used, while taking into account the media's right to report legal proceedings.

6. *Children

i) All pupils should be free to complete their time at school without unnecessary intrusion.

ii) They must not be approached or photographed at school without permission of the school authorities.

iii) Children under 16 must not be interviewed or photographed on issues involving their own or another child's welfare unless a custodial parent or similarly responsible adult consents.

iv) Children under 16 must not be paid for material involving their welfare, nor parents or guardians for material about their children or wards, unless it is clearly in the child's interest.

v) Editors must not use the fame, notoriety or position of a parent or guardian as sole justification for publishing details of a child's private life.

7. *Children in sex cases

1. The press must not, even if legally free to do so, identify children under 16 who are victims or witnesses in cases involving sex offences.

2. In any press report of a case involving a sexual offence against a child –

   i) The child must not be identified.

   ii) The adult may be identified.

   iii) The word "incest" must not be used where a child victim might be identified.

   iv) Care must be taken that nothing in the report implies the relationship between the accused and the child.

8. *Hospitals

i) Journalists must identify themselves and obtain permission from a responsible executive before entering non-public areas of hospitals or similar institutions to pursue enquiries.

ii) The restrictions on intruding into privacy are particularly relevant to enquiries about individuals in hospitals or similar institutions.

9. *Reporting of Crime

i) Relatives or friends of persons convicted or accused of crime should not generally be identified without their consent, unless they are genuinely relevant to the story.

ii) Particular regard should be paid to the potentially vulnerable position of children who witness, or are victims of, crime. This should not restrict the right to report legal proceedings.

10. *Clandestine devices and subterfuge

i) The press must not seek to obtain or publish material acquired by using hidden cameras or clandestine listening devices; or by intercepting private or mobile telephone calls, messages or emails; or by the unauthorised removal of documents or photographs; or by accessing digitally-held information without consent.

ii) Engaging in misrepresentation or subterfuge, including by agents or intermediaries, can generally be justified only in the public interest and then only when the material cannot be obtained by other means.

11. Victims of sexual assault

The press must not identify victims of sexual assault or publish material likely to contribute to such identification unless there is adequate justification and they are legally free to do so.

12. Discrimination

i) The press must avoid prejudicial or pejorative reference to an individual's race, colour, religion, sex, gender identity, sexual orientation or to any physical or mental illness or disability.

ii) Details of an individual's race, colour, religion, gender identity, sexual orientation, physical or mental illness or disability must be avoided unless genuinely relevant to the story.

13. Financial journalism

i) Even where the law does not prohibit it, journalists must not use for their own profit financial information they receive in advance of its general publication, nor should they pass such information to others.

ii) They must not write about shares or securities in whose performance they know that they or their close families have a significant financial interest without disclosing the interest to the editor or financial editor.

iii) They must not buy or sell, either directly or through nominees or agents, shares or securities about which they have written recently or about which they intend to write in the near future.

14. Confidential sources

Journalists have a moral obligation to protect confidential sources of information.

15. Witness payments in criminal trials

i) No payment or offer of payment to a witness – or any person who may reasonably be expected to be called as a witness – should be made in any case once proceedings are active as defined by the Contempt of Court Act 1981. This prohibition lasts until the suspect has been freed unconditionally by police without charge or bail or the proceedings are otherwise discontinued; or has entered a guilty plea to the court; or, in the event of a not guilty plea, the court has announced its verdict.

*ii) Where proceedings are not yet active but are likely and foreseeable, editors must not make or offer payment to any person who may reasonably be expected to be called as a witness, unless the information concerned ought demonstrably to be published in the public interest and there is an over-riding need to make or promise payment for this to be done; and all reasonable steps have been taken to ensure no financial dealings influence the evidence those witnesses give. In no circumstances should such payment be conditional on the outcome of a trial.

*iii) Any payment or offer of payment made to a person later cited to give evidence in proceedings must be disclosed to the prosecution and defence. The witness must be advised of this requirement.

16. *Payment to criminals

i) Payment or offers of payment for stories, pictures or information, which seek to exploit a particular crime or to glorify or glamorise crime in general, must not be made directly or via agents to convicted or confessed criminals or to their associates—who may include family, friends and colleagues.

ii) Editors invoking the public interest to justify payment or offers would need to demonstrate that there was good reason to believe the public interest would be served. If, despite payment, no public interest emerged, then the material should not be published.

The public interest

There may be exceptions to the clauses marked * where they can be demonstrated to be in the public interest.

1. The public interest includes, but is not confined to:
   i. Detecting or exposing crime, or the threat of crime, or serious impropriety.
   ii. Protecting public health or safety.
   iii. Protecting the public from being misled by an action or statement of an individual or organisation.

iv. Disclosing a person or organisation's failure or likely failure to comply with any obligation to which they are subject.

v. Disclosing a miscarriage of justice.

vi. Raising or contributing to a matter of public debate, including serious cases of impropriety, unethical conduct or incompetence concerning the public.

vii. Disclosing concealment, or likely concealment, of any of the above.

2. There is a public interest in freedom of expression itself.

3. The regulator will consider the extent to which material is already in the public domain or will become so.

4. Editors invoking the public interest will need to demonstrate that they reasonably believed publication – or journalistic activity taken with a view to publication – would both serve, and be proportionate to, the public interest and explain how they reached that decision at the time.

5. An exceptional public interest would need to be demonstrated to override the normally paramount interests of children under 16.

Appendix 3
Schedule 1 to the Defamation Act 1996

Qualified privilege [see ch. 21, pp. 286–291, Qualified privilege by statute]

This is the text of Parts 1 and 2 of Schedule 1 to the 1996 Act, paragraphs 1–16, as amended by various subsequent legislation including section 7 of the Defamation Act 2013.

Part 1—Statements having qualified privilege without explanation or contradiction

nition
ourt',
para. 16
ue
edule

1 A fair and accurate report of proceedings in public of a legislature anywhere in the world.

2 A fair and accurate report of proceedings in public before a court anywhere in the world. [*Para. 17 makes clear that this includes the European Court of Justice, the European Court of Human Rights and any international criminal tribunal established by the United Nations or by an international agreement to which the UK is a party.*]

3 A fair and accurate report of proceedings in public of a person appointed to hold a public inquiry by a government or legislature anywhere in the world.

4 A fair and accurate report of proceedings in public anywhere in the world of an international organisation or an international conference. [*Para. 17 limits these definitions to a conference attended by representatives of two or more governments or an organisation of which two or more governments are members, including any committee or other subordinate body of such an organisation.*]

5 A fair and accurate copy of or extract from any register or other document required by law to be open to public inspection.

6 A notice or advertisement published by or on the authority of a court, or of a judge or officer of a court, anywhere in the world.

7 A fair and accurate copy of or extract from matter published by or on the authority of a government or legislature anywhere in the world.

8 A fair and accurate copy of or extract from matter published anywhere in the world by an international organisation or an international conference. [*Same definitions as for para. 4.*]

Part 2—Statements privileged subject to explanation or contradiction

9   (1)   A fair and accurate copy of, extract from or summary of a notice or other matter issued for the information of the public by or on behalf of—

    (a)   a legislature or government anywhere in the world;

    (b)   an authority anywhere in the world performing governmental functions;

    (c)   an international organisation or international conference.

   (2)   In this paragraph "governmental functions" includes police functions.

10   A fair and accurate copy of, extract from or summary of a document made available by a court anywhere in the world, or by a judge or officer of such a court.

11   (1)   A fair and accurate report of proceedings at any public meeting or sitting in the United Kingdom of—

    (a)   a local authority or local authority committee;

    (aa)   in the case of a local authority which are operating executive arrangements, the executive of that authority or a committee of that executive;

    (b)   a justice or justices of the peace acting otherwise than as a court exercising judicial authority;

    (c)   a commission, tribunal, committee or person appointed for the purposes of any inquiry by any statutory provision, by Her Majesty or by a Minister of the Crown, a member of the Scottish Executive, the Welsh Ministers or the Counsel General to the Welsh Assembly Government, or a Northern Ireland Department;

    (d)   a person appointed by a local authority to hold a local inquiry in pursuance of any statutory provision;

    (e)   any other tribunal, board, committee or body constituted by or under, and exercising functions under, any statutory provision.

   (1A)   In the case of a local authority which are operating executive arrangements, a fair and accurate record of any decision made by any member of the executive where that record is required to be made and available for public inspection by virtue of section 22 of the Local Government Act 2000 or of any provision in regulations made under that section.

   (2)   In sub-paragraphs (1)(a), (1)(aa) and (1A) "local authority" means—

    (a)   in relation to England and Wales, a principal council within the meaning of the Local Government Act 1972, any body falling within any paragraph of section 100J(1) of that Act or an authority or body to which the Public Bodies (Admission to Meetings) Act 1960 applies,

(b) in relation to Scotland, a council constituted under section 2 of the Local Government etc (Scotland) Act 1994 or an authority or body to which the Public Bodies (Admission to Meetings) Act 1960 applies,

(c) in relation to Northern Ireland, any authority or body to which sections 23 to 27 of the Local Government Act (Northern Ireland) 1972 apply; and

"local authority committee" means any committee of a local authority or of local authorities, and includes—

(a) any committee or sub-committee in relation to which sections 100A to 100D of the Local Government Act 1972 apply by virtue of section 100E of that Act (whether or not also by virtue of section 100J of that Act), and

(b) any committee or sub-committee in relation to which sections 50A to 50D of the Local Government (Scotland) Act 1973 apply by virtue of section 50E of that Act.

(2A) In sub-paragraphs (1) and (1A) "executive" and "executive arrangements" have the same meaning as in Part II of the Local Government Act 2000.

(3) A fair and accurate report of any corresponding proceedings in any of the Channel Islands or the Isle of Man or in another member state [*that is, a European Union member nation*].

11A A fair and accurate report of proceedings at a press conference held anywhere in the world for the discussion of a matter of public interest.

12 (1) A fair and accurate report of proceedings at any public meeting held anywhere in the world.

(2) In this paragraph a "public meeting" means a meeting bona fide and lawfully held for a lawful purpose and for the furtherance or discussion of a matter of public interest, whether admission to the meeting is general or restricted.

13 (1) A fair and accurate report of proceedings at a general meeting of a listed company.

(2) A fair and accurate copy of, extract from or summary of any document circulated to members of a listed company—

(a) by or with the authority of the board of directors of the company,

(b) by the auditors of the company, or

(c) by any member of the company in pursuance of a right conferred by any statutory provision.

(3) A fair and accurate copy of, extract from or summary of any document circulated to members of a listed company which relates to the appointment, resignation, retirement or dismissal of directors of the company or its auditors.

(4) In this paragraph "listed company" has the same meaning as in Part 12 of the Corporation Tax Act 2009 (see section 1005 of

that Act). [*'Listed company' means a company (a) whose shares are listed on a 'recognised stock exchange'—that is, recognised by the UK tax authorities—and (b) which is neither a close company nor a company that would be a close company if it were UK resident. So, the 'listed company' definition means—according to the Explanatory Notes to the Defamation Act 2013—UK public companies and 'public companies elsewhere in the world'.*]

14   A fair and accurate report of any finding or decision of any of the following descriptions of association formed anywhere in the world or of any committee or governing body of such an association—

(a) an association formed for the purpose of promoting or encouraging the exercise of or interest in any art, science, religion or learning, and empowered by its constitution to exercise control over or adjudicate on matters of interest or concern to the association, or the actions or conduct of any persons subject to such control or adjudication;

(b) an association formed for the purpose of promoting or safeguarding the interests of any trade, business, industry or profession, or of the persons carrying on or engaged in any trade, business, industry or profession, and empowered by its constitution to exercise control over or adjudicate upon matters connected with the trade, business, industry or profession, or the actions or conduct of those persons;

(c) an association formed for the purpose of promoting or safeguarding the interests of a game, sport or pastime to the playing or exercise of which members of the public are invited or admitted, and empowered by its constitution to exercise control over or adjudicate upon persons connected with or taking part in the game, sport or pastime;

(d) an association formed for the purpose of promoting charitable objects or other objects beneficial to the community and empowered by its constitution to exercise control over or to adjudicate on matters of interest or concern to the association, or the actions or conduct of any person subject to such control or adjudication.

14A A fair and accurate—

(a) report of proceedings of a scientific or academic conference held anywhere in the world, or

(b) copy of, extract from or summary of matter published by such a conference.

15   (1) A fair and accurate report or summary of, copy of or extract from, any adjudication, report, statement or notice issued by a body, officer or other person designated for the purposes of this paragraph by order of the Lord Chancellor.

(2) An order under this paragraph shall be made by statutory instrument which shall be subject to annulment in pursuance of a resolution of either House of Parliament.

16   In this Schedule—"court" includes—

(a) any tribunal or body established under the law of any country or territory exercising the judicial power of the State;

(b) any international tribunal established by the Security Council of the United Nations or by an international agreement;

(c) any international tribunal deciding matters in dispute between States;

"international conference" means a conference attended by representatives of two or more governments;

"international organisation" means an organisation of which two or more governments are members, and includes any committee or other subordinate body of such an organisation;

"legislature" includes a local legislature; and

"member State" includes any European dependent territory of a member State.

Glossary

Absolute discharge A decision by a court after conviction that the offender should not be punished for the crime.

Affidavit A statement given on oath to be used in court proceedings.

Alibi A claim by an accused that he/she can show he/she was not at the scene when a crime was committed and is therefore innocent.

Allocation The procedure at magistrates' courts to determine whether an **either-way** criminal case is dealt with by magistrates or by a Crown court. Also known as the **mode of trial hearing**.

Arraignment The procedure at Crown courts when charges are put to defendants for them to plead guilty or not guilty.

Automatic, automatically Terms used for reporting restrictions which ban publication of certain information if no court order is needed to put them into effect in respect of a particular case or individual. Statutes specify the circumstances in which they operate.

Bail The system by which a person awaiting trial, or appeal, may be freed by a court pending the next hearing. *See also* **Police bail**

Bailiff A court official who enforces its orders.

Case law The system by which reports of previous cases and the judges' interpretations of the common law are used as precedents where the legally material facts are similar.

Circuit judge A judge appointed to sit at a Crown court or county court within a circuit—one of the regions of England and Wales into which court administration is divided. Unlike High Court judges, circuit judges do not go on circuit—that is, travel to various large centres dispensing justice.

Claim form The document which begins many forms of civil action.

Claimant The person who bring an action in the civil court.

Committal for sentence, committed for sentence When a defendant at a magistrates' court who has admitted an offence or been convicted at trial is sent to Crown court to be sentenced because the magistrates decide their powers of punishment are insufficient. (There are no reporting restrictions on committals for sentence.)

Common law Law based on the custom of the realm and the decisions of judges through the centuries rather than on Acts of Parliament.

Community punishment An order that an offender must carry out unpaid work in the community under a probation officer's supervision.

Concurrent sentences Two or more sentences of imprisonment imposed for different offences; the longest one is the sentence actually served.

Conditional discharge A decision by a court that a convicted defendant should not be punished unless he/she re-offends—the condition of the discharge being that if he/she commits another crime within a specified period, for example a year, he/she can be punished for both the new and the original offences.

Conditional fee agreements (CFAs) 'No win, no fee' agreements—their use was extended to defamation cases in 1998 under the Conditional Fee Agreements Order 1998.

Contra mundum An **injunction** or order which binds all those who are aware that it has been made. The Latin means 'against the world', but such orders only have effect within the jurisdiction in which they are made.

Copyright The law which protects the rights of the creators of original literary, dramatic, musical and artistic works, including photographs.

Counsel Barrister (singular or plural), not solicitor.

Disclosure and inspection The process whereby each side in a court action serves relevant documents on the other, which has the right to inspect them.

District judge A county court judge who also decides smaller cases, family law cases, presides at public examinations in bankruptcy and deals with cases under the informal arbitration procedure.

District judge (magistrates' courts) A full-time legally qualified magistrate.

Editors' Code of Practice Code of ethics enforced by the Independent Press Standards Organisation (Ipso) as regulator for newspapers, magazines and their websites.

Either-way offence One triable either summarily at magistrates' court or by a jury at Crown court. In an either-way case a defendant who has indicated a plea of not guilty has the right to opt for jury trial at Crown court. But if he/she opts for summary trial, the magistrates may decide that the case is too serious for them to handle and must be dealt with at Crown court. *See* also **allocation**; **mode of trial hearing**

Evidence-in-chief The main evidence given by a witness before he/she is cross-examined.

Ex parte *See* **Without notice**

Excluded material Material that is exempt from compulsory disclosure under the Police and Criminal Evidence Act 1984 (PACE). It includes **journalistic material** that a person holds in confidence and which consists of documents or records.

Fair dealing The limited use of **copyright** material for reporting news or current affairs, or for criticism or review or quotation, under which the work is properly identified and attributed to its author.

Honest opinion A defence to a libel action, formerly known as 'honest comment' or 'fair comment'; the defendant does not have to show the words were fair, but must show they were an honestly held opinion.

In camera Proceedings in a courtroom which are heard in secret, with the media and public excluded (for example in Official Secrets Acts or terrorism cases).

In chambers Used to describe the hearing of an application which takes place in the judge's room. If there is no legal reason for such a hearing to be held **in private**, journalists who want to report it should be admitted if 'practicable'.

In private A term used of a court hearing **in camera** or one **in chambers** which the press and public are not entitled to attend.

Indictable offence A charge which may be tried by a jury at Crown court, which will therefore be either an **indictable-only offence** or an **either-way offence**.

Indictable-only offence One which can only be tried by a jury at Crown court.

Indictment A written statement of the charge(s) which is put to the defendant at the **arraignment** at Crown court.

Information A written statement alleging an offence which is presented or laid before a magistrate who is then asked to issue a summons or warrant for arrest.

Inherent jurisdiction The powers of a court deriving from common law rather than statute. The inherent jurisdiction of lower courts, for example magistrates' courts, is more limited than that of the higher courts, for example the High Court.

Injunction A court order requiring someone, or an organisation, to do something specified by the court, or forbidding a specific activity or act.

Interdict A Scottish law term meaning an **injunction**.

Journalistic material Material acquired and created for the purposes of journalism. Special protection is given to journalistic material in the sections of the Police and Criminal Evidence Act 1984 that lay down the procedure whereby the police may search premises for evidence of serious arrestable offences.

Judicial review A review by the Queen's Bench Divisional Court, part of the High Court, of decisions taken by a lower court, tribunal, public body or public official.

Legal aid Public money provided to pay for legal advice and legal representation in court for a party in a civil case or a defendant in a criminal case, if his/her income is low enough to qualify for such aid.

Malice In law not only spite or ill-will but also a dishonest or improper motive. Proof of malice can be used by a **claimant** in a libel action to defeat a defence of qualified privilege.

Mitigation A plea for leniency in the sentence due to be imposed, citing extenuating circumstances, which is made in court or on behalf of a convicted offender.

Mode of trial hearing The hearing at a magistrates' court to decide whether an **either-way case** is dealt with by that court or proceeds to a Crown court. Also known as the **allocation** procedure.

Narrative verdict/narrative conclusion A short statement by a coroner or inquest jury detailing the circumstances and manner of a person's death which takes the place of the traditional 'short-form' verdicts.

Newton **hearing** A hearing involving a defendant who has pleaded guilty but offers a substantially different version of events to that alleged by the prosecution, at which the court hears evidence so it can decide which version its accepts as forming the basis for the sentence. Newton was the defendant's name in the relevant precedent case.

Ofcom Broadcasting Code Code of ethics used by Ofcom to adjudicate on complaints against broadcasters.

Police bail The system administered by police whereby a person under on-going investigation can be released from arrest on conditions, including that they return to a police station on a later date, at which time they may be questioned again, charged, or be told there will be no charge. They can be arrested if they breach the conditions. After being charged, they can be bailed by police to attend court or may be taken there in custody.

Preliminary hearing A hearing, before any trial, at a magistrates' or Crown court.

Prima facie Literally, 'at first sight'. In criminal law a 'prima facie case' is one in which a preliminary examination by a court has established that there is sufficient prosecution evidence for it to proceed to trial. In journalism ethics the term 'prima facie grounds' means that preliminary inquiries have established there is sufficient evidence or sufficient ground of suspicion to justify use of deception or undercover tactics in an investigation.

Prior restraint The power which courts have to stop material being published.

In defamation law there is a general rule against prior restraint, and judges are extremely reluctant to ban publication of material which the media argue can be successfully defended in any future trial.

Privilege A defence, absolute or qualified, against an action for libel which attaches to reports produced from certain events, documents or statements.

Public interest The phrase 'in the public interest' is used by judges to define when an individual's rights, for example to privacy, can legally be infringed if this produces a sufficiently major benefit to society, for example from investigative journalism. But judges may also decide that a general 'public interest', for example in the confidentiality of medical records, needs to be upheld against media activity. Codes of ethics use the phrase too, to indicate when journalists may be justified in infringing people's rights.

Recorder An assistant judge at Crown court who is usually appointed to sit part time (for example for spells of a fortnight). Barristers and solicitors are eligible for appointment as recorders.

Remand An individual awaiting trial can be remanded on bail or in custody.

Robbery **Theft** by force or threat of force. The word 'robbery' is often wrongly used to describe simple theft.

Sending for trial The procedure by which an **indictable-only offence** and, in the **allocation** procedure, some **either-way offences** are sent from the magistrates' court to a Crown court.

Skeleton arguments The documents in which each side in civil or criminal court proceedings sets out the bases of their cases. Journalists should normally be allowed to see them to help them report the proceedings.

Spent conviction A conviction that is no longer recognised after the time (varying according to sentence) specified in the Rehabilitation of Offenders Act 1974. After this time, a media organisation referring to the conviction might not have available some of the normal defences in the law of libel.

Statements of case Documents including the **claim form**, particulars of claim, defence, counterclaims, reply to the defence and 'further information documents' in a civil action—reports of which are now protected by **privilege**.

Statute An Act of Parliament—that is, primary legislation created by Parliament.

Statutory instrument Secondary legislation which can be enacted without parliamentary debate by a Minister to make detailed law (for example rules and regulations) or amendment to the law, under powers given earlier by a statute. Statutory instruments are also used to phase in gradually, for administrative convenience, legal changes brought about by Acts.

Strict liability A strict liability offence does not require the prosecution to show intent on the part of the accused. Statutory contempt of court is a strict liability offence.

Sub judice Literally 'under law'. Often applied to the risk which may arise in reporting forthcoming legal proceedings. Frequently used by authority as a reason for not disclosing information. But this is not the test for strict liability under the Contempt of Court Act 1981.

Subpoena A court order compelling a person to attend court to give evidence.

Summary offence A comparatively minor offence which can usually only be dealt with by magistrates.

Summary proceedings Cases dealt with by magistrates. At the end of a summary trial of an **either-way offence**, however, magistrates can, if they consider their powers of sentence insufficient, **commit for sentence**.

Summary trial A trial at a magistrates' court.

Supreme Court The name originally given to the Court of Appeal, the High Court and the Crown courts as a combined system. However, from October 2009 the House of Lords appellate committee (the court commonly referred to merely as 'the House of Lords') became the UK Supreme Court.

Surety A person, usually a friend or relative of the defendant, to whom a court entrusts the responsibility to ensure that the individual, having been released on **bail**, returns to court on the due date. The surety may pledge a sum of money as the guarantee that the defendant will answer bail and risks losing it if the defendant fails to do so.

Taken into consideration The system under which a defendant admits having committed offences with which he/she has not been charged, thus clearing the slate and avoiding risk of subsequent prosecution for those offences.

Theft Dishonest appropriation of another's property with the intention of permanently depriving the other of it.

Tort A civil wrong, such as defamation or medical negligence, for which monetary damages may be awarded.

Truth The defence in defamation actions that the words complained of are substantially true.

Warranted Term used in the **Ofcom Broadcasting Code** to indicate that an ethical norm can be breached if there is a public interest justification or some other exceptional justification.

Without notice Previously known as *ex parte*, meaning 'of the one part'. An injunction without notice is one granted after a court has heard only one side of the case. An order granted *inter partes* is one made after a hearing at which all sides involved were represented.

Book list

Chapter 1, Introduction
Free Speech, Eric Barendt (Oxford University Press, 2nd edition, 2007)
Media Law and Human Rights, Andrew Nicol, Gavin Millar and Andrew Sharland
  (Oxford University Press, 2nd edition, 2009)

Chapter 2, Press regulation
*An Inquiry into the Culture, Practices and Ethics of the Press: Executive Summary and
  Recommendations*, Lord Justice Leveson (The Stationery Office, 2012, and at http://
  webarchive.nationalarchives.gov.uk/20140122145147/http://www.official-documents.
  gov.uk/document/hc1213/hc07/0779/0779.asp)
Privacy and Media Freedom, Raymond Wacks (Oxford University Press, 2013)
Journalism Ethics and Regulation, Chris Frost (Routledge, 2015)

Chapter 3, Broadcast regulation
'Fair enough? Ethics and regulation in broadcast journalism', Tony Harcup, ch. 22 in
  Broadcast Journalism: A Critical Introduction, Jane Chapman and Marie Kinsey
  (Routledge, 2008)
Journalism Ethics and Regulation, Chris Frost (Routledge, 2015)
Media Regulation: Governance and the Interests of Citizens and Consumers' Peter Lunt
  and Sonia Livingstone (Sage, 2012)

Chapters 4–8 (on crime and the criminal courts system)
Blackstone's Criminal Practice 2016, David Ormerod and David Perry (lead authors)
  (Oxford University Press, 2015)

Chapter 12, Civil courts
Civil Litigation 2015–2016, Susan Cunningham-Hill and Karen Elder (Oxford University
  Press, 2015)
Civil Litigation 2015/2016, Margaret Catlow and Kevin Browne (College of Law,
  2015)

Chapter 13, Family courts
The Family Court Practice, Lady Justice Black, Anthony Cleary and Lord Wilson of
  Culworth (eds) (Jordan, 2014)
The Family Court without a Lawyer: A Handbook for Litigants in Person, Lucy Reed
  (Bath, 2nd edition, 2014)
Court of Protection Handbook: A User's Guide, Alex Ruck-Keene, Kate Edwards,
  Anselm Eldergill and Sophy Miles (Legal Action Group, 2014)

Chapter 14, Open justice and access to court information

Media Law, Geoffrey Robertson and Andrew Nicol (Penguin, 5th edition, 2008)
Open Justice: A Critique of the Public Trial, Joseph Jaconelli (Oxford University Press, 2002)

Chapter 16, Coroners' courts

Coroners' Courts: A Guide to Law and Practice, Christopher Dorries (Oxford University Press, 3rd edition, 2014)

Chapter 18, Contempt of court

Arlidge, Eady and Smith on Contempt, Sir David Eady and A T H Smith, Team Contributors One Brick Court Chambers (Sweet and Maxwell, 4th revised edition, main work and supplement 2015)

Chapters 19–24 (on defamation and related law)

Duncan and Neill on Defamation, Sir Brian Neill, Richard Rampton, Heather Rogers, Timothy Atkinson and Aiden Eardley (LexisNexis, 4th edition, 2015)
Blackstone's Guide to the Defamation Act, James Price and Felicity McMahon (Oxford University Press, 2013)
Gatley on Libel and Slander, Patrick Milmo, Richard Parkes, Godwin Busuttil, Clive Walker and Adam Speker (general eds) (Sweet and Maxwell, 12th edition, main work and first supplement, 2015)
Carter-Ruck on Libel and Privacy, Alastair Mullis and Cameron Doley (general eds) (LexisNexis, 6th edition, 2010)

Chapter 25, Breach of confidence

Confidentiality, Charles Phipps and Roger Toulson (Sweet and Maxwell, 3rd edition, 2012)

Chapter 26, Privacy

Privacy and Media Freedom, Raymond Wacks (Oxford University Press, 2013)
Celebrity and Royal Privacy, the Media and the Law, Robin Callender Smith (Sweet and Maxwell, 2015)
Tugendhat and Christie: The Law of Privacy and the Media, Mark Warby and Nicole Moreham (eds) (Oxford University Press, 3rd edition, 2016)
Privacy and Freedom of Expression, Richard Clayton and Hugh Tomlinson (Oxford University Press, 2nd edition, 2010)
Carter-Ruck on Libel and Privacy, Alastair Mullis and Cameron Doley (general eds) (LexisNexis, 6th edition, 2010)
Privacy Injunctions and the Media: A Practice Manual, Iain Goldrein (Hart, 2012)
Media and Public Shaming: Drawing the Boundaries of Disclosure, Julian Petley (ed) (Reuters Institute for the Study of Journalism, 2013)

Chapter 28, Data protection

Data Protection Law and Practice, Rosemary Jay (Sweet and Maxwell, 4th edition main work and supplement, 2014)

Data Protection: A Guide to UK and EU Law, Peter Carey (Oxford University Press, 4th edition, 2015)

Chapter 29, Copyright

Copinger and Skone James on Copyright, Nicholas Caddick, Gillian Davies and Gwilym Harbottle (Sweet and Maxwell, 17th edition, 2016)

Chapter 30, The Freedom of Information Act 2000

Freedom of Information: A Practical Guide for UK Journalists, Matthew Burgess (Routledge, 2015)

Blackstone's Guide to the Freedom of Information Act 2000, John Wadham, Kelly Harris and Eric Metcalfe (Oxford University Press, 5th edition, 2014)

The Law of Freedom of Information, John Macdonald and Ross Crail (eds) (Oxford University Press, 3rd edition, 2016)

Chapter 33, Official secrets

The Snowden Files: The Inside Story of the World's Most Wanted Man, Luke Harding (Guardian Faber, 2014)

Media Law, Geoffrey Robertson and Andrew Nicol (Penguin, 5th edition, 2008)

National Security and the D-Notice System, Pauline Sadler (Dartmouth, 2001)

Official Secrets: The Use and Abuse of the Act, David Hooper (Coronet Books, 1988)

Secrecy and the Media: The Official History of the D-Notice System, Nicholas John Wilkinson (Routledge, 2009)

Chapter 35, The risks of being charged with bribery, misconduct, hacking or intercepting

Hack Attack: How the Truth Caught up with Rupert Murdoch, Nick Davies (Vintage, 2015)

Beyond Contempt: The Inside Story of the Phone Hacking Trial, Peter Jukes (Cadbury Press, 2015)

Chapter 40 (www.mcnaes.com online), Terrorism and the effect of counter-terrorism law

Terrorism and the Law, Clive Walker (Oxford University Press, 2011)

Blackstone's Guide to the Anti-Terrorism Legislation, Clive Walker (Oxford University Press, 3rd edition, 2014)

Table of cases

Table of statutes

Table of statutory instruments

Index